Tony Jones is one of the ABC's most respected journalists, with more than twenty years' experience in radio and television news and current affairs. Tony began hosting the award-winning news and current affairs program *Lateline* on ABC Television in 1999. He has received four Walkley awards, including two for Best Broadcast Interviewing in 2004 and 2007. He is also the host of a new program called *Q & A*, which will be broadcast on ABC Television in May 2008.

Best and
Purly
2008

The Best Australian Political Writing 2008

Edited by
Tony Jones

MELBOURNE
UNIVERSITY
PRESS

MELBOURNE UNIVERSITY PRESS
An imprint of Melbourne University Publishing Limited
187 Grattan Street, Carlton, Victoria 3053, Australia
mup-info@unimelb.edu.au
www.mup.com.au

First published 2008
Introduction © Tony Jones, 2008
Guy Rundle article © Guy Rundle and *Arena Magazine*
Text © for other articles remains with individual authors
Design and typography © Melbourne University Publishing Ltd, 2008

Designed by Alice Graphics
Typeset by Megan Ellis
Printed in Australia by Griffin Press

National Library of Australia Cataloguing-in-Publication entry:

The best Australian political writing 2008 / edited by Tony Jones.
Carlton, Vic.: Melbourne University Publishing, 2008.

9780522854213 (pbk.)

Australian essays.
Political culture—Australia.
Australia—Politics and government—2001–

Jones, Tony.
994.07

Contents

Introduction

What's left of that epic year, 2007? All the agonising and the ecstasy, McKew's beaming grin, Howard's gritted teeth, a cup of tea, an Iced Vo Vo and it's over …

But who really *got* it? Who best read the tea leaves? Who understood what was actually going on in the electorate's collective mind?

Maybe you'll find some of the answers buried in a pile of magazines in a friend's bathroom, a few penetrating insights before you reach for the chain. But most likely the evidence has already been carted away for recycling. If you search hard enough you'll find the electronic footprints of a year's punditry and analysis somewhere on the internet. But they're like tracks in the sand and sooner or later a tide will come in and wash them away.

It could be the rising tide of inflation that's threatening to inundate the new government, or the high tide of debt already up to the necks of the battlers who voted for change, or, even worse, an economic tsunami triggered by the US sub-prime detonation. That fearful image of 'a huge tsunami' starting in China and flooding through the world's financial markets was thrown up by Peter Costello in his last months as treasurer as a futile warning to the Reserve Bank against raising interest rates during the campaign. If that wave comes now there'll be little time to examine whether Costello left us vulnerable. Those of us left clinging to the wreckage will be focused on Kevin Rudd's untested and palpably nervous team, and the whiteness of their knuckles.

Clearly politics has its own momentum but you have to keep one eye on the rear-vision mirror. That's where the lessons of history are to be found and by any measure the election of 2007 was political history.

At *Lateline* I was lucky enough to have a ringside seat at the year's events: to Kevin Rudd's short march to power and the decline and fall of John Howard; the return of David Hicks and the forced departure of Dr Haneef; the ongoing culture wars; the Northern Territory intervention and the reporting of child sexual abuse in remote Aboriginal communities that prompted it; the emergence of climate change as one of the defining issues of our time and the flawed attempt of a sceptical English filmmaker to prove the whole thing is nothing more than a Great Global Warming Swindle.

By the end of such a year so much has been said and written that the winnowing process for a book such as this is gruelling. Not everyone will agree with our choices but what stands out for me is that the best writing from all corners of politics is provocative, forensic and uncompromising. We've brought together in this collection the prophetic pieces, those that added depth to our understanding, subtlety and new perspectives, and those whose undeniable passion just make you stop and think.

In the opening section you'll find an edited version of David Marr's *Quarterly Essay* 'His master's voice', a polemic born out of years of pent-up rage that concludes that 'Howard's Government has been the most unscrupulous corrupter of public debate in Australia since the Cold War's worst days', and that our passivity and trust have let this happen. In Marr's view self-deception, along with 'boredom, indifference and fear', are at the heart of this: 'Australians trust authority ... It's bred in the bone. We call ourselves larrikins, but we leave our leaders to get on with it'.

But as early as January the social researcher Hugh Mackay had sensed a stirring, a restlessness, in the national mood. The trust in Howard's authority had become fragile. Mackay had the feeling that Australians were emerging from a period of political disengagement that bordered on somnolence. By March, that prolific chronicler of the Howard years, Judith Brett, was attuned to the mood swing. While some streams still ran Howard's way, powerful currents pulled in another direction, 'deeper than the surface froth of political debate'. Brett pointed more specifically to three potential turning points that indicated support was shifting from the incumbent to a fresh face. These were, she wrote, from age to youth; from fear to hope; from private withdrawal to public engagement.

Both Brett and Mackay singled out global warming as an issue that defined John Howard as out of touch. 'Everyone knows he has been denying the reality of climate change for the past decade at least', Brett claimed, 'and everyone knows that the politics of this situation are changing fast'.

So too the politics of David Hicks had changed under Howard's feet. Musing on the Newspoll showing 71 per cent of us wanted Hicks brought home, Hugh Mackay suggested 'the fifth anniversary of his incarceration without trial has jolted us'.

A relentless stream of opinion polling from the moment of Kevin Rudd's ascension late in 2006 confirmed the government was in trouble across a range of big issues, from WorkChoices to health and education. Leadership was at the heart of it. Despite the boom-time economy, many people had simply stopped listening to John Howard. Eventually, even the rusted-on right started flaking off.

'Time to turn the dial because voters seem bored to sobs by Howard after 11 years', cried *The Herald Sun*'s Andrew Bolt as he jumped ship. 'It's over and it's personal.' *The Australian*'s Janet Albrechtsen soon penned 'one of the hardest columns I will write', her own 'Dear John' letter, echoing Bolt's plea for him to step aside for Peter Costello.

Abandoned by old friends, blitzed by polls, harried by *The Chaser* as he hunched into his Vodafone Wallabies trackie, John Howard marched on regardless. An ageing general drawing on the lessons of past battles, he began plugging the gaps in his lines, reinforcing and attempting to repair the damage to his defences in a drawn-out campaign of attrition. He may have been headed for his own Waterloo but he was as alert as Napoleon to the chance for a fresh offensive. Halfway through the year he found it in the most unlikely of places and launched his federal intervention into the Northern Territory.

I pause here, for fear of trivialising that decision, for while it's undoubtedly true that John Howard needed a political circuit-breaker, he was also confronted in the *Little Children Are Sacred* report with the most graphic evidence yet that child sexual abuse was endemic in the Territory's Aboriginal communities. The reasons for this run so deep I can think of no other moral crisis to equal it in modern Australia. Those comfortably removed from the consequences need only ask themselves how they would respond if this were happening in their own suburbs. Howard was right to treat it as a national emergency but the nature of the intervention inspired a profound debate and, in my opinion, some of the best writing of 2007.

I have in front of me the photograph of an Aboriginal boy taken in 1901 at the Alice Springs Telegraph Station by the pioneering ethnographer Baldwin Spencer. It's titled 'Arrernte boy wearing cast off clothing' and includes Spencer's observation that 'any child who owned a discarded garment of a European child was greatly envied'.

'Once on,' he writes, 'no garment was ever removed, day or night until the fragments could hang on no longer and it fell off, bit by bit'.

The boy looks to be about ten. His eyes are in shadow, his long hair matted, his jaw set. Spencer notes that every time he set his camera down, carefree, laughing children would suddenly become as solemn as judges. In this case the boy's unsmiling face adds a strange gravitas. We assume he's a fringe dweller at this remote outpost of the newly formed federation. The rags hang off him, shredded into strands that barely cover his sturdy frame. It is easy to believe he would wear them until they literally fell from his body.

And it's easy to believe that covering himself in these threads of the dominant European culture was the closest he would come to being part of it.

In Baldwin Spencer's startling images of a largely extinct tribal world we see the ghosts of Federation. The man behind the camera believed he was recording a dying race. 'The time in which it will be possible to investigate the Australian native tribes', Spencer wrote in 1899, 'is rapidly drawing to a close'.

So much energy has been exhausted in the culture wars arguing questions of blame, of cause and effect and historical responsibility, that we've ended up in a moral maze.

In the first century of the Australian nation we've gone from Spencer's boy in rags to the *Little Children Are Sacred* report. And we have gone from traditional communities to 'outback ghettoes' like Noel Pearson's hometown of Hope Vale, which he describes as 'a hellhole where whirring fans and airconditioners in the concrete block houses drown out the noise, including the screams'.

The historian Robert Manne does not much like Baldwin Spencer. He writes in his essay 'Pearson's gamble, Stanner's dream' that Spencer looked at Aboriginal ceremony 'as if he was peering through the glass of an aquarium'. That was rather typical, says Manne, and it was not until the more enlightened anthropologist AP Elkin called, in 1934, for 'a positive policy' for Aboriginal welfare that government experimentation began.

Manne's essay maps the shifting foundations of Indigenous policy since that time and examines the philosophy that underpinned the first real policy, which was labelled 'assimilation'. One principal architect of assimilation was the Menzies-era minister Paul Hasluck, who conceived of it as a destination, a place and time wherein all 'Aborigines and part-Aborigines will attain the same manner of living as other Australians'.

But devastating short cuts were made in the attempts to reach that destination, the consequences of which were set out in the 1997 *Bringing Them Home* report into the Stolen Generations. Children were taken by the state for many reasons, but the forcible removal of mixed-blood children from their families and communities, on the assumption they would be more easily absorbed into white society, had the bleakest impact. One woman who was put into care at the age of eight, with her three sisters, told the inquiry: 'We were completely brainwashed to think only like a white person'. But in the end she concluded that the removed children were rejected by both societies because they were 'neither black nor white. They were simply a lost generation of children. I know. I was one of them'.

The Northern Territory intervention last year spawned both a new debate from the right about assimilation and attempts to rehabilitate Hasluck. Those atmospherics inspired great caution from Robert Manne when he came to consider the intervention.

'Like the majority of Australians, I was relieved that a decision for action had finally been taken', he writes, while being simultaneously dismayed by 'the arrogant disregard for Aboriginal people and their leaders'.

But one leader was not disregarded. In fact, the ideas of Cape York's intellectual revolutionary Noel Pearson underpin the intervention's welfare changes. This is Pearson's 'gamble', referred to in Manne's title, a plan to break the ideological stalemate over Aboriginal policy 'by marrying the idea of rights with the idea of responsibilities', and despite his reservations Robert Manne concludes it's the most coherent policy ever offered.

But to really understand where Pearson is coming from, his own long essay 'White guilt, victimhood and the quest for a radical centre' is required reading. It's a distillation of seven years of his thoughts about Aboriginal suffering and solutions.

Pearson writes on the fortieth anniversary of the 1967 referendum that empowered the federal parliament to make laws about Aboriginal issues. More than 90 per cent of Australians voted 'Yes' in that referendum, a flowering of goodwill that bloomed into a social movement and was eventually instituted as government policy. Four long decades later, Pearson subjects that goodwill to forensic scrutiny and plots the development of a perversely interdependent culture of 'white guilt' and Aboriginal 'victimhood'.

This is the best outline until now of the evolution of Pearson's political philosophy. The nuances therein, his commitment to detailed, difficult thinking and the force of his argument make it clear that Noel Pearson's ideas, made concrete in his Cape York social experiment and adopted piecemeal by the intervention's planners, will continue to have a profound influence on government policy.

That being the case, the debate between Indigenous leaders is likely to harden. In 'Whatever happened to reconciliation?', Patrick Dodson, for example, refers to the intervention as 'cultural genocide' and accuses Pearson of being 'recklessly naive in aiding and abetting the Howard Government's agenda'. By contrast, Marcia Langton in 'Stop the abuse of children' calls on the Rudd Government to continue the intervention and 'to stop the plague of child rape, abuse and neglect in Aboriginal communities'.

Langton was writing in the wake of last December's ghastly reports from the Cape York town of Aurukun. As I write this there's still no adequate explanation as to how a judge could possibly justify her decision to return nine males to the community after they admitted to gang-raping a 10-year-old girl.

Russell Skelton's 'Tortured history of violence' takes us into the ravaged township, where traditional culture has been replaced by 'a form of social anarchy and madness', while Tony Koch, who broke the story in *The Australian*, examines the shattered life of the now 12-year-old rape victim in 'Born of grog violence to child tragedy'.

The girl was born with foetal alcohol syndrome in 1995 and a paediatric surgeon says: 'She's probably functioning as a five- or six-year-old'. When she was five she was taken from her family after being sexually abused by a close family member; at seven she was raped by up to five youths; then at ten she was gang-raped over six weeks by nine males. Wandering the streets she was raped 'on at least six other occasions' and contracted gonorrhoea.

Without a hint of irony, the paediatrician observes: 'She's very difficult to control—she's very rebellious, she's got a foul temper, and I'm well aware numerous carers have had huge problems with her behaviour'.

I am old enough to remember watching at close quarters as Bob Hawke made his 1987 election promise in the Sydney Opera House that 'no child will live in poverty'. It was a grand gesture made during an almost operatic campaign launch. No child will live in poverty. But its all-too-evident failure leaves the impression it was no more than political rhetoric.

For his part, Bob Hawke now says it was 'a silly shorthand thing to say' and that even though his government did give extra money to low-income families, many of them simply 'pissed it up against the wall'.

This summer I thought to ask him more about this when I saw him in his electric-blue trousers and white shoes promenading with friends to the southern point of Palm Beach, to watch the freak waves generated by the storm surge. When he did a double take of half-recognition to my 'G'day Bob' and offered up 'How's the cricket going?' I lost my nerve.

To be fair, besides the roiling surf, the wacky weather and its implications, cricket was on many minds because of claims a Sikh spinner had racially abused an Australian player of Afro-Caribbean heritage by calling him a monkey. But, in the light of his long-ago pledge, what I really wanted to ask Bob Hawke about was the *Little Children Are Sacred* report and how he thought the new Labor Government should respond to it.

We are still being buffeted by the effects of that political storm surge last November. Here we are, fully twenty years after Bob Hawke promised to save the children, with a new Labor Prime Minister who's actually taken the trouble of laying out the underpinnings of his moral philosophy in a detailed essay. Of course, it was Kevin 06 who wrote that. It was Kevin 07 who won the election and we're still waiting to find out about Kevin 08.

So what should we expect of our strangely enigmatic new Prime Minister? For clues beyond his speeches and policy documents, there are two less than brilliant biographies, a veritable library of interview transcripts, some TV profiles, a filmed Kokoda trek with his cultish '*Sunrise* family', his globally broadcast earwax consumption, his conversational Mandarin, his text messages and his own influential essay on Christian philosophy and its political implications, penned just before taking the Labor leadership.

To add to that swag of biographical data we have included here Simon Mann's 'The making of Kevin Rudd', which tracks the evolution of the Queensland wunderkind from when he was right-hand man to Premier Goss. The 32-year-old Rudd was one of the 'boys in suits', derided by Labor's old guard but promoted by Goss when the party won office after a generation in the wilderness. Running the premier's cabinet office, Rudd was the policy gatekeeper in a government that 'disgorged years of pent-up reforms, articulated in reams of legislation'. A brilliant and driven technocrat, Rudd was feared by some as the 'baby-faced assassin' or 'Dr Death', but his team of young, university-educated policy wonks became the engine room of the Goss Government. The words used to describe him in those days are useful markers for future reference: formidable, meticulous, driven, conservative, arrogant, rude, an intellectual force.

Missing from that list is 'Christian', which is strange when you consider that Kevin Rudd is the most overtly religious Prime Minister we've had in modern times. Wondering how that might be reflected in policy, Andrew West in 'More than just a light on the hill' looks to Rudd's hero, the German theologian Dietrich Bonhoeffer, who was martyred for his opposition to Nazism. Bonhoeffer thought it a Christian duty to identify with the 'marginalised, vulnerable and oppressed' and, true to his hero, Rudd has focused early on the plight of the homeless, earning the media title 'Prime Minister of hard knocks'. So where will the economic conservative who described Howard's Australia as a 'Brutopia' lead us? Would he dare to repeat Bob Hawke's promise? His decision to apologise to the Stolen Generations (albeit without the compensation recommended by the inquiry) has immense symbolic significance, but what concrete measures will follow? And how would he go about dispensing Christian charity to a damaged and uncontrollable 12-year-old girl from Aurukun?

One thing that's certainly exercised his mind in recent years is the Christian concept of a 'just war'. In that regard Kevin Rudd was in two minds about Iraq, but Labor policy is clear: Iraq is an unjust war, Afghanistan is a just war—so just, so vital to the War on Terror, that the Labor Government may well send more troops there even though that's where Australian soldiers are dying. But before the diggers in Iraq are transhipped from the Gulf to fight the Taliban in Oruzgun province, we get a reality check from two of our writers. In 'Misguided US policy a gift to bin Laden', Paul McGeough reports from Pakistan, home of the Al Qaeda leader, while in 'Mission drift' Chris Masters reports from Afghanistan, where Australian troops now confront the Taliban, Al Qaeda's key ally. Neither reporter finds reasons for optimism.

On the fourth anniversary of the Iraq invasion, as jihadis celebrated Osama bin Laden's fiftieth birthday, McGeough reflected on the disastrous failings of a War on Terror that has in fact inspired a global blossoming of terrorism. At precisely the same time, the Australian Government was preparing to repatriate a citizen who'd been trained by Al Qaeda in Afghanistan.

It took years but eventually David Hicks's long detention without trial at Guantanamo Bay had become a serious political embarrassment, and, as Leigh Sales details in 'Inside the Hicks deal', that embarrassment was also being felt in Washington as the State Department and the Pentagon wrangled over the fate of an imprisoned Australian citizen.

Even anti-terror hardliner Michael Costello condemned the Australian Government for not protesting 'the whole jerry-built, ramshackle, ad hoc treatment of prisoners at Guantanamo', and when Hicks was finally charged and hauled before a military commission to plead guilty, Robert Richter, QC, described it as a charade that 'would have done Stalin's show trials proud'.

Perhaps the public tolerance for secret hearings and detention without trial had reached some kind of limit by the time Dr Mohamed Haneef was detained as a terror suspect in Brisbane after his cousin attempted a car bombing at Glasgow airport. Paul Kelly concludes there was by then a 'crisis of trust', but as the case for holding Haneef was unravelled by lawyers and journalists, the lack of trust appeared warranted. David Marr, in 'Just an ordinary life', traces the disintegrating trail of evidence linking Dr Haneef to his cousin's plot.

All the while a parallel debate on 'Australian values', sprouting from the fear of radical Islam and global terror, ran hot. As many Australians began to sympathise with that Anglo convert to radical Islam, David Hicks, a woman born to the faith contemplated her own role as one of those most fear-inducing of hyphenated identities: a Muslim-Australian. The status of Australians, writes Randa Abdel-Fattah in 'Veils and Vegemite', 'feeds off the un-Australian status of others'.

Australian identity is also explored by Mark McKenna in 'The Anzac myth'. He plots the rise of a particular kind of nationalism in Howard's Australia, which he characterises as 'unreflective, earnest and often sentimental'. Meanwhile, Thomas Keneally, in 'Flattened by a falafel', offers a historical perspective on how race and ethnicity have long been invoked in this country for political purposes. Keneally wonders why there is 'so little faith in the breadth of what Australia is, in its capacity to go on?'

It was part of John Howard's longstanding agenda to reverse what he regarded as a false interpretation of Australia's history as 'a litany of intolerance, bigotry and narrow-mindedness'. The values debate was just one front of the culture wars he initiated.

In 'Conservatives are no longer losing the culture wars', *The Australian*'s Tom Switzer declares a victory of sorts that, he says, many on the right have not fully realised: 'I would suggest that there has been something of a political and cultural realignment of the nation'. A stretch, you say? Well, take a look at Guy Rundle's scathing indictment of Australian left-liberalism in 'Goodbye to all that' and you might think again.

In 'Right-wing warriors who changed the workplace', Michael Bachelard profiles Ray Evans, the most spectacularly successful and most battle-scarred veteran of that philosophical fight. Evans was a co-founder of the HR Nicholls society (with Peter Costello)—it was he who dreamed up the name. At the time, Ray Evans was an executive officer at Western Mining, having been hired by Hugh Morgan, as he freely admits, to 'engage in the culture wars and provide him with feedback'. Those revolutionary backroom meetings were the genesis of the WorkChoices legislation.

But Ray Evans's influence was not confined to industrial relations. His zeal was franchised to another outlet, the Lavoisier Group, to promote climate change scepticism.

I met the engaging Mr Evans while moderating a live debate after the screening of *The Great Global Warming Swindle*. Hugh Morgan once described his relationship with Ray Evans as 'a twenty-year seminar', but one sensed a waning of Evans's influence as he struggled to come to terms with the fact that the articulate young woman sitting next to him in the panel, passionately arguing that climate change is a real and present danger, was actually there representing the coal industry.

As to 'the Swindle' itself, many climate change sceptics saw the Martin Durkin documentary as a prime-time opportunity to derail the scientific consensus on global warming. Durkin clearly sees himself as a culture warrior. He wrote in an op. ed.: 'I could not have upset the soft-left, soft-green middle classes more if I had crept into their kitchens and snuck genetically modified tomatoes in their paninis'. It was certainly getting hot in the kitchen.

We've included Durkin's antipodean loyalist, geologist Bob Carter, to indicate the temperature of the debate that was seen by some as the last gasp of climate change denial. Clive Hamilton responds with 'Who's being swindled here?', raking over Durkin's record as an activist filmmaker, his links to a Trotskyist splinter group and 'the concoction of scientific distortions in *Swindle*'.

While Marian Wilkinson details the political history of the Australian climate change debate in 'Delayed reaction', in 'Take me to the river' novelist Chloe Hooper visits a sun-blasted Mallee town in north-western Victoria and talks to farmers whose children have never seen 'proper rain'.

While climate change became the environmental motif of the election campaign (with a few whales thrown in), Mark Latham's politically fatal conversion by Bob Brown in 2004 ensured that Tasmania's forests would be off-limits for Labor, but one writer managed to put the issue back on the agenda. Richard Flanagan's searing and at times mournful essay 'Out of control' inspired a public debate about the Gunns pulp mill that briefly threatened to derail the long-term ambitions of then Environment Minister Malcolm Turnbull.

As it transpired, Turnbull was one of the few Coalition ministers to emerge unscathed from the eventual Ruddslide, and we are only now learning in detail of the role that he and others played in trying to have John Howard stand down on the eve of the campaign.

In one of a series of increasingly pessimistic *Lateline* interviews, Howard loyalist Tony Abbott told me last May that he feared Australians were 'sleepwalking' to electoral change 'in a fit of absent-mindedness'. Now we know the analogy was better applied to a government that was sleepwalking to oblivion—or even 'annihilation', if you prefer the word John Howard chose in his famous party room warning.

Retrospectivity is a fine thing.

Alexander Downer now tells us that, by September, Mr Howard was no longer issuing mere rhetorical warnings. Nor was he sleepwalking. He was wide awake to the prospect of defeat. As Paul Kelly details in

'The defeat', the Prime Minister floored Downer during APEC with the following private revelation: 'My best judgment is that we will lose the election and I'll lose my seat of Bennelong as well'.

We may have to wait a long time to hear Mr Howard's own version of events. But as the long shadows of summer turn 2007 into history, we reprint the electoral post-mortems of Howard's bitterest enemy, Paul Keating, and one of his closest friends, Geoffrey Blainey. In 'Divisive leader who squandered Australia's hopes', the politician tells of his relief that 'the toxicity of the Liberal social agenda' is over, while in 'From triumph to a tragic' the historian asserts that 'in the end, John Howard will be seen by vast numbers of Australians as one of the great prime ministers'.

If Blainey is right, John Howard will first have to survive the judgement of his own party, now at its lowest ebb since Menzies founded it. The final word, therefore, goes to Pamela Williams, who assesses how the Liberals' 'Royal Family' led the party into a right royal mess.

There are many other writers included in this collection but not mentioned so far. Political prognosticators of the calibre of Michelle Grattan, George Megalogenis, Phillip Adams, Glenn Milne and Paul Sheehan are woven through the collection, along with social commentators like David Burchell and the playwright Louis Nowra. And it is with sadness that we include here one piece from our most insightful modern parliamentary sketchwriter, Matt Price. To say Matt's death was untimely simply doesn't cover it. He lived to see John Howard's bamboozlement turn into gracious acceptance of defeat on election night. Matt texted his congratulations to Kevin Rudd and died the following morning. Honoured by both sides of politics, his sudden illness focused the press gallery, commentariat and politicians alike on the stuff that really matters.

It's obviously true that these journalists and essayists do not qualify as instant historians, but anyone hoping for a real understanding of the events of 2007 will do well to regard *The Best Australian Political Writing* as key source material.

Tony Jones
January 2008

1

All the Way to the Lodge

Hugh Mackay

A stir from slumber: Waking up or just rolling over?
The Sydney Morning Herald, 27 January 2007

Straws in the wind. Hints. Possibilities. Nothing more. But it's hard to escape the feeling that the Australian electorate might be emerging from its dreamy period. Sitting up. Taking notice. Ready, perhaps, for a little nourishment.

Some of us have been lulled by sweet talk of a resources boom. Others have been inhibited by fear of what might happen to us if the terrorists have their way. But the effect has been the same: we haven't been paying attention. In everything from our TV viewing to our voting behaviour, we have been trying to ignore the big picture in favour of the miniatures of our private lives.

We couldn't get enough TV programs about backyards and home renovations, because that's where our heads were. Our narrow, inward focus excluded the things we half-knew needed our attention, ranging from our continuing involvement in Iraq to the anti-terrorism and industrial relations laws; from the rising tide of prejudice to the apparently intractable problems of poverty, drug abuse and the crisis in our public hospitals, schools and universities.

For these past five years or more, our disengagement strategy seemed to work. When we opened our newspapers, we were more interested in the lifestyle supplements than the headlines. When we had to vote, we returned every federal, state and territory government with an increased majority (except Queensland, where the Beattie Government's majority was too large to increase)—not because this is a golden age of political contentment, but because we'd been disengaged from politics to the point of somnolence.

But now, for some reason, there's a stirring. A restlessness. A gnawing sense that we'd better take another look at the big picture.

Those of us interested in tracking the mood of Australia have long wondered what might provoke this kind of re-engagement. A terrorist attack? A bird flu epidemic? A crash in commodity prices that would burst our economic bubble? A painful rise in interest rates?

If there is, indeed, a turning of the tide, it appears not to be the result of a single, sudden crisis, but a confluence of several unrelated factors.

The environment tops the list. Not since the late '80s has there been such widespread openness to the possibility that the planet is sending us a message. A drought that seriously threatens the water supplies of our capital cities, bushfires that rage out of control for months and have seasoned experts shaking their heads, and the scary prospect of global warming all suggest there's an issue here we can't ignore.

Even the sceptics who see climate change as part of the inexorable swing of a global pendulum are starting to wonder whether this latest swing might have been accelerated by human activity. From water restrictions to car use, we are starting to engage with the idea that tough remedial action might be called for.

Then there's the "values" question. Ironic, really, that politicians have tried to hijack this one: the issues are real enough, but they have nothing to do with defining distinctive Aussie values or deciding whether "mateship" somehow distinguishes us from other cultures (the French, after all, claimed fraternité long before we did). But deeper values-based questions are engaging our attention: have we become too materialistic for our own good? How can we lead more balanced lives? Can we revive our communities and our sense of belonging to them? Is the Australian way of life in danger of being hijacked by American values and culture?

Multiculturalism has again become an issue for us. The Cronulla riots, ethnic violence among spectators at the Australian Open and the news that Tamworth had turned its back on a group of Sudanese refugees have made some of us wonder whether the multicultural game is up. It isn't, of course: how could it be when 50 per cent of us were either born overseas or have at least one parent born overseas, and when we are creating such a brilliantly successful society out of people who've come here from more than 150 different birthplaces?

But disturbing signs of ethnic tension—including the unleashing of anti-Islam prejudice—remind us that multiculturalism is a fragile edifice that requires commitment, goodwill and a healthy curiosity about our differences. To succeed, our bold experiment needs more diversity, not less. It also needs some imaginative and reassuring leadership.

Our changing attitudes to David Hicks look like another symptom of a mood shift. An authoritative Newspoll survey has revealed that 71 per cent of us think Hicks should be brought home. Six months ago, I doubt if enough of us were paying attention to have an opinion, but perhaps the fifth anniversary of his incarceration without trial has jolted us. Even our involvement in Iraq seems set to attract renewed, more critical, interest.

Kevin Rudd's accession to the Opposition leadership adds another item to the list of things re-engaging us. Can Labor win in 2007? Who knows? But the question has suddenly become more interesting, the contest more lively.

It will be six months before we'll know whether the electorate has emerged from its dreamy period. If it has, no incumbent government will feel as safe as it did a year ago: voters who are wide awake tend to notice things that pass them by when they are curled up in little cocoons of self-absorption.

Judith Brett

The turning tide
The Monthly, March 2007

"There is a tide in the affairs of men / Which, taken at the flood, leads on to fortune." But tides also recede. The big question for observers early in this election year is: Has the tide finally turned?

Still running John Howard's way are the economy and the resources boom, as well as the momentum of incumbency. But there are also powerful currents pulling the other way, deeper than the surface froth of political debate and the play of issues. There are three turning points with the potential to shift the basis on which Howard has built his political success: from age to youth; from fear to hope; from private to public.

From age to youth

This is the most obvious. When he turned 65, Howard promised to stay in the job for as long as the Liberal Party and the voters wanted him. And he reiterated the promise when Costello challenged last year. There is a deep disingenuousness in this promise. Taken at face value—and this is how Howard wants it taken—it disavows personal ambition and puts him at the service of the party and the nation. But it also says, If you want me to leave, you will have to throw me out. Hence Keating's rather improbable image of Howard as a coconut glued to his chair, and his reminder of the brutality of his own disposal of Hawke. "You know, prime ministers have got Araldite on their pants, most of them. They want to stick to their seat. And you either put the sword through them or let the people do it."

Howard, of course, will argue for the benefits of experience and a wise head. But whatever he says or promises, he cannot escape the fact that he is getting old. And all of a sudden, with Rudd rather than Beazley as his opposite number, he looks it. Howard turns 68 in July this year. When the next election comes round, in 2010, he will be 71. What is he to say to the electorate about his intentions? Elect me and I promise to stay on till I'm 71, and then I may even run again, like my hero Robert Menzies, who stayed on till he was 72! Or: Elect me, and at some unspecified date before the next election, I will retire and pass the leadership on to my loyal and patient deputy, he of the down-turned mouth, who lacks the common touch and already looks worn out from all those hard years in Treasury.

Old leaders often believe that after them, the deluge: it seems to be a hazard of the psychology of ageing. So, on the whole, they stay on too long. It would have been much better for Menzies' subsequent reputation had he lost the credit squeeze election in 1961 (which he won on Communist preferences); for Margaret Thatcher not to have waited till she was pushed; for Mao Zedong not to have launched the Cultural Revolution. At stake here is not just the age of leaders and their waning physical and intellectual energy, but their inevitable disconnection from the social and cultural worlds of people born 20, 30, 40 and even 50 years after them—and from their futures. Sometimes, ageing leaders are reckless with their country's future because they won't be around to bear the consequences. So Howard seems remarkably unworried about the consequences of global warming, responding to it more as a political challenge to be managed than a real-world danger.

From fear to hope

Critics of Howard argue that much of his political success is due to the way he has used fear: fear of asylum seekers, terrorists, rising interest rates, loss of jobs and so on. The most sustained argument for this is found in Carmen Lawrence's book *Fear and Politics*, and it is a standby of the so-called Howard-haters. I don't completely agree with this position: it is overblown, and relies on a sloppy conflation of Howard's characteristics with those of the Australian people. Because it interprets Howard's political success in essentially negative terms, it fails to engage with the full range of reasons why voters have supported the Coalition. The Coalition has always been the preferred party of the cautious, and caution is not the same as fear. However, I think a slightly different and more complex claim takes us to the heart of Howard's prime ministership.

Howard's leadership style is shaped around combat and control. He thrives in a crisis, is quick to point out threats in the environment and to create division between friends and enemies. He believes that one should stick to one's guns, never give ground, stay till the job is done, and so on. Howard has embraced the war in Iraq with such enthusiasm because war suits his leadership style, and he focuses on enemies real and imagined, because he needs them. Real terrorists are a boon, but his obsessive battle with a largely imaginary left-wing educational establishment shows that there is more going on here than a hard-nosed confrontation with a nasty reality. It is a timeworn cliché, but if he didn't have enemies, he would need to invent them. Howard needs the war in Iraq and the War on Terror at the top of the political agenda because this is his psychological home ground.

His foolish attack on the American Democratic candidate Barack Obama, in an interview with Laurie Oakes on the *Sunday* program, shows this clearly. He said, "If I were running Al Qaeda in Iraq, I would put a circle around March 2007 and pray as many times as possible for a victory, not only for Obama, but also for the Democrats." Obama's position on Iraq is shared by many American politicians and by most of the American public. So why was it Obama he singled out? I think Obama is such a threat to him not because of his different position on Iraq, but because he works with a very different psychological palette. "We can build a more hopeful America," Obama told the crowds at his campaign launch. "And that is why, in the shadow of the Old State Capitol where Lincoln once called on a house divided to stand together, where common hopes and common dreams still live, I stand before you." Howard knows that if the political mood in the US and Australia shifts from fear to hope, he is done for.

Harold Stewart and James McAuley's Ern Malley put into the mouth of Lenin a truth political leaders mostly ignore: "The emotions are not skilled workers." Sometimes, no matter what the penalties in their AWAs, people simply down tools and go looking for a different boss who will allow them to feel things differently.

As my late friend and colleague Graham Little showed in his work on political leadership, all leadership styles are unstable. Each has a particular emotional and psychological shape, but each also casts the shadow of the emotional possibilities it excludes. Strong leaders, like John Howard, are emotionally organised for survival in a difficult world. They thrive on competition and stress the virtues of independence, individual responsibility, hard work and tough decisions. Competitors are often treated as enemies, even if they are only the mild-mannered members of the parliamentary Opposition. When real enemies appear, such leaders rally their team behind them for the fight. Graham Little contrasted strong leaders with group leaders, who pay attention to the many ways human beings need and depend on each other and believe in the creative possibilities of collective action. Group leaders specialise in the politics of sympathy and compassion; strong leaders dismiss them as weak and not to be trusted with the tough tasks of national leadership. They, in turn, see strong leaders as uncaring and many of the dangers that they guard us against as delusional.

Little also had a category of inspiring leaders, leaders who are able to break through the habitual stand-off between strength and compassion and suggest that perhaps we can find political solutions that encompass both. This is a less coherent leadership style than the other two, a sort of midpoint, but it captures the way some leaders can break through with the promise and hope of solutions.

Each of Little's leadership styles has characteristic strengths, and characteristic ways of failing. The danger for strong leaders is that they become too rigid, demand too much repression of individual initiative in the name of loyalty or security, invent enemies and stifle the new ideas needed to respond effectively to a changed world. They may offer a safe pair of hands, but the hands are often only holding solutions to yesterday's problems.

The characteristic shortcomings of strong leadership are displayed on our television screens every time Howard has to discuss the challenge of climate change. Human-induced climate change is a new and urgent problem, and it transcends all the battlelines and solutions of the old politics. Facing up to it, Howard squares his shoulders, sets his chin and stares resolutely into the camera. Everyone knows he has been denying the reality of climate change for the past decade at least, and everyone knows that the politics of this situation are changing fast. But he can only do what he can do—so he gives ground slowly and reluctantly. Having been forced to accept the scientific consensus that carbon emissions are causing the earth's climate to change, he refuses to admit any link between either of these and the drought, even though a connection is highly probable. He searches for enemies to attack: global panic merchants, loony greenies. And he tries to turn the problem into a conventional conflict of economic interests. In this scenario, he presents himself as the guardian of a national economy pitted against other national economies. And he turns the challenge from one of the long-term sustainability of life on the planet to short-term issues of economic prosperity, and the threatened jobs of coalminers. You can almost hear the cogs whirring as he calculates the margins in the Labor electorates with coalmines.

It is abundantly clear that Howard simply does not *get* climate change, and certainly that he has no solutions. He may well be able to win the next election by targeting voters with jobs in the old energy sector, but this is not a solution to climate change.

From private to public

Obama called for more than hope in his launch speech. He called for generational change, and "an awakened electorate". "It hasn't been an absence of sound plans that has stopped us," he said, "but the failure of leadership, the smallness of our politics. People have looked away in disgust and disillusion. We're here to take politics back."

Hugh Mackay reports that among the people he's interviewed over the years, there is a widespread nostalgia for the Whitlam era—and this from people who disliked Whitlam, as well as from the fans. The nostalgia, he argues, is for the political intensity of the times, the sense of engagement and that politics mattered. It's much like the nostalgia sometimes expressed for World War II, that it brought people together, lifted them out of their small lives into an enlarged sense of collective purpose. In an elegant little book called *Shifting Involvements*, the political economist Albert Hirschman has argued that there is an oscillation in modern Western political history between periods of engagement with collective and public purposes, and periods of retreat into the concerns of private life and the pursuit of individual material wellbeing. This oscillation, he says, can only partly be explained by outside events and crises; there is also a psychological dynamic at play in such turnabouts, which can be very rapid. Hirschman was writing in the wake of 1968, when a new political engagement appeared, as if from nowhere, and swept large numbers of people into public action. And then this spirit ran its course. Disappointed with the inevitable failures of activism, people went back to the more manageable but smaller concerns of their private lives, leaving politics to the professionals.

There is a match between a strong leader and a disengaged polity. The strong leader's message is, Leave it to me, I'm in charge. He may, as Howard has done with the anti-terrorist legislation, demand to be given more power, but he does not ask for more involvement. His peacetime purpose is to provide the safe shield behind which people can get on with their lives. Obama offers a different relationship, inviting people back into public life and the exciting possibilities of public action. Obama's critics point out that he is short on policy specifics. And people may well not heed the invitation—or not quite yet.

But they may. The looming environmental crisis is one which confronts us with our interdependence, not just on the environment but on each other, and so it is likely to propel increasing numbers of people into public action to seek collective solutions to a collective problem. It is becoming blindingly obvious that the West cannot go on as it has done, consuming resources as if there is no tomorrow, year after year, decade after decade, into an open-ended future which is simply more of the same. Popular culture, with its fascination with disasters, knows this. Global business leaders know this. Politics is paralysed.

Many people, I am sure, feel as I do, that they are living in two clangingly discordant timeframes. In one, life goes on as usual, turning on lights and taps, driving cars, complaining about the weather, organising holidays, bringing up children, calculating superannuation ...

In the other, we know that the scientists are right, are haunted by images of polar bears swimming between melting ice floes, and feel powerless to do anything. The enthusiasm with which water is being saved shows that people know things have to change. But most of the solutions are far beyond anything people can do as individuals, and if you think too much about the future, you just get depressed. Howard says he prefers to be optimistic about the future. So would we all.

What Howard doesn't seem to get is that on climate change, our preferences are irrelevant. If the climate is changing, it is changing, no matter what he would prefer or how he describes it. And this is not a problem that can be turned into a conflict between us and them. He can fire insults at the messengers as much as he likes, but if the message is right, there will be simply be more messengers.

Much of Howard's political success has come from the intensity of his focus on the minutiae of day-to-day politics. He knows the margins in all the electorates and the names of his backbenchers' children; he dominates the media; he calculates the days till the next election; he devises handouts for disgruntled groups and keeps money in the coffers for government advertising campaigns; he studies his opponents to find their weaknesses and public opinion polls to craft his arguments. And he has won again and again. But none of this tells us anything about whether the long-term public interest is being served by his victories. Keeping his eye so firmly on the present, Howard seems unable to focus on the long-term future of the nation, let alone the planet.

Howard knows his strengths, and in the coming year, he will play to them. He will warn us of the threats of terrorism and Labor's mismanagement of the economy, try to wedge Labor on climate change among blue-collar workers, blame the Labor states as much as possible for health crises and the skills shortage. He will stress the inexperience of youth against the wisdom of age; he will pour scorn on the illusory and insubstantial promises of hope; he will promise that with him as prime minister, our individual prosperity will continue for ever and ever, and that global warming can be dealt with by the pragmatic politics of incrementalism, in which no one will be a loser. He will fight to keep the election on his chosen ground. It will be a remarkable feat if he can pull it off.

The turning points from age to youth, from fear to hope and from private withdrawal to public engagement have their own separate dynamics. But they also overlap with and reinforce each other. If they start to run together, they will sweep Howard from office. And he knows it.

Simon Mann

The making of Kevin Rudd
The Age, 21 April 2007

Gary Sturgess can't recall the year exactly, but he remembers the moment. It was at the annual gathering of the prime minister and state premiers, their top bureaucrats and assorted minders, the so-called Special Premiers' Conference. In fact, it was 1990. And in Brisbane.

Kevin Rudd was there, mop-haired and bespectacled, working alongside newly elected Queensland Labor premier Wayne Goss. Sturgess, the head of the NSW Cabinet Office, was the right-hand man of Liberal premier Nick Greiner.

Tensions had arisen between the two—Johnny-come-lately apparatchik Rudd and the man who had long pulled strings for Greiner—though Sturgess can't recall exactly why. "Whatever it was," says Sturgess, "I have to say I'd reached the point where I thought: 'He's a rude bastard.'"

Some time later the telephone rang in Sturgess's Sydney office. It was Rudd. "He was going down to Canberra for something, and said: 'Let's get together for dinner in Sydney on my way back.'" So the pair headed to a restaurant near the Rocks on Sydney's waterfront, Sturgess not quite sure of what to expect.

The talk was "frank", he admits, "and we discovered we had similar backgrounds and saw the world in pretty similar ways. In fact, it was the beginning of a very close relationship."

Now a London-based consultant, Sturgess says Rudd's "cold call" to him more than 16 years ago offers a clue about how the Labor leader operates, about the way he meets challenges and works to build strategic relationships and his willingness to compromise if necessary. "Kevin was very good at that, and him coming in and sitting down and eyeballing me that day and saying 'You know, this is actually extremely important; let's you and I talk', is a classic example of Kevin addressing not just the content but also the process."

It is also, perhaps, an example of the power of connections—a year or so later, Sturgess sat on a three-member panel that chose Rudd as the inaugural head of Goss' new Cabinet Office, a carbon copy of Greiner's.

There are varying accounts of Rudd's operating style in the inner sanctum of the reformist Goss government, firstly as the premier's chief of staff, then as the director-general of its cabinet office.

Those five or so years in the early-to-mid-1990s reveal much about the man who wants to be PM and much too, perhaps, about what sort of prime minister he would likely make. This was Rudd at the coalface of executive power, privy to a sleeves-rolled-up take on government in action. How did he operate in the cauldron of everyday decision-making as he morphed from political sidekick into policy maestro, and how did he cope with the wrench, ultimately, of defeat—firstly, with the Goss government's demise, then with his own ill-fated first tilt at Federal Parliament? What did he make of that intense period, and what did he learn from it?

Methodical, process-driven and naturally conservative, Rudd was to many people the proverbial man on a mission. Many found his style abrasive and uncompromising, and Goss himself has conceded that Rudd was at times during those torrid years in Queensland a bit of a bastard, "because sometimes you have to be if you want to make a difference".

Labor's enemies derided Rudd as the "power behind the Goss throne", "chief cruncher" and the "Dr Death" of a regime that made no apologies for wanting to plunge a stake deep into the heart of "Old Queensland", a state characterised by political ineptitude, cronyism and corruption, and a public sector whose policy skills had atrophied.

But former colleagues and close mates such as Glyn Davis, now vice-chancellor of Melbourne University, nominate Rudd as the "intellectual force" of the time. And Sturgess reckons the brash and somewhat nerdy mandarin could not have endured in Queensland "without also having some fairly sophisticated skills".

Certainly Rudd made an impact at those early premiers' conferences. He was a resolute negotiator—"I thought 'Gee, this guy's pretty sharp,'" recalls one senior bureaucrat—and, in an era of unprecedented federal–state co-operation on a national power grid, business regulation and competition, Rudd proved himself an integral player adept at finding common ground among disparate interests.

It's why some Rudd observers expect that Kevin Rudd, PM, would be a champion of a new federalism, harnessing national co-operation, especially in response to things such as water and climate change and on national productivity drivers. (Rudd frequently signposts as much by insisting he wants to "end the blame game" played between governments in light of an "increasingly dysfunctional federation".) They see him as a likely change agent, not so much radical but consensual. And they see in Rudd, in 2007, a much mellowed version of the raw, fresh-faced Queensland Cabinet Office head.

"What you do at age thirtysomething and what you do at 50 is likely to be different for all of us," says Patrick Weller, of Griffith University's department of politics and public policy, while sounding caution about drawing too much inference, good or bad, from those early years. "There was something written the other day which seemed to suggest that everything that had happened in Queensland after 1989 was Rudd's fault, which it wasn't."

Even so, scars run deep. Rob Borbidge, who became premier in the Nationals–Liberal Party minority government that succeeded Goss in 1996, says a lot of Rudd's time has been "glossed over". "My view is he is a formidable opponent, but I do believe his record during that period does require closer scrutiny because it's the only experience that's on the record about Kevin Rudd ... They were wild times and, interestingly, they were uncomfortable times for a lot of the true believers."

Kevin Michael Rudd is a Queenslander. Should he scale the ultimate political peak, Rudd would be the fourth Queenslander to do so but possibly only the second to have a real crack at it. Labor's Andrew Fisher had three goes totalling almost four years, his last term in 1915. Then there was the 40-day reign in 1941 of Arthur Fadden, of the Country Party, and Frank Forde's caretaker eight days following John Curtin's death in 1945. Fisher was 46 when he first took office: Rudd turns 50 in September.

Rudd seems to have been driven from the outset, despite tough early years when he lost his father and was packed off for a time to a Catholic boarding school in Brisbane, where he is said to have been miserable. He was smart, too. He was dux in 1974 of the local high school at Nambour, home of the "Big Pineapple" on Queensland's Sunshine Coast. Wayne Swan, the shadow treasurer, went to the same school, but was a few years ahead of him. Rudd went on to Canberra's Australian National University, where he studied Chinese language and history, and where he met his wife, Therese Rein, now an independently wealthy businesswoman, before entering the diplomatic corps in 1981. There was a first-up posting in Sweden, where he was involved in talks on nuclear safeguards agreements, and later a stint in Beijing.

But the ambitious Mandarin-speaking young diplomat appears to have been looking for high-octane adventure, eschewing a further posting to London for a role alongside barrister-turned-Queensland opposition leader Goss, whose political fortunes were rising fast. He answered an advertisement in a Brisbane newspaper, famously asking his prospective employer whether it would be OK to have Sundays off, a line Goss happily trots out as evidence of Rudd's focus and commitment.

There was mutual admiration then, and there remains so: Goss, chairman of Deloittes in Brisbane, sits on the board of Therese Rein's job placement company, Ingeus, and likes to hint that he remains a Rudd confidant. "Oh yeah, I talk to Wayne quite a lot," Rudd tells *The Age*. "He's a great guy," though he says he never really "seeks advice" from anyone outside of the normal political process. "I just chat ... I find in the process of conversation with people you trust and people who have experience that your own ideas come to you."

Within a year or so of their first meeting, Goss and his bright new chief of staff were in office. It was December 1989. "And then all shit happened," says a former department director-general, partly in jest but partly, too, in horror at the subsequent upheavals within the bureaucracy.

Context is a key. The Queensland to which Rudd had returned in the late 1980s was in turmoil and much of the Goss government's agenda was, in fact, being written by others such as Queen's Counsel Tony Fitzgerald, who handed down his report on police corruption six months ahead of the 1989 state election, an investigation that had evolved into a forensic inquiry into the body politic in Queensland. Four former ministers and a police commissioner were subsequently sent to jail.

Goss committed to setting up the Public Sector Management Commission, "to make government work", as he put it. Headed by academic Peter Coaldrake, the commission conducted a searing review that led to Queensland's 27 government departments being reduced to 18. All but one or two departmental heads were replaced, many having their jobs advertised before losing out to a new breed of bureaucrat. Mud flew: supporters describe it today as "cleaning out the stables", opponents as politicisation.

As change swept Queensland, Goss' new team was derided by some, including by Labor's old guard, as "the boys in suits", while its youthfulness led to charges of impudence and arrogance. At the time of his election Goss was just 38. So was Coaldrake, while Labor's then state secretary, Swan, was 35 and Rudd 32. Barely 30 was another up-and-comer, academic Davis, who joined Coaldrake's commission. Goss had been five when Labor last ruled the state, Rudd not yet born.

As the new premier's right-hand man, Rudd found himself at the vanguard of the Goss revolution—and in the firing line of recalcitrant public servants, as well as ministers and their staff, some of whom almost certainly envied the wunderkind's close relationship with the premier. But the job at hand was to deliver the Goss agenda, and Rudd set about doing so with single-mindedness.

It didn't take long for the sobriquet "Dr Death" to be coined. Years later Rudd would acknowledge the moniker, adding that he was heartened to know that his opposite numbers in other state governments were similarly damned as "Pol Pot", "Rasputin" and "Morticia". "In my callow youth, I might have been sensitive about these sorts of things but you tend to become hardened over time," he once said.

There are varying accounts of how the title came about. Ministers used to complain that Rudd would kill off submissions before they got to cabinet; others say it was because it was often Rudd who delivered bad news to key public servants. "The nickname arose because if you got called in to see him it wasn't a good look," says a former minister. "And that's when people would say with some dread: 'I've got an appointment with Dr Death.'"

Some of those removed from top jobs by the government were sent into isolation, where they were left to "sharpen pencils and not much else", according to one ex-director-general. The repository, named the "research unit" but known as the "gulag", was an old state-owned building said to have housed lepers a century before. It was a richly symbolic gesture, and by early 1990 at least eight senior public servants had been dispatched there on full pay but with nothing to do, only to find themselves being portrayed in the media as indolent fat cats. The tactic was meant to force resignations and avoid costly redundancies.

The bureaucrats blamed Rudd for their plight. "The general belief around the place was that it was the baby-faced assassin," recalls one, who was summarily sent to the gulag two days before Christmas Day 1989. "Kevin Rudd was the mastermind of the gulag." The former "inmate" still smarts at the humiliation. "It was a really shitty thing. They treated people in the most inhumane way," he says. "It spread a climate of fear … We were fodder for a political message they wanted to send out to the public service."

Resentment lingered long. On wresting the premiership in 1996, National Party leader Borbidge referred scathingly to "the place where Rudd, Coaldrake and (Goss) sent some of this state's most senior and longest-serving public servants to rot", telling Parliament: "The conditions of their separation from the public sector were haggled over. Health broke, families fell apart and careers were utterly destroyed."

Rudd says now: "No one ever gets it completely right. I certainly didn't. You try your hardest, do your best." But as for individual decisions, some things might have been done better. "I think, for example—this is the government generally as opposed to just me personally—the way in which reform of the public service was carried out was rougher than it needed to be."

Some observers thought Rudd relished the label of "Dr Death", a bit like notches on a career belt. "Certainly, if you have the view that you're ambitious and have the right answers, being criticised for that is something that you rather welcome," says Roger Scott, who headed up the Education Department during the Goss years.

"I think the representation of him was coloured by his personal style," Scott adds, "because the role he played as a major instrument for reform was an important role and he played it successfully."

It was mid-1991 when Rudd was elevated from political minder to policy driver as director-general of the newly created Cabinet Office.

"Among the central agencies, I am very much conscious of being new kids on the block," Rudd, not yet 34, told public administrators 10 days into the life of the new office. "And you see a number of things can happen to new kids on the block—they can get bashed up by the older kids, they can become ostracised or they themselves can turn into neighbourhood thugs."

Rudd had no intention of getting beaten up. He had the premier's imprimatur, and the office was the gate-keeper of the government's policy program. Its role was to review all submissions to cabinet, seeking comment from other departments where necessary, then advise the premier of any points of dispute as well as a suggested way forward. Departmental officers bringing items to the table had to know their stuff and be prepared to face a grilling.

"It was about bringing for the first time some serious discipline around government priorities being delivered in a co-ordinated way," says Michael Roche, then principal policy adviser to treasurer Keith De Lacy. "And that was pretty new to Queensland, where it wasn't unknown for ministers to roll up to the cabinet room with their submissions literally in their back pocket."

Rudd set a cracking pace as the Labor government disgorged years of pent-up reforms, articulated in reams of legislation. The office grew to a staff of more than 80. They were university-educated and young. (By 1995 their average age was 35 and average length of service two years.) In fact, "turnover was encouraged and was high," noted Griffith University's Weller in a book analysing the "engine room" of the Goss government.

"Rudd was there to make sure things happened," he says now.

> By definition, the Office of the Cabinet reflected the interests of the premier. If the premier wants advice you get it, if the premier wants action you move it. And Rudd is very hard-working, he's got a good brain, he doesn't suffer fools … And he distills it all into a set of proposals for Goss.

Former ministers and directors-general describe the process as rigorous, the scrutiny as potentially withering. Unprepared, department heads could be made to feel that they were in an ejector seat with the finger of Goss, or Rudd, hovering over the button. "I wouldn't put it as crudely as that," says Ruth Matchett, who was appointed director-general of family services, Aboriginal and Islander affairs. "But people would quiz you, certainly." The flip side was that when policies did get to the Cabinet Office there was wide inter-departmental consultation. "That hadn't happened in the past."

But Rudd was also seen in some quarters as a brake on more ambitious policy, applying a pragmatism that stifled ideology. The government's land rights legislation was a case in point, criticised as falling short on its promise of delivering real control of land to Queensland Aborigines.

The initial draft came out of Matchett's department but Rudd took the lead. "That was a decision taken fairly early in the process," says Matchett, now an academic at Queensland University of Technology, "to ensure that we got a whole-of-government approach, so balancing the interests of the mining industry and the pastoralists and not allowing the people in the social policy area to run it from a one-eyed perspective perhaps."

Others felt Rudd betrayed some key people in the process, however. Aboriginal activist and academic Marcia Langton quit her role as a senior adviser in the Goss government, accusing it of inherent racism. In a farewell epistle, published in Brisbane's press, she claimed the real strategy behind Rudd's round of consultations was "to warn industry about the 'lunatic radicals' who would endanger their economic aspirations … (assuring them) that land rights in Queensland would be 'minimalist, like a dot painting'."

Leading activist and lawyer Noel Pearson also fell out with the government over its "miserable legislation", having joined a taskforce to help frame a response to Paul Keating's native title legislation in 1993. He noted recently that Rudd had dealt with industry and civic leaders, and lobbyists "with breathtaking verve and skill" but that his arrogance was "equal to his abilities".

Writing on the eve of Rudd's election as federal Labor leader last year, he noted that

> even in the depths of my detestation of what I considered to be his
> mealy political trimming when dealing with issues that had been on

Labor's policy platform, I have never been able to deny a grudging regard for Rudd. After all the expletives and bile would come: 'Yes, but this man is formidable.'

Anne Warner, Aboriginal affairs minister at the time, says Rudd's mission was about delivering results. "I don't remember Kevin being the big stickler (on land rights). He was simply trying to get a workable compromise. He was good at getting all the players around the table at the same time and making sure that everybody's interests were met to some degree."

Of Rudd's style generally, she adds: "He is a conservative individual, he's socially conservative, his whole manner is conservative. He's not a zealot or a hot head … He was just meticulous, and he was very good at that co-ordination process. At the time it was irritating but in retrospect it was good for us." Some programs Rudd appeared particularly keen on, including a raft of women's initiatives. One of the first moves of the Goss government was to establish a register of women suitable for appointments to government boards and statutory bodies, and within a short time the appointments trebled in number. Extra money was found for a range of women's initiatives, too, on health issues, domestic violence and sexual assault programs.

Former education head Scott also acknowledges Rudd's support in the education field, particularly his successful push at those early premiers' conferences for a National Training Authority as well as the wider introduction of Asian languages in schools, a program subsequently axed by the Howard Government.

In fact, observers of varying political hues are quick to cite those successful early inter-governmental forums as a measure of Rudd's intensive policy work. And, having flagged his intention to step down as Cabinet Office chief to contest the seat of Griffith in the impending federal election, Rudd received a send-off from Jeff Kennett at the 1994 premiers' conference in Melbourne, replete with plaudits and a bottle of Kennett's infamous Cabinet Chardonnay, the drop the premier once flogged controversially for a fund-raiser from his Spring Street office.

Kennett is inclined to play down the admiration now.

> We didn't dine together or anything of that sort. But I always respected
> him as a senior public servant, as I respected others … You can't be

a hermit premier and you've got to recognise those around you. So I'd like to think (the send-off) was a sign of good grace more than necessarily trying to be cynical or suggest that he was about to become Lord Kerthumpian of the Wet Wipe islands.

Rudd's departure paved the way for Glyn Davis to succeed him as director-general in 1995. In a move courting condemnation from Opposition ranks, Rudd then worked for Davis as a consultant while building his election platform. Most people noted a distinct change in the Cabinet Office's operating style. Davis was more consensual and less directive, they say. Adds Roger Scott: "It was quite striking ... but Glyn was hugely popular and well liked and I think he was just as effective (as Rudd)."

Davis, who had worked for Coaldrake in the Public Sector Management Commission, had for a time in 1992 also worked closely with Rudd while seconded to the Cabinet Office.

> He drove himself hard and he drove everyone else hard. That's his style. And people understood if you wanted to work for him and with him you had to keep up ... If you weren't adding value he'd lose interest in you pretty quickly. So there were people who were hurt because they didn't meet his standards and they felt they would have liked more time or more opportunity and he would basically move on, because it was never about the people; it was about the process.

Rudd and Goss were peas in a pod, adds Davis. "We used to joke about them being Germanic. It was very much lists of things to be done, strict sequences, a certain amount of information had to be acquired ... that's what they were both like."

Davis, who has headed Melbourne University for the past two years and is an obvious recruit for a Rudd-driven national tertiary advisory body, says much of the commentary on Rudd's time in Queensland has been politically driven and inaccurate. "I would call him the key intellectual force of the Goss government ... (But) no single person can put their stamp on every part of government." If the matter wasn't essentially about policy or intergovernmental issues, then Rudd most likely wasn't involved.

Of the times generally, Peter Coaldrake, now vice-chancellor of Queensland University of Technology, says: "There was a lot of criticism at the pace of change that occurred in that period, and I'm sure that that's a reasonable comment but what I will not easily accept as criticism was that in some ways the agenda was radical." He believes Rudd could draw legions from his experience of the machinery and operations of government, and in terms of federal-state interplay. "It's got to have been very good preparatory territory," he says.

Others see in the Rudd ascendancy parallels with the popular rise of Goss in Queensland, and it seems not at all coincidental that the Labor leader has surrounded himself with a group of aggressive young minders, not to mention their intense—and sometimes overzealous—media management, which has manifested itself in TV chat show appearances, soft magazine profiles and staged picture opportunities. Overall, it's a "softer", jazzier-looking and more amenable Labor leader these days. Even Borbidge senses a more mature operator, and puts it down, in part, to Rudd having absorbed a few political knocks along the way.

Davis cites the pain of the Goss government's defeat as transforming for Rudd. He had seen the government's vote collapse in 1995 and finally dissolve early in 1996 when a crucial re-vote in the electorate of Mundingburra turned into a mini-referendum on the government's plan to build the so-called "koala road", a highway from Brisbane to the Gold Coast that was to be threaded through vital habitat—and several marginal Labor seats.

Rudd and Davis both found themselves in the cross-fire of Labor recriminations. And within a month Rudd also lost his bid for a seat in Federal Parliament in the election that swept John Winston Howard into office. Rudd had harboured high hopes. As a public servant he'd felt stymied. "The only way you can participate in a full way on future directions is by being in the public domain yourself," he had said.

Both losses were "profoundly shocking", says Davis. "They forced him into a serious period of reflection and evaluation." At the same time Rudd joined KPMG as a China consultant, while keeping his eye on a renewed political assault.

"He took defeat personally," says Davis. "That is: 'I was defeated. I must have done something wrong.' He reflected on what it meant about his own skill set, and he went out and systematically built the skills to make sure it didn't happen again."

Indicative was the way Rudd tackled his next campaign, in 1998— meticulously. "He'd become more flexible and more understanding of how politics operated and how it was fundamentally different from the world that he'd known," says Davis. "He was much better on the hustings, he'd learnt to do all that; he'd studied the art as it were. He was a better speaker. He'd built his alliances in the local area ... And he took that seat, in a jog, and he never looked back."

In subsequent elections, and with a little help from a favourable redistribution, Rudd has built his margin in Griffith from 2.4 per cent to more than 8.6 per cent. And with it has crystallised Rudd's ambition for the nation's top job, something he brushed off 12 years ago when he first raised his hand for political office.

"I believe in a substantial apprenticeship," he told a newspaper on announcing his original intention to run. "After some years, I would value the opportunity of serving as a minister." But asked about the prime ministership, he replied: "I don't believe I have the goods to be prime minister."

Was it false modesty? Just honesty, suspects Professor Weller of Griffith University. "Probably quite genuine at the time," he says, just as his pitch for PM now was equally genuine because Rudd believes he IS the goods. Weller makes the point that should Rudd succeed Howard he would be a prime minister with the most hands-on, high-level public sector experience ever, understanding "from the inside" how the public service works, and sensing perhaps what's possible.

> The thing about politicians is that they tend to be dominated by the political system, the political fight, the political processes. Because of his career, his languages, lived here, worked there, but been in embassies, been a self-employed consultant ... He actually does understand, I suspect, a wider range of things.

Those who worked closely with Rudd in those heady and revolutionary days of the Goss government, do not doubt his intensity, ability and sense of purpose. Says Carolyn Mason, former Goss government women's policy adviser: "He had his own inimitable style. A very determined man.

And so when I knew that he was going for the (federal) leadership, I said to everyone: 'Kevin would not be doing that unless he had the numbers three times over.'"

Mason was on the money. Rudd had done his homework, and on December 4 last year, by 49 votes to 39, Kevin Rudd overpowered Kim Beazley and took a further step in his ultimate political quest.

Phillip Adams

Fears of a clone perturb ALP faithful
The Australian, 17 April 2007

I had never heard—or heard of—Paul Keating before I first encountered him hammering away in a parliamentary debate late in the Whitlam era. His vitality and verbal venom showed him to be a force to be reckoned with; no surprise that he went on to become a most complex and creative prime minister.

A few decades, governments and Labor leaders later, while ring-mastering a radio program starring some snarling MPs, I felt a similar sense of discovery. Whose was that voice from Queensland? Forensic in his use of language, icy calm where the others were overheated, Kevin Rudd was utterly different in style from Keating, yet as instantly impressive. Finding that friends in the party were iffy about him (too cool, too ambitious, a god-botherer), I nonetheless made a note of the name.

In the post-Keating era, Labor flopped and floundered. Simon Crean bombed, as did the Bomber, and Mark Latham was a bomb. As I wrote when Latham was contesting the leadership, the only question was whether Mad Mark would explode before, during or after the election. Like Doc Evatt, whom Latham physiologically and psychologically resembled, he proceeded to detonate nonstop.

This column would urge Rudd on the caucus before every leadership tussle, hoping to head off the amorphous Kim Beazley and the lethal Latham. I'd praise Rudd's intelligence and sense of high moral purpose. When neither attribute seemed congenial to the comrades, I'd change tack, suggesting that he was the one potential leader who could knock off John

Howard because he was so like Howard. Now I'm getting emails from true believers worrying that he's too much like Howard.

Bespectacled and earnest, neither Kev nor John are heavily burdened by charisma. While a Keating or a Latham would bend the stylus on any Richter-style measure of political potency, Kev seems to have a calming effect and proffers the illusion of business as usual.

In any biopic of the incumbent PM, Rudd could be cast as the young Howard. Give Kev a track suit and a fake hearing aid and get him doing early-morning jogs, and you'd give the voters a sense of security, of change without change.

I've always reckoned a lot of people will vote for Rudd by mistake.

As for the god-bothering, we live in an era when Christianity has made a political comeback. The born againers were essential to the Bush ascendancy, while locally your Howards, Costellos and, most of all, your Abbotts beat their religious pectorals. Trips to Hillsong are mandatory while Family First and the Exclusive Brethren flex their muscles and their finances. So, having a Labor leader who speaks Christian as well as Mandarin has to be advantageous. Particularly when Rudd's a Bonhoeffer brand of Christian, one who believes strongly in social justice. Someone who might remind Australian Christians that Jesus didn't vote conservative. Note Abbott's agitated response to Rudd's attempts at reconciliation with the religious Right.

Pushing Rudd's barrow was a lonely task, but once over the line he instantly justified my enthusiasm. Who could have imagined such a surge of support for such a nerdy newcomer? Of course, Howard was our secret weapon. After a decade, voters realise that what I'd been saying about him for 10 years was 110 per cent true.

In 2007 perhaps even Simon Crean could beat Howard. Or Bill Hayden's drover's dog. Clearly Howard will be defeated by Howard, although having Rudd around will certainly help.

But Labor sceptics are increasingly worried by the new leader and email me their doubts and worries. They're more concerned to learn that Rudd had lunch with *The Daily Telegraph*'s right-wing columnist Piers Akerman than they were by his breaking of bread with Brian Burke. And they're alarmed when Rudd follows Howard's enthusiastic endorsement of Alan Jones with a diagonal nod to the beleaguered broadcaster.

I respond to readers with soothing noises about realpolitik and the demands of electioneering, but wish Kev wasn't quite so quick to be populist in, for example, his stern denunciation of well-known stand-up comic Taj Din al-Hilali. After all, his public utterances are only marginally sillier than what you hear from your average Anglican archbishop or Catholic cardinal.

I'm not too worried by the gaffe of a pre-dawn dawn service, but wish Rudd wasn't so quick to open the gap on Howard by closing the gap on policy differences. Thus far his campaign seems reminiscent of Beazley's small-target strategy. For example, while taking comfort in Kev's holding the line on industrial relations, I'd prefer bolder initiatives on climate change.

Having come to know Rudd pretty well, I retain my respect for his IQ and enjoy his humour: something too rarely on public display. He'll never do one of Keating's Placido Domingo performances, nor risk the tantrums of a Latham. Like Howard he'll restrain his emotions and try to minimise tactical error. Yet Rudd still has to satisfy many Labor supporters that he has the right stuff. They want some fire with the ice.

David Marr

Yes, Prime Minister—We're a nation in authority's grip

The Sydney Morning Herald, 2 June 2007

At the heart of democracy is a contest of conversations. The tone of a democracy is set by the dialogue between a nation and its leaders. For the past decade, Australia has had a prime minister almost superhumanly reluctant to engage in frank debate. Of course, debate ploughs on in Australia. Hansard is fatter than ever. The Prime Minister is always at the microphone. But after being belittled for most of his political career, John Howard came to power determined public debate would be conducted on his terms. These are subtle, bizarre and at times brutal.

Since 1996, Howard has cowed his critics, muffled the press, intimidated the ABC, gagged scientists, silenced non-government organisations, neutered Canberra's mandarins, curtailed parliamentary scrutiny, censored the arts, banned books, criminalised protest and prosecuted whistleblowers.

This is not as Howard advertised himself on arrival. Then he spoke proudly of his party's tradition of defending individual liberty and the rule of law. He still does. He painted his victory as a repudiation of "stultifying political correctness" that left Australians able "to speak a little more freely and a little more openly about what they feel". The ravings of Pauline Hanson he represented as a triumph of free speech over stifling orthodoxy. And after Aboriginal protesters burnt the flag on Australia Day last year, he rejected calls for their prosecution. "Much in all as I despise what they did, I do not believe that it should be a criminal offence," he told Neil Mitchell of radio 3AW. "I do hold to the old Voltairean principle that I disagree with what he says but I will defend to the death his right to say it, and I see that kind of thing as just an expression, however offensive to the majority of the community, an expression of political opinion."

The Old Voltairean has fallen a bit short. He leads a Government notably uncomfortable with freewheeling debate. Uncomfortable is too kind a description: the dislike is profound. For a decade now, public debate has been bullied and starved as if this were an ordinary function of government. It's important not to exaggerate the result. Suppression is not systematic. There are no gulags for dissidents under Howard. We reserve them for refugees. The occasional victories liberty wins in Canberra are illuminating. There are limits. But Howard's Government has been the most unscrupulous corrupter of public debate in Australia since the Cold War's worst days back in the 1950s.

We haven't been hoodwinked. Each step along the way has been reported, perhaps not as thoroughly and passionately as it should have been, but we're not dealing in dark secrets here. We've known what's going on. If we cared, we didn't care enough to stop it. Boredom, indifference and fear have played a part in this. So does something about ourselves we rarely face: Australians trust authority. Not love, perhaps, but trust. It's bred in the bone. We call ourselves larrikins, but we leave our leaders to get on with it. Even the leaders we mock.

We've watched Howard spin, block, prevaricate, sidestep, confound and just keep talking come what may through any crisis. Words grind out of him unstoppably. He has a genius for ambiguity we've almost come to applaud, and most of the time he keeps himself just this side of deceit. But he also lies without shame. Howard invented the breakable or non-core promise; the first was to maintain ABC funding five years before those children weren't thrown overboard. The truth is we've known he was a liar from the start.

Howard can admit error, but it is extremely rare. Apologies are almost unknown. More than any law, any failure of the Opposition or individual act of bastardry over the past decade, what's done most to gag democracy in this country is the sense that debating John Howard is futile.

One response has been to turn away and wait for him to disappear, in the belief that Australia will once again be what we remember it was: free, open, principled, fearless, fair etc. It wasn't. Most of what troubles us now about the state of public discourse began under Labor. Many of us complaining now did not complain loudly enough back then as Paul Keating bullied the press, the public service and the Parliament. But Howard has come to dominate the country in ways Keating never could. To the task of projecting his voice across Australia, he brought all the ruthless professionalism that marks his Government. Perhaps the man has now exhausted his welcome, but even when the Howard years are long gone, we will be left confronting the damage done and the difficult question of how we let this happen.

We roll with the insults, threats and suppression because we have come to expect Howard's Government to behave like this. We're habituated. Christian warriors fighting sex on the screen demand film censors serve brief terms for fear exposure to all that filth will "desensitise" them. After a decade, Australia is desensitised to John Howard. So why doesn't Labor rally the nation to fight Canberra's bullying in the name of free speech? Because the party's heart isn't in it and Australians have only the patchiest record of becoming passionate about great abstractions, even the greatest of them, liberty.

We've never fought to be free. Vinegar Hill was a convict break-out easily and brutally suppressed. The officers who overthrew Bligh spouted liberty to trade in rum. Shorn of the colour, Eureka was a bunch of miners who didn't want to pay tax. The great issue that drove self-government for the colonies was seizing control of land. We were as much a part of the British Empire after Federation as we were before. And each step away from Britain had to be forced on Australia until the great Mother of the nation finally turned her back on us and walked into Europe. Australia surprised itself by refusing to accept Menzies' tyrannical plans to ban the Communist Party. But only just. Referendums opposed by any of the big parties always lose, and usually heavily. Liberty was preserved in 1951 by 50,000 votes in a nation of millions. The barricades have rarely been manned since.

We aren't the larrikins of our imagination. Australians are an orderly people who obey authority. We grumble instead of challenging it. We despise politicians. Belittling them as a class is a cover for our own passivity. We elect leaders much as we hire electricians: we may whinge about the job and haggle over the bill, but essentially we leave them to get on with their work. The historian John Hirst writes:

Australians think of themselves as anti-authority. It is not true. Australians are suspicious of persons in authority, but towards impersonal authority they are very obedient. This is a country which for a long time closed its pubs at 6pm and which pioneered the compulsory wearing of seatbelts in cars. Its people since 1924 have accepted the compulsion to vote. Its anti-smoking legislation is so tough that smoking is prohibited in its largest sporting stadium, the Melbourne Cricket Ground, though it is open to the skies.

Many puzzles of this subtle country can be solved by remembering how British we remain. It's structural. We have voted to keep the Crown. Our courts are British down to the horsehair wigs. The ethic of government is shifting from Westminster to Washington, but the framework remains British. We have a British suspicion of open information. Freedom-of-information legislation hasn't challenged an instinct for secrecy deep within government, justice and business. We were together in the rearguard of democracies opposing guarantees of citizens' rights, particularly American notions of free speech. With Britain now absorbed reluctantly into Europe's human rights regime, Australia remains the last Western democracy without any national bill of rights. Polls tell us we'd like to have one, but we're not particularly concerned. It's another struggle for liberty we're not busting to fight.

David Malouf has a wonderful notion that Australia and America were made such different places by the English we carried in our baggage. To America, settlers took a language of high abstraction:

> Passionately evangelical and utopian, deeply imbued with the religious fanaticism and radical violence of the time, this was the language of the Diggers, Levellers, English Separatists and other religious dissenters of the early 17th century who left England to found a new society that would be free, as they saw it, of authoritarian government by Church and Crown.

By the time Australia was colonised, the language had changed. What came with the First Fleet was the English of the Enlightenment: "Sober, unemphatic, good-humoured; a very sociable and moderate language; modern in a way that even we would recognise, and supremely rational and down to earth."

That could almost be John Howard's portrait of himself: the leader uncomfortable with high principle who prefers to deal in practical solutions. Over the last decade, "practical" has become a key Howard word used to stop debate in its tracks. Try to explore the principles behind his politics, and more often than not his talk turns to practical options, initiatives, outcomes, consequences, points of view, guidance, solutions, partnerships and so on. Perhaps the most famous phrase he's uttered in office is "practical reconciliation"; his cover for shredding the notion that white Australia had particular moral obligations to Aborigines.

Ask him why asylum seekers who arrive by plane aren't also thrown into detention and he replies: "The practical circumstances are different." Ask why he hasn't signed Kyoto and he replies: "What we need to do is embrace practical measures."

Australians find this deeply attractive. As Malouf recognised, we don't live in a country and we don't use a language that revels in abstractions. Liberty and freedom are not subjects of continuing public debate. We hear nothing like the great arias sung by American politicians in praise of fundamental freedoms.

John Howard is, in his own eyes, a champion of liberty leading a nation whose commitment to freedom is "on a par with or better than the other great democracies of the globe". In the innocent days before September 11, he fought for the freedom of small businesses to sack; the freedom of parents to send their kids to private schools; the freedom of stevedores to employ non-union labour; the freedom of unionists to vote against strikes; the freedom of students not to join university unions. The preamble he and the poet Les Murray drafted for the constitution in 1999 guaranteed nothing while declaring Australians "free to be proud of their country and heritage, free to realise themselves as individuals, and free to pursue their hopes and ideals".

Despite reiterated claims over the years that Australia and America are at one in their commitment to freedom, Howard remains a resolute opponent of the document that guarantees that liberty in the United States. Hitler's Germany and Stalin's Soviet Union prove his point that even the most "beautifully written" bills of rights can fail utterly. Even trying is dangerous. "I believe that if you try and institute a bill of rights, you run the danger of limiting, rather than expanding, freedoms," he told ABC radio in Melbourne. "All you'll do is open up yet another avenue for lawyers to make a lot of money being human rights specialists and practitioners." But the three institutions Howard claims guarantee liberty in this country are three he has worked to curtail almost from the day he took office: parliament, the courts and "a strong free press".

On paper, no country's prime minister could be more devoted to press freedom. Howard declares he's an "uncompromising supporter" of the cause and opposed to "any kind of censorship". He says he believes that "if you have a strong, free, on occasion rambunctious ... press which is willing to have a go and is not in any way intimidated by the political process, then you are far more likely to have a strong, robust, virile democracy than with a bill of rights". Yet under Howard, the press has found itself misled, intimidated and starved of information. On coming to power, Howard set about making sure the tactics he had used so brilliantly to claw down his rivals would not be turned against his Government. There would be minimal tolerance for dissent within the party, the Government and the bureaucracy. The great leaker would stop the leaks. Senior bureaucrats who survived the purge of the first weeks were instructed to report all calls by journalists to the Prime Minister's press office. Stories were doled out as rewards. More than ever under Howard, the press would win access through favourable coverage. The new communications minister, Richard Alston, was soon lashing the ABC over budgets and bias. Journalists were locked out of stories, particularly those involving the military and refugees, in ways Americans would find inconceivable.

On Australia Day 2002, the Woomera detention centre was in turmoil, with inmates on hunger strikes, rioting and sewing their lips. A large number of press stood about in the desert that night watching. When ABC journalist Natalie Larkins questioned a police direction to fall back 200 metres from the camp perimeter, she was arrested. Other journalists and photographers were threatened with arrest if they did not move.

Sydney's *Daily Telegraph* condemned the police operation as "the latest and lowest example of Canberra's censorship. This pattern emerged during last year's federal election campaign ... the scenes at Woomera on Saturday night would not have been out of place in the countries from which the asylum seekers have fled". But the Prime Minister mocked the idea that these scenes contradicted his sweeping support for media liberty.

I'm concerned the press have total freedom in this country and people who pretend that because of what happened in Woomera yesterday that there's some restriction on press freedom, there's some attempt being made by the Government to cover up what is occurring in detention centres, I mean that is just ridiculous.

By this time, the twin towers had come down and Howard was wrestling with a new kind of rhetoric both tough and reassuring. "We should never sacrifice basic civil liberties in pursuit of terrorists," he told Australian journalists gathered in Washington in June 2002. "Equally, we should never squirm from enacting new and strong laws simply because they may unreasonably offend some people." He promised he would never overturn "fundamental" or "generic" rights, but it was never clear which rights these were. Once habeas corpus went in 2005, it was difficult to see what bedrock rights remained. As each piece of security legislation fell into place, Howard would claim: "We think we've got the balance right."

Attempts to understand how he weighed the scales proved futile. Instead of explaining himself, Howard pleads for sympathy as he tries to resolve, in these difficult times, the "eternal dilemma" between security and freedom. "We are a society that respects the right of people and encourages people to exercise their freedoms to the full. And free societies always find striking that balance difficult. But that doesn't absolve us of the obligation to defend the freedoms that make us different."

The result has been a steady attack on the liberty of the media that meant Australia plunged to 35th place, behind many former Soviet Bloc countries, in the latest press freedom index compiled by Reporters Without Borders. A dozen senior journalists in the Canberra press gallery confirmed the slide when they spoke to Helen Ester for the collection of essays *Silencing Dissent*. Ester wrote:

The interviews highlighted issues such as control and surveillance, and paint a picture of cumulative deterioration in sources of political news and information, describing new layers of disempowerment, frustration and disinformation. Most of the interviewees noted that the Howard Government had ushered in a decade of unprecedented executive control over political communication.

The Paris watchdog, the Canberra press gallery, the Australian branch of the Commonwealth Press Union and the journalists' union, the Media Entertainment and Arts Alliance, all concur: the Government is squeezing public debate. As evidence, they most frequently cite four cases:

- The long pursuit of journalists Gerard McManus and Michael Harvey for refusing to divulge the source of a story, which leaves them awaiting sentencing for contempt of court.
- The chilling effect of bans on reporting contained in federal anti-terrorism laws passed since 11 September 2001, particularly the five-year prison sentences for reporting the detention without trial of suspects and witnesses.
- Difficulties placed in the way of reporting on refugees and asylum seekers who reach Australia by boat.
- The failure of freedom-of-information laws, which the High Court last year confirmed gives federal ministers virtually a free hand to withhold documents from the public. Calls for reform of the FoI laws by the press, NGOs, lawyers' groups and the Commonwealth Ombudsman have all been ignored.

Governments have claimed since the beginning of time that the last thing they're doing is censoring. There's always some explanation for information withheld: security, morality, respectability, order, fair play, care for the vulnerable, the rights of business, the rights of government.

It's the same list of excuses used all over the world. But for a supposedly larrikin people, Australians are easily persuaded and oddly blind to the violations of principle these excuses cover. In the new political correctness of the Howard years, Australians are never racists and Australia is always free.

Commentators fill opinion pages arguing the opposite. More ink than ever has been spent in the past few years defending the nation's liberties. The recent slew of reports, books and articles on the state of freedom in this country is evidence of growing discontent. There's never a night when some decent bunch isn't gathered somewhere discussing the bill of rights we have to have.

But the steady constriction of public debate under Howard has aroused no deep concern in Australia. Only the little parties will touch the issue. Labor's indifference is colossal.

We've accepted this as we've accepted so much in the past decade— not with enthusiasm, but with resigned forbearance. Isn't it just what governments do?

This edited extract, published in The Sydney Morning Herald, *was taken from* Quarterly Essay 26: His Master's Voice.

Michelle Grattan

Eyes on the prize
The Age, 23 April 2007

Even in the political world, where "ambition" is stamped on your membership card, Kevin Rudd is seen as extraordinarily driven. He is also disciplined, organised, focused, ruthless and unbelievably energetic. That much is clear. But, equally, this is a man whose core is hard to define.

Nicholas Stuart, one of two authors (the second is another journalist, Robert Macklin) working on biographies of Rudd, says: "He is a mystery wrapped inside an enigma—the further you go, the more questions you end up with."

Former NSW premier Bob Carr describes him as "the 100 per cent political professional, even more focused than John Howard", adding that "he will learn from every mistake with lightning speed and be back on track, like a heat-seeking missile".

Rudd's political views are centrist, his underlying values soundly mainstream. He may or may not have gilded the lily about what happened in his boyhood, but the darker recesses of his character are not black, only shades of grey. No one has found any serious skeletons in the Rudd personal cupboard, although the Government works hard at promoting to the media the negative stories disputing his claims about his childhood.

In public, Kevin Rudd is careful not to show a temper that can be nasty, but recently it has been inconveniently "outed". Asked at his National Press Club lunch last week about his abuse of the *Sunday Telegraph* editor over the story about *Sunrise*'s ill-fated plan for an Anzac ceremony at Long Tan, he gave an answer that reveals quite a lot about his style. Confessing that on media relations "we've got to turn a new leaf", he said: "The whole question of what's right and what's wrong, what's accurate and inaccurate, can be handled differently ... We have had a long discussion internally within the office about that and I'm responsible for it and for executing that change ..." Here was Rudd treating the bullying charge as a management problem rather than a behavioural one. He had previously brushed off criticism over the heavy-handed attempt by him and his staff to suppress a *Sun-Herald* story disputing his account of his family being evicted after his father's death. But after the bruising *Sunrise* incident, Rudd knew he needed a better tack. So he said he would organise things better.

The "managerial" approach characterises Rudd's politics. If something is a problem, have a meeting, get out the duster and wipe it off the board. Or sweep it under the carpet? This can leave an unsettling impression. Rudd as Opposition Leader may now swear off bullying, but would he be a recidivist if he became PM? Very likely.

It's become a cliche to see Rudd as a Labor version of Howard. For both, ambition was an addiction fed early. Howard became a frontbencher less than a year after entering parliament. When Rudd arrived in Canberra in 1998, his first goal was to become foreign affairs spokesman. Laurie Brereton, who had the job, backed Rudd to chair the caucus foreign affairs committee. From there Rudd was well placed to stalk Brereton, whom he replaced in November 2001.

Rudd trailed his coat in the leadership contests of December 2003 and January 2005 but didn't run when he clearly didn't have the numbers. Those who thought this meant he would never have the guts to challenge were wrong, although he tells *The Age*: "The toughest thing I had to do was to walk in ... and tell Kim I was going to challenge him ... It was very tough. I liked him. And like him. I didn't resolve to come in here and do it until ... that morning. That's the absolute truth." But it is known the plotting had been months in the making.

"Kevin operates at 200 kilometres an hour," says a source close to him. "The guy never stops. He has an ambition and he's determined to get there." On a typical parliamentary day he is in his office by 6.15am, reading papers with a couple of senior staff, scoping out the day. At 7am he normally goes to the gym for a 45-minute workout. An 8.30am tactics meeting includes deputy Julia Gillard, shadow treasurer Wayne Swan, manager of opposition business Anthony Albanese; there's another tactics session at 11.30. The time between is packed with meetings with colleagues, groups, dignitaries, business people. He likes to write parliamentary speeches himself, often between the second tactics meeting and question time at 2pm.

Splice in media interviews and events and work on the never-ending stream of policy announcements, and you get an idea of the pace. Often there's a dinner, and when he leaves for the night, about 10 or 10.30, he'll take briefing papers back to the Canberra apartment he shares with a right convener, Victorian Anthony Byrne. Byrne reports Rudd's light is frequently on at 1 or 2am.

He'll ring staff—and radio stations—at all hours. "You certainly need to keep the phone on," says deputy Julia Gillard. "There can be calls at 11.30 on Saturday morning, 5.30am Sunday." Or a teleconference with "shadows" at 10pm.

One of the strengths of Team Rudd is that he has forged a comfortable and easy relationship with Gillard, with whom he hadn't been close (they saw themselves as potential rivals), and a good working one with Swan, previously a Beazley ally and Rudd enemy. Gillard says: "I've found him tremendously consultative and open with me. I feel it's a genuinely shared endeavour."

While these three are soldered together for the good of the party, Rudd can be more discriminatory towards some others. In his reshuffle he promoted those who brought him the numbers to be leader, and some who voted against him feel that's not forgotten even now. He's organised and (usually) strong on detail. "He's very good at structuring issues to be resolved," says Bruce Hawker of the Labor-oriented lobbying firm Hawker Britton, and a personal friend of Rudd's.

"You see it in private and public moments. He carries that with him all the time." Hawker adds, "It's the ones who leave no stone unturned who have the best chance of winning an election."

Kim Beazley says of the man who put him to the knife: "Walter Bagehot (19th-century author of *The English Constitution*) once said that great prime ministers are a product of commonplace opinions and uncommon administrative abilities. Kevin's opinions are not all that commonplace but he does have uncommon administrative abilities."

When, as shadow foreign minister, Rudd was prosecuting the AWB bribery scandal, he had a staff member sit in on the Cole inquiry hearings so nothing was missed. He's also plugged in and tactically astute. He often knows or senses what the Government is coming up with and makes pre-emptive strikes, as he has done on water and education.

It goes without saying he likes to be in control of everything (making it all the harder to understand how he apparently failed initially to question his staff properly about who knew what of the *Sunrise* plan). One big difference between Rudd and Beazley is Rudd's appearance of energy, quite apart from the reality of it. Beazley was way behind him in both appearance and reality.

Rudd is a skilled "spinner", another way of saying he's tactically smart.

When he felt he had to quit *Sunrise* after the Anzac fiasco and because he was getting caught in the commercial rivalries between Seven, Nine and the News Ltd tabloids, he ensured he took Joe Hockey, his sparring partner of five years, off the program with him and "spun" it as partly helping his "mate". Hockey told their last *Sunrise* program that he had developed a "mateship" with Rudd out of their Kokoda trek last year. Rudd doesn't seem to have too many "mates" in politics, at least not in caucus, where most MPs are, however, delighted that he has become their possible vehicle to victory.

A Labor MP who dislikes Rudd says: "He doesn't have friends. That's because the guy's working all the time. I think the guy has the personality, the grit, the get-up-and-go to give Howard the s----- because he's a chameleon, he's a mini-Howard.

"The punters think he's terrific, because he's not heavy, not over-the-top. He's resonating." Others attest to this. An MP who likes Rudd says he has still been surprised at his popularity with people in the street. Tony Maher, from the mining section of the CFMEU, concluded after seeing Rudd with miners at a Labor function in Mackay, "I don't think he's had a lot of experience with blue collar people—but he goes over all right. He's a likeable enough fellow." Maher was especially impressed when he saw Rudd arrange to sign up the waiter for Labor. Pressed on friendships, Rudd says "I am really close to my family." Wayne Goss does fall into the "friend" category. When asked whether he seeks advice from Goss, Rudd gives an insight into how he soaks up information from him and others. "If you chat through things ... in an intelligent conversation (with) people who are familiar with the subject ... and people, most importantly, that you trust, I find that's a very helpful process to clarify your thinking."

Rudd sups mostly on success but his limited experience of defeat has seared into his consciousness—and given him a certain human sensitivity. When Michelle O'Byrne, now a Tasmanian minister, lost her federal seat in 2004, Rudd went to great trouble to meet up with her months later. "Kevin and I weren't extremely close," she says. "He told me he wanted to come and see me because 'I remember when I lost my first election (he failed to win Griffith in 1996), I contemplated writing a book called *When the Phone Stops Ringing*. I didn't want you to think because we don't call you we don't think about you'." O'Byrne says she had indicated she wouldn't run federally again, so there was nothing in it for Rudd. It was simply "a genuinely nice thing to do".

Rudd has the boldness and audacity that is a necessary condition for good leadership. Knowing he must throw everything at this election and that others have little choice but to fall into line, he is using his authority to the full, although so far not wilfully. He pushed through caucus with minimal consultation the plan to dip into the Future Fund to finance a high-speed broadband network. He is willing to intervene to have ACTU secretary Greg Combet shoehorned into a seat, replacing a sitting member. On Friday he slapped down comments on his industrial relations policy from left union leader Doug Cameron, declaring he "needs to get used to the 21st century".

A Labor MP identifies as a quality of successful leaders that "they may not always be right but they've got to have a view and back their judgement—and he does". Like most others in the party this MP is pleased with the progress of the Rudd express. But he sounds a warning. "The margin for error when you're going at 200 kilometres an hour is very small."

Matt Price

Rudd does a good JFK to Howard's Johnson

The Weekend Australian, 26 May 2007

I'm halfway through a thick but fascinating biography of Lyndon Johnson and the contemporary antipodean parallels raised a smile. It's 1960 and Johnson is weighing up whether to nominate for president. The ambitious senator from Texas enjoys a growing support base among southern Democrats but has profoundly underestimated the nous of the much younger candidate, John Kennedy.

"It was the goddamnedest thing," LBJ conceded afterwards:

> Here was a young whippersnapper, malaria-ridden and yellah, sickly, sickly. He never said a word of importance in the Senate and he never did a thing. But somehow with his books and his Pulitzer prizes he managed to create the image of himself as a shining intellectual, a youthful leader who could change the face of the country. He looked awfully good on the goddamn television screen and through it all he was a pretty decent fellow, but his growing hold on the American people was simply a mystery to me.

John Howard much prefers Republicans, but I suspect our besieged and bamboozled Prime Minister would sympathise with these sentiments about young, goddamned whippersnappers with mysterious holds on voters.

And there was this lovely morsel for Peter Costello, who has been complaining Kevin Rudd is shamelessly stealing most of the Coalition's economic policies. When Johnson met Kennedy in a nationally televised debate, JFK seriously flustered his rival with an opening gambit which included: "I don't think senator Johnson and I disagree on the great issues that face us." Whether the duelling Democrats declared themselves fiscal conservatives wasn't recorded.

KMR hails from the north, not the south, but this young whippersnapper is ripping through the federal Coalition like a knot of rampaging cane toads. I've written before how colleague Christine Jackman extracted this spectacular quote from Rudd in her February magazine profile of the fledgling Labor leader: "It will be fun to play with his [Howard's] mind for a while." Notwithstanding his wife's business dealings, we can presume Rudd is thoroughly enjoying himself.

Only last week the PM speculated absurdly that punters might just be joking telling pollsters they preferred Labor. By Monday, Howard admitted voters were contemplating a change of government, hardly a stunning concession but, in this delirious political climate, big news nonetheless. Within 24 hours, contemplation had been super-sized to annihilation as the PM warned his troops all could be lost.

Clearly there was a strategic side to Howard's rhetorical flourish; having fired most of its heavy artillery and failed to wound Rudd, the Coalition wants us all to vividly confront the nightmare of life under Kevinistic rule.

What's fascinating, however, is the PM constantly feels compelled to protest that what he's saying is true, not tricky. There's nothing remotely contentious about Howard's assessment; annihilation is a perfectly apt description of the Coalition's fate under present poll trends.

"I was telling the truth," the PM exclaimed afterwards. "There was no hidden meaning or, you know, sort of dark message that I was trying to convey. It was a statement of fact ... It's got nothing to do with sending signals."

That Howard is required to explain himself when stating the bleeding obvious is testimony to two reliable maxims; one about strengths becoming weaknesses, the other about the importance of unyielding repetition in selling a political message.

Long regarded and often admired as the nonpareil of guile and artifice, a perception of Howard as too-tricky-by-half seems to be embedding itself in the national psyche. Not least because Labor has been banging on and on about it for years and years.

I remember ridiculing Kim Beazley over damning Howard with faint praise for being "just brilliant" at politics, hardly a liability for a PM (don't be fooled; Rudd, by any definition, is also a brilliant politician). But this relentless branding of the PM by senior Labor figures as clever and cunning has stuck. "The Australian public is getting sick of this tricky Prime Minister and his Treasurer," Bomber said in 2005, "even to the point of disbelieving them on occasions when perhaps they ought to be believed." Exactly.

Unsurprisingly, there has been a bout of public harrumphing about the preposterous significance afforded polling. Timothy Watson of Melbourne wrote to *The Australian* this week: "I'm sick of all this discussion about opinion polls. Why do we waste so much time discussing who is going to win the next bloody election?" Many would doubtless agree.

But imagine there was no public polling.

For starters, we'd all be running around in a cloud of delusion, intoning "it's the economy, stupid" and anticipating a fifth-term Coalition landslide. Plus, it's been exquisite watching allegedly sensible politicians turn to jelly trying to rationalise the emergence of Kevinism.

Andrew Robb thinks people may be flirting with Labor because they've been overloaded with far too much politics. Which is completely at odds with the emerging conventional wisdom—or wishful thinking—supported by most of cabinet that has the overwhelming majority of punters cheerfully disengaged from politics, hence not really thinking straight when they support Rudd.

Tony Abbott trusts the innate common sense of the Australian people. Except, according to the Health Minister, we're in danger of "sleepwalking" to the election and accidentally ousting the Coalition. "There are two parallel universes out there," Abbott complains. "This has been a very good Government, it's just at the moment the polls don't seem to be measuring that."

For all his cleverness and cunning, the PM has no rabbits, no hats and absolutely no idea what's hit him. He seemed to be following Glenn Milne's advice as dispensed in Monday's *Australian*: when in doubt, panic and concede near-certain defeat. Luckily, annihilation got a very good run, otherwise the PM might have been forced to stand atop the Sydney Harbour Bridge screaming: "We're all completely Wilson Tuckeyed."

Milne, incidentally, provided easily the best explanation for the dramatic shift in political fortunes when he told ABC's *Insiders* "we're in a mid-paradigm situation".

I've no idea what that means but it sounds entirely plausible.

As we speed through the parallel universes towards a paradigm situation, Howard at least will appreciate LBJ's rather more earthy theory of crisis management: "Being president is like being a jackass in a hailstorm. There's nothing to do but stand there and take it."

George Megalogenis

The small picture men
The Weekend Australian, 16 June 2007

Economic management is the oxymoron of modern politics. The notion that federal governments manage the economy in the same way that a chief executive would run a business is, frankly, delusional.

Remember, the reforms of the past two decades were designed to take prime ministers and treasurers out of the marketplace. Governments no longer fix the currency or interest rates; fiddle with tariffs; oversee a centralised wages system; own airlines; or place caps on the number of home loans issued each year.

All that's left is fiscal policy, but thanks to the China-led resources boom it is hard to get that wrong at the moment. The latest intergenerational report says the federal budget will remain in structural surplus for at least another 15 years. It is important to understand these humble facts as John Howard and Peter Costello and Kevin Rudd and Wayne Swan rumble over economic management.

Ask either side to spell out what they mean by economic management and they are quickly reduced to comic book slogans. The Prime Minister and Treasurer say Labor will raise interest rates and restore the trade union monopoly. The Opposition Leader and shadow treasurer say the Coalition will raise interest rates and give business a free hand to rip off workers.

These competing caricatures assume the electorate is a touch stupid. Somehow we are supposed to believe that the Reserve Bank doesn't set interest rates and that Australia is still crouched behind the tariff wall where class war is being waged by boss and worker.

Howard and Rudd understand the first point, and voters were reminded of it again on Thursday when Reserve Bank governor Glenn Stevens suggested interest rates may or may not rise before the election. But our leaders fail to grasp the second point and their collective failure helps explain why the national debate has become so incoherent lately.

Labor can't revive trade unionism any more than the Coalition can deliver business a blank cheque. Neither scenario is possible in a globalised economy such as ours because no government can afford to pick the winner between labour and capital. Businesses that surrender to trade unions will go under just as surely as those who short-change their staff in a near-full employment economy. Labor can't go back even if it wanted to because the market will always throw up a rival firm prepared to strike the balance between a happy workforce and a cheap, reliable product.

Howard and Rudd are caught in a time warp. Less than six months out from the election, they argue the minutiae of workplace relations as if they really matter. Remember how simple Rudd's message was before Labor's national conference in April? He wanted to restore a sense of balance, to give families back their Sundays and public holidays, and to protect the pay and conditions of those workers without bargaining power. The Labor argument resonated so clearly that it formed the basis of Howard's so-called fairness test. Howard now agrees with Rudd that battlers shouldn't go backwards in their negotiations with employers. And Rudd always agreed with Howard on the perils of trade union power. Nothing much will change in the workplace whoever wins the election, yet neither man knows how to move on to another debate.

Listen carefully to Rudd now. He is couching his election appeal in the negative, as in don't trust the other bloke. Howard, in Ruddspeak, is past his prime. Rudd, in Howardspeak, is a lightweight. Sadly, both men have a point. Neither leader is seeking a positive mandate because they share a blind spot. They talk about the past, about economic management, because they have yet to figure out the proper role of government beyond the tariff wall.

What should governments do to keep the population match-fit for globalisation while maintaining social cohesion? The question doesn't nag the political class here in Australia in the way it does in Britain and the US.

Check out the essay departing British Prime Minister Tony Blair penned for *The Economist* magazine on what he had learned after 10 years in office. "The role of the state is changing," he wrote in the June 2 edition. "The state today needs to be enabling and based on a partnership with the citizen, one of mutual rights and responsibilities."

It got a bit muddled from there, but at least Blair asked himself the threshold question about the role of government now that it no longer commands the economy. His successor Gordon Brown will no doubt try to answer it.

Perhaps the question doesn't get posed here because the Australian economy is too wealthy and our national character too laid-back to force this level of introspection on our leaders.

But the issues that should trigger such a discussion are already apparent. Here are four obvious examples. Our cities are chronically short of water. Our telecommunications sector can't deliver a national broadband network. The immigration program is producing more skilled workers than our tertiary education system. The number of people going on to disability benefits is rising faster than the number who are moving off the dole.

These are post-deregulation debates. They demand a new framework for government. But each is being dealt with on the old crisis management model, through handout and spin.

For this blame Rudd and his predecessors for failing to take up the challenge to Howard. The Opposition never made the case to change the way government operates because it assumed, wrongly, that the Hawke–Keating era was somehow ahead of the world policy curve: that is, Labor rebuilt Australia between 1983 and 1996 before Bill Clinton and Blair went looking for the "third way" between 1992 and 2007. The flaw in Labor's thinking is that it denies the true sequence of events. Britain and the US began their deregulation projects a couple of years earlier than Australia with the ascensions of Margaret Thatcher in 1979 and Ronald Reagan in 1981. Clinton and Blair could only ponder the third way after the British and US economies were opened up.

The reason Rudd and Howard have their eyes fixed firmly on the rear-vision mirror is that neither man knows how to talk to the electorate beyond the banalities of interest rates and workplace relations. It is easy to understand why Howard would frame the election as a referendum on economic management. After 11 years in office and a 16-year run of national prosperity, all the PM has left going for him is fear of change. But why is Rudd caught in the same bandwidth, simply playing the shock-horror card against Howard?

If Labor is to win and become a decent government, it needs a reason for claiming power. Pitching Rudd as a younger version of Howard may deliver an election victory. But what would the point be for the nation if Rudd became a young-fogey version of Howard in office?

Glenn Milne

The wrong time, the wrong man
The Australian, 15 October 2007

Sometimes the incidental atmospherics of politics are defining. Thus it was on Saturday night as John Howard returned to Canberra, head bowed into the cold night wind as he descended the stairs of the VIP jet onto the Fairbairn tarmac. The Prime Minister suddenly looked very much alone.

And for the next six weeks he largely will be. This, however, is not just an observation about the isolation of leadership. It is also a summation of how many senior figures in the Government now regard Howard.

With the election finally under way there is a view that he really is now on his own; that having twice made the judgment when confronted with the option of leadership transition that he represented the Coalition's best chance of winning another term, it is now down to him to vindicate that judgment.

This reflects the context of Howard's latest and ultimate self-assessment, when at the time of the APEC summit he rejected the view of the majority of his cabinet that he should stand aside in favour of Peter Costello. Howard will have a reckoning at the bar of history for this resolution.

This was the moment when he set himself on the course of either vindication and a fifth term, or humiliation and a graceless exit from public life.

Yes, the coming campaign will see the cosmetics of the half-hearted shared leadership with Peter Costello. And the emphasis on the cabinet team as a way of highlighting the inexperience of the line-up behind Kevin Rudd.

But the tone as to how Howard intends to really conduct this campaign—and how some of his key colleagues now plan to leave him alone to conduct it—was set by the bizarre nature and dynamics surrounding his Sydney Institute reconciliation speech of Thursday night last.

Many in his ministry watched that speech with a sense of disbelief at the depth of its miscasting. Here was Howard—obviously desperate to get a toehold on Kevin Rudd's moving walkway to the future—unilaterally turning the election, on the eve of its announcement, into a referendum on him, his relevance and his failings. Precisely what the Government does not want the next six weeks to be about.

The brutal fact is that when it comes to symbolic acts recognising Aboriginal hurt Howard is exactly the person voters who care about such things don't want to hear from.

The rest were just confused. After 11 years, and longer, of decrying the meaninglessness of such gestures, coming from Howard, the Sydney Institute initiative was simply unbelievable. And the smarter heads in the Government know it.

If Howard had really wanted to maximise the Government's chances of re-election it should have been Peter Costello who made that speech. With his deputy having made it and claiming it as his own Howard should have acknowledged it as the Treasurer's vision for the future and locked in behind it.

Instead of the jaundiced reception Howard got, voters might, just might, have greeted the idea of an indigenous preamble in the Constitution coming from Costello as a genuine attempt to begin a sketch of a post-Howard Coalition government. After all it was Costello who walked for reconciliation in 2000, not Howard.

Not on your Nelly. No, Howard, who is so closed over with scar tissue after 30 years in politics that some colleagues complain they can no longer have a meaningful social conversation with him outside politics or cricket, hoarded his Sydney Institute enterprise so closely none of his ministers got a decent look-in. If they had they might have warned him it was a folly, fatally contaminated by the imminence of the election, which as we now know was clearly in Howard's own mind.

Those kept in ignorance included Indigenous Affairs Minister, Mal Brough. Asked on the *Sunday* program yesterday as to when Howard informed him of his intentions, Brough revealed that it was the day of the night Howard made the speech.

There are other ministers too who believe that Howard has missed vital chances to send a message that the future under the Coalition is no longer primarily about him. Malcolm Turnbull, for one, has told others that it would have been in the Government's best interests for him, and not Howard, to take the central role in major climate change announcements.

Instead, Howard made his reconciliation speech as much about himself as it was about righting indigenous injustice. It is probably the most intimately personal contribution to public life he has ever made. And what did he use it to do? To acknowledge that he had been the captive of his own generational limitations.

"For my generation," Howard declared, "Australians who came of age in the 1950s and 1960s—it (Aboriginal injustice) has been ever present, a subject of deep sorrow and great hope."

"The challenge I have faced around indigenous identity politics is in part an artefact of who I am and the time in which I grew up." Given that Kevin Rudd has made this election about "fresh leadership", Howard could have chosen a better word to describe himself than "artefact". That's what happens when you write speeches alone, without consulting anyone else.

Politics, you see, is not only about "right" policies. It's about "right" policies at the "right" time. The year 2000 would surely have been a better time for Howard to move on symbolic as well as practical reconciliation. Even the 40th anniversary of the 1967 referendum four months ago could have worked.

But 72 hours out from an election campaign was exactly the "wrong" time for Howard to finally arrive at his self-defined "right" position on indigenous issues.

Because winning elections is fundamentally about creating a narrative for the electorate to follow, creating a story worth supporting. Rudd's current ascendancy is based on Howard's spectacular failure to do this. And it's not that he hasn't in the past. In 1998 the story he told was about continuing economic reform through the GST. In 2001, in the shadow of 9/11 and the *Tampa* it was about national security. And 2004 was won off the back of guarantees about personal economic security.

And 2007 is about ... what exactly? It certainly isn't about reconciliation. And it can't be about Howard, because he's already admitted he won't be around. That's what stops him from having a coherent conversation with voters about the future. Having conceded under pressure of losing his leadership that he won't be part of that future voters have every right to discount most of what he says about it.

Viewed that way, the Prime Minister's Sydney Institute speech wasn't part of any cogent narrative, past or future. Worse, it jarred fundamentally with the story Howard has created about himself for 11 years. It was like a chapter that he had consciously left out of his biography and suddenly rediscovered. But having discovered it, he just hurriedly pasted it in, out of context, meaningless.

In the broadest sense Howard now has just six weeks to rewrite that ending. The final reviews will then be in.

2
The Lucky Country?

Noel Pearson

Vale hope in outback hellhole

The Weekend Australian, 17 February 2007

On a recent Friday night I walked out on to the lawn of my mother's house in my home town. It was after 2am and though my family lives a kilometre away, I could hear loud music booming from several stereos in various parts of what I would have called a village in my youth, but which more accurately answers to the description of an outback ghetto today.

The music emanated from houses known as party houses, where numbers of men and women congregate to binge drink, share marijuana, often out of what are called bucket bongs, laughing, shouting, singing and dancing and seeking sexual partners—consensual and otherwise.

By midnight the bonhomie of the early evening descends into tension, as various bingers develop dark moods, vent anger, resentment and suspicions at those to whom they earlier professed love. Arguments and fights ensue, over the smallest slights and often over ownership of and access to the dwindling supplies of alcohol.

While parties rage at a number of notorious locations throughout the town, with erstwhile hosts boosting their stereos with specially bought amplifiers, often placed at windows facing outwards as if for the benefit of the rest of the inmates of this sad place, it is hard to maintain the fiction that this place is a community.

It is a hellhole where whirring fans and airconditioners in the concrete block houses drown out the noise, including the screams.

This Friday night was the third night in a row of parties, beginning on Wednesday evening following the receipt of Family Tax Benefit payments, which continued at a lower gear over the next day and got back into top gear on Thursday night following the receipt of CDEP work-for-the-dole payments. The number of people missing from work has led almost every community to declare Fridays as the unofficial start of the weekend. School attendance collapses from already low levels earlier in the week. This has led to many proposals over the years from educators to reduce school days in Cape York Peninsula schools to four days, as if that would be a solution.

As I drove around the streets at 3am, I passed by drunks stumbling from one party house to another. I passed groups of young teenage girls walking around or sitting on the kerbside. For too many of them, sexual activity begins young at Hope Vale, very young. Who knows the circumstances of their first experience, but the incidences of abuse that come to light are only the tip of the iceberg of sexual assault, unlawful intercourse with minors, and incest.

That older men should be able to have sexual relations with the young girls I pass in the street in exchange for alcohol, marijuana or esteem, is water off the moral backs of our people. Young men may jump through windows to rendezvous with their paramours, but it is as likely they do so to interfere with women and children.

My home town looks and feels like a ghetto. The mango trees, frangipanis and old wooden church still evoke the mission of my early youth, but the fibro and weatherboard cottages built by the hands of our own local carpenters have been replaced by welfare housing, increasingly built by outside contractors. The uniform rows of kit homes and Besser Block houses are of course much more expensive and have better amenities (at least at first, because they do not last for long), but they look squalid. The once lovingly tended gardens with topiary, gardenias and fruit trees are scarce today, and the plastic bags, VB cans, old motor cars and general rubbish spill out of the homes and on to the streets.

With the eyes of someone who returns to his home town for holidays and occasional weekends, I marvel that the people who live here do not see the shit in front of their eyes. Despite vastly improved levels of funding and infrastructure the place is a mess compared with the village of my childhood.

I drove past the place where my parents brought up our family in a small fibro cottage with no hot water and a pit toilet out the back. We got electricity when I was in Year 4 but I did not see television until I went to college. Now they have Austar and adults carelessly expose children and young people to their pornographic videos and DVDs.

Earlier in the afternoon at the roundabout I saw the shocking sight of a beautiful puppy that had been run over by a vehicle, in a pool of blood on the bitumen. As we say in the language of this place, Ngathu wawu baathi, my soul cried for this lost life.

In my nocturnal drive I passed the puppy in the same place. The binge drinking will continue to daybreak, and on through Saturday. Bingers pass out and catch some sleep, before waking again to resume the fray.

The parties change gear during the course of the four days as participants come and go, supplies run out and fresh supplies are brought in from Cooktown.

The beauty of electronic banking is that welfare and CDEP income is dropped into keycard accounts automatically, and Centrelink will assist recipients to stage the time at which payments are made to members of a household. So Jimmy can get his on Wednesday and Sally can get hers on Friday. There is money for drinking and drugs over a longer stretch of the week.

Centrelink's intention of course with flexible payment plans is to assist people to manage their income to purchase food and pay their bills, but the reality is that it makes more money available for binge drinking over a longer period of time.

As I drive down to the beach early on Saturday morning I see the young children emerging out of the houses, as if from a war zone. Yes, there are children and young girls in the homes of the hosts of the binge drinking parties. How they fare through these weekly episodes depends on whether their often inebriated parent is nevertheless able to keep an eye on their welfare, because the chance that molesters are among the party people is very high. Older children may run off and stay with sober relatives, particularly grandparents, but what happens to the ones left behind? Some of the young people sitting on the kerbside at 3am are simply scared to go back home.

On Sunday things will be quiet. "They run out of grog," people explain to me. The town will be mostly quiet for the next two, and if you are lucky, three days. The bureaucrats from Peter Beattie's Government will do their business with the people and organisations of Hope Vale in the sane part of the week. Certainly the communities of Cape York Peninsula during the quiet days can give the impression of being pleasant if untidy "communities". You can excuse the rubbish and the ubiquitous high barbed wire fences and iron cages that have to be constructed around almost every public facility, because after all this is an Aboriginal community.

But the public servants and politicians only visit for the day and never sleep in the town. They never have anything other than the official conversations down in the administration offices, so they too easily have the view that "this place is not too bad", "we just need to co-ordinate the programs" and "we have a demand reduction plan" for the alcohol problem. The underbelly of these so-called communities is not intriguing like a David Lynch movie, it is Hobbesian.

Meanwhile in public policy land three relevant events take place. First, journalist Margaret Wenham reported in *The Courier-Mail* on February 8 as follows:

> Hundreds of impoverished indigenous people in remote communities have been hit with fines totalling nearly $600,000 for breaking Queensland's controversial alcohol management laws. Figures, released this week by the Justice Department, also show that seven people have been jailed and six vehicles confiscated since December 2002 when AMPs were phased into the state's 19 discrete indigenous communities. Reports of the penalty tally were greeted with dismay by Aboriginal leaders who said most people could not pay the fines and the AMPs were not working to curb violence.

The problem with Wenham's argument and that of any Aboriginal leader to whom she refers, is that if you divide $600,000 worth of fines between 19 communities over 3½ years, the average fine for each community is about $9000 per annum, or less than $200 per week.

The liquor licensing authorities in Queensland do not release liquor sales figures from each community, and no one tracks alcohol purchases from outside of the communities, but if you make a rough estimate of alcohol expenditure per week I would say an average of $10,000 per week would be extremely conservative.

So if an average community spends $520,000 on alcohol, how can you say that $9000 worth of fines is causing or even compounding impoverishment? Is it not the spending on alcohol that is causing poverty?

Second, on Monday this week the National Drug Research Institute at Curtin University released a study which showed that in the period from 2000 to 2004, an estimated 1145 indigenous Australians died from injury, disease or suicide caused by drinking.

The study found that many indigenous people died very young from diseases that do not exist among young non-indigenous people. A third of the deaths investigated were female. The second biggest alcohol-related killer of indigenous women was haemorrhagic stroke, and the average age of the deceased was only 25 years. Among non-indigenous people, stroke is a disease of the elderly.

The worst alcohol-related killer of indigenous people, alcohol liver cirrhosis, on average shortens indigenous sufferers' lives to 54 years. The other major causes of death—suicide, road traffic injury, assault injury, stroke—mainly kill indigenous people in their 20s and 30s.

Third, Premier Peter Beattie met the mayors of Queensland's indigenous shire councils to discuss the problems besetting indigenous communities.

The Premier emerged saying his Government would be making various investments in the communities and he expected the community leaders to take greater responsibility for alcohol.

One problem with the Premier's hopes is that these councils are still the owners and operators of the canteens which sell alcohol to their people. The councils are as addicted to the profits from the canteens as the Queensland Government is to gambling revenues. Tony Fitzgerald recommended in his Justice Study report to Beattie in 2002 that the nexus between alcohol profits and councils be broken, but the nexus remains.

Typically it is the justice groups that want to maintain AMPs while shire councils want them to be watered down. In fact the Government is considering proposals from councils to allow weekend trading and takeaways, against the opposition of local justice groups.

Beattie's minister responsible for the issue, Warren Pitt, has already weakened restrictions in some communities. Beattie and Pitt need to spend an anonymous night or two in at least one, preferably a couple, of these communities. They need to be in the town on the binge-drinking nights, and they need to take a quiet drive or walk around the town and hear and see the nightmare that the sober people and children have to endure.

Last year Hope Vale's Mayor Greg Mclean invited a delegation of children from the local primary school to present their views to a large roundtable of assembled bureaucrats and community leaders. In plain English the children pleaded to these black and white adults that they wanted the drinking and violence in their community to stop.

As I drove through my home town on the Sunday evening on my way back to Cairns, I saw the dead puppy still in the street. I thought about the distance between being inured to the fate of a puppy that didn't see the car coming, and being inured to the fate of our own children.

Louis Nowra

Culture of denial

The Australian Literary Review, March 2007

In 2005 I spent several days in the Alice Springs hospital after falling ill while attending a friend's wedding. I shared a ward with a middle aged Aboriginal man who was quite proud that he had raped a 13-year-old girl. As he said, "She wouldn't say yes, so I f---ed her hard."

It did not surprise me. A few years before, I was in Alice Springs talking to two Aboriginal men in their early 70s. They were preparing to go into town to buy plastic toy dinosaurs. This was to pay a 12-year-old girl for having sex with both of them at the same time.

What amazed me was their lack of shame or even simple embarrassment. What disturbed me even more was that the most common sight in the hospital was Aboriginal women and girls with severe injuries suffered during domestic violence. Some of their faces looked as though an incompetent butcher had conducted plastic surgery with a hammer and saw. The fear in their eyes reminded me of dogs whipped into cringing submission. The confronting evidence of what men had done to the women was almost unbearable.

About 20 years ago an Aboriginal woman told me she had been raped at the age of seven by her uncle and grandfather on a town rubbish tip. As I was to discover as my circle of Aboriginal friends and acquaintances grew, sexual abuse was not uncommon—and in some communities it was rife—from the 1960s onwards.

Another friend told me that at the age of 10 he had been thrown into a wardrobe where his uncle masturbated him and then forced him to perform oral sex. Several other "uncles" also abused him through the years. I heard of many more such incidents and not one of these men ever had to go to court for their actions.

After I had recovered from my stay in Alice Springs hospital I was alarmed to read of a middle-aged Aboriginal man who anally raped a 14-year-old girl whom, he said, had been promised to him. Northern Territory Chief Justice Brian Martin sentenced him to detention for the duration of the court session.

It seemed to me that Aboriginal men were using the defence of cultural traditions to get away with rape and murder. But it's not only that. The statistics on Aboriginal domestic violence and sexual abuse are so much worse than in the general population, as has been highlighted in the 40 reports produced on the issue since 1999. All the statistics and case studies I refer to in this piece are sourced from federal and state government reports, court proceedings, newspaper articles and books, and are expanded on in my new book, *Bad Dreaming* (Pluto Press), which also contains an extensive bibliography.

The Alice Springs hospital provides a clear example: about 800 Aboriginal women were treated for domestic assault last year, up from 351 in 1999. The rate of domestic assault in indigenous communities is eight to 10 times that of non-indigenous communities and the sexual abuse of girls is so widespread that one-third of 13-year-old girls in the NT are infected with chlamydia and gonorrhoea. In fact, the situation has become a calamity.

But even more disturbing is that while some Aborigines are being recognised as wonderful painters, photographers, actors, filmmakers, footballers and dancers, indigenous communities are breaking down under the strain of male violence and sexual brutality. As Aboriginal elder Mick Dodson has said: "This is not just our problem; this is everyone's problem."

After the arrival of the First Fleet explorers and settlers wrote about the violence they saw Aboriginal men inflict on women. They also observed how the men kidnapped women from other tribes, raped them and forced them to become their wives.

By the end of the 19th century, the new discipline of anthropology began to study Aboriginal culture and society in detail, and with much sympathy and respect. It is in these studies that we gain a clearer picture of the relationship between Aboriginal men and women.

Betrothal was universal across the continent, with some marriages arranged before a child was born. A feature of Aboriginal life was that of the considerably older man, a middle-aged elder, marrying a girl barely into her teens. Polygamy was also practised.

A. W. Howitt, who wrote the influential *The Native Tribes of South-East Australia* (1904), summarised what he had learned about the marital situation in traditional society as "a man had power of life and death over his wife".

Despite local variations, there is a consistent pattern of traditional Aboriginal men's treatment of women that could be exceedingly harsh and sexually aggressive (gang rape, for instance). Given its pervasive nature across Australia, we can say that it was ancient and long-lasting.

Anthropologist Phyllis Kaberry, author of the seminal *Aboriginal Women Sacred and Profane* (1939), sums up Aboriginal men's attitude to women: "[The men] generally attribute a series of undesirable qualities to women. They are held to be faithless, untrustworthy, sexually insatiable, and talk too much."

One of the most depressing exercises in Australian history is to map the march of white settlement. Invariably, the arrival of white men meant the quick destruction or near dissolution of Aboriginal groups as a result of disease (including venereal disease as a result of rape), violence and dispossession. Later came the deliberate removal of mixed-blood children from their families, and state and federal governments' benign neglect or callous indifference towards Aborigines. Missionaries undermined traditional culture but there were some customs indigenous women were pleased to see fade away. One has only to read Oodgeroo Noonuccal's poem 'The Child Wife' ("They gave me to an old man, / Joyless and old, / Life's smile of promise. / So soon to frown") to understand why.

If cases of Aboriginal men murdering their women were reported in newspapers, it was merely to confirm that Aboriginal ways were primitive and their actions and behaviour were very different from white societal norms.

For example, in the mid-1960s, an Aboriginal man killed his wife in central Australia. A Department of Aboriginal Affairs welfare officer explained to the judge that it was customary for the men to punish their wives or partners with "considerable beatings". After listening to this explanation, the judge sentenced the man to a year in jail, justifying the short jail term as making "allowance for racial customs". This episode is related in Joan Kimm's 2004 book *A Fatal Conjunction* (Federation Press).

Customary law or traditional law began to be used as a common defence. In 1980, justice John Gallop in the Northern Territory Supreme Court accepted the argument from evidence given for an accused man

> that rape is not considered as seriously in Aboriginal communities as it is in the white communities ... and indeed the chastity of women is not as importantly regarded as in white communities. Apparently the violation of an Aboriginal woman's integrity is not nearly as significant as it is in the white community.

Occasional reports in the '80s began to detail some alarming trends. For instance, in Western Australia, sexual assault by Aboriginal men increased tenfold between 1961 and 1981. Audrey Bolger, in her 1990 book, *Aboriginal Women and Violence*, writes that if all reported and unreported assaults are taken into account, about one-third of the female population in the NT is assaulted every year. Bolger further points out that the number of murdered Aboriginal women exceeds the number of indigenous men who have died in custody.

It is not necessary to exaggerate the dystopian quality of some Aboriginal communities. The poverty and squalor can be overwhelming. Alcohol, kava, marijuana (according to the police, almost every house on Groote Eylandt has a bong) are pervasive drugs that, with petrol-sniffing, render some indigenous communities totally dysfunctional. Viewing pornography is commonplace and children are constantly exposed to it. Nepotism means regular financial corruption and the misuse of public funds. "Big men" control their communities by thuggery.

The poor health of Aborigines results in a life expectancy 20 years shorter than that of non-indigenous Australians. As regards education, the 1999 NT government report *Learning Lessons* pointed out that indigenous students in the territory were less literate and numerate than their parents or grandparents.

Violence is so much a part of Aboriginal life that a town such as Alice Springs has a murder rate 10 times the national average. An Aborigine is seven times as likely to be murdered and about 10 times as likely to be jailed. These conditions spawn a hideous environment where women are subjected to brutal sexual indignities, physical wounds and murder and where child sexual assault is endemic. Indigenous theatre director Wesley Enoch recently summed up the situation: "I don't know any Aboriginal who hasn't had to deal with physical and-or sexual abuse."

Since the release of the report by the Queensland Aboriginal and Torres Strait Islander Women's Taskforce on Violence in 1999 there have been about 40 official inquiries into domestic violence and sexual abuse in indigenous communities. The Aboriginal Child Sexual Assault Taskforce's *Breaking the Silence* report, released last year, found that the sexual assault of indigenous children in NSW was so widespread that not a single family in the 29 rural and urban communities surveyed was unaffected by it.

Such reports contain many graphic examples of the appalling violence meted out to women. Let's take some at random.

Last year Alice Springs crown prosecutor Nanette Rogers reported a case in central Australia in which the wife of an elder was repeatedly bashed and stabbed through the years. Eventually her husband beat her to death, tied up her corpse and left it on an ant's nest for a week.

Two years ago, at Araru outstation on the Coburg Peninsula, Trenton Cunningham beat his wife, Jodie Palipuaminni, to death after she failed to bring him a cup of water while he was burying his dog. On the night before she died, people heard her screaming. Rather than help her, relatives told Palipuaminni and her husband to shut up. She was later heard crying out, "Please stop."

At the time of the attack Cunningham, 27, was on parole for assaulting his wife with a steel bar and pouring boiling water over her, resulting in skin grafts to 20 per cent of her body. Palipuaminni had been promised to Cunningham soon after being born and they had four children.

These men assault their women for sometimes the most minor reasons. Sometimes the reasons are almost unbelievable. In her 2005 book *Balanda: My Year in Arnhem Land* (Allen & Unwin), Mary Ellen Jordan relates that in Maningrida, a community in the far north, it was common for men to bash their wives when the women returned from a trip just in case they had done anything wrong while they were away.

Nurses and doctors in the outback see countless examples of domestic abuse. Kate Napthall once worked at the small Tennant Creek hospital.

She remembers one Friday night working in the emergency department from 5pm until 8am and seeing 28 cases of domestic assault and, as she remarked, these were the ones who had sought help.

"The case I recall with the greatest sadness," she told a newspaper interviewer last year, "is that of a young woman, probably 28, who had a saucepan of boiling water poured over her face, scalding her eyes beyond recognition. When I looked in her files, she had between 40 and 50 similar presentations of assault against her by her husband."

It's also worth remembering that many of these violent acts occur in public but no one steps in to help the woman, not even relatives. As one woman related to the 1999 taskforce: "I've seen women on the ground being kicked in the belly and in the head and no one went to help her. You just didn't do that. You could watch, but weren't allowed to butt into people's fights."

The number of assaults on women is rising dramatically but the brutality of the attacks is escalating, too, with spears, rocks, knives, bottles and bricks being used.

The 2002 Gordon report into child abuse and family violence in Aboriginal communities in Western Australia makes it quite clear that rape has become more common, especially gang rape.

The violence associated with these rapes is increasingly ferocious and sometimes beggars belief. Victims are viciously gang-banged, during which they are smashed with iron bars, rocks, pieces of concrete or lumps of wood that cause extensive physical injuries and permanent facial deformities.

A particularly nasty strain of this violence that is showing an alarming increase is the number of women being set on fire. Russell Skelton wrote in *The Age* last year about the case of a young man who doused petrol on his 18-year-old girlfriend's stomach and genitals and set her clothes on fire when she refused to have sex.

It has been the recent publicising of child abuse in Aboriginal communities that has shocked the non-indigenous community most. I don't want to dwell on the details of such abuse but I will note a few cases that are indicative of what is happening to Aboriginal girls.

A seven-month-old baby was taken out of her home and raped. She needed surgery under general anaesthetic. A six-year-old girl was playing in a waterhole when an 18-year-old petrol sniffer grabbed her, pulled her under and simultaneously anally raped and drowned her. A 10-year-old girl was tied to a tree for several weeks and raped repeatedly. Then there was the case of a three-year-old girl who had been sexually assaulted by three men. If that wasn't enough, 10 days later another man raped her twice, once using a mangrove stick.

The *Breaking the Silence* report notes that the sexual abuse of children is at least four times more likely in Aboriginal communities and that the reported levels of abuse "grossly under-represent the reality".

If the sexual abuse were not enough, many of these girls are infected with sexually transmitted diseases by the perpetrators. In WA, the rate of gonorrhoea for Aboriginal children aged 10 to 14 is an astonishing 186 times the non-Aboriginal rate. In late 2005, four underage girls in the NT, the youngest being just seven, were found to have serious sexually transmitted infections that included chlamydia and resilient strains of gonorrhoea and syphilis.

Indigenous homosexuality has always been an uncomfortable topic to discuss, for Aborigines and their supporters. The reasons are complex but we know that it was practised traditionally, both as a sexual release for teenage boys and young men who couldn't find female sexual partners, and in initiation ceremonies.

Because of the secrecy around the subject the abuse of boys has been overlooked; but there is no doubt that some men are raping boys under the guise of the act being part of Aboriginal culture. Researcher Gary Lee says that boys as young as eight are being used for sex. "It seems to have almost a cultural sanction," he says, adding that everyone in the community knows it is happening but that there is "a real reluctance to talk about it". He believes the main perpetrators are elders or older relatives.

The situation is so bad in the Tanami Desert that mothers have banned their sons from going into the bush for initiation camps.

We also know that Aboriginal boys are 10 times more likely to be sexually assaulted than the rate for the rest of Australia. In a 2006 survey of indigenous men in Queensland and the NT, 10 per cent of participants had been raped before reaching the age of 16.

It is a mistake to think that this only happens in remote or rural areas. About 70 per cent of the indigenous population lives in urban areas. The Sydney Aboriginal communities at La Perouse, Woolloomooloo, Mount

Druitt, Blacktown and Redfern have high rates of domestic violence and sexual abuse, too, as the *Breaking the Silence* report points out.

A few years ago, at La Perouse, Lani Brennan fled from her partner after he tried at least four times in their three-year relationship to kill her. She left him after one incident when he bashed her with a baseball bat and golf club, raped her, then tried to hang her. She said the La Perouse community knew what was happening but did nothing to stop it.

"It's not just happening in some Aboriginal community in Western Australia or the Northern Territory; it happens in Sydney," she said after her husband's trial. "A lot of Aboriginal people are 'Hear no evil, see no evil'. There's a lot of alcohol, a lot of sexual assaults and a lot of really terrible violence. It's a normal thing in an Aboriginal community."

This abuse of children is disturbing, but so is the constant threat of its occurrence. It must create a state of permanent tension and fear that permeates the childhood years of many young Aborigines. One of the contributing factors to the high suicide rate among indigenous children is sexual molestation.

Henry Councillor, chairman of the National Community Controlled Health Organisation, has said: "One of the experiences we are finding is that a lot of youth suicide under the age of 18 is a result of child sexual abuse."

Perhaps the worst outcome is that the abused child ends up becoming an adult abuser, making the terrible cycle a permanent feature of indigenous life in Australia.

Traditional Aboriginal society expressed anger through aggression, but the violence and sexual behaviour was tightly structured through ritual, ceremony and proscribed procedures. But with the influence of alcohol and acculturation, some of these customs have become a pathological distortion of those that were the basis of traditional life.

Even so, some Aboriginal men use the notion of custom and tradition to get their own way. Journalist Paul Toohey has written of how indigenous men in the NT fallaciously claimed that tribal law justified their raping of Aboriginal girls and women. The truth is that most, if not all, of these rapes occur because of lust and alcohol, not because the girls and women have committed a traditional offence.

Even when Aboriginal men go to court, many receive lenient sentences when using the defence of intoxication combined with customary law.

Cunningham was convicted of manslaughter, not murder, yet no alcohol was involved in the crime and he was breaching the conditions for his parole at the time.

There is no doubt that some judges still consider that Aboriginal men's treatment of their women should be viewed differently from how the rest of society treat women. The defence does work. Last year NT Chief Justice Martin conceded he was wrong to sentence the elder to a month's jail for having anal sex with a 14-year-old promised to him as a wife. He admitted he had placed too much emphasis on the elder's belief that under tribal law he had the right to teach the girl to obey him.

There are other problems with this defence. The most important one is that it is always the man's view of customary law that prevails in court. Women remain victims of men's versions of indigenous customs and culture.

Women have not only been at the mercy of men's violence but also captives to the idea that they do not represent Aboriginal culture; that only men do. Is it any wonder that indigenous women despair of their own Aboriginal legal services, which still continue to push the defence of customary law?

In May last year, Marcia Langton, an indigenous professor at the University of Melbourne, spoke for many women when she asked: "Are the Aboriginal legal services which supposedly work for us ever going to stop arguing that rape is traditional law?"

It's not only in law courts where indigenous men take precedence over their victims but in their communities, where many elders wield authority through physical intimidation and bullying and by using bureaucratic powers given to them by state and federal governments.

The Gordon report concluded that "Some elder groups or councils are part of the reason why indigenous communities are having little success in creating less violent, more positive communities with male elders hindering prevention initiatives because of their own involvement in violence."

A prime example is Robert Bropho, an influential elder who had for years effectively banned child welfare workers and the local Aboriginal medical service from the Swan Valley Nyoongar camp. His indifference to the plight of abused girls was disgusting. He was eventually jailed for sexual matters involving a girl under 13.

These men not only intimidate their own people but the white health workers, bureaucrats and others who work in these communities. Lara Wieland, a former flying doctor who spent three years in far north Queensland, said last year that public servants who reported abuse were themselves verbally abused and threatened by men in positions of power:

> Some of these men were considered by many in the community to be perpetrators of child abuse themselves. Yet time and time again we saw them wield the power and control in the communities and saw government departments and officials cower in fear, turning a blind eye rather than [be] accused of being a racist by these men, which was their common ploy.

Another way these violent men maintain control is through the use of the permit system that allows some indigenous communities to refuse entry to visitors. Men use the permit system to continue their abuse undetected and unreported by the wider community. *The Australian*'s Nicolas Rothwell has commented that "there is a striking correlation between the levels of violence in a community and the tightness of its closure".

In any community it takes much courage to report domestic violence and sexual abuse, but in Aboriginal communities women and children face other enormous obstacles.

Retribution by relatives of the accused is common. One woman told the 1999 taskforce: "Extended family came around and got into me. They went for me at the court after he was found guilty of attempted murder on me."

Sometimes the whole community will protect a vicious abuser. In November last year, NSW District Court judge Michael Finnane, in sentencing Aboriginal rapist Phillip Boney to 23 years' jail, criticised the Moree Aboriginal community who refused to help police find the rapist after his first attacks on a woman.

By protecting him, the community allowed Boney to rape her again. Within the space of one month, he kidnapped the woman on three occasions, assaulted her and raped her five times.

As Finnane remarked in his judgment, "Aboriginality does not provide any justification for his obsessive and cruel behaviour."

But as far as many Aboriginal men are concerned, it does. Kinship ties are strong. Men will not condemn perpetrators whom they are related to by kin, and because these communities often see violence and sexual assault as a normal way of life, the dire situation is frequently hidden to protect family members and the perpetrators.

The most important commodity in any society is its children. After all, they are the future. The problem with this is that, despite the high numbers of Aboriginal children being removed from their communities and families (in 1990, indigenous mental health specialist Ernest Hunter reported that heavy drinking had been so destructive of family life that there were fewer Aboriginal children in Western Australia being reared by their biological parents than in the days of forced assimilation), many other at-risk children are not being removed.

The reason, as Sue Gordon, National Indigenous Council chairwoman, has remarked, is that "government agencies across the states and territories charged with the statutory responsibility for children's issues have, I believe, taken the softly-softly approach to child abuse, [whether it be] emotional, physical neglect or sexual, because they have been frightened of creating another stolen generation."

The most pressing need is that these children be rescued. Education has to be a priority. This may mean children are sent away from their communities to separate them from the corrupting influence of grog and the welfare mentality. Some communities, like those on Cape York, aware they need a new generation of leaders capable of dealing with the outside world, are sending their boys to Sydney boarding schools.

Indigenous communities have to recognise that it is impossible to hide from a globalised world behind an ossified sense of tradition. They have to realise they are part of Australian society as a whole and they have to face up to the high rate of social crisis among them. Indigenous communities cannot argue that they are not part of Western culture when they are eager devourers of it, consuming drugs, television, pornography, alcohol, junk food, cars and rap music.

Last year Rosalie Kunoth Monks, who chairs the Batchelor Institute of Indigenous Education, said Aboriginal people were on a path of cultural suicide and needed to accept some blame for the choices they had made. She added that land and culture were no longer sufficient to sustain identity and that people must accept change. "To be part of the economy and a contributing member of society we have to take that journey," she said. "It is my belief that the confusion will only be resolved through a new sense of identity and that comes through when you connect with other people, look at future pathways and not be so internalised."

Yes, there are considerable health issues; yes, there are too few police in remote communities; yes, there is a shortage of women's shelters; yes, one of the main problems is alcohol, yet it has been successfully banned in some communities. But one of the most insidious and intractable problems is welfare. Most of these communities have no employment and people exist on welfare their whole lives. As a result, a large number of men have nothing to do.

To put it quite simply, an idle man is a dangerous man.

It is curious that while researching *Bad Dreaming* there were many solutions put forward to combat these issues, yet men were rarely mentioned. But they are the problem and the solution. The men not only have to realise their behaviour is undermining Aboriginal culture but also that they are creating a generation of boys without good role models.

There is another aspect to all of this: Aboriginal society is oriented towards a sense of collective obligation rather than individual responsibility, but men may have to confront the perpetrators of violence, even though many of them may be elders and relatives. This may be the hardest task of all.

Furthermore, men need to accept that certain aspects of their traditional culture, and customs such as promised marriages, polygamy, violence towards women and male aggression, are best forgotten.

Above all, there should be one law for all and a recognition that human rights come before cultural rights. If the men refuse to do anything, they will be responsible for the slow death of aspects of their culture and their communities will continue to be on a nightmarish treadmill to cultural oblivion.

Robert Manne

Pearson's gamble, Stanner's dream: The past and future of remote Australia

The Monthly, August 2007

In 1934 the Professor of Anthropology at the University of Sydney, AP Elkin, published a small pamphlet which called for "a positive policy which aims at the welfare and development of the aborigines". To us, Elkin's words seem anodyne. For his contemporaries, they had a galvanising effect. Before Elkin's pamphlet, Aboriginal policy had passed through just two phases. In the first, the Aborigines, an impediment to the steady expansion of the pastoral economy, were subdued. By the end of this phase, as a result of disease, removal from hunting grounds and water sources and the impact of armed force, perhaps half of the 500 or so tribes that existed at the time of the arrival of the British settlers had vanished altogether from the face of the Earth. In the second phase, those Aborigines who had survived the initial onslaught were segregated, either voluntarily on government stations, Christian missions and reserves or involuntarily in detention camps, and protected by an ever-tightening net of special laws that controlled movement, marriage, sexual behaviour, the fate of children, employment, savings and the consumption of alcohol. At the time of Elkin's pamphlet most Australians believed it was only a matter of time before the surviving remnant would die out. Following his call for a positive policy, a 70-year journey of government-led policy experiments to build a future for the Aborigines began. The mood of these experiments has since lurched erratically between rather pessimistic realism and over-optimistic hope. The most recent experiment was the decision in June to dispatch police, troops and medical workers to protect Aboriginal children on the remote settlements of the Northern

Territory. The Howard government has now altogether abandoned the hopes embedded in the language of reconciliation. Realism once more rules. How did we arrive at this point?

It took a decade and a half for the first positive policy to be formulated clearly. It was labelled assimilation. The postwar Minister for Territories in the Menzies government, Paul Hasluck, was its philosophical driving force. For Hasluck, assimilation was not a set of administrative devices but a destination. The destination was this: "All Aborigines and part-Aborigines will attain the same manner of living as other Australians, as members of a single community enjoying the same rights and privileges, accepting the same responsibilities, observing the same customs and influenced by the same beliefs, hopes and loyalties as other Australians." The policy was frankly paternalistic, although the word was not used. Hasluck described welfare work among Aborigines as "sheltering, protecting, guiding, teaching and helping, and eventually, as the perhaps most difficult act ... quietly withdrawing without any proud fuss when the Aboriginal entered the Australian community". The policy was also gradualist. Hasluck assumed that the destination might not be reached for all Aborigines for three generations or more. He did not believe that assimilation implied racial inter-marriage and biological absorption, as many inter-war Australian native administrators did. He did not believe that it was necessary that all Aborigines would ultimately leave their ancestral homelands, although he thought that as a matter of fact very many would.

But where he was insistent was that Aborigines had no future as a distinct or separate people. The government might not actively work to destroy Aboriginal language and culture, but Hasluck believed that eventually both would have to go. In a letter to a churchman he put the point like this. Australians could not "have it both ways". If the aim was to facilitate eventual Aboriginal entry into the wider Australian society "on equal terms", such an ambition was quite simply "incompatible with full and active preservation of their languages and culture without any changes".

Towards the end of his life, after his policy had been discredited, Hasluck stated his case about the inevitable end of the Aborigines as a distinct people, about assimilation as their inevitable fate, with uncharacteristic polemical sarcasm. Were Aborigines, he asked in *Shades of Darkness*, to be living museum pieces? Or a sort of fringe community whose quaint customs are stared at by tourists? Will the drone of the didgeridoo, the clicking of the boomerangs and the stomping in the red dust in the red centre of Australia still be the sufficient employment for the grandchildren of the people of Ularu? Will the separate development that is being pursued with a beneficent purpose today have the result that after two or three generations persons of Aboriginal descent find that they are shut out from participation in most of what is happening in the continent and are behind glass in a vast museum, or are in a sort of open-range zoo?

Aborigines were, in his vision, destined to be nothing more than an ethnicity. At most, Aborigines would have vague memories of what their people once had been. For Hasluck, the idea of a separate people was separatism; apartness was apartheid. He stared at the total destruction of the way of life of the people the British had encountered in Australia, and did not blink.

During the late 1960s and early '70s the policy of assimilation was abandoned. The most general explanation for this was the impact in Australia of the profound revolution in sensibility which took hold in the West at that time: the belated recognition of racism as a dimension of Western civilisation. Perhaps only now had the meaning of the Holocaust been grasped. Europeans and European settler societies realized that their history had for centuries been sullied by the assumption of their superiority and the barbarous actions which had been granted permission as a result. In the US the civil-rights movement grew. Western opinion became increasingly sympathetic to the anti-colonial liberation struggles of the peoples in the European empires. White dominance in South Africa and Rhodesia came to seem intolerable. And in Australia, not only were the cultural assumptions underlying the assimilation policy questioned; more deeply, the fate of the Aborigines, which had interested a small segment of the educated public since the 1930s, now became for the first time a matter of general political significance. The old indifference lifted. It was as if, from this moment, many Australians came only now to see with moral clarity what had been in front of their noses since the arrival of the

British: what their presence had meant for the original inhabitants, what they and their forebears had actually done. Nor was recognition of racism all that was required of Australians. It seems plausible to suppose that all nations yearn for a noble myth of origin. As Australia was founded by an act of dispossession, coming to terms with what had been done was to prove unusually hard—far more difficult, for example, than for Americans eventually to come to accept the ignominy of black slavery.

Grasping the true meaning of what had occurred in the settlement of Australia required something far less abstract than what I have written so far implies. It required an intimate understanding of the nature of the people which had been dispossessed. For this understanding Australians relied on the work of the anthropologists. Although many were important—Howitt and Fison; Spencer and Gillen; Walter Roth; Radcliffe-Brown; Elkin; Ronald and Catherine Berndt—in this vital task of national education, no one was of more significance than WEH Stanner, in my opinion if not the greatest of the anthropologists (I am in no position to judge), then certainly the most interesting writer on Aboriginal society Australia has ever seen.

The older anthropologists had looked on the Aborigines they studied as a Stone Age people on the edge of extinction. Baldwin Spencer, for example, introduced his two-volume 1928 memoir, *Wanderings in Wild Australia*, with these words: "Australia is the present home and refuge of animals, including man himself, that have elsewhere become extinct and given place to higher forms." Stanner, by contrast, never tired of trying to convince his readers that the Aborigines were a contemporary people. To think of history as "a linear sequence", with the primitive Aborigines at the beginning and Europeans at the end, he wrote as early as 1958, and to suggest that "all we have to do is to instruct them in the manifest virtues of our style of life" and wait for them to "'unlearn' being Aborigines in mind, body and estate", was a malignant and self-centred "fantasy", whose consequences were to be seen "in a thousand miserable encampments around the continent".

The older anthropologists never doubted their superiority to the people they studied. "The idea of putting any of their beliefs to the test of experiment never entered their heads," Spencer typically informed his readers during a discussion of magic. This was a tone of which Stanner was incapable. Perhaps the finest essay ever written by an Australian is

Stanner's portrait in *White Man Got No Dreaming* of one of his lifelong Aboriginal friends, Durmugam. In it, Stanner sails assuredly between the customary rocks of peril waiting for writers on Aborigines—condescension and sentimentality. It is hard to convey the flavour of the essay, but here are snatches from its final pages:

> He was for me the most characterful Aboriginal I have known ... I am sure he was deeply moved to live by the rules of his tradition as he understood it. He wanted to live a blackfellow's life, having the rights of a man, and following up the Dreaming ... He venerated his culture ... I do not believe he ever formed a deep attachment to any European, myself included. He knew I was making use of him and, as a due for good service, he made use of me, always civilly, never unscrupulously or importunately ... [One] young man's remark, 'If I live I live, if I die I die' had seemed to Durmugam monstrous. To him, how a man lived and what he lived for were of first importance.
>
> But he himself had in part succumbed. He now spent much time playing poker (there were five aces in one of his pack of cards) ... He still went bootless, but wore a hat and well-kept shirt and trousers ... Durmugam came to good terms with Europeanism, but found it saltless all his days and, at the end, bitter too ... it never attracted him emotionally, it did not interest him intellectually, and it aroused only his material desires.

Baldwin Spencer and Frank Gillen's *The Native Tribes of Central Australia* is probably the most influential book ever written by Australians. It provided the source material for Freud's *Totem and Taboo* and Durkheim's *Elementary Forms of Religious Life*. And yet, when Spencer wrote of Aboriginal ceremony it was as if he was peering through the glass of an aquarium. These passages are taken from his memoir:

> The ancestor is rarely represented as doing anything more interesting than looking around, wriggling his body in an extraordinary way, or perhaps eating something ... The natives were very anxious that we should see everything, which sometimes resulted in our spending a good many uncomfortable hours watching dreary performances of no special interest.

WEH Stanner's most important work concerned Aboriginal religion. For him there is no aquarium glass: "While at song, the celebrants vie rather than compete ... The men's faces take on a glow of animation and tender intent. At the last exclamatory cry—*Karwadi, yoi*—everyone shouts as with one voice. An observer feels that he is in the presence of true congregation, a full sociality at the peak of intimacy, altruism and union." Because Stanner does not feel superior to what he is observing or to the people he is among, he is capable of entering the Aboriginal world of meaning in a quite extraordinary way. No one has explicated more lucidly for outsiders the metaphysic of the Dreamtime, for which he coined the neologism "everywhen". No one has taken us more profoundly to an understanding of the Aboriginal world view:

> Murinbata religion might well be described as the celebration of a dependent life which is conceived as having taken a wrongful turn at the beginning, a turn such that the good life is now inescapably connected with suffering ... The Murinbata, like all the Aborigines, gave the impression of having stopped short of, or gone beyond, a quarrel with the terms of life.

And no one other than Stanner could capture the Aboriginal sense of life more vividly, and in a single phrase: "A joyful thing with maggots at the centre."

Stanner's 1968 Boyer Lectures are probably the most influential radio broadcasts in our history. For one thing, Henry Reynolds tells us that it was only after hearing them that he decided to study Aboriginal history. Most famously, Stanner identified and analysed what he called the Great Australian Silence on the dispossession. "Inattention on such a scale cannot possibly be explained by absent-mindedness ... Simple forgetting of other possible views turned under habit and over time into something like a cult of forgetfulness practised on a national scale." But he also captured the depth of Aboriginal attachment to country more powerfully than had any writer until that time:

> No English words are good enough to give a sense of the links between an Aboriginal group and its homeland ... A different tradition leaves us tongueless and earless towards this other world ... What I describe as

"homelessness", then, means that the Aborigine faced a kind of vertigo of meaning.

In the lectures Stanner provided the most devastating critique of the policy of assimilation that had yet been given by a non-Aborigine: "We are asking them to become a new people but this means that we are asking them in human terms to un-be what they now are." And, in addition, he provided the most plausible explanation of why the Hasluck policy of assimilation would eventually be rejected:

> Just as in the nineteenth century a sense of physical and biological principle steadily permeated the public mentality so a sense of what I will broadly call "anthropological principle" may be permeating our own century's mentality. I mean by that a steady awareness that there are no natural scales of better or worse on which we can range the varieties of men, culture and society.

AP Elkin stood, in sensibility, halfway between Spencer and Stanner. He could write movingly of the enchanted Aboriginal world, but also about the Aborigines as a primitive people and the supposedly smaller size of the Aboriginal brain. As mentioned, he was the original source of the positive policy that ended in the idea of assimilation. For both these reasons I found very telling indeed an incident recorded in the biography of Elkin by Tigger Wise. Elkin had invited Paul Hasluck to address the 1959 annual congress of Australian and New Zealand anthropologists. In his speech, Hasluck told the audience: "Looked at from one point of view the weakness of the old Aboriginal society ... is an advantage. The more it crumbles, the more readily may its fragments be mingled with the rest of the people living in Australia." Elkin was agitated. Wise tells us that he saw in these remarks "all his ideas twisted and misapplied". He took to the rostrum to deliver a rebuke: "The Aborigines themselves will observe a partial and voluntary segregation—an apartness for an unpredictable period ... This apartness is a sense of belonging ... Our task is to see that the phase of apartness does not become apartheid ..."

Elkin had spent his life studying the Aborigines. He had come to admire deeply their way of life. Faced with light-hearted talk about the end of Aboriginal Australia, even Elkin, the intellectual father of assimilation, blinked. So did the political leaders of Australia in the 1970s—Malcolm

Fraser no less than Gough Whitlam—as the policy of assimilation was abandoned in favour of a policy of self-determination and reconciliation.

There were very real achievements in the new, post-assimilation era. Land rights were granted by statute throughout Australia. In the Mabo and Wik judgements native title was discovered to exist in common law. In 1975 the *Racial Discrimination Act* was passed. In the new school of history pioneered by Charles Rowley and Henry Reynolds, the Great Australian Silence was shattered. The reports of both the Royal Commission on Aboriginal Deaths in Custody and the Human Rights Commission on Aboriginal child removal shook the nation. In 1991 a formal structure aimed at achieving reconciliation was established.

Yet it must be stressed that the generation educated by WEH Stanner, which had finally opened its eyes to the full moral meaning of the dispossession, now hoped for more than this. What this more consisted of is best revealed in the thought of the most influential intellectual figure of the post-assimilation era, the former Treasury head Nugget Coombs, Stanner's close friend and political collaborator. Coombs believed that through the policy of allowing Aborigines self-determination or, as he often preferred to call it, their autonomy, the traditional way of life of the Aborigines need not die. He advocated government support for hundreds of small, decentralised Aboriginal communities in what he called their homelands. He hoped these communities would be formed, so far as possible, according to the pre-conquest divisions of language, tribe and even clan. He hoped for nothing less than the rebirth of the Aboriginal world.

Coombs was not the kind of Rousseauian, 'noble savage' dreamer that his ideological enemies on the Right invariably suggest. He did not believe that these re-established groups would be unaffected in a multitude of ways by the undeniable fact of the dispossession, and by the existence alongside them of an advanced Western materialist-industrial civilisation. This presented no insurmountable problem. He argued that far from being hidebound or inflexible, Aboriginal culture was dynamic, flexible and adaptive. Coombs imagined a future for the homeland communities where traditional hunting and gathering would be able to be combined with a monetary economy based on welfare payments and small-scale market activities, like cattle raising, emu or crocodile farming, land management, and the production and sale of arts and crafts. He did not deny that all Aboriginal children needed an education that equipped them for some participation in the contemporary world by providing them with basic modern skills. In one of his essays he wrote that he had yet to meet an Aboriginal parent who did not want his or her children to be literate and numerate. Nor did he ignore altogether the evidence of the social ills affecting the remote Aboriginal communities he knew. Coombs wrote from time to time about male violence against women, the indiscipline of the younger generation and the problem of alcohol. After visiting Yuendumu with Stanner, the pair accepted that there was need for a police presence to deal with "brawls and other disorder arising out of ... abuse of drink".

And yet, if Coombs' critics on the Right, like Peter Howson or Helen Hughes, offer a distorted picture of him as nothing but a utopian collectivist fantasist, his defensive friends on the Left, like Tim Rowse, now offer an even more distorted portrait of Coombs as a moderate economic rationalist, eminently capable of passing a contemporary neo-liberal respectability test. In the last two decades of his life Coombs was a critic of Western materialist civilisation, capable, for example, of calling it the "beer and Coca-Cola" culture, or quoting with approval a description of it as "life without reverence for the past, love for the present or hope for the future". Because he was open to such a bleak view about his own society, it is not surprising that he often wrote as if he genuinely believed that the Aboriginal way of life was superior to the one in which he lived: "That human beings are at home in a hunter-gatherer society is not surprising. They have been adapted to it for more than 500,000 years." Nor is it surprising that he was fiercely opposed to the imposition on Aboriginal children of a Western world view. On one occasion Coombs described purely Western education for Aborigines as "cultural genocide". On another he expressed opposition to the idea of compulsory school attendance. Rather, Coombs advocated a "two-way education", with not only a Western but also an Aboriginal dimension. This would help, he believed, to "decolonise" the Aboriginal mind. Coombs also wanted to "Aboriginalise work". He was enthusiastic about the possibilities offered by the Fraser government's Community Development Employment Projects (CDEP) scheme, which allowed Aborigines to be paid while continuing their hunting and gathering, and gave them time to devote to their religious ceremonies. He supported the re-institution, wherever possible, of Aboriginal customary law. He regarded attempts to interfere with traditional punishments, like leg spearing or the system of "pay-back", as "ethnocentric".

Coombs believed that in the era of self-determination and land rights an authentic revival of Aboriginal life was indeed occurring. "There are," he wrote, "widespread reports of increasing activity in Aboriginal ceremonial life." Distinctive forms of education were, he believed, thriving: "There is a quality of enthusiasm, indeed exuberance, about Yolngu education at present." As traditional life revived, he thought the problems of young people fell away: "Almost universally the problems of delinquency appear to decline and disappear." While alcohol abuse might presently be a problem, he seemed convinced that it was coming under control. Indeed, "Aboriginal concern and action in this matter," he wrote on one occasion, compared "favourably with that in Western society". In the conclusion to his collection of essays, *Aboriginal Autonomy*, published about the time that John Howard regained the leadership of the Liberal Party, Coombs summarised the meaning of all this in the following way:

> In the years since the apparent "consensus" in approach by the Whitlam and Fraser governments, the direction of change has inexorably been towards greater independence for Aboriginal Australians. Despite the repudiation of that "consensus", Aboriginals have made by their own initiatives, intelligence and dedication, remarkable progress in the achievement of a lifestyle more healthy, more creative and more characteristically Aboriginal than has previously been possible since their dispossession.

A miracle was occurring. Traditional Aboriginal life was in the process of revival. At the time, few members of the left-liberal intelligentsia would have disagreed strongly with these words.

In the 1960s the British anthropologist David McKnight first began fieldwork on Mornington Island, in the Gulf of Carpentaria. He continued regular visits over a period of 30 years. In 2002 he published a study of social life on Mornington Island, *From Hunting to Drinking*. It is the most remarkable portrait of an Aboriginal community in the age of self-determination I have read. For McKnight, by far the most significant event during the period of his visits was the opening of the canteen in 1976. For the vast majority of Mornington Islanders drinking now became the "main social activity". McKnight noticed that those who used to go hunting until dusk now returned by two in the afternoon, so as not to miss the opening of the canteen. "It felt," he tells us, "as if all the people were drunk all of the time or at least most of the people were drunk most of the time." Dreadful alcohol-related deaths soon began occurring: "Teddy Bell and his brother were drinking and in the middle of the night Pat Bell woke up and discovered that Teddy was drinking methylated spirits. He tried to stop him and in the resulting struggle Teddy accidentally stabbed himself to death."

By the '90s, of the 900 or so Indigenous inhabitants, McKnight calculated that there were 40 women and eight men who did not drink. Most drunk to wild excess. McKnight also calculated that by the '90s, on average 50% of income was spent on alcohol. The effects on health were catastrophic: "After ten years of drinking people were dying at such a rate that the carpenter built spare coffins." Wild drunken fights became common. Fights had once been about something—kinship loyalty or women—but now they were about nothing. Although McKnight continued to do so, it was now dangerous to walk about the community at night. Going to a film had been a pleasant experience when McKnight first came to Mornington Island. Because of the likelihood of a violent drunken incident, it ceased to be. The cinema was closed.

Children were badly affected. Babies were often neglected. Girls became vulnerable to sexual abuse. Although the community was awash with money, cases of malnutrition occurred. After ten years of schooling most children were illiterate. Even more, some could barely speak. Marital relations deteriorated badly: "Women appeared to be treated as objects, as if they were things." Rape had not been a problem in the past. It became so now, especially for white women or Indigenous women who associated with whites. Among the three tribal groups on Mornington Island—the Lardil, the Yangkaal and the Kaiadilt—suicide was unknown before the arrival of Europeans. Before the 1980s it remained virtually unknown. Yet between 1996 and 2000 there were 22 suicides on Mornington Island.

In Queensland the rate of suicide for these years was 13.7 per 100,000; on Mornington Island it was 466. Between 1914 and 1978 there was one homicide on Mornington Island. Since the opening of the canteen there had been 15. All but one of the killers were male. Most of the victims were wives.

McKnight is an anthropologist. He offers some cultural explanations for this disaster. The Mornington Islanders were not a "moderate" people. They lived traditionally on "the edge", with dancing, initiation ceremonies, violent clashes. Drinking is also an exciting activity, with people living for the time at a heightened pitch. The Mornington Islanders have egalitarian traditions. Drink drags everyone down to the same level; no one is better than anyone else. They have no tradition of regulated consumption; everything available was and is instantly consumed. They were also a single-activity people. Once they were hunter-gatherers; now they are drinkers. Yet he also offers more political explanations. Work under CDEP has become meaningless. What the Mornington Islanders have learnt, he tells us, is that "a job not worth doing is not worth doing well". Ironically, in the age of so-called self-determination, almost everything is done by the whites who bowl in to work for the shire. They establish less human connection with the Indigenous Mornington Islanders than did the missionaries. The Mornington Islanders, especially the men, feel powerless and humiliated. Life has been stripped of meaning. A people that once lived vibrantly as hunter-gatherers is now profoundly, existentially, bored.

It is difficult to know how typical Mornington Island is of remote Aboriginal communities, at least of those where for some time alcohol has flowed; how far McKnight's terrifying portrait is coloured by his sceptical and sardonic disposition; and whether life has improved on Mornington Island since attempts began in recent years to restrict alcohol there. But there is one thing at least that seems clear. The contradiction between what McKnight and many others observed in remote Aboriginal communities, and what Nugget Coombs and a generation of left-liberals imagined was happening in such communities and, even more, what they dreamt might eventually happen there—nothing less than the revival of a healthy and authentic Aboriginal life—would sooner or later require some new and radical thinking to be done.

It was Noel Pearson who broke the ideological stalemate over Aboriginal policy and the remote communities. Pearson had been a land-rights activist and a man of the Left. At one memorable moment in the early years of the Howard government, during the political skirmishes surrounding native title, he had labelled his conservative opponents "racist scum". In 1999 he shifted gear. Pearson now acknowledged that over the past quarter-century or so the communities at Cape York had experienced what he would call "a descent into hell". For the Left, insofar as problems of violence, sexual abuse, suicide, alcoholism, drug dependency, petrol sniffing, gambling, illiteracy, truancy and child neglect were acknowledged, the historic process of colonisation and the trauma associated with the dispossession were blamed. Although this explanation might in the most general sense be true, for Pearson it was not only useless—by explaining everything it explained nothing—but also misleading. Pearson had grown up on the Lutheran mission of Hope Vale. He knew that conditions then were far less grim. In the early '70s not one Hope Vale Aborigine was in prison. Thirty years later, there were a dozen who were either in prison or had narrowly escaped that fate. Murder on the Cape York of his childhood was unknown. "In one of our communities," he wrote in 2000, "there were three murders within one month."

The Left was committed to Aboriginal rights. It focused, for example, almost exclusively on the provision of legal aid to Aborigines charged with criminal offences, and was neglectful of the fate of the women and children who suffered abuse at their hands. The Right was responsive to talk of Aboriginal responsibilities but was hostile to Aboriginal rights like native title, the cause for which Pearson had been struggling in recent years. At one level, Pearson's breaking of the ideological log-jam in 1999 was an attempt to refashion the agenda of Aboriginal politics, by marrying the idea of rights with the idea of responsibilities. Yet this formulation is somewhat misleading. In ideological politics, activists are invariably more hostile to the camp from which they have defected than they are to the camp of the former enemy, even when they keep their distance from it. Although Pearson was theoretically opposed to the Right, he was far more emotionally engaged in his conflict with the Left. For their unwillingness to confront the reality of the remote Aboriginal communities, he held the soft-headed Left to blame. Even though he remained committed to native title and Indigenous rights, he postponed the resolution of his differences with the hard-hearted Right for a later day.

What then was to be done? In Pearson's analysis, there were three inter-connected causes of the post-1960s catastrophe of the communities: alcohol, the poison of passive welfare, and disconnection from the real economy.

Pearson believed that the Left saw alcohol as a symptom of deeper problems. For him, it was vital to interpret the emergence of the alcohol epidemic not as a symptom but as a cause. In part, this was because the grog culture on a small community developed a momentum of its own, becoming increasingly difficult for individuals to resist. And in part, it was because seeing alcohol as a symptom of something deeper provided splendid justification for the easy option of inaction. Pearson advocated total prohibition on the communities, total abstinence, rehabilitation programs for drinkers and tough criminal sanctions for those who brought the alcohol in. He saw alcohol abuse as a paradoxical consequence of the citizenship rights won in the '60s. And he saw how the traditional hunter-gatherer ethic of kinship and reciprocity could prove disastrous under conditions of modernity when it was grog rather than food that was being shared.

For Pearson the liberation of Aborigines from the poison of welfare dependency and their return to the real economy was as vital as alcohol control. Here his thought developed. In 2000 he offered a social-democratic distinction between the virtue of the redistributive welfare state and the vice of a life of complete welfare dependency. This year, with the help of seconded Treasury officials, his Cape York Institute completed *From Hand Out to Hand Up*, a sophisticated, fully neo-liberal plan for the future of his people. The plan recommends that all welfare payments be made conditional. Those who are convicted of drug or drink offences, who fail to pay their rent, or who fail to care for their children or ensure their regular school attendance will lose control of family welfare payments, which are to be redirected to those who will act responsibly. The system is to be administered by a Family Responsibilities Commission with both Indigenous and non-Indigenous members. Welfare payments, including CDEP, will be reduced to remove what are called perverse incentives against employment. Worthwhile CDEP activities, like teaching aids, will be converted into real jobs. CDEP will not be available to anyone under 21. Various attempts will be made to let children break out of the cycle of inherited social breakdown. The talented will attend boarding schools. Those seeking work training outside the communities will be supported. Although native title will in general be staunchly defended, residents will be encouraged to purchase their present homes or newly built ones, which taxpayers will heavily subsidise. Businesses will be attracted to the communities with 99-year leases. Because it is accepted that there will never be sufficient employment available in the communities, many members will have to "orbit" in and out, throughout their lives. "Orbiters," we are told, "are people who periodically return to their communities or homelands and thereby retain their cultural heritage, their languages, their hunting skills, their rituals and cultural rights." In this way, the very idea of community is re-defined. Membership will consist not of those who live in a settlement but of those who feel connected with it in some way.

Pearson's plan is not merely an audacious (and very expensive) neo-liberal blueprint for the revival of Aboriginal community and the adaptation of Aboriginal identity to conditions of modernity. It is based on the paradoxical belief that the sticks and carrots of a transformative, interventionist policy of social engineering can create the character of the responsible, acquisitive individual on which the philosophy of neo-liberalism is premised. This is Pearson's gamble. It is very far indeed from Stanner's dream—many will think too far. Yet for the hope of the survival of autonomous and viable Aboriginal communities, it seems to me the most coherent policy which has yet been offered. If it too fails, it might turn out to have been the last throw of the dice.

As Noel Pearson was handing his report to the enthusiastic Minister for Aboriginal Affairs, Mal Brough, the prime minister, after reading another report into the sexual abuse of Aboriginal children on the remote communities of the Northern Territory, decided to declare a state of national emergency and to send in the troops, police, administrators and doctors. Like the majority of Australians, I was relieved that a decision for action had finally been taken. I am absolutely convinced that the crisis in the communities is real. The analogy drawn by some between this intervention and the children-overboard affair struck me as absurd. I opposed Howard over the question of the detention or military repulsion of asylum seekers because of the almost unbelievable cruelty it showed especially towards vulnerable children. On this occasion the aim was to protect children from abuse. Nonetheless, like many of those who support passionately the idea of reconciliation, I was dismayed but not surprised at the arrogant disregard for Aboriginal people and their leaders revealed by the failure even to pretend to consult over issues as sensitive as land rights and the permit system for communities.

There is a Napoleonic streak in the present prime minister. As with the *Tampa* 'crisis' and the blank cheque commitment to the US in the War on Terror, he has a capacity for advancing basic policy trajectories through apparently instinctive and improvisatory acts. Although much of the policy over the Northern Territory settlements showed signs of being made on the run, behind it the Howard government's new remote communities strategy was advanced. Those who wish to grasp the general direction of the government's policy should read Helen Hughes's new book, *Lands of Shame*. Hughes is a senior fellow of the Centre for Independent Studies, the most important ideological engine room for Australian neo-liberalism and the Howard government. Hughes supports the elimination of passive welfare and the introduction of private home ownership. In the short run, she advocates the liquidation of most of the settlements but continued support for a small number where decent education and medical services can be delivered, through a population-concentration policy. In the long run, she shows sympathy to the views of the Canadian conservative John Ibbotson, who recently advised young indigenous Canadians living on their settlements to pack their bags and permanently leave. Although Hughes thinks she is sympathetic to traditional Aboriginal values, it turns out that she is hostile to customary law and regards what Stanner called the Aboriginal "low culture" as little more than contemptible superstition. The policy Hughes outlines—cogently and persuasively, it must be said—is generally unsympathetic to land rights and self-determination, frankly paternalistic, opposed to those who presently exercise power in the Aboriginal communities and openly assimilationist in its ultimate ambition. *Lands of Shame* undoubtedly reflects the general thrust of the thinking of the Howard government and conservative Australia.

The considerable overlap between this and the neo-liberal dimension of the thought of Noel Pearson is clear. Yet the differences between Pearson and Howard are no less important. Pearson supports land rights and native title. Howard is hoping for their erosion. Pearson supports genuine, not phoney, Aboriginal self-determination. Howard supports assimilation, in fact if not in name. Pearson detests Windschuttle's denialist history of the dispossession. Howard is the country's most influential supporter. Pearson regards the rights of indigenous peoples as politically fundamental. In a recent essay in the *Griffith Review*, he tells us that when he discussed first peoples' rights with a senior and sympathetic member of the Coalition government, he was told, "I just don't understand the Indigenous-rights stuff." Pearson's life has been dedicated to the struggle for the survival and health of the remote Aboriginal communities. There is no reason to suppose that Howard would be concerned if they all eventually collapsed.

In the final essay of *White Man Got No Dreaming*, WEH Stanner, a supreme realist, warned against the temptation of pessimism. I take the warning seriously. My present hope is that in the next few months, if Labor is elected, Noel Pearson will be able finally to act upon his fundamental differences with Australian conservatives and join cause with Aboriginal leaders like Pat and Mick Dodson, Lowitja O'Donoghue and Patricia Turner and, as importantly, with a new generation of leaders, in their common struggle for the future of the remote Aboriginal communities.

Noel Pearson

White guilt, victimhood and the quest for a radical centre
Griffith Review 16: Unintended Consequences

Back in those days the Boss had been blundering and groping his unwitting way toward the discovery of himself, of his great gift … nursing some blind and undefined compulsion within him like fate or a disease.

—*Robert Penn Warren,* All the King's Men *(New English Classics, 1946)*

The audacious idea of a Barack Obama presidency emerged when the first-term black Senator from Illinois was invited by John Kerry to deliver the keynote to the 2004 Democratic Convention. From a gatecrasher without a pass at the previous convention in Los Angeles four years earlier, Obama's exceptional charisma navigated by a (politically) precise moral compass led to the fortuitous invitation from Team Kerry. Good for Obama, maybe not so good for Kerry. It must have been akin to asking a before-he-was-famous Bill Clinton to introduce the paler, less gifted candidate. Like sending Jesus before John the Baptist.

From his star turn in Boston, Obama stirred the American imagination with the prospect of a first black presidency, and in a flash his 1995 biography *Dreams from My Father* (Three Rivers Press) was reprinted and in the bookstores. The beautiful writing promised to live up to the blurb, and with anticipation I read of Obama's work as an organiser in the projects of Chicago, hoping it would reveal deep insights into how extreme social dysfunction and deprivation might be tackled. Alas, the insights were lean and the rhetorical wind soon failed to sustain its ambitious sails. It took an effort to finish the book.

I well understand Joe Klein's assessment in his *Newsweek* cover piece: Obama is a bit thin on the ideas, a fact which charisma and mesmerising oratory cannot completely disguise. He is no wonk in the Bill, Hillary, Tony (and Kevin) class, but policy paucity is no disqualification for the world's highest office. It is his native lack of proximity to power: a dummy born to power can rule, but outsiders need more than extraordinary talents—they must, amongst other things, be capable of extreme ruthlessness when the time requires. Will Obama be prepared to do the equivalent of refusing clemency to a (black) mentally retarded "death rower" on the eve of the primaries? Hillary and Bill were outsiders with cold steel veins; it remains to be seen whether Obama is prepared to have blood on his hands when called for. Hillary's blood in a bowl, courtesy of the (nice) tall, dark, handsome man, is probably what America will need if the Rubicon to a black presidency is to be crossed.

Obama's application for his 2008 candidature is set out in last year's bestseller *The Audacity of Hope* (Crown), where he does nothing less than boldly set out his "thoughts on reclaiming the American dream". It is an impressive statement of beliefs, characterised by its intelligent analysis, a candour that may not be completely calculated and a carefully calibrated self-deprecation. It is counter-weighed by an understandable, but nevertheless disturbing, absence of doubt about whether the contradictions of America can really be resolved: the over-promise of leadership. Obama attributes the audacity of hope to the salt-of-the-earth characters he parades throughout his book (he uses this device with almost toast-masterish sincerity), but there is no doubt—it is really the audacity of his own ambitions that he has in mind.

Obama's great talent is that of Bill Clinton: a keen public moral compass that can provide persuasive direction through the dialectical thickets of modern conundrums, and a near-peerless capacity for summoning "the better angels of our natures" even as the GOP's Lee Atwater and Karl Rove brought American (and therefore the world that follows) electoral politics to new pitiless nadirs, where devils are casually conjured from the body politic in pursuit of power. I am reminded of Robert Hughes' early rebuke of what would become the neo-conservative versus (by then old) New Left culture wars of the 1990s when he wrote in

Culture of Complaint (Harvill, 1992): "Against this ghastly background, so remote from American experience since the Civil War, we now have our own conservatives promising a 'culture war', while ignorant radicals orate about 'separatism'. They cannot know what demons they are frivolously invoking. If they did, they would fall silent in shame." But alas, the mutating lexicon of American political campaigning since Pat Buchanan first gave expression to wedge politics by advising Richard Nixon "If we tear the country in half, we can pick up the bigger half" has not paused for shame. America is riven.

My concern with Barack Obama is to ask whether he represents "the radical centre" of the great dialectical tension in black leadership philosophy in the United States, between the omnipresent legacies of black American leaders Booker T. Washington (1856–1915) and William Edward Burghardt Dubois (1868–1963). Washington exhorted black Americans to work their way up from the bottom of society. He argued that moral self-improvement, vocational training, and securing the trust and co-operation of white Americans and government were necessary first steps, not confronting discriminatory laws. Washington fought discrimination behind the scenes, but Dubois emerged as the public face of black protest. Dubois argued that higher education and removal of discrimination should be more aggressively pursued, and he offered structural and social explanations for black crime, arguing that crime diminished as blacks' social status improved.

The history of the Washington–Dubois dialectic continues to be the prism through which policies for the alleviation of oppression (what we are given to calling in this country—perhaps euphemistically—"disadvantage") might best be understood. If Rev Jesse Jackson is Dubois's heir, and Condoleezza Rice heir to the Washingtonian tradition, then Obama may be the closest thing there is to a synthesis: the radical centre. Black Americans have been mostly subscribers to the Duboisian tradition, the tradition in which Dr Martin Luther King Jr stood and Rosa Parks sat: it is the predominant model of black advocacy for uplift. Booker T. Washington's disciples, on the other hand, have been mostly silent, living ordered and industrious lives, valuing education and enterprise, bringing up strong families who desire to take their share of a country much built on the enslavement of their ancestors. When the doors of citizenship opened and Jim Crow was outlawed, these families quickly emerged as the nascent black middle class, using their sober sense of individual and family responsibility (and yes, a keening sense of class) to lower their buckets into the deep opportunities of America. Today they are a minority, but they are not small and their achievements are far from mean: five chief executives of Fortune 500 companies, two successive secretaries of state of the world's only superpower attest to this.

If Obama ("I've never had the option of restricting my loyalties on the basis of race, or measuring my worth on the basis of tribe") does transcend the Dubois–Washington paradigms, then his capacity to defy the enormous gravitational pull of the Dubois orthodoxy probably stems from his unique biography: the son of a white American mother ("to the end of her life [she] would proudly proclaim herself an unreconstructed liberal") and an absent Kenyan father (now both deceased), with an Indonesian sister from his mother's second marriage. Obama is an African-American, but not part of the long history that began with slavery. The stigma associated with the Washingtonian legacy—the allegedly Uncle Tomish belief that American opportunity will reward discipline and responsibility—does not shackle Obama.

My only reservation about the capacity of Obama to transcend the Washington–Dubois paradigm is that, while his rhetoric is capable of embracing the validity of the Washingtonian responsibility thesis, he is by background, education, work experience (a civil rights lawyer and "community organiser") and temper, a liberal whose starting point is the Duboisian rights thesis. He moves from Dubois to Washington, and not the other way around. Are the economic power and individual responsibility (and the limits of government) parts of Obama's philosophy just rhetorical genuflections and not innate conviction?

Let me explain my reservation with reference to Opposition Leader Kevin Rudd's critique of what he describes as the neo-liberal fundamentalism of the Howard Government: "Modern Labor ... argues that human beings are both 'self-regarding' and 'other-regarding'. By contrast, modern Liberals ... argue that human beings are almost exclusively self-regarding." Rudd concedes that the self-regarding values of security, liberty and property are necessary for economic growth. He argues that the other-regarding values of equity, solidarity and sustainability must be added in order to make the market economy function effectively, and in order to protect human values such as family life from being crushed by unchecked market forces.

My reservation about this analysis is that it is mainly concerned with those who are not deeply disadvantaged in a cultural and intergenerational way. Kevin Rudd's father was a sharefarmer, and his untimely death brought hardship to his widow and children. But hard work and appreciation of education were passed on to Rudd from his parents. Rudd's ideological manifesto is concerned with the effects of neo-liberal policies on people who may have less bargaining power than the most sought-after professionals, but who are nonetheless firmly integrated into the real economy—not only because they have jobs, but because they are culturally and socially committed to a life of responsibility and work. I welcome the debate Kevin Rudd sought to revitalise about the long-term effects on most working people of neo-liberal policies: what will the effects be on family life, on people's sense of security and purpose, on social cohesion? How great is the risk that families of the lower strata of the real economy will descend into the underclass?

These are real issues, but the important question from an African-American or Aboriginal Australian perspective is: what is the correct analysis of self-regard and other-regard in the context for those already disengaged from the real economy? Disengagement is the problem in Cape York Peninsula and in dysfunctional African-American communities.

The moderate left, as represented by Kevin Rudd, would probably argue that neo-liberal dominance increases the number of disengaged people and the difficulties of returning them to the working mainstream. This may well be true. However, disadvantage can develop and become self-perpetuating, even without neo-liberal government policy. In Australia, Aboriginal disadvantage has become entrenched during decades when social democrats, small-l liberals and conservatives influenced policy; many policies for Indigenous Australians have been liberal and progressive.

The insight which informs our work in Cape York Peninsula is that disengagement and disadvantage have self-perpetuating and cultural qualities—problems not covered by Rudd's analysis. These are the problems of the underclass, people who are psychologically and culturally disadvantaged. (Rudd does not spend time thinking about the underclass.

In the scramble for the political middle, who does?) His is an analysis of the prospects of the upper 80 or 90 or 95 per cent of society, and how they will fare under social democrat or neo-liberal regimes. If Rudd's analysis were extended to the truly disengaged, his model would probably be interpreted like this: some people are successful and, as well as being self-regarding, they should be other-regarding. And then there are the disadvantaged.

The problem is that it is assumed that the life chances of the disadvantaged depend on the other-regard of the successful—either a precarious dependency in the absence of state institutions, or an institutionalised dependency which my people have come to know as passive welfare. In reality, *what is needed is an increase of self-regard among the disadvantaged*, rather than strengthening their belief that the foundation for their uplift is the welfare state and the other-regard of the successful. This, I think, is a deeply Washingtonian view.

Washington versus Dubois

I remembered the legend of how he had come to the college, a barefoot boy who in his fervour for education had trudged with his bundle of ragged clothing across two states. And how he was given a job feeding slop to the hogs but had made himself the best slop dispenser in the history of the school; and how the Founder had been impressed and made him his office boy.
—*Ralph Ellison,* Invisible Man *(Penguin, 1952)*

Born a slave in Virginia in 1856, Booker T. Washington would ascend via an industrial education to be the first president of the famous Tuskegee Institute (now University) in Alabama. Washington became the most powerful black American in the post-bellum era, connected with philanthropists and industrialists: 5,000 common schools would be established as a result of his advocacy. He was consulted by politicians and presidents on black matters, and had a decisive say over appointments to government positions. The "Tuskegee Machine" was renowned for its powerful influence in black politics.

Washington's star rose with his Atlanta Compromise speech at the Cotton States and International Exposition on September 18, 1895. His thesis was that blacks should secure their constitutional rights through their own moral and economic advancement in the booming economy of the South rather than through legal or political channels ("Our greatest danger is that in the great leap from slavery to freedom we may overlook the fact that the masses of us are to live by the productions of our hands."). His central metaphor was both literary and instantly folkloric:

> A ship lost at sea for many days suddenly sighted a friendly vessel. From the mast of the unfortunate vessel was seen a signal, "Water, water; we die of thirst!" The answer from the friendly vessel at once came back, "Cast down your bucket where you are." ... The captain of the distressed vessel, at last heeding the injunction, cast down his bucket, and it came up full of fresh, sparkling water from the mouth of the Amazon River. To those of my race who depend on bettering their condition in a foreign land or who underestimate the importance of cultivating friendly relations with the Southern white man, who is their next-door neighbor, I would say: "Cast down your bucket where you are" ... Cast it down in agriculture, mechanics, in commerce, in domestic service, and in the professions ...

Although Washington's approach angered some blacks, many approved, including W.E.B. DuBois, the man who would later became the other important protagonist in the policy conflict. Washington's major achievement, however, was to win over diverse elements of the southern white population, without whose support the economic programs he envisioned and subsequently created would have been impossible. Washington's depreciation of political activism, and his acceptance of social segregation, was the key to the compromise with southern whites.

DuBois was born free in 1868 in Massachusetts. Aided by family, friends and scholarships, he was able to attend university and ultimately received a doctorate from Harvard. The main feature of DuBois's academic work, after the completion of his university studies and a short period of teaching, was that he closely studied disadvantaged black neighbourhoods. He was a founder of modern social sciences in the United States, and developed structural explanations for inequality. As he recalled in his autobiography *A Soliloquy on Viewing My Life from the Last Decade of Its First Century* (International Publishers, 1968), he advocated "ceaseless agitation and insistent demand for equality" and the "use of force of every sort" to remove racism and discrimination. In 1905, DuBois solicited help from others for "organised determination and aggressive action on the part of men who believe in black freedom and growth", and the Niagara Movement was launched from the meeting that took place on the Canadian side of the famous falls. This was subsequently superseded by an organisation formed in association with white liberals, the National Association for the Advancement of Colored People (NAACP).

DuBois's eloquent and often vitriolic calls for action during his period as editor-in-chief of the NAACP's *Crisis* magazine were politically influential, but he would be frustrated at the lack of progress in removing discrimination in America. He then embarked upon a pan-Africanist crusade against colonialism, believing that the freedom of blacks in America was contingent on the freedom of blacks in Africa. He would die a citizen of Ghana in 1963. DuBois's biographer, David Levering Lewis, wrote in *The Fight for Equality and the American Century 1919–1963* (Owl Books, 2001) that DuBois "attempted virtually every possible solution to the problem of twentieth-century racism—scholarship, propaganda, integration, cultural and economic separatism, politics, international communism, expatriation, third world solidarity".

The Washington–Dubois conflict is well-known. But it is critical to understand how *close* they were, despite their fundamental differences. Dubois had congratulated Washington on his Atlanta compromise speech, which set out the accommodationist framework. Early in Dubois's career, they were engaged in a courtship that included the possibility of him joining Washington at Tuskegee. In the first cordial decade of their relationship they corresponded on legal strategies, planned conferences and sought ways to use each other to the advantage of each. The history of their relationship tells us that DuBois understood and appreciated Washington's strategy and did not wholly disapprove. He knew the context and the limitations of black advancement as much as Washington. It is also now much better known that Washington devoted significant time, money and effort to surreptitiously fighting the race system behind the scenes through back-door lobbying, law suits and editorials, including financial assistance to DuBois who was well aware of Washington's private opposition to the Jim Crow system, but also Washington's unwillingness to risk his influence through public agitation. DuBois was a much more balanced and generous commentator and critic of Washington than many others who shared his view that discrimination had to be confronted.

But already in the 1890s DuBois's relationship with Washington had begun to degenerate, and differences deepened in 1903 when DuBois wrote *The Souls of Black Folk* (Dover, 1994), which contained a critical chapter entitled "Of Booker T. Washington and Others". When Washington died in November 1915, DuBois's judgement was harsh: "In stern justice, we must lay on the soul of this man a heavy responsibility for the consummation of Negro disfranchisement, the decline of the Negro college and public school, and the firmer establishment of colour caste in this land."

Whether or not DuBois was right in this judgement, the salient question is not what Washington intended his (necessarily) one-sided advocacy to achieve, but what effect it had in practice. If it had the effect DuBois contended, then this was not just the result of Washington's strategic folly but the inability of the advocates of the other side of the dialectic to produce a strong rights antithesis to Washington's responsibility thesis.

Washington's public conciliatory position brought him, especially in the latter part of his career, into direct conflict with black militants who sought to challenge white America. As the clash between these two approaches intensified, Washington and Dubois found themselves on opposite sides of a polarised debate, which pitted militancy against conciliation, separatism against assimilation, and a "Talented Tenth" focus on higher education against Washington's preference for trade school training that would equip the other nine-tenths who he understood must work by their hands. It was an irreconcilable dichotomy that would shape the race debate in America for the next century.

I can make no judgement as to this history; there is much evidence to support the modern black despisers of Washington and his faith that the white America which welcomed his Atlanta Compromise would open the doors to participation. White America simply did not deliver on the bargain. There was little black progress until after the Second World War when government social redistribution efforts started registering progress amongst blacks. I only wish to posit some of my own convictions about those aspects of Washington's philosophical conviction that were right at the time he expressed them, and I believe are still right today. In his famous address Washington had two compelling lines, the first of which was: "It is at the bottom of life we must begin, and not at the top."

For a downtrodden people Washington's preference for improvement was a policy relevant to every black person ("No race can prosper till it learns that there is as much dignity in tilling a field as in writing a poem…"). I don't think Washington disagreed that the black community would need its Talented Tenth to succeed. I think what he disagreed with was deprecation of the more humble learning and achievement. He declared: "Excellence is to do a common thing in an uncommon way". The excellent pig slop dispenser would one day have a child in Harvard. His second compelling line was: "Nor should we permit our grievances to overshadow our opportunities." This is a psychological point about how a people might deal with grievances of the past and the present, including the injuries sustained from racism. The best insurance is to become socially and economically strong by capitalising on opportunities.

Destroying the civil rights promise

You're investing in steam control. And you're getting value for money … People own the boilers, but that don't do 'em a bit of good unless they know how to control the steam.

—*Tom Wolfe*, Bonfire of the Vanities *(Bantam, 1987)*

Shelby Steele, according to the shallow taxonomy of American political culture, is a black conservative. In his book *White Guilt* (HarperCollins, 2006), Steele tells how disconcerting it was for someone with his background—son of civil rights campaigners, young Afro-haired wannabe campus radical of the 1960s, fellow traveller with high hopes for Lyndon Johnson's Great Society—to be tagged with this label. That he came to question the post–civil rights trajectory of black America, and to advance a compelling interpretation of the strange twist in the aftermath of the civil rights victories—how retching defeat came from the bowels of victory—earned him the most dreaded black classification: Uncle Tom.

But even as Harry Belafonte denounced Colin Powell and Condoleezza Rice as "White House niggers" in 2002, a critique was growing in black America that challenged the progressive consensus around race which has prevailed since the constitutional foundations of Dr Martin Luther King's dream were finally secured in 1964–65. Shelby Steele is one of the intellectuals leading this critique of the progressive orthodoxy. He raises troubling issues for those who see themselves as the heirs of the radical side of the dichotomy I described above.

Steele opens his book with reflections on the Monica Lewinsky scandal, and President Clinton's infamous denial: "I did not have sexual relations with that woman." Steele was surprised when he realised "not only might [Clinton] survive his entire term but also that his survival ... spoke volumes about the moral criterion for holding power in the United States". If similar behaviour had been made public in the 1950s, it would almost certainly have resulted in the resignation or removal of a president. Steele then asked himself what would have happened if President Clinton had been accused of using the word "nigger"—as President Eisenhower was rumoured to have done. Would the same relativism protect Clinton? *No way.* In America today, there is no moral relativism about race. No sophisticated public sentiment recasts racism as a "personal choice" or a "quirk of character". Instead, America is unwavering in its stance on racism—Eisenhower's flippant use of the word "nigger" would almost certainly have destroyed Clinton.

How is it, Steele asks, that the moral preoccupation of America shifted away from personal (sexual) virtue and came to focus on issues of social import? He answers this by drawing attention to the legitimacy of institutions and of government being earned and sustained through fidelity to democratic principles. These principles include freedom of the individual, equal rights under the law and equality of opportunity. Freedom, Steele asserts, is what follows from adherence to these principles. It is not a state-imposed vision of the social good, but the absence of an imposed vision, which allows individual choice.

Freedom is eroded or lost, he argues, when societies decide that some social good is so important that it justifies suspending the discipline of democratic principles. America's imposition of white supremacy is the pertinent example: "White Americans presumed that white supremacy was a self-evident divine right, so freedom's discipline of principles did not apply where non-whites were concerned." Over time, however, the moral authority of American democracy and its institutions was undermined by this failure. The turning point for America, and what Steele refers to as the "disciplining" of the country's democratic principles, was the civil rights movement. This movement established that race could not undermine individual rights. Multi-racial democracies demand that race (along with gender, ethnicity, class and sexual orientation) cannot obstruct rights. This was, then, the "concept of social good that would make democracy truly democratic, and thus legitimate".

The crux of Steele's thesis comes from looking at the effects of the civil rights movement on institutions and figures of authority in mainstream America. By the mid-1960s, he argues, following acknowledgement of racial hypocrisy, institutions across America suffered a moral authority deficit. He recounts an occasion in his youth when he and a gang of black students burst into the office of his college president with a list of demands. Expecting to face resistance, even disciplinary action, Steele describes the experience as revelatory: he realised the college president "knew that we had a point, [and] that our behaviour was in some way connected to centuries of indisputable injustice. The result was that our outrage at racism simply had far greater moral authority than his outrage over our breach of decorum." This was one of Steele's first encounters with *white guilt*— the notion that past injustices perpetrated on a group of people absolve subsequent generations of that group of standard responsibilities.

For Steele, white guilt is a product of the vacuum of moral authority that comes from knowing that one's people are associated with racism. Whites—and, he asserts, American institutions—must acknowledge historical racism to atone for it. In acknowledging it, however, they lose moral authority over matters of social justice and become morally—and, one could argue, politically—vulnerable. To overcome this vulnerability, white Americans have embraced a social morality, designed to rebuild moral authority by simultaneously acknowledging past racial injustices while separating themselves from those injustices. Steele calls this dissociation.

Where white guilt forces white Americans to acknowledge historical injustices, social morality may absolve them of it, restoring authority and democratic bona fides. With authority restored, power relations may continue as before. Critically, Steele argues, "social morality is not a dissident point of view urged ... by reformers; it is the establishment morality in America. It defines propriety ... so that even those who harbour racist views must conform to a code of decency that defines those views as shameful."

But Steele does not limit his analysis to white America. He expands his argument to assess the effects of white guilt on the freedoms—tangible or otherwise—of black Americans. In a critique of the "black consciousness" which challenged traditional American authority, Steele draws a connection between increasingly militant messages of black power and burgeoning manifestations of white guilt. For a generation of black leaders, racism existed within this context—in a society suffering a lack of moral authority. The new black leaders (adopting a neo-Marxian structural analysis) redefined racism as systemic and sociological. Racism was larger than individual acts, and defined social and political events and decisions.

Because racism, as it was interpreted by militant black leaders, did not manifest on an individual level, the mere absence of an overtly racist act—using the word "nigger", for example—was not enough to prove that racism was not in operation. Even a hint of racism proved the rule, and the only way to address it was a systemic solution. So, Steele notes, despite the fact that current generations of black students across America have not suffered the oppression or subjugation of their forefathers, "much less been beaten by white policemen", they enjoy affirmative action (the systemic redress) with a clear sense of entitlement. Black entitlement and white obligation have become interlocked.

Steele's thesis contends that racism became valuable to the people who had suffered it because it "makes the moral authority of whites and the legitimacy of American institutions contingent on proving a negative: that they are not racist". The power of white guilt is that it functions in the same way as racism—as a stigma. White Americans and American institutions are stigmatised as racist until they prove otherwise. What began as "an almost petulant alienation from traditional authority", Steele asserts, has now evolved into a sophisticated manipulation to elicit an increasing sense of obligation. In a perversion of civil rights–era aspirations, racism is no longer a barrier to individual black Americans, but one of the factors contributing to the assurance of their rights.

Pushing the argument one step further, Steele unpacks the effects of the interplay between black consciousness and white guilt. Black consciousness, he argues, led many black Americans to talk themselves out of the personal freedom won by civil rights activism, for the sole (and unworthy) purpose of triggering white obligation. In a reactionary drift, race became seen as more important than individuality, the primary determinant of a person's ability to advance. One's identity became primarily that of the group (race) rather than that of an individual, one of whose characteristics was colour. In this way, identity played a destructive role in the advancement of black Americans.

Few who live in liberal democracies today would contest the idea that freedom is crucial to a decent life. A related—although perhaps more frequently debated—assertion is that only by being responsible for one's life can one assume agency for it. Agency, Steele believes, is what makes us fully human. With the rise and rise of black consciousness, however, the idea that black Americans must take personal responsibility to get ahead was subverted by the idea that responsibility was a tool of oppression and white America was responsible for black American advancement.

The first step in that argument—that responsibility was a tool of oppression in the age of racism—is not without historical justification. Steele's father, born in the American South in 1900, had "plenty of responsibility"—the same responsibilities as whites—"but not much possibility". He could not join the union, and therefore had to raise a family on a lower wage. Steele calls this a "crucible", "an absurd bind that … denies one the opportunities to meet adequately the burden of responsibility one must carry". "Thus," Steele continues, "a heavy and often futile responsibility was the primary *experience* of racial oppression … this Sisyphean struggle with responsibility was the condition of oppression itself into which all the other indignities—discrimination, intimidation, humiliation—were absorbed."

When his peers raised their consciousness and embraced the neo-Marxian theories of institutionalised racism, Steele argues they began to think of responsibility as something that made blacks complicit in their own repression. Paradoxically, this historically justified insight started influencing black American ideology at the same time as discrimination and oppression were rapidly and formally being removed from the society.

The realisation that white America had a diminished moral authority to tell black Americans to be responsible led many—black and white—to conclude that white America was *obliged* to demonstrate its reformation by taking on the burden of responsibility for black Americans. White America—as in President Johnson's Great Society and the introduction of affirmative action policies by the American college system—thus assumed considerable responsibility for improving the socio-economic status of blacks. Underpinning this was the unspoken assumption—rooted in America's history of racial injustice—that it was morally wrong (or unnecessary) for blacks to bear full responsibility for "their own advancement".

Having drawn out these ideas, Steele examines how they are connected: the new social morality, underpinned by white guilt, dictated that black Americans, as victims of racial oppression, could not be expected to carry the same responsibilities as others: "American society no longer had the moral authority to enforce a single standard of responsibility ... [and] no-one—least of all the government—had the moral authority to tell me to be responsible for much of anything."

The devastating effect of this redistribution of responsibility for black advancement to (white) institutions, however, is to perpetually project blacks as weak and incapable of achieving advancement on their own merit. Nevertheless, white Americans and American institutions promote policies of affirmative action to demonstrate their social morality, and at the same time legitimise their own moral and intellectual authority. No group in human history, Steele asserts, has been lifted into excellence or competitiveness by another. No group has even benefited from the assistance of others without taking responsibility for itself. And herein lies the nub of his thesis: that social justice is not a condition of, but an agent or mechanism for, an equitable world. In other words, it cannot be delivered in the same way as basic services. It cannot be absent one day and present the next. Social justice requires work and collaboration; if it is not accompanied by *individual* efforts to "get ahead" it is unlikely to generate a better life.

In America, then, social morality has become more important than individual morality, effectively de-linking social justice and individual responsibility in the quest to improve the socio-economic conditions of black Americans. White guilt now underpins a sense of white obligation to lift blacks up, with disastrous effects. In a 1999 *Harpers* essay, Steele nailed his argument:

Right after the '60s civil-rights victories came what I believe to be the greatest miscalculation in black American history. Others had oppressed us, but this was to be the first 'fall' to come by our own hand. We allowed ourselves to see a greater power in America's liability for our oppression than we saw in ourselves. Thus, we were faithless with ourselves just when we had given ourselves reason to have such faith. We couldn't have made a worse mistake. We have not been the same since.

Australian paradox after 1967: Black rights become white responsibilities

You sharpen your axe on the hardest stone.

—Kevin Gilbert, The Cherry Pickers *(1968)*

There are compelling parallels between what happened with black Americans from the time of civil rights and voting rights in 1964–65, and black Australians from the time of the 1967 referendum, when 90.2 per cent of Australians voted to amend the Constitution to count Aboriginal people in the census and to empower the Commonwealth Parliament to make laws in respect of Aboriginal and Torres Strait Islander people.

The American rights guarantees were substantive: they provided freedoms and protections denied to black Americans since the abolition of slavery. So, from the time of their passage, blacks in America could invoke federal law in order to combat discrimination in respect of a wide range of civil rights. The Australian changes did not immediately provide any substantive rights; the Commonwealth Parliament was merely empowered to make laws—a power previously the exclusive province of the states. Protection from racial discrimination was not available to black Australians (or anyone else) until the Commonwealth Parliament passed the *Racial Discrimination Act* in 1975.

Nonetheless, the symbolic significance of the 1967 referendum, which was the culmination of a concerted ten-year public campaign and redressed the complete exclusion of Australia's Indigenous peoples from the federal compact of 1901, marked the beginning of a new era in Indigenous history and policy. It was a hopeful and positive event, and is still mostly seen as such.

Substantive rights and protections for Indigenous Australians were enacted in the years before and after the referendum. Voting rights, where they did not already exist, were granted from 1962, although Queensland lagged until 1965; an attempt to protect Indigenous Queenslanders from discriminatory laws was legislated in 1975, as was protection against racial discrimination; land rights were legislated for the Northern Territory in 1976; legislation establishing the Human Rights Commission was enacted in 1986; and a range of state legislation outlawing discrimination was also promulgated in the 1970s and 1980s. But legislation providing affirmative action and access to educational and other institutions was never introduced in Australia. Affirmative action programs have only ever occurred as voluntary policy decisions by public or private institutions. There has been no Australian law to compel affirmative action.

It is not these rights and recognition events of the 1960s that I (or Shelby Steele and the growing like-minded critique in the United States) question. They were seminal achievements; it is their aftermath that requires reconsideration.

In the aftermath of the civil rights victories, the politics of "victimhood" became the predominant methodology of black advocacy and the reigning paradigm of public policy thinking. Victimhood relied on a phenomenon within the dominant white societies that had two faces: *white guilt* and *moral vanity*. The rise of victim politics meant that, even as there was increased recognition of black rights in the post-citizenship era, there was also a calamitous erosion of black responsibility.

I have often reflected on the downside of the events surrounding citizenship, at least for the remote communities of northern Australia with which I am familiar—particularly Cape York Peninsula. In the light of the problems with which we are grappling today, I see three factors as decisive contributors to the descent into hell three decades later. These factors appeared to be positive developments designed to address inequities, but whose unintended consequences—particularly for Aboriginal men—were negative:

- The equal wages decision of 1966, which mandated equal payment for Aboriginal stock-workers, contributed to the large-scale exodus from the long-standing employment and lifestyle Indigenous people had carved out in the pastoral industry of northern Australia (and elsewhere). The removal of Aboriginal people to the fringes of country towns and into missions and settlements meant that young men had lots of *idle time*.

- The Commonwealth Government's solution for Aboriginal people displaced from the pastoral industry was to provide access to social security payments, and the relevant government department undertook a drive through the 1970s to sign people up to income support. This provided young men with *work-free income*.
- Citizenship brought to Aboriginal people the *right to drink*.

Young men with idle time, free income and the right to drink led to the start of an alcohol abuse vortex which would increase in terms of the chaos it caused and its negative impacts, and would widen out to later include women and older people who had not previously been drinkers. I saw this pattern spread in the three communities with which I am intimate, from my childhood in the late 1960s to the present.

Equal wages, access to social security income support and giving Aboriginal citizens the right to enter pubs and to drink alcohol were progressive measures. Not all the consequences of these measures were unforeseen: it had been clear to the Commonwealth Government in the hearings before the Australian Conciliation and Arbitration Commission that a ruling in favour of equal wages would result in the large-scale removal of Aboriginal stock-workers from the stations of northern Australia. The Commonwealth's solution was to make social security available. The Commission ruled:

> If any problems of native welfare whether of employees or their dependants, arise as a result of this decision, the Commonwealth Government has made clear its intention to deal with them. This is not why we have come to our conclusion but it means we know that any welfare problems which arise will be dealt with by those most competent to deal with them.

The then President of the Commission, Sir Richard Kirby, would later tell his biographer Blanche d'Apulget (*Mediator*, MUP, 1977) that the case would "be seen as the greatest contribution he and other members of the Commission made to Australian society".

The story of the past four decades is, of course, more complex than this. There were other factors driving the decline in the pastoral industry. The dismantling of the systems of social and administrative control by governments and missions led to growing social chaos. Even where strong and functional social and cultural norms were maintained by Aboriginal people themselves, their maintenance was broken down by values and standards imported from the wider society and the shutting down of Aboriginal authority through the intrusion of the legal system. Legal Aid services to Aboriginal offenders probably did more to undermine the authority of elders and other local justice mechanisms (in Queensland, the Aboriginal Courts presided over by local Justices of the Peace) than any other intervention. A workable system of social order based on moral and cultural authority was forced to comply with legal authority—and ultimately had to defer to the law. This moral and cultural authority which had provided structure to life in the settlements withered away.

The decline of religion and the influence of the churches in the communities are also part of this story, including the historically problematic role of the churches in the administrative management of Aboriginal communities. In the case of my hometown, I served on the Hope Vale Aboriginal Community Council when the last vestiges of the Lutheran Church's administrative involvement in the affairs of our people were removed in the late 1980s. We cut these last ties with a relishing sense of historic reckoning. The awful truth is that we threw the baby out with the bathwater: the role of the church in the secular and spiritual life of our community was conflated; both the church and our people should have found a way to move beyond the paternalism of the past without destroying the moral and cultural order which had been such a strong quality of our community. But the transfer of moral responsibility that Shelby Steele identified in the United States also played out here. We now repent a social and moral wreckage.

But these are details. The larger context was the growth of the culture and politics of victimhood, which came to be the accepted basis of the relationship between Aboriginal people and the rest of the country.

Prior to reading Shelby Steele's thesis on white guilt—and how the success of civil rights transmogrified into the failure of victim politics—I had been thinking about the various positions Indigenous and non-Indigenous

Australians take in relation to questions of history and race. There is a dichotomy in popular discussion of racism. It is assumed that people and ideas come from one of two possible sides: those who are racists and those who are not, those who are subject to racism and those who are racists, those who believe that racism is a major social ill and those who do not, and so on. In Australia, the divide is generally seen as being one between those who believe Australia has a problem with racism, and those who believe that Australia is not a racist country.

Since the 1960s, heavily influenced by international norms established by the United Nations, decolonisation in Africa and Asia, and by the civil rights movement in the United States, Australians from the left and right have altered their views on racism for the better. Whilst, historically, racism was widely acceptable across Australian society (the "White Australia" policy was championed by the Australian Labor Party), political opinion and social values shifted fundamentally towards an understanding that overt racism, at least, was unacceptable.

Today, whilst leading conservatives and liberals (notably former Prime Minister Malcolm Fraser) are avowed opponents of racism, the polarity between those who consider racism a serious problem and those who do not is generally seen as a left–right split. As progressive people predominately come from left of the cultural and political divide, the ALP (and the progressive minor parties) are generally regarded as opponents of racism, whilst the Liberal and National Parties are considered racist—or at least indifferent to racism. Individuals from both sides often contradict this generalisation.

This dichotomous view of racism is simplistic and misleading. My analysis looks at six positions which Indigenous and non-Indigenous Australians take in relation to race and history concerning the country's original peoples. This is an arc for non-Indigenous Australians that goes from denial to moral vanity, to acknowledgement and responsibility. For Aboriginal people, this arc ranges from separatism to victimhood, and to pride and principled defence.

There is a strong tradition of *denial* in Australia. The eminent ethnographer W.E.H. Stanner named this tradition in the country's historiography up to the late 1960s the "Great Australian Silence" (Boyer Lecture, 1968). There is a very large constituency which denies that the treatment of Indigenous people in Australia's colonial history (and up to the present) was as bad as those historians who have contributed to the genre known as "Aboriginal history" demonstrate. These people deny that racism in Australia against the country's Indigenous peoples is a serious problem. Keith Windschuttle's refutation of massacres and violence on the frontiers, and Pauline Hanson's galvanising resentments against alleged preferences to Aboriginal people (and other racial minorities) are just the most egregious representatives of a wide constituency which adopts a position of denial. Denial is a strong word. It is only a general characterisation of a spectrum of views amongst non-Indigenous Australians which range from David Irving–style ideological denialism to those who acknowledge the depredations suffered by Indigenous people through history and the racism in our society, but who minimise its nature and extent ("we shouldn't dwell on the past"). Many join this constituency because of political and cultural affiliations with the political right.

There are two important things to understand about this constituency. First, most of them are defensive about their own identity and heritage. The accusation that they are racist and their colonial heritage is a catalogue of shame and immoral villainy—and they should therefore feel guilt for racism and history—makes them defensive. If race and history are raised in such a sharply accusatory and unbalanced way, then people who may otherwise be prepared to acknowledge and take responsibility for the truth end up joining the hard-core ideologues. There is some truth in the proposition that "political correctness" has had this effect. There is also truth in the proposition that the political right has deliberately and wilfully galvanised this defensiveness by mischaracterising the progressive position as being about guilt, rather than what former Prime Minister Paul Keating referred to as "open hearts" in his landmark 1992 Redfern speech. This has provided great fodder for the right in their prosecution of the culture wars.

The denialists also keenly understand how debilitating it is to adopt the mentality and outlook of victimhood. It is easy for them to say that victimhood is worthless, as it grows out of their ideological contempt for interventionist social policy that seeks to ameliorate the impact of the market even on the most vulnerable, but this does not make them wrong. Those on the cultural and political right are therefore more correct than their opponents in recognising the folly of the impact of policy that turns people into victims.

The second major constituency in contemporary Australia is *morally vain* about race and history. Its members largely come from the liberal left and are morally certain about right and wrong and ready to ascribe blame. For them, issues of race and history are a means of gaining the upper hand over their political and cultural opponents. The primary concern of the morally vain is not the plight or needs of those who suffer racism and oppression, but rather their view of themselves, their understanding of the world and belief in their superiority over their opponents. There are two things about this constituency which need to be understood. This constituency contributes most to, and actively supports, the outlook that casts Indigenous people as victims. Its members have no understanding of how destructive, demoralising and demeaning this mentality is. Their most telling catchphrase in rebuke of their opponents, whenever there may be a suggestion made about the personal responsibility of Indigenous people (or indeed the disadvantaged at large), is "don't blame the victims". They excuse and provide a justification for those on whose behalf they advocate, in order to avoid responsibility. They infantilise Indigenous people by not allowing those whom they seek to protect to face the consequences of their actions: Indigenous people's status as victims means they require protection from the real world.

Moral vanity is perhaps an unfair characterisation. There is a broad spectrum of views within this group, and many within this broad spectrum have decent motivations. They empathise with the plight of Indigenous people who face racism and other real injuries; they acknowledge what has happened through history and recognise that the present is not unconnected with the past. They understand the hypocrisy of the prescription to forget the past, especially in a country whose most famous lapidary exhortation reads: Lest We Forget. But at some point empathy and acknowledgement turn into moral superiority, and the relative failures of one's cultural and political opponents become the basis of accusations of insensitivity or racism. At this point, race becomes a useful club to beat the Neanderthals from the right, and racism serves the cultural and political purposes of the progressive accuser rather than the humanity of those subjected to it.

Let me offer an example: the enforcement of laws to prevent drinking in public places which results in "homeless" Aboriginal people binge drinking in the parks (policies that are tried in Australia) could be combined with controlled management of income support to "homeless" people so that accommodation, food and other essentials are provided and cash for alcohol is not (policies that have not been tried in Australia). If this were proposed, it would be characterised as racist by morally vain progressives and vehemently opposed. Indeed, these people run campaigns on behalf of "long grassers" to the effect that the homeless have a "right to sleep". Long grassing is romanticised as some kind of final act of resistance against authority, but patently people do not "choose" to live like this.

Rather than denial or moral vanity, the optimum position for non-Indigenous people to take is that of *acknowledgement*—of the past and its legacy in the present, recognising that racism is not a contrivance, that Indigenous people endure great hurt and confront barriers as a result of racism. They need to take *responsibility* for the fact of racism, and work to answer and counter it.

On the Indigenous side, the extreme position is that of *separatism*. In the United States, black nationalists such as Marcus Garvey actively pursued separatist agendas. The separatist rhetoric and strategy of Malcolm X was real. There has been no such equivalent in Australia, despite rhetorical flourishes and stunts such as the Aboriginal Provisional Government. Separatist posturing has largely been a tactical device in Australia, not entirely without (tactical) effect; however, separatism has not been the subject of a real and serious strategy, despite a profound sense of alienation experienced by many Indigenous people.

The largest constituency on the Indigenous side subscribes to *victimhood*. Again, this is a strong term which covers a broad spectrum of outlooks. People will object to my interpretation of the dimensions of victimhood because what many of our people regard as radical, separatist and resistance politics, I say is victim politics. Further, what many of our people regard as pride and necessary defensiveness against racism is, I believe, victim politics. Argument arises here because of the dynamic way in which the cultural and political currents of political economy evolve and change over time: what may have been a truly radical act at one time, such as the Tent Embassy in 1971, degenerates into a sad symbol of defeatist, victim politics as is plain with the squalid demountables at the Tent Embassy site in 2007.

Argument arises because it is one thing to properly analyse whether some outlook, mentality or action proceeds from victimhood, and another to analyse the political or social effectiveness or utility gained from it. I am not saying the politics of victimhood have not (and do not still) yield returns. They have and do, but at an enormous cost that is sometimes hard to recognise. As Shelby Steele has explained, *white guilt* is a resource blacks in America and Australia have learned to mine.

I want to talk about two problems with victimhood. The first is that we pay a high price for casting ourselves as victims in the morality field. The tactic of victimhood moves from an outlook and a mentality to become an identity. The long grassers and under-the-bridge dwellers are the most visible, end-stage subscribers to this tragic and self-harming tactic. It damages our people wherever they are—from the young student who believes that academic achievement at school is "acting white" and defeats him or herself with such a pernicious outlook, to those who tolerate domestic violence because it is "understandable" given the history of the people concerned.

We indigenes of Australia are confused in our cultural understanding of victimisation and victimhood. Yes, individuals and groups in our society are *victimised* in a variety of ways. But it is a terrible thing to encourage victims to adopt a mentality and outlook of victimhood, to see themselves as victims. To adopt this mentality is fatal because it concedes defeat, and it can also literally kill. Victims do not take responsibility for what they eat and drink, for their health and mental well-being; their families become dysfunctional and their children are damaged even before they are born. The worst indulgence is to take away the one power victims need to survive, to defy victimisation. To say: "Yes, I have suffered victimisation—but I'm not giving in by becoming a victim!"

This is the difference between the responses of Rosa Parks and Vincent Lingiari to the racist victimisation they endured—and the victim politics which the post–civil rights and post-citizenship leadership cultivated. The gap between members of the NAACP in the United States and the Federal Council for the Advancement of Aborigines and Torres Strait Islanders (and like organisations) in the lead-up to freedom and the generation that followed became profound.

The second problem with victimhood is that the access and opportunities it produces are of mixed quality. Whether it is education or other opportunities, the "soft bigotry of low expectations" tends to characterise the quality of what is yielded to people who are taken to be victims. In America the hot button issue is affirmative action. If you take Steele's view, affirmative action is a policy constructed for victims which does not help them rise out of their victimhood. I will not engage in a discussion of affirmative action here, other than to say that three thoughts are on my mind in relation to it. Firstly, I think Steele is right about the problematic consequences of affirmative action for black Americans: the disincentive effects are serious. Secondly, black Australian participation and achievement is even worse than that of black Americans, and we have never had affirmative action, and I am not convinced that all doors open from the outside. Thirdly, if we consider affirmative action for Australia, it should be aimed at breaking class barriers rather than race barriers.

Characterising Indigenous people as victims leads to an emphasis on the need for recognition of rights—human rights and land rights—which are undeniably good things. The rights question is complicated in the Australian context. In America, it focused on recognition of formal equality between blacks and other citizens. In Australia, it is not so simple: Indigenous people possess certain rights that flow from their unique position as the first Australians. Therefore their rights to land, language and other matters concerning their status necessarily involve different rights to those guaranteed other citizens. Where rights could be enjoyed as a result of political and legislative fiat, there were beneficial developments. But where they could not be simply granted (such as better education and better health outcomes), and where state-provided service delivery could not achieve better outcomes without behavioural change, the behaviour of the victims simply could not be confronted because victims could not be responsible. This is what Shelby Steele calls blameless poverty, and it characterises many Aboriginal communities today.

So, instead of confronting behaviour—even when the first wave of programs did not work, and indeed produced a set of secondary problems—the welfare state builders of the original Great Society simply increased their commitment to the idea that the victims could be rescued from deep poverty through co-ordination of service delivery. This is still the dominant response today, even as the failure of passive welfare is apparent.

Of course, the leadership that campaigned for the 1967 referendum gave way to what would become the new victim leadership of the 1970s. Thomas Wolfe's perspicacious observations of the radical chic posturings of morally vain whites, and the mau-mauing of the flak-catchers by the angry "radicals" in America all played out here too, right through the 1970s and '80s. Acquisition of an undergraduate command of some key ideas in international and human rights law led to the new language of "sovereignty". I was once told a hilarious story by the late Charlie Perkins of an Indigenous gathering in a Returned Services League hall in a country town where the entire morning was spent debating whether a portrait of Her Majesty Queen Elizabeth II should remain gazing down at the proceedings as the owners of the establishment intended it to. Those seeking to make a point about the wrongful usurpation of Indigenous sovereignty by the Crown succeeded in their motion, and the rest of the day was spent looking for another venue because the gathering was immediately ejected from the premises.

In my (relatively) short experience, I have endured my fair share of fanciful separatist rhetoric—and plenty of inane stunts and speeches—founded on vague and insufficiently grasped theories. As long as some key words and concepts are sprinkled amidst the denunciations, then any lunatic can be a leader. I've often had the sense that we are playing delusional games in our own obscure little sandpits. We want our sovereignty recognised by the International Court of Justice, and in the meantime I'm off to the TAB and the pub.

During my law studies in Sydney in the late 1980s, I expressed my interest in seeking work in an Indigenous organisation to a white trade unionist, who was well acquainted with some key figures of the 1970s Indigenous leadership. I was taken by this kindly man to the separate work offices of two of the pioneers of the post–Tent Embassy leadership, now "running things" like Leo and Giovanni Casparo (aka Johnny Casper) in the Coen Brothers' film masterpiece *Miller's Crossing*. Nothing came from my introductions. But my most vivid memory is sitting in the office of one of these characters, dressed in a black skivvy and smart sports jacket, smoking a cigarette through an elegant cigarette-holder. It could have been a scene out of a "blaxploitation" film starring Jim Kelly across 110th Street circa 1975.

All of this was victim politics, no matter the radical pretence. It was scratching bark, not digging out the roots. A prideful and principled defence against racism is what we need as a people. Many ordinary Indigenous people possess this dignity and strength. We must make it the dominant outlook of our people.

Peoplehood

An inclusionary and involuntary group identity with a … shared history and distinct way of life … everyone in the group, regardless of status, gender, or moral worth, belongs.

—*John Lie,* Modern Peoplehood *(Harvard University Press, 2004)*

There is one respect in which the discussion of Indigenous Australian policy differs from the African-American discussion: the question of Indigenous "peoplehood". In this sense the position of Native Americans is more relevant. The African-American struggle is for socio-economic advancement and equality. Steele describes the aspiration to "advance through education, skill development, and entrepreneurialism combined with an unbending assault on any continuing discrimination". Steele believes that the main obstacles to African-Americans taking their rightful place have been removed, and that "blacks are no longer oppressed in America", that the main burden weighing them down is the advocacy of flawed policies and ideologies.

Steele does not see African-Americans as a minority people. Although some radical African-Americans have advocated separatist policies and argue that they constitute a separate people with national rights, that view is not widely held. Generally, African-American issues are thought of as "race relations" with a goal of ending public programs and practices which recognise African-Americans as a distinct group. Americans to the left of Steele argue that policies which go beyond the abolition of official discrimination and the elimination of overt racist attitudes are necessary, but they do not advocate perpetual special measures; rather, they see them gradually disappearing as irrational racial prejudice recedes and equality increases.

The Indigenous Australian struggle is for socio-economic advancement and equality, but it is also about the recognition of status and rights as a people. The goal here is to preserve and win legal recognition of cultural distinctness as well as citizenship. Indigenous Australian political issues are "peoplehood issues". It is regrettable that this word is so little used in English-language debate. Berkeley professor John Lie has defined it as "an inclusionary and involuntary group identity … It is not merely a population—an aggregate, an external attribution, an analytical category—but, rather, a people—a group, an internal conviction, a self-reflexive identity."

The word peoplehood is needed in the analysis of national issues because it unambiguously conveys this concept. We are all familiar with the "inclusionary and involuntary" identity which Lie describes, but we have no generally accepted word for it. The word "ethnicity" is sometimes used to cover the hole in our linguistic map, but this word suffers from connoting, in Lie's words, "external attribution"—an anthropological origin. One can imagine people claiming their rights as "Yorta Yorta people", but hardly as "the Yorta Yorta ethnic group". Nor is "nationhood" the word we need, because it confuses the issue that needs to be discussed—namely the tension between the current world order of approximately two hundred sovereign states, and the several thousand distinct peoples who have demonstrated their desire for recognition. "Nationhood" is more or less synonymous with the creation of a sovereign nation state, and is therefore misleading and unhelpful. The term peoplehood, if it came into common usage, would be perfect. It is self-explanatory and refers to something other than nation states and formal citizenship. It is also likely to convey two desired connotations: "outcome[s] achieved through the efforts of the population itself"; and "result of a historical process".

As a result of a global historical process, diverse populations have developed a "self-reflexive identity", an "internal conviction" about the bond that unites them. The notion of peoplehood has evolved and become politically more important. As a consequence of the rise of nationalism, the relationships between peoples forced to coexist within the borders of sovereign states deteriorated during the nineteenth and twentieth centuries and today are a chief source of some of the world's most intractable conflicts.

I strongly object to the modern tendency to categorise people according to a system of exclusive identities. Nobel Laureate Amartya Sen has called this "the illusion of singular identity" (*Identity and Violence*, Norton, 2006). We labour under impoverished conceptions of identity. The identity of a group is assumed to be singular—arising from some salient characteristic. The identity of an individual within an ethnic group is also assumed to be singular—again arising from some salient feature of the group. Instead Sen argues that we should recognise "competing affiliations" or "competing identities". His choice of words is unfortunate; I have proposed a better metaphor: "layers of identity". These layers include identification with cultural and linguistic groups; citizenship; religions; places of birth, upbringing, residency and death; local and regional geographic communities; regional, provincial and national polities; and professional, literary, recreational, philosophical and other sub-cultural groups.

A Rugby Union–following Lutheran Aboriginal with a love for the literature of England shares much with many other Australians that he does not share with his closest kin—but he does share an identity based on peoplehood. A pluralist and united world is one which has strong bonding identities between those who know each other, and bridging identities with strangers.

Indigenous Australian issues are peoplehood issues. The main difference between Australian and American policies is that the basis for Australian policy is (or should be) the legitimate claim of Indigenous Australians to their recognition as a distinct people with constitutionally recognised rights. The point of this essay is that the black American comparison is germane—because race relations are relevant here too.

Unintended consequences

If we want things to stay as they are, things will have to change.

—*Guiseppe Lampedusa*, The Leopard (Pantheon)

"Unintended consequences" is a concept derived from liberal economics: positively, the consequences of choices made in the marketplace are never certain and cannot be completely anticipated; negatively, they are the inevitable product of state planning. By impeding and superseding decision-making in the market, ambitious rationalist social planners cause unintended consequences by using the state to plan good societies and good futures for citizens, when they do not have the capacity to do so.

Unintended consequences can therefore be seen as a liberal critique of statist socialist planning. As Friedrich von Hayek might have said, the road to serfdom is paved with good intentions.

There is also a possible Marxist explanation for the phenomenon: the ruling forces that dominate society inexorably transform progressive movements into regression. The opaque nature of the ideological and cultural superstructure built on society's material base means that movements that might be viewed as progressive may be regressive when the question is asked: "What is the objective effect of this movement?" Unintended consequences arise when radicals fail to maintain an objective analysis, and naively maintain a subjective view of what is progressive.

It is not necessary to decide which is correct—liberals and Marxists can agree that there is a ubiquitous phenomenon in the history of human policy that unintended consequences occur. A theoretical explanation of the phenomenon is not my principal concern. I indicate the framework only to introduce a policy analysis I have become convinced about: that the distance between good and bad policies is most often very fine—not poles apart. People from either side of the cultural and political divide usually believe the distance between their own correct policies and their opponents' wrong policies is substantial. Politics is given to stark caricatures. Intellectual discussion in service of politics is also similarly inclined.

This polarisation leads to problems—a failure to distinguish between a potentially correct policy (policing relatively minor misdemeanours to restore order to crime-ridden, disadvantaged neighbourhoods) and an obviously incorrect one (police harassment and violence). Typically, the left opposes zero-tolerance policing, although it would be truly progressive to restore social order to disadvantaged neighbourhoods, and such policing is probably critical to achieving this. So the champions of certain reforms end up being the opponents of the means needed to achieve them. I see this time and time again in my consideration of the plight of the disadvantaged people who are my concern, Indigenous Australians. (This was the theme of my essay in *Griffith Review 2: Dreams of Land*.)

This polarisation leads to a failure of the left to appreciate the correctness of policies promoted by the right (and vice versa) because the fine difference between the correct and the incorrect policy is too subtle for (and I use the following phrase advisedly) usual public discourse, which only sees stark tensions that suggest bald contradictions rather than close, more intense tensions that suggest paradox and potential synthesis.

The tensions involved in the policy debate on crime in neighbourhoods centre around the question of freedom and social order. (Obviously) too much social order undermines freedom. (Less obviously) too much freedom with low social order in fact undermines freedom. People who live in optimally free and ordered communities often fail to appreciate the fact that it is the high degree of social order which underpins the freedom they enjoy. Libertarians are either blind to (or careless of) the advantages they take from the strong social order provided by invisible social norms: this is why classical libertarians come from privileged classes. (Lower-class libertarianism is, of course, the very definition of social dysfunction.)

Where black people are involved, then the tensions of racial discrimination/non-discrimination and advantage/disadvantage are also intertwined in the freedom and social order dialectic. Where the existing problem in disadvantaged neighbourhoods is high rates of blacks offending, then measures aimed at strengthening social order (such as zero-tolerance policing) actually deliver advantage and freedom in the long run. The argument against such measures is that they will result in even greater rates of imprisonment of black people. And indeed, in the short and intermediate term they will. There will be a spike. But if we want black neighbourhoods to enjoy freedom, we need to ask the question: "What is it about advantaged neighbourhoods that guarantees freedom for their denizens?" The answer is: "They have social order". If we don't take the hard policy decisions to increase social order where it is weak because we fear that black involvement in the criminal justice system will increase, then we will never solve the egregious (and, in the case of my home state of Queensland, increasing) over-representation of black people in prison. Not until we have socially ordered neighbourhoods.

The "radical centre" may be defined as the intense resolution of the tensions between opposing principles (in this example, the principles are freedom and social order)—a resolution that produces the synthesis of optimum policy. The radical centre is not to be found in simply splitting the difference between the stark and weak tensions from either side of popularly conceived discourse, but rather where the dialectical tension is most intense and the policy positions much closer and more carefully calibrated than most people imagine.

Before I turn to my thoughts on the radical centre in policy and leadership, I should make some final points. First, it is intellectually difficult to analyse and identify the correct (radically centrist) policy because commanding ideologies hold sway and limit the capacity of people to abandon wrong policies and search for better ones. But even where the right policies have been identified and adopted, their implementation is susceptible to distortion. The correct policy can easily turn sour because of incompetent implementation, because the calibration is lost: if a police force does not understand the aim of restoring social order to crime-ridden communities and that racism and sharp practice must not be tolerated, policy will degenerate into abuse and victimisation. Even when optimal policies are competently implemented, one must be mindful of the dynamic nature of social, political and economic currents. A progressive measure at one time can produce regressive results later. Policy must take account of the effluxion of time and the stage of historical development.

The radical centre in policy and leadership

When a team is running in attack, the key player is not the player with the ball but the player off the ball—that is, the player he will pass it to. He is the one under pressure to be in the best possible position to receive the ball … The player running in support has to decide whether to go inside or outside, whether to run close or wide and when to call for the ball. Furthermore, before he calls for the ball, the player running in support has to manoeuvre himself into a position from which he will be able to do something constructive with the ball once he receives it.

—*Mark Ella*, Running Rugby *(ABC Books, 1995)*

I initially considered the role of dialectical tension in creating the radical centre when I thought about leadership. My first official job was on a taskforce appointed by Queensland Premier Wayne Goss in 1991—led by his *wunderkind* head of the cabinet office, Kevin Rudd—to develop Aboriginal land rights legislation. In opposition since time immemorial, the fledgling Labor government dreaded its commitment to introduce land rights legislation in the most conservative of states. In dramatic circumstances, at a national conference hosted by Premier Goss as part of Justice Tony Fitzgerald's Fraser Island Inquiry, the Premier announced the government's intention to develop land rights legislation. I was there with a delegation of Cape York elders and colleagues; I had begun my own trajectory in pursuit of land rights for the people of Cape York Peninsula by forming the Cape York Land Council the year before.

Kevin Rudd and Wayne Goss eventually produced miserable legislation—an opinion that I have not changed sixteen years later. The new law provided for a slightly different form of title to replace that previously granted by the National Party government of Sir Joh Bjelke-Petersen. The practical effect of the title transfer was negligible and did not grant any more land than that already under Aboriginal ownership. Most of these title transfers have still not taken place.

Provision was made for Aboriginal groups to claim lands on the basis of their traditional affiliation or historical association, or economic and social need. National parks and vacant Crown lands were the only land that could be claimed before a specially established Land Tribunal—but only those parcels of land that the executive government had decided were available. This provision, which Kevin Rudd designed, enabled the government to control what could be claimed, and when it could occur. There was no right to claim land other than what government determined. In the sixteen years of this legislation, very few parcels of vacant land were ever gazetted for claim: I know of only one claim that went through the process. Around a dozen national parks were made available—principally in Cape York but also the Great Sandy Desert National Park in the south-western corner of Queensland—and they were all successfully proven before the Land Tribunal.

I represented the traditional owners in the first claim to the Flinders Islands and Cape Melville National Parks in 1993. The claim was successful. However, the Yiithuwarra traditional owners have still not received title to the park. They have no role in its management, and not one of them is employed by any of the plethora of government agencies responsible for the "natural resource management" of these lands and seas. The managers are all white. Half of the Yiithuwarra who gave evidence in the 1993 claim, including almost all the elders, are now dead. The implementation of the original commitment to hand over title and management of national parks to traditional owners has been in abeyance during the three terms of Premier Peter Beattie's government. The government fears an electoral backlash if it proceeds with the Goss–Rudd scheme.

I recount this story first to make the point that if I had a dollar for every time I heard that phrase "social justice" fall easily from the lips of a Labor politician in my home state, I would be an extremely wealthy man.

My first experience of the *realpolitik* of fighting for Aboriginal rights was bitterly hard. The most shameful thing occurred on the day Premier Goss tabled the Bill. It contained nothing to distress the miners or the farmers, whose interests were fully accounted for. Then Anglican Archbishop of Brisbane Peter Hollingworth duly came out and gave the government's paltry legislation his extraordinary blessing. It was the Premier's language that was shocking. He and his advisers had determined that the best way to sell the new law to an unsympathetic Queensland public was to make it clear he was not giving any free handouts to the blackfellas. The grab on the evening news was to the effect that the provision for the payment of royalties for mining would not allow any Aboriginal "sheiks" to drive around in Rolls Royce motorcars. It was appalling. True to his promise, the minor provision for the payment of royalties for mining applying to only one of Queensland's numerous mines—the Cape Flattery Silica Mines owned by Mitsubishi on the land of the Hope Vale community—has not paid one cent of royalties to the community sixteen years later.

I learned a bitter truth through this experience: that Aboriginal people are lepers in the Australian democratic process. I have watched with awe how the progressive lobby turned al-Qaeda recruit David Hicks into a relentless, irrecusable and finally triumphant national cause—from Taliban terrorist to latter-day Nelson Mandela of Guantanamo Bay. It has (occasionally) been said that it is not the man, it is the principle. There is a much clearer principle involved in the breach of the *International Convention on the Elimination of All Forms of Racial Discrimination* by operation of the Australian Government's *Native Title Act*, but this could not be made a *cause célèbre*. In terms of marketability, it is easier to sell a terrorist than an Australian Aborigine subjected to ongoing racial discrimination by the country's laws relating to native land title. Australia's democracy is telegenically allergic to blackfellas.

This got me thinking about pragmatism and realism in political leadership. The new breed of Labor apparatchiks running state governments after the disasters of the 1980s were more hard-headed about the imperatives of holding on to power: no more Whitlam-esque indulgences, no more socialism. Goss, Rudd and Swan were the new pineapple heads of the Sunshine State. I understood that Aboriginal causes were political hard-sell. I felt at the time that Premier Goss could have produced more just legislation without cutting his government's throat in the process. I thought about low-level, poll-driven pragmatism versus ideals. Wayne Goss had been part of the Labor lawyer brigade who had spent time working in Aboriginal Legal Aid, yet in two electorally handsome terms his government did nothing to improve the lot of Queensland's most abject people.

Later the albatross of Australia's lepers hung around the throat of Paul Keating's prime ministership in 1996. Never before, and likely never again, would indigenes be invited in from the woodheap to sit at the main table as they did during those Keating years. This just confirmed the opinion that Aborigines are electoral poison. No more bleeding hearts. No more prime ministerial insistence that the blackfellas come in from the cold.

We are prisoners of our metaphors: by thinking of realism/pragmatism and idealism as opposite ends of a two-dimensional plane, we see leaders inclining to one side or the other. The naïve and indignant yaw towards ideals and get nowhere, but their souls remain pure. The cold-eyed and impatient pride themselves in their lack of romance and emotional foolishness: pragmatism and a remorseless Kissinger-esque grasp of power make winning and survival the main prize every time. Those who harbour ideals but who need to work within the parameters of real power (as opposed to simply cloaking lazy capitulation under the easy mantle of righteous impotence) end up splitting the difference somewhere between ideals and reality. This is called compromise. And it is all too often of a low denominator.

I prefer a pyramid metaphor of leadership, with one side being realism and the other idealism, and the quality of leadership dependent on how closely the two sides are brought together. The apex of leadership is the point where the two sides meet. The highest ideals in the affairs of humans on Earth are realised when leadership strives to secure them through close attention to reality. Lofty idealism without pragmatism is worthless. What is pragmatism without ideals? At best it is management, but not leadership.

As one rises above the low denominator compromise, it takes skill, creativity, strategy, careful calculation as well as bold judgement, prudence and risk, intelligent analysis, insight, perseverance, as well as preparedness to alter course, belief and humility, great competence, and an ability to make good from mistakes to bring ideals closer to reality. One must be hard-headed in order to never let go of ideals.

Idealism and realism in leadership do not constitute a zero-sum game. This is not about securing a false compromise. It need not be a simple trade-off where one splits the difference. The best leadership occurs at the point of highest tension between ideals and reality. This is the radical centre. If the idealism is weaker than the realism, then optimum leadership cannot be achieved. And vice versa. The radical centre is achieved when both are strong.

Otherwise, you get the problem of skewing. This occurs when one side of (what I will call) a classic dialectical struggle is weak and the other pronounced. Skewing also occurs through history; the balance of tensions may be optimal at one point, but it can change over time. As we have discussed earlier, even ideal policy is not static and what might be truly progressive policy at one time can become regressive. To refer back to an earlier example, Legal Aid for Aboriginal offenders has treated wrongdoers as victims and contributed to the undermining of social order and norms within Aboriginal society. Legal Aid pointed to the criminal justice system as the principal problem, not the behaviour of Aboriginal people towards their kith and kin, and resulted in a vicious spiral downwards with even more offenders appearing as a consequence of the breakdown of social order.

Skewing occurs not just because the intellectual analysis is faulty or weak, but because of the issues involved in working out interests in the real world and the great challenges of reality for any policy and leadership seeking a better resolution in the radical centre. No leadership is immune from the forces that impel confrontation with reality and ideals. Leaders are buffeted by reality and must contend with it—they cannot choose it. Leaders' ideals are not just innate qualities: they are often forced by events and by those around them who most ardently press such ideals. Some of the greatest leaders achieve their apex as much by being compelled by external forces as by their own preferences.

My example may be predictable: Abraham Lincoln. Like Winston Churchill, he brought together the highest ideals and the hardest realism. Lincoln starts with his First Inaugural Address ("I have no purpose, directly or indirectly, to interfere with the institution of slavery in the States where it exists. I believe I have no lawful right to do so, and I have no inclination to do so.") and ends up leading the country towards emancipation. The journey is not Lincoln's alone: leaders are not gods. As Doris Kearns Goodwin's perspicuous account (*Team of Rivals,* Simon & Schuster, 2005) shows, Lincoln's competitors for the Republican nomination (Salmon Chase, William H. Seward and Edward Bates) led the President to a better result than he would otherwise have achieved, but his decision to bring his rivals into his team marked the nature of the man's leadership.

There are at least ten classic dialectical tensions in human policy: idealism vs realism, rights vs responsibilities, social order vs liberty, individual vs community, efficiency vs equality, structure vs behaviour, opportunity vs choice, unity vs diversity, nature vs man and peace vs war. This list traverses an entire universe and history of philosophy, policy and politics, and it is not my purpose to set out a prolonged discussion of each of them here.

My contentions are these. First, it is important to correctly identify the fundamental dialectical tensions that define human policy and political struggle. Second, the resolution of each of these tensions lies in their dialectical synthesis, and not through the absolute triumph of one side of a struggle or a weak compromise. Third, other subsidiary struggles fall out of these classical conflicts. Fourth, complexity arises because questions of human policy are not confined to the neat and isolated categories of a ten-point list. Rather, they involve a number of tensions simultaneously.

I have discussed the tension between idealism and realism and between social order and liberty. Economist Arthur Okun set out the basic quandary between social and economic policy in capitalist democracies in his classic 1975 essay, *Equality and Efficiency: The Big Tradeoff* (Brookings): too much equality is inefficient and too much efficiency drives inequality. The discourse on rights and responsibilities is so ubiquitous as to be almost sterile—but the fact that two tribes still face each other on either side of the ideological divide between rights and responsibilities demonstrates that, while the radical centre may make common sense analytically, it is uncommon to see it emerge in practice. The predominant view in Australian Indigenous policy, from a progressive and Indigenous perspective, remains that rights are the real imperative and responsibilities are an ideological diversion. Their opponents hold exactly the contrary view. I will return to this when I come to discuss my own contribution to this discourse.

I will leave the last three on the list, but will briefly discuss the tension between opportunity and choice and structure and behaviour because they are germane to this essay. In our reform work in Cape York Peninsula, we have come to greatly appreciate the insight of Nobel Laureate Amartya Sen in *Development as Freedom* (Oxford University Press, 1999), who believes that it is not enough to say individuals have the right to choose their own path—they require some basic capabilities, such as good health and education, to be able to make real choices. Sen's theory is an important gloss on the powerful principle of individual choice, for without capabilities, choice can be a bare conceit. In Western democracies, whilst the power of individual choice has largely been accepted, there is a social democratic insistence that there be "opportunity" to make choice real (indeed during the long reign of the pre-Hayekian consensus in the twentieth century, even large-L liberals and capital-C conservatives came to accept the notion of universal opportunity). Social democrats look to the (welfare) state to ensure universal opportunity, yet the welfare state's provision of opportunity has had mixed success. What I call classical welfare has been undeniably successful, but passive welfare has not only failed to spread opportunity, but has increased the incapacity of certain sections of society. Putting aside the debates as to how the universal guarantee of basic opportunities might best be delivered, there is a strong consensus in Western democracies that opportunity must accompany choice.

Sen has put an important gloss on choice, and I propose a similar gloss on "opportunity": it must be accompanied by responsibility. Opportunity alone will not produce capability. Rather, individuals, families and communities must fulfil their responsibilities if opportunities are to become real. This was a strong conviction of Booker T. Washington: that his people had to take responsibility so that whenever opportunities came knocking, they would be able to capitalise on them. He deprecated opportunity without responsibility. Indeed, Washington's support for property qualifications being attached to suffrage—provided that blacks with those qualifications could also vote—underscores his tremendous belief that no opportunity or right should accrue without responsibility. Whether it is correct to make rights and opportunities conditional on responsibility, it is nevertheless true that without responsibility they do not produce the capacity that enables people to make the choices needed to pursue better lives.

Finally the dialectic between structure and behaviour: Shelby Steele points to the malignant effect of theories that underpinned leftist politics on black race thinking and politics from the 1960s: "The Marxian emphasis on structures and sub-structures gave the new militant leaders of the time an infinitely larger racism to work with, a systemic and sociological racism that was far more 'determinative' than the simpler immoral racism of Martin Luther King's era." Steele is dismissive of structural explanations which absolve individuals from personal responsibility and agency, and which have made race such a heavy burden and an insuperable barrier to opportunity in America.

He is correct in identifying the baleful and shallow theories on which the New Left constructed a cultural and social folly, but this does not mean that there is not a structural dimension to black problems; they are both behavioural and structural. For example, welfare dependency is clearly a behavioural issue, but it also has a structural explanation; similarly, welfare dependency came about for structural reasons but became a behavioural issue. Taking another example, there is a passive welfare industry within government bureaucracies and non-government organisation "service deliverers" with an entrenched interest in cultivating and maintaining behavioural dependency by their many clients. Tackling welfare dependency is not just a behavioural challenge: it is a massive structural and institutional challenge.

The problem with discussing structures is that it can become an excuse for failing to deal with behaviour. People are absolved from their behaviour because of the sheer daunting scale and nature of the structural explanation. This is what Steele means when he talks about "social determinism": structures are so omnipresent and overwhelming that there is no possibility of human agency and responsibility. Progressivist thinking in this area has failed to distinguish between explanation and the policy prescription which occurs in the light of such explanation. It is one thing to have a greater understanding of the reasons for certain behavioural problems, but it does not by itself suggest a solution. The problem may have a history, but illumination is not itself a solution. We will still need to deal with dysfunction and poverty as much as we seek to tackle those structural dimensions that can be reformed.

Some explanations, such as structural violence in history, are beyond contemporary policy reach in any case: we have to deal with what we face now. Some structural problems, such as racism, may not be amenable to reform, and if we premise black progress on its elimination or substantial diminution, we might be waiting until kingdom comes. In other words, we are liable to leave ourselves impotent and defeated in the face of racism, and this is infinitely more tragic if we have imagined the barriers of racism to be greater than they really are.

It is one thing to have a structural analysis, but at the end of the day it is through individual agency that structures can be challenged and reformed. Behaviour is ultimately about agency—first personal and then social. The mistake of the structural analysis of the black predicament in America and Australia is that race has been treated in the same way as class. Race is really only an instrument of class. It is an easy and more convenient marker than others.

Flannel shirts, mullet hairstyles and "hotted up" cars marked the "plebs" when I attended private boarding school in Brisbane. "Rat-tails" and other ghastly markers declared the class identity of their innocent offspring. Race is just more explicit. The privileged college I attended was adjacent to a less privileged high school, and the two main roads from these schools met at a Y junction that led to the train station and shopping centre. Students from my college with regulation haircuts, carrying violins and book bags and dressed in hats, ties and blazers, met their nemeses at this junction, in a spirit of mutual contempt and abuse. I recall walking down our side of this road one day with some students from my hometown when a group of unruly white kids on the other side of the road, half-dressed in an indeterminate school uniform and long hair, started calling us—who were smartly dressed in blazers and ties—"Abos" and "Coons". After an initial shock, we shouted back "Plebs" and "White Trash". We urged them to "Get back to Inala", the symbolic home of the lower classes in Brisbane in my youth where, in fact, a large Aboriginal population lived in fibro homes that looked dreadfully similar—but were in fact superior—to our families' fibro homes back at the mission.

I began to learn then that race matters, but it is not destiny. Class matters more, but it also need not be destiny. The most profound debility caused by racism is not the externally inflicted harm, but the internalised acceptance of its power as destiny, which can become an excuse. If you want "black consciousness", it is the consciousness of Bill Cosby, Shelby Steele and John McWhorter that is sorely needed, not the victimhood and false separatist consciousness of post-'60s black leadership.

I will finish by setting out some reflections on my experience of driving an agenda of rights and responsibilities in Indigenous policy. By the end of the last millennium, it was not possible to continue in this area without facing up to the gaping responsibility deficit. It was a deficit of which I had long been aware, but the prevailing currents were averse to this particular R word. Two other Rs—rights and reconciliation—were ruling. I have never doubted the correctness of our claim to rights; I have made a contribution to the struggle for the rights of my people in Cape York Peninsula, and have continued this contribution. Our rights to our traditional lands, to our languages and our cultures, our identities and traditions are a constant part of our work for a better future for our people.

When I decided that we could no longer go on without saying that our people held responsibilities as well as rights, is was not a repudiation of rights. It was just that all of the talk, all the advocacy, all the analysis, all the leadership, and all the policy and politics was about rights. There was no talk about responsibility. So when we talked about child malnutrition, we spoke of the rights of the children and the responsibility of governments, but we didn't talk about the responsibilities of parents. We didn't ask "how come children are malnourished?" It can't be because the parents have no money, because in Australia the government provides money to all those who don't have an income. It can't be because there is no food available—there are shops in these communities where the malnourished children live, as well as bush food.

There was a widespread refusal to even think about responsibility. If there were no practical consequences to our failure to talk about responsibility—and strong strategic reasons not to make the responsibility concession to the political right—then this situation could have continued. But there are practical consequences galore! It is simply not possible to see how any social or economic problem can be solved, or opportunity seized, if we don't first accept responsibility. No progress can be made without filling the gaping deficit.

My view is that the main reason why people have refused (and still refuse) to talk about responsibility is not for strong strategic reasons, but because they actually believe that better health and better education and better housing and better life expectancy and better survival of traditional languages are rights that can be enjoyed if other people—specifically governments, but also the wider society—take the necessary actions to make them materialise. It amounts to this absurdity: my rights depend on you fulfilling your responsibilities to me. Who in world history has ever been saved by anyone in the way we hope whitefellas will save our people?

This absurdity drove my campaign for responsibility and my thesis: we have a right to take responsibility.

It is a thesis in which I firmly believe. When it all boils down, the most important right we have is the right to take responsibility for ourselves. The misery we endure and have endured as virtual wards of a state which has taken over our responsibilities points clearly to the urgent need for our right to take responsibility to be restored to us.

Our responsibility agenda of the past seven years has led us to tackle the largest immediate problems facing our people: substance abuse and the reform of welfare. We aim to tackle these problems at the level of individual responsibility, because addicts and their addictions, welfare recipients and their passivity are behaviours that must be tackled. We also aim to tackle these problems at the structural level: the policy, legislative and administrative structure of the income support system, and the passive welfare services delivered by governments and non-government organisations. We aim to be radical in our reforms, in that we seek to tackle the root of the problems that we say are the cause of the responsibility crisis among our people.

We have cut through with our advocacy and our policy analysis. We have contributed to a wider discussion on welfare reform and social disadvantage—a discussion which is not unique to Indigenous affairs, and certainly not unique to Australia. The responsibility agenda is now ascendant. However, while my own experience of talking with Indigenous people in communities confirms that there is widespread resonance with the responsibility agenda, the effective weight of Indigenous leadership is, at best, silent on it. There is still, I suspect, a yearning for the ascension of the old paradigm.

The problem is that, with the rise of the responsibility agenda, there has been a corresponding collapse of the rights discourse. While there has been a lot of talk about "the rights agenda" in Australia over the past decade, there has been no effective leadership with impactful advocacy, policy and strategy. It is not enough to stubbornly keep up the talk. There has to be *impact*. And in order to have impact, there must be new thinking, new strategies, new tactics—to cut through. For discourse to penetrate the social and political currents of society, we have to get beyond preaching to the converted, and complaining in our in-house forums about the failure of wider forums to take up our hammers. Influence is not conferred on all discourse as if it is an equal opportunity exercise. We have to fashion hammers with impact.

We therefore have the problem of skewing in Indigenous policy in Australia. The tensions of the responsibilities agenda are ascending, but the tensions of the rights agenda have receded. There is at present no effective rights leadership and advocacy. This is not to say there is no competent intellectual analysis of the rights agenda (though I have doubts about the quality of the intellectual ballast supporting the rights agenda), but there needs to be more than compelling analysis; there must be a capacity to increase the necessary dialectical tension.

My experiences have led me to three conclusions about the prerequisites for syntheses which allow societies to transcend conflicting tensions and take a historical leap forward: the political analysis must be right; it is not possible for the same actor to play several roles in the dialectical process; and apparently contradictory principles must be carried by strong societal forces.

Shelby Steele has described how faulty analysis can derail promising development. The twin phenomena of "white guilt" and a problematically conceived "black consciousness" prevented the United States from achieving a historical breakthrough that would have benefited all Americans. (I do not subscribe to the quasi-radical analysis that white Americans benefit from the current plight of black Americans.) You have to get the analysis right.

The second conclusion is that it is difficult for the same actor to play several roles in the dialectical process. It is possible for the same person to have an overall intellectual analysis, but practical politics and the production of theory are not the same thing. For example, in a socially and economically successful country, there is competition between interests and forces which represent capitalist principles on the one hand, organisations which represent communal and socialist ideas on the other, and inspired political leaders who perform the synthesis between these contradictions. It is possible for an individual to have an intellectual appreciation of this, but that individual can hardly play all three roles.

Only the primary leaders of a whole society can "triangulate", to use the crude practical terminology of Clinton's adviser Dick Morris in *Behind the Oval Office* (Renaissance, 1999), during his most effective "third way" period—from mid-term disaster at the hands of Newt Gingrich's Republican revolution in 1994 to re-election against the odds in 1996—to move players to a radical centre on vital issues such as welfare reform. People with lesser vantage can only advance one side of a dialectical tension.

I and my associates in Cape York Peninsula decided to champion the Indigenous responsibility agenda, because this was the most under-developed area in the then Australian discourse. The side-effect of our decision is that we are perceived to represent only the principle of responsibility; in a political and societal sense, we are largely limited to this role, despite our continued work and ongoing practical achievements in securing rights for our people.

This leads to the closely related problem: a successful synthesis will not occur unless the rights agenda is equally developed and cutting through. Perhaps this was W.E.B. Dubois's great shortcoming—that he had the analysis, but not the capacity to increase the necessary dialectical tension.

Australian Indigenous rights consist of both socio-economic rights (which may be referred to as "race relations" and which we share with African-Americans) and rights derived from our "peoplehood". A successful Australian synthesis must reconcile these rights with Indigenous responsibility, and the interests of non-Indigenous Australians. But the

Indigenous rights agenda is so weak that non-Indigenous Australians seem unaware of the nature of our people's aspirations. This might seem a strange contention almost two decades after the *Mabo* decision on native title, but it is becoming clear that our opponents do not understand our point.

Six words struck me like a bolt of lightening when I read Shelby Steele's book. Reflecting on the decision of boxing authorities to strip Muhammad Ali of his world heavyweight title when he refused to fight in Vietnam, Steel wrote: "When he said, 'I ain't got no quarrel with the Viet Cong', *even his enemies understood his point* [my emphasis]. Where was the moral authority to ask this black man, raised in segregation, to fulfil his responsibility to the draft by fighting in a war against a poor Asian country?"

Recently we hosted a senior federal minister so that we could explain our reform plans and seek support for them. The minister was supportive, amiable and intellectually astute. He observed the relevance of our work for his portfolio, and I have no doubt he will support our plans. Indeed, I have no doubt he desires our people to rise up in the world. However, as he left he commended our work but said: "I just don't understand the Indigenous rights stuff."

The minister was not expressing conscious enmity or opposition to my people's aspirations. His remark was a symptom of the fact that the Indigenous rights agenda is politically irrelevant. Tension between rights and responsibilities is impossible, and therefore no synthesis can be achieved. Warren Mundine and I (and many others) are carrying the Indigenous responsibility leadership. There is no sign of effective carriage of the Indigenous rights leadership. There is no sign of a primary societal leadership that is interested in finding the radical centre—where rights and responsibilities are synthesised.

There is a growing insight in the United States about the nature of their problems—importantly by black intellectuals and leaders—and a successful synthesis of the traditions of Booker T. Washington and W.E.B. Dubois is likely to emerge. I eagerly await Shelby Steele's forthcoming book on Barack Obama and Steele's views on whether Obama has "the right stuff".

Pat Dodson

Whatever happened to reconciliation?
Crikey, 13 September 2007

The tragedy of the Howard Government's eleven-year hold on power is that Indigenous policy has focused on destroying the potential for this nation to respect and nurture the cultural renaissance of traditional Indigenous society. Public policy that celebrates Indigenous culture has been shunned.

We are left with a vague sense that the problems of the present-day crisis have no history and that the way forward is for Indigenous people to abandon their identity and be absorbed into European settler society. Any casual glance at Aboriginal people living in Redfern, Mt Druitt or Perth will tell you that there is no paradise for those in the Northern Territory to pass over into the Promised Land on the other side that is mainstream Australia.

The current battle ground of the assimilation agenda is located on that vast new region of northern and central Australia where Indigenous people maintain their languages, own their traditional lands under Western legal title, and practise their customs whilst seeking to survive on public sector programs whose poor design has resulted in entrenched dependency.

This is where the Howard Government is implementing its radical agenda of deconstructing and denying the abilities of Indigenous people to live in their settlements on traditional country. It is setting out to remodel them into mine labourers, small business people and private entrepreneurs. This is an existence already questioned by many debt ridden Australians.

The policy agenda is increasingly asserted in both rhetoric and funding programs. Communal ownership and collective decision making will give way to private land and home ownership and a new mobile Indigenous individualism that will need to seek employment opportunities dictated by market forces at distant locations.

In this conservative worldview, population movements from remote communities or welfare dependent towns to urban environments with economies struggling with or sustained by the global market are simply par for the course. Such communities sink or disappear. Forty thousand years of a society founded upon different presuppositions to the Greco-Roman tradition and the Protestant work ethic of industrialisation is finally colliding head on with the believers of the meteor called the global market economy.

The benign use of government language—mainstream services, practical reconciliation, mutual obligations, responsibilities and participation in the real economy—cloaks a sinister destination for Australian nation building.

The extinguishing of Indigenous culture by attrition is the political goal of the Howard Government's Indigenous policy agenda. Our nation is confronted with a searing moral challenge.

A cultural genocide agenda has been foisted on the Australian public in the context of extensive media coverage about the social collapse of Indigenous communities, centred on sexual abuse of children and rampant violence fuelled by alcohol and drugs.

Rather than explaining the human tragedy caused by decades of under-investment by governments in capital and social infrastructure, the Howard Government has promoted a neoconservative public discourse in which Aboriginal people's failure to take responsibility has become the central tenet of the debate.

In these circumstances, the Howard Government's policies of coercive intervention and dismantling of the building blocks of self-determination have been broadly painted as correcting three decades of progressive liberalism that have resulted in degrading welfare dependency.

Some Indigenous voices in this debate, motivated by the urgency of ending the suffering in Indigenous communities, have been recklessly naive in aiding and abetting the Howard Government's agenda. The struggle for Indigenous people's cultural survival amidst overwhelming destructive historical forces cannot be constructed as a contemporary political debate with contrived theatre to forge a middle path acceptable to mainstream Australia.

The advocacy for recognising Indigenous people's cultural survival has unimpeachable integrity that cannot be compromised in the face of historic European settler hostility and frontier violence. Indigenous advocates, campaigning for structural change in government relationships that aim to liberate their people from the tyranny of welfare dependency and control, have misread the Indigenous political struggle.

Economic development has been a central component of the Indigenous struggle for land rights and decolonisation. This is why the capacity for Indigenous people to negotiate with governments and resource developers over the use of their lands has been so critical to self-determination.

The debate on welfare reform and the capacity of Indigenous people to take responsibility for nurturing and supporting their families and communities must be part and parcel of self-determination. It should be recognised that investing in the reconstruction of Indigenous society through traditionally based governance structures, customary land owner-ship and internal reconciliation and healing are critical to ensuring social cohesion through the interconnected obligations and responsibilities on which Indigenous societies are based.

The recognition, respect and resourcing of Indigenous authority by the dominant society is fundamental to dealing with the scourge of grog and drugs that have caused such incomprehensible damage to Indigenous communities.

Tragically, the Indigenous public policy debate in recent years has been framed by imperatives that are oppositional to Indigenous systems of belief. The value of individualism has been elevated above the value of community and collective decision making.

Policy prescriptions about wealth generation through employment and individual home and land ownership are argued for by influential voices as the new basis of civil society within Indigenous communities. The misguided logic of this view is that communal land ownership and Indigenous collective decision making is responsible for the social collapse of Indigenous communities.

The ravages of alcohol and drugs, violence and child sexual abuse, and the endemic community malaise are the result, they argue, of separating

Indigenous settlements from the mainstream Australian economic and social system. This argument plays into the hands of conservatives who have long advocated that Indigenous people should be assimilated into the dominant society.

Any special measures designed to achieve any level of equity with mainstream Australia are now characterised as a denial of the rights of the colonial inheritors. This perspective then sets like cement in the minds of the average punter as a dictate that there is nothing noble about the Aboriginal race.

The Howard Government has used the growing welfare reform debate it has intentionally fuelled, and the conservative ideological critique about the social implosion of discrete Indigenous communities, to escalate its political goal to dismantle the structures that support Indigenous self-determination.

This has not suddenly occurred as a result of accusations of rampant sexual abuse of children in Indigenous communities. In its eleven years of power, the Howard Government has laid the political groundwork for a dramatic change of policy which promotes the absorption of Indigenous communities into Anglo-dominant Australian society.

This has not occurred through persuasive articulation of its policy agenda but through drawing on the cancer of settler hostility to Indigenous people that bubbles beneath the surface of Australian civil society. It should never be forgotten that throughout much of the twentieth century the formal policy of governments was to administer the extinguishment of Indigenous people by historical attrition, to first smooth the dying pillow and then assimilate to end cultural difference.

This extract, published in Crikey, *was taken from* Coercive Reconciliation—Stabilise, Normalise, Exit Aboriginal Australia, *edited by Jon Altman and Melinda Hinkson.*

Russell Skelton

Tortured history of violence
The Age, 22 December 2007

Silas Wolomby pauses, deep in thought. His milky eyes suggest faded vision, but he has little difficulty recalling the savagery that stalks Aurukun's streets. "It was Monday the 17th of September, I ended up in hospital."

That day the Wik elder had his jaw broken in two places. Some say a house brick hit him. He says he was bashed from behind by two youths with an iron bar.

I had asked this proud, elderly man what had put him in hospital. "I'll tell you what my problem was," he began. "I don't have two eyes in the back of my head, I don't see it coming. Next thing I was in the Cairns hospital."

On that day, two of Aurukun's five clans had taken to each other with iron bars, fence posts, rocks and knives. An estimated 200 men, women and children brawled viciously up and down the red dirt streets. Anybody, even a revered 79-year-old Wik elder, was fair game.

Silas Wolomby said that when his granddaughter and grandson were being attacked in front of his house he had no choice but to intervene, to do his best to get them out of harm's way. "I feared the worst, I didn't know what was going to happen. Nobody is safe in Aurukun at the best of times."

His wife, Rebecca, a 75-year-old pensioner with a shock of grey hair and a quick mind, says Aurukun's community of 1100 people (a third of whom are children) live in constant fear, never knowing where the next assault on them or their property may come from. "I never, never let my 16-year-old granddaughter out at night. We don't trust anyone. Bad things happen. Our dogs protect us at night but the gangs come into our front yard."

Rebecca and Silas Wolomby, who share some 50 grandchildren and great grandchildren, are dismayed at the recent dark events that have made Aurukun headline news around the world. They cannot understand why nine indigenous males—six of them juveniles—were set free after raping a 10-year-old intellectually impaired girl.

"Those boys should be punished. If it had happened to my granddaughter, there would be trouble." The elderly man shakes his head in disgust.

He says the loss of traditional culture has opened the way to a form of social anarchy and madness. Several decades ago troublesome kids would be taken out bush by the senior law men and sorted out. Child sex was taboo and offenders were punished. But these days, he says, young mothers and fathers go to the tavern, leaving children to the mercy of whoever may come along. The lucky ones are left with their grandmothers or elder sisters.

The tragedies here are ones that have been repeated, and reported, across indigenous communities from Western Australia to Queensland over the past 15 years. Alcohol and petrol abuse, the failure of self-determination policies, welfare dependency and whispers of an inherent violence within the indigenous psyche itself have all been variously used—or rejected—in attempts to explain or justify the dysfunction of these communities.

Harriet Pootchemunka, a member of the community's justice group that liaises with the courts and the school, believes the council-owned Three Rivers Tavern, which operates on restricted hours through an alcohol-management scheme, should be closed to curb the violence. But she says closure is unlikely because too many people want it open and any council that closed it would be voted out of office:

> People are fighting all the time. It all comes down to alcohol. I am probably the only person in my clan who refuses to take sides and is friendly with everyone. Education should be the main priority here and learning about the outside world. People think this life is normal, they know nothing else.

When *The Age* visited Aurukun this week the place seemed peaceful enough, possibly exhausted by months of street violence. A woman followed a man up the street. He had a bandage on his fist, she dabbed a bleeding mouth with a tissue. A lonely young figure hobbled towards the river. He had lost his leg to diabetes. The tavern was closed to keep heads cool, and payback over the rapes to a minimum.

So what is Aurukun? As one regular visitor to the community put it:

> Aurukun is a place where people come together to fight, go to funerals and go to the tavern. Young men define themselves by fighting for their clan or their family. You haven't made it until you do time at Cleveland or Candle River prisons. They draw esteem from serving jail time, they don't want to be known as black drunks.

Like many of the people who have emerged as community leaders and councillors, Pootchemunka was educated at a boarding school in Cairns, which allowed her to break the cycle of drinking and fighting. Ralph Peinkinna, chairman of the community justice group and a Uniting Church minister, also attended boarding school. He spent 11 years there before returning to the community to take up a position as court clerk.

"We must look seriously at the issues," he says. "We need people on call 24 hours a day to stop the violence, we need to get the kids to school, we need to get parents involved. Little kids see the young men who steal cars and fight as role models."

Perched on the western side of Cape York and surrounded by grasslands, Aurukun is a two-hour drive from the mining town of Weipa. The community is yet another confronting monument to the comprehensive failure of indigenous policy in Australia and chronic shortcomings of the Queensland justice system.

The presiding judge in the gang rape case, Sarah Bradley, had visited Aurukun many times. As *The Age* revealed this week, she had been fully briefed by the justice group on the breakdown in law and order yet she let the rapists avoid jail.

Her decision is being appealed against and reviewed by the Queensland Attorney-General, Kerry Shine. Nobody has come to the judge's defence. Peinkinna insists the gang rape was an unusual case for Aurukun, that "it doesn't happen all the time".

Depressingly, Aurukun fits the notorious indigenous community paradigm. Binge drinking at the tavern (drinking is restricted to just three hours a day) fuels an ongoing crime wave. Of the 200 school-age children, only 50 turn up regularly for class and only 10 every day. Five teachers have recently cancelled contracts with the school because of the negative publicity surrounding Judge Bradley's sentencing.

The community-run store posted a loss last year of about $1 million after years of trading profitably. For several months this year, residents claim the store was without fresh food. The Auditor-General is investigating community claims that funds were mismanaged and misappropriated.

The swimming pool is empty. About 60% of the town is employed on Community Development Employment Programs (CDEP), accumulating some 4000 hours on cleaning up rubbish and other meaningless work. The majority of men and women have never had a real job. Alternative jobs are rare.

But it is the unrelenting violence and constant destruction of public property that hampers any form of social progress. The community is home to eight convicted murderers. Community sources said one man who had served five years for murder had recently been charged over the death of another person. In the magistrates court this week, well over 130 charges were being heard against members of some of the community's most well-known families.

Most prominent on the court lists were relatives of the town's Mayor, Neville Pootchemunka (Harriet's cousin), whose son Ian Koowarta was one of the nine convicted rapists. Five other members of the Pootchemunka family faced charges of assaulting and obstructing police, unlawful wounding, possession of a knife and breaches of the liquor act. Anywhere else in Australia, Neville Pootchemunka would have been forced to resign.

When *The Age* visited the Mayor's home last weekend, his de facto spouse said he had gone fishing. Plenty of people think he should resign even though he has said his son should have been jailed over the rape. "Neville is not setting a good example that's for sure, but his children should respect him more," was how one resident summed up the situation. Most alarming is the large number of juveniles charged with stealing, damage to public property, assault and carjacking. The rate of sexually transmitted infections is believed to be among the highest in the state, along with the juvenile crime rate.

But Aurukun is not a place without hope. The giant Chinese mining conglomerate Chalco (the Aluminium Corporation of China) has plans to mine bauxite just north of the community. The $3 billion project is expected to provide about 700 jobs in the construction phase. Commitments have already been given to maximise employment opportunities for the local community.

Wik Way woman Gina Castelain is deeply involved in the environmental and social impact assessment process to be conducted over the next two years. A 23-year-old master's student at Monash University, she has been involved in community politics since the age of 10. She believes the project, if properly managed, can provide skilled jobs to replace the demeaning CDEP work. Already, a small number of Wik people have been hired to liaise on the assessment stage. But Castelain says: "The challenge is to build capacity into the community so people can take advantage of the job opportunities. Education is going to be the key to that."

Although she doesn't say it, Castelain believes that the community is in desperate need of new leadership and that the Mayor, for a start, should stand down. "This project is going to create lots of spin-off opportunities, but kids are not going to school and we have to change that."

Silas Wolomby couldn't agree more but believes that is going to require a significant change of attitude for many. "You have to stop the fighting and I don't believe that is going to happen until I am dead and gone. This was a happy place in the 1960s, it is shameful what has happened."

Marcia Langton

Stop the abuse of children
The Australian, 12 December 2007

The latest heart-breaking tragedy—the freeing of three adult and six juvenile Wik males who pleaded guilty to gang-raping a 10-year-old Wik girl in the Aurukun community—has brought to the fore the urgency of dealing with the conditions in which these horrors occur.

The notorious Queensland criminal justice system, along with the system that purports to protect children, has demonstrated again (so soon after the Mulrunji Doomadgee case) that it is incapable of anything approximating justice, for offenders or victims. In imposing 12-month probation orders and refusing to record a conviction against any of the nine who pleaded guilty, Queensland District Court judge Sarah Bradley has expressed utter contempt for this little girl and for the basic norms of humanity.

So is it acceptable in Queensland to suspend the laws of the state when dealing with convicted felons of Aboriginal ethnicity? Apparently so, according to Bradley, who has disregarded the Criminal Code of Queensland, which makes sex with a minor a crime, and the laws of that state, which make it clear that a minor is not deemed to be capable of giving consent.

The eventual result of this ultimate race-hate practice is the rewarding of serial rapists and murderers.

Instead of jail sentences that would apply to any other member of an ethnic group, they are freed immediately after a laughable lecture from judge or magistrate, or sent to a prison for a few months. They are then released back into the communities where their crimes were committed and where recidivism takes on a special meaning: the younger sisters or cousins of their original victims are the next in line to be raped.

One may be forgiven for believing reports of abuse and rape of Aboriginal children in the Northern Territory had not occurred, nor a commission of inquiry resulting in the report *Little Children Are Sacred*. Perhaps Bradley does not read the newspapers. Perhaps she has not heard of crown prosecutor Nanette Rogers. Perhaps she just doesn't give a damn about the gang rape of a 10-year-old Wik girl.

A week ago, I appealed to the newly elected Rudd Government to continue the NT emergency intervention and to maintain the strategies that are likeliest to stop the plague of child rape, abuse and neglect in Aboriginal communities.

I was attacked and pilloried by Aborigines, spruiking the usual sentimental, blame-shifting nonsense.

Their views were also posted on the web page of Women for Wik, a group of high-profile women supporting Aboriginal rights.

I have spoken during the past few years to other young Wik women who have been the victims of incest and rape. I have reported these matters to the authorities.

If it were in my power, I would immediately close the alcohol canteen in Aurukun and send more police into the community, including a special police taskforce to interview women and children victims, health workers and suspected offenders, and increase powers to detain and arrest suspected offenders. I would send in a police taskforce to inspect airline charters, cargo and luggage, confiscate all drugs, illicit substances and sly grog and the equipment, vehicles and associated paraphernalia. I would increase the penalties for grog runners and drug dealers and ensure jail sentences that befit the harm caused by their crimes.

As is so typical in such cases, several of the rapists are from the ruling families of Aurukun, where anti-social behaviour, which varies from day to day only in its intensity and detrimental outcomes, is graced with labels in the media, such as riot.

Imagine if the regular occurrences of dysfunctional behaviour were merely riots, rather than murder, rape, incest, assault, suicide, alcohol and drug abuse, and non-stop gambling. Then there would be no justification for the recommendations made through the years for an end to welfare payments without conditions and government funding without positive outcomes.

It would be a fair bet that each of the adults who pleaded guilty to raping this child was receiving a government social security or Community Development Employment Program payment. It is difficult not to draw the conclusion that dysfunctional Aboriginal behaviour is financially supported by federal and state government funding.

I have two questions for the Women for Wik (and the cowardly men who hide behind their skirts): What suggestions do you have that could prevent incidents such as this one that took place in the heart of Wik country? And will you cease using the name of the once proud Wik people, now reduced into a vicious, violent and miserable existence by failed sentimental policies such as those you advocate and that utterly dehumanise them?

Tony Koch

Born of grog violence to child tragedy
The Weekend Australian, 15 December 2007

She was a child of Aurukun's beer bottle era—a violent, drunken 13-year experiment into the officially sanctioned sale of alcohol.

When she was born in August 1995, the town's alcohol canteen was five years old, and her mother was a raging alcoholic.

Now aged 12, she is a multiple gang-rape victim whose story has been told around the world, a symbol of the moral decline of Australia's Aboriginal communities and the deeply flawed mainstream indigenous policies that have failed them.

At first glance she is just another bubbly and pretty Aboriginal girl—bright eyes, laughing smile, a shock of unkempt dark, curly hair. But she was born with fetal alcohol syndrome, which left her intellectually and emotionally unable to cope with the trauma of life in the remote, dysfunctional community of Aurukun on western Cape York.

"She's probably functioning as a five- or six-year-old—very little attention for anything you tell her," said a pediatric surgeon who examined the girl in Cairns after the most recent rape.

"She seeks attention by sexual acts with other people. She's desperately attention-seeking and she's well aware that by opening herself up to sex, she gets the attention she thrives on.

"She's very difficult to control—she's very rebellious, she's got a foul temper, and I'm well aware numerous carers have had huge problems with her behaviour.

"She's been seen by pediatricians and psychiatrists, trials with stimulant medication, Experidrome—which is another behavioural management drug—and none of them have benefited her," the pediatrician said.

"I think her constant moving from pillar to post with no firm carer in her life has not helped her behaviour."

Before she was five, the girl was sexually abused by a close family member, and she was taken from the family by the Queensland Department of Child Safety and placed with indigenous foster parents.

There were many placements because she was a difficult child. She was slow to learn—everything except talking, which she does almost constantly.

At age seven in Aurukun she was raped by up to five youths, suffering severe genital trauma. From that assault she was flown to Cairns base hospital for treatment, and the cycle of being placed in foster homes resumed.

Finally, in 2005, frustrated that the girl was making little progress, the department placed her with a non-indigenous foster family in Cairns, where she remained for almost a year.

All reports show this was an inspired placement. The family had another foster child, and this little Aboriginal girl appeared to be fitting in well. She was attending school, and the father took a year off from his public service job to give her constant supervision because he and his wife saw there was a little person worth saving hidden behind all that confusion and grief.

But in May last year, a distant relative in Aurukun died and the girl's blood family said it was culturally imperative she return to attend the funeral. Department of Child Safety representatives were advised and the child was put on a plane for the hour-long trip to the community, where she was met by her aunt and grandmother.

During the course of the next six weeks the girl was gang-raped by nine males, but was also raped on at least six other occasions. And yet no adult reported the matter.

A senior medical officer with experience in Aurukun told a committee investigating the case that earlier experiments with alcohol has ripped the heart out of the community. "You must understand that there's been a loss of parenting skills due to the beer-bottle era between 1990 and 2003, when alcohol management came in," he said. "Aurukun was (then) described as a second Beirut and that's even more applicable at the moment. Before the alcohol management program, 90 per cent of our work was alcohol-related trauma and domestic violence."

It was in this environment that the girl found herself, wandering the streets, being stalked by males who knew no better. Even when she sought help, the rapes did not stop. When she walked into Aurukun clinic and asked for a pregnancy test she was not taken into care.

Almost a week later results of tests came back from Cairns confirming she had gonorrhoea. But two welfare workers from the Department of Child Safety dallied, with one later telling investigators she did not act immediately because she was making inquiries to establish if gonorrhoea could be contracted by any means other than intercourse.

The same worker did not pass on the report of the sexual activity from the clinic to the police as was her statutory obligation. In fact, police heard about the crimes from other sources in the community almost by chance. And when police insisted the girl be flown to Cairns and placed in care, the welfare worker said that would not happen as she had organised for the girl to have a weekend away in the bush with relatives. The officer warned the Child Safety worker that, should harm come to the girl over the weekend, she would be responsible.

History shows that the weekend in the bush did not eventuate and the girl was raped again.

Suggestions the nine males who subsequently pleaded guilty to rape—only to walk free—were able to commit their crimes because it was "culturally acceptable" is challenged by Aboriginal activist Gracelyn Smallwood.

"If culture was invoked here, all nine of those who pleaded guilty to raping this poor little girl would have been taken out and speared and murdered," she says.

Meanwhile the young girl with the mind of an infant still struggles to understand why others have caused her so much hurt when, as the doctor said, all she wanted was to be noticed.

3
The Heat Is On

Marian Wilkinson

Delayed reaction
The Sydney Morning Herald, 24 March 2007

Reassuring cool air greeted David Kemp as he entered the Nusa Dua hotel on a hot Bali morning in June 2002. Inside, the leaders of the World Wildlife Fund were assembled to celebrate World Environment Day by bestowing their most prestigious honour on Australia's environment minister—the "Gift of the Earth" award for preserving the natural beauty of the wetlands. A gracious Kemp, who was sharing the honour with his counterparts from Indonesia and Papua New Guinea, remarked with pleasure that the award "highlights the fact that the environment is everybody's business throughout the world".

But in Canberra, the Prime Minister, John Howard, was about to deliver a World Environment Day message of his own that would ricochet around world capitals. Rising to his feet in Parliament he pronounced that Australia had formally decided not to ratify the Kyoto agreement on climate change. "For us to ratify Kyoto would cost us jobs and damage our industry," Howard said. "The national interest does not lie in ratifying Kyoto."

Almost five years on, that single decision still defines Australia's stand on climate change in the eyes of many. Internationally, Australia is lumped alongside the US as a rogue state in the fight against global warming. We are attacked for being, per head, the largest emitters of greenhouse gases in the world.

Today, as Australians look anxiously at their parched landscapes, evaporating rivers, declining rainfall and record temperatures, Howard is facing a national revolt over his stand on climate change. In the past year, the public, prominent business leaders and the state premiers have all rejected the simple, immutable doctrine he pursued for almost a decade: that he would not act to put a price on greenhouse gas pollution caused by the industries that have enriched Australians as surely as they have caused global warming.

Paul Anderson, who once led the resources giant BHP and now sits on the board of BHP Billiton, warns bluntly that Australians will soon have to face reality. "The first step is we want less carbon dioxide and there is going to be a cost," he told the *Herald* from his home in Maine, in the US. It is a warning echoed by the head of the Australian energy giant AGL, Paul Anthony, and the Australian of the Year, Tim Flannery, who now spends his days briefing Australian companies, including mining companies, on climate change.

"You can see the social licence to operate conventional coal-fired power stations around the world being withdrawn virtually by the week," says Flannery. "Mining companies see what is happening. The world has moved on and Australia finds itself in the position where it is very vulnerable because there's been no action. We've lost a decade."

Until last year, Howard was driven by two fundamental beliefs. He and some key ministers, including Kemp, were never fully convinced by the science that climate change was caused by human activity. As a result, Howard gave less weight to scientific, public service and community opinion in deciding his response. Instead, he set great store by advice from a small group of corporate leaders in Australia's resource industries, among them the former Western Mining boss, Hugh Morgan, and successive heads of Rio Tinto, Brian Horwood and Charlie Lenegan. Documents, emails and interviews with many of the key players over the past decade lent weight to this.

Kemp, who has since retired from politics, told the *Herald* last week that during his three years as environment minister he always had doubts that climate change was caused by human activity, and he remains sceptical today.

"There was no doubt about the fact that the climate was shifting," Kemp said. "The extent to which that change was due to human agency was much less clear in the data. There were aspects of the data that appeared to conflict with that hypothesis."

The CSIRO's leading atmospheric scientist at the time, Graeme Pearman, recalls Kemp's scepticism when he was briefing the minister on a major report on climate change. "I always felt he was sceptical and it is clear he was the not the only senior member of the Liberal Party who was," Pearman says.

This scepticism inside the Government led it to pursue what was called the "no regrets" policy on climate change. "Any action that Australia took should be on a 'no regrets' basis," Kemp said. "It meant, where it is possible to take action without damaging Australia's economy and without adding to the inefficiencies of the economy, then action should be taken."

Put another way, policies were largely rejected if the business advisers Howard trusted could mount a convincing argument against them. From the start, Morgan and his allies argued against Kyoto because it did not compel developing nations such as China, India and Brazil to cut their emissions. This, they said, would severely penalise Australian companies if Kyoto was ratified. While few business leaders were as forthright in public as Morgan, their lobbyists delivered the same message to Canberra.

Records of meetings between Howard and these key business figures reveal his determination to avoid putting a cost or tax on carbon dioxide pollution. What was lacking was advice giving the Government a detailed cost on the price of not taking action on climate change.

Now, as Howard and his new Environment Minister, Malcolm Turnbull, scramble to fashion a new policy, many are asking: will the Government's trusted business advisers essentially still determine Australia's climate change policy as they have in the past? And will what emerges be too little, too late?

Few Australians remember that in 1997, Howard's first environment minister, Robert Hill, signed the Kyoto Protocol on behalf of Australia, calling it "a landmark agreement for the global environment" and "a win-win" for the country. Hill not only set up the Australian Greenhouse Office but argued for Australia to put a price on greenhouse gas pollution by setting up a carbon trading system—a policy Howard and Turnbull have resurrected 10 years later.

Then, the world's leading scientists on the Intergovernmental Panel on Climate Change had found that "the balance of evidence suggests a discernible human influence on global climate". It was this momentous finding that led the world's leaders to draft the Kyoto Protocol to cut carbon emissions.

"Hill was an extremely good minister," Pearman said. "He identified the difference between the mainstream science on climate change and the so-called sceptics and made a decision he was going to trust the mainstream science. I think we've gone backwards since then."

From the outset, Hill faced an unrelenting campaign led by Morgan, who not only had Howard's ear but had earned respect in the Liberal Party as a prodigious fund-raiser. Morgan did not respond to the *Herald*'s request to be interviewed for this piece. But while much has been written about a "greenhouse mafia" who ran Australia's policy behind closed doors, Morgan and his allies argued their case not only in the back rooms but in the boardrooms, newsrooms and lounge rooms of the country, openly, loudly and publicly.

Morgan co-chaired a showdown conference in Canberra in 1997 with the head of the conservative US lobby group Frontiers of Freedom, whose supporters included American fossil fuel industries. Taking the microphone at the conference, Hill stood his ground, telling the sceptics bluntly: "I have stated many times, and will do so again, that Australia accepts the balance of the scientific evidence which suggests that human activity is accelerating the increase in the Earth's average temperature."

And he warned prophetically: "No country can ignore the potential ramifications—least of all Australia, which is already so vulnerable to natural climatic extremes of drought and flood associated with El Nino ..." But Hill would be the last Howard environment minister to so forcefully put the case against the sceptics until Turnbull was appointed almost a decade later.

Morgan began backing prominent science sceptics in Australia, most famously the Melbourne-based Lavoisier Group, which starkly warned Liberal backbenchers that the Kyoto agreement was "the most serious challenge to our sovereignty since the Japanese fleet entered the Coral Sea on May 3, 1942".

But Morgan's real success was not in the propaganda war but in the boardroom battle. In 2000 the Business Council of Australia was struggling to come to grips with the challenge of climate change. Anderson, then chief executive of BHP and a key member of the council, called a meeting of the leading business players to discuss their response.

"I held a party and nobody came," he says. "They sent some low-level people that almost read from things that had been given to them by their lawyers. Things like, 'Our company does not acknowledge that carbon dioxide is an issue and, if it is, we're not the cause of it and we wouldn't admit to it anyway.'"

While Anderson was no fan of the Kyoto agreement, he was convinced climate change was real and BHP should get out in front on the issue. He believed the solution was a carbon tax that would put a cost on greenhouse gas pollution to force down emissions.

Others backed Hill's idea for a carbon emissions trading system, a market-driven scheme that Hill had successfully argued for at Kyoto. Stripped of its complexity, an emissions trading scheme allows companies to trade their polluting emissions with others who are making cuts. This lets the market put a price on carbon dioxide pollution. But it only works in bringing down greenhouse gases if the government sets a firm, measurable target that cuts the country's overall emissions.

The majority of Australian companies, however, simply didn't want any price put on greenhouse gas emissions. In the end, they were saved by Washington. In early 2001, George Bush took control of the White House and announced that the US would not ratify either. Howard made it clear that without US support, Australia would not ratify Kyoto. When he went to the polls in 2001 he was ready to abandon it. In his new ministry, Hill was moved to defence and Kemp, a sceptic, was given environment.

While the sceptics rejoiced in Canberra and Washington, scientists around the world were increasingly gripped by the urgency of climate change. That year the Intergovernmental Panel on Climate Change had intensified its warning that greenhouse gases were rising, "as a result of human activities", causing surface air temperatures and subsurface oceans temperatures to rise.

In March 2002 satellite pictures showing the collapse of the massive Larsen B ice shelf in Antarctica sent shock waves among scientists, who attributed the collapse to rising temperatures. Many Australian scientists not only rejected the sceptical view coming from their new minister, they were fearful that climate change was accelerating at an alarming rate.

Kemp and Howard knew their challenge was to come up with a credible post-Kyoto plan. As scientific and public alarm was mounting, so, too, were the concerns of many business leaders, premiers—led by NSW's Bob Carr—and public servants. In 2003 the head of Kemp's department, Roger Beale, put together a strategy—supported by his counterparts in Treasury, the Industry department and Foreign Affairs—to again examine how a carbon trading scheme might work for Australia.

While Morgan had by now parted ways with Western Mining, he remained ferocious in his opposition and Howard listened to him. As one key Government figure put it: "There was no doubt that Hugh was a person who had very high respect within the Government and he didn't have to say very much to be very influential." By August 2003 Howard had killed off the Beale plan and the Government was left scrambling to come up with a replacement strategy.

"Greenhouse policy is in a state of chaos," the then head of the Australian petroleum lobby group, Barry Jones, emailed colleagues. "It appears there was no fall-back option to the emissions permit trading package that cabinet rejected a fortnight ago."

But Howard and Kemp had been working on ambitious plans with Washington which the Prime Minister discussed with industry players, led by the Rio Tinto executives Brian Horwood and Sam Walsh. According to a leaked account of the meeting written by Walsh, "technology would be the long-term solution to greenhouse issues …".

Working closely with Washington and the leaders of Rio Tinto, Alcoa, BHP, Boral, Orica and other energy companies, the strategy was to rely heavily on pouring millions of taxpayer and investment dollars into "clean coal" technology. Australia and the US would lead the way in clean coal, a technology that captures emissions from coal-fired power, compresses them into a liquid form and pumps them into long-term storage deep underground. The technology was, and still is, hampered by its costs, its feasibility and the years it will take to become available on a large scale. But Bush and Howard persuaded China, Japan, South Korea and India, the world's biggest polluters, to sign up to the strategy.

Howard was sold on the idea by Rio Tinto's top scientist, Dr Robin Batterham, who had produced a report called *Beyond Kyoto*, arguing the viability of clean coal technology as the long-term solution to the greenhouse problem. Batterham was also the Government's chief scientist, despite complaints of a conflict of interest.

As one business leader wrote in a confidential email to his colleagues: "PM gets on well with Batterham—and has accepted his prescription as the central and (looks like) sole policy response to GHG [greenhouse gases]."

In May 2004 the resources-based companies led by Rio Tinto met Howard, his industry minister, Ian Macfarlane, and senior public servants to discuss the new greenhouse strategy. Notes of that meeting reveal Howard told them he wanted to set up a $500 million low emissions energy fund, focused on "accelerating Super Dooper [the Prime Minister's words] technology progress aimed at significantly reducing emissions".

A month later, Howard unveiled his energy white paper centred on the energy fund, which included $75 million for a solar cities project and $134 million for renewables technology. But Howard would not raise the mandatory target for renewables from 2 per cent, which would force a quicker transition to wind and solar. Nor would he put a cap on Australia's greenhouse emissions or support a carbon emissions trading scheme or a tax.

While Howard's statement was applauded by some in the resources sector, other business leaders and scientists were alarmed. "It was terrible," Pearman says. "It was just not a strategy, it was a hodgepodge of ideas. It is built on the assumption that we have plenty of time to adapt. And we don't."

But despite mounting public and business concern, Howard stuck to his strategy until last year, when, almost without warning, Australians reached a tipping point and began turning against the Government on the issue.

The seismic shift began in April, when a frustrated group of corporate leaders from the Business Roundtable on Climate Change released a report on the cost of climate change to Australia. Breaking the silence over the debate, they issued a stark warning that Government inaction would put at risk billions of dollars invested in tourism, livestock, wheat and insurance.

The report's sponsors included the head of BP Australia, Gerry Hueston, the head of Westpac, David Morgan, and the head of Insurance Australia Group, Mike Hawker, who had all worked with the Australian Conservation Foundation. They called on the Government to set up "a long, loud and legal framework" that would finally set a price in Australia for carbon dioxide pollution.

Their warning was supercharged when, just months later, Sir Nicholas Stern released his report for the British Government. Stern concluded that climate change was the greatest market failure in history and unless countries were prepared to sacrifice 1 per cent of their global wealth to mitigate the effects of climate change, the costs would be "on a scale similar to those associated with the great wars and the economic depression of the first half of the 20th century".

Adding to the pressure on Howard, the premiers released a report supporting a carbon trading system.

By late October, a rattled Howard began shifting position. He would later admit that his views on the science changed about this time. On the ABC's *Lateline* program he was asked by Tony Jones: "When was it that you ceased being a climate change sceptic and became, in effect, a true believer?" Howard replied: "I can't put an exact time on it, it wasn't a Damascus road conversion. I've always accepted that greenhouse gas emissions, carbon emissions, were potentially damaging. I think the scale of it has become more apparent as a result of the research."

At the Business Council of Australia's annual dinner last November Howard said he would set up a task group to look at carbon emissions trading—10 years after his first environment minister pushed for it.

But two days later, when he brought leaders from Rio Tinto, Woodside and Shell and some of his business critics together to discuss the idea, Howard said: "I am not going to see this country's economic advantage thrown away in some panicky response to something that may not turn out to be as bad as many people are predicting."

The task force and its advisory group is confined to business leaders, lobbyists and public servants. Already the business council and companies such as Rio Tinto have tentatively supported a trading scheme, but the devil is in the detail. Ian Dunlop, the former oil executive who first advised Hill on his scheme, is worried that unless there is a tough, mandatory cap or target for Australia's emissions, a trading scheme will not be effective.

Turnbull insists that Australia "has led the world on climate change", saying that Europe intends to follow his recent announcement that incandescent light bulbs will be phased out. Like Howard, he defends the decision not to ratify Kyoto and says Australia is one of the few countries on track to meet its Kyoto targets. But Carr points out that this is not because Australia has cut its industry emissions. It is only possible because Australia was given a breather at Kyoto by being allowed to offset emissions by stopping large-scale land clearing in Queensland and NSW. This has now run its course and Australia is about to begin an uphill battle to control rising emissions.

Since Howard reopened the debate on an emissions trading scheme, Turnbull has given it his backing, saying he has "no doubt that there will be a price on carbon". But, like Howard, he has so far refused to discuss any new emissions target. The public is not yet convinced that the Government is moving quickly enough and is questioning whether a solution worked out almost solely with industry leaders is still tenable.

Chloe Hooper

Take me to the river
The Monthly, February 2007

Twice a day, David Hill records the weather in the Mallee town of Warracknabeal, in north-western Victoria, for the Bureau of Meteorology. A tall, lean man with sandy orange hair and moustache, his weather station—latitude 36° 15' 41" S, longitude 142° 24' 18" E—is outside the Agricultural Machinery Museum. At 9 am and 3 pm he walks through a dry, dusty paddock where corellas have been scratching for seed. Raised above the ground is a white slatted box, paint peeling, padlocked and surrounded by chicken wire. It looks like a beehive, but is actually a temperature screen containing a wet-and-dry bulb thermometer, which shows the day's highest and lowest temperatures. Like some shaman of old, Hill estimates visibility, the height of the clouds, where the clouds are coming from, the direction of the wind and its speed in kilometres per hour. The bureau's customised record sheet also requires a description of "phenomena". *Circle observation known to have occurred*, it reads, before listing the following possibilities: *Hail, Snow, Thunder heard, Frost, Dust storm, Mist, Haze, Smoke, Fog, Dew, Strong wind, Gale*. Sometimes Hill circles four phenomena in the morning alone.

Then he must record the rainfall, or lack of it. The water gauge is a 30-centimetre aluminium tin set in the ground with a plastic beaker inside. As if in a Beckett sketch, Hill checks it each day, knowing there'll be no water. "It tried to rain last night," he explains, "but as the locals say, you could walk between the drops." These drops now barely register and that is how it's recorded: "trace". He believes some local children have never seen proper rain.

Inside the foyer of the museum, David Hill opens a ledger from 1969, the year the weather station opened, and says of the rainfall, "Those were the good old days." The ledger's blue pages are inscribed with neat copperplate. Victoria has about 30 manual climate stations, which are increasingly joining the ranks of the 70-plus automated stations as people such as Hill, who is 57, retire or move away. "Just like fish in a pond when it dries up, we're buggered," he says. "Once farmers are affected, towns are affected and then these small towns die in the backside."

The museum's display area is filled with wagons and harvesters and tractors from around the world. ("You can always tell who owned a certain tractor," Hill claims. "They walk in and cringe when they look at it.") The tractors, with their enormous wheels, give the visitor the sense they've shrunken and are walking through a maze of giant toys. The Mallee was named after the hardy mallee scrub that covered the region before settlement in the early twentieth century. In what was regarded as an epic battle in the cause of progress and putting the small man on the land, farmers were contractually obliged to clear as much land as fast as possible, using fire, winches, axes and horse-drawn logs. These brightly coloured machines of the '50s also pulled logs, then scrub rollers, then chains, obliterating any remaining native vegetation, and look so full of optimism you could imagine Doris Day was driving.

Leo Tellefson's family have been farming in the Mallee, near Donald, for a hundred years. "My father was given tax breaks to cut trees and I'm given tax breaks to plant them," he says. Like many of the pioneers' descendants, Tellefson, 56, is now battling chronic soil erosion and salinity, problems made worse by the lack of rain. He remembers droughts that endured for a year, perhaps two, but there was then a wet year afterwards. "There were always hot days, but not this continual dryness." Nor has he ever witnessed such a strange suite of what meteorologists now call 'weather events'. For the first time, a frost last winter killed all his grass overnight, "every blade dead". There is now no moisture in the soil. On some parts of his farm, he has to switch his ute to 4WD setting, as the ground crumbles beneath him. Tellefson, a man of preternatural enthusiasm, has been trying to find ways to boost Donald's tourism: he plans to build a giant duck on the town's fringes, possibly funded by a series of tug-of-war contests. He recently visited Melbourne for a weekend and stayed in a hotel opposite the new Southern Cross Train Station. It rained, and it was painful watching so much water falling unharnessed from the multi-million-dollar roof.

As you travel further into the scorched country, you sense and see the multiplying nature of the drought. You pass over bridges with signs marking dried-up streams and creeks. Their flow is carved into the ground, but they are gone. Three hours from the Mallee, outside Echuca, farmer Max Marchetti, 32, showed me the site of a swamp which a decade ago was home to brolgas, pink-eared ducks, straw-necked ibis, parrots and "herds" of swans. In the 1982 drought, he sent his father's cattle there to drink. *Murphy's Swamp*, the sign over a dustbowl reads.

Marchetti was driving his truck back from a nearby abattoir after unloading stock. Although he isn't a regular churchgoer, he had an old prayer card of Jesus, its edges curling, stuck to the dashboard, "to give the driver some peace", with a tiny Australian flag on a toothpick tucked inside. "Our farm, our business, our family: that's our church," he says.

Murphy's Swamp once irrigated 18 farms. It now irrigates three, including Marchetti's, but he has not seen a drop of water since June. Marchetti was "born and bred" on this land where, like a modern-day Old MacDonald, he farms cows, sheep, goats, pigs, geese and chickens. He has been trying to keep heritage breeds of pigs from becoming extinct, but the drought has suspended those ambitions. These days, he is just trying to keep his breeding stock alive, with feeding costs rising to impossible heights and "not one blade of green feed on the property".

Malcolm Turnbull, the unofficial minister for water, told the National Press Club in November, "This year the inflows into the Murray River will be only 9% of the long-term average; half the previous all-time low." "By April," Turnbull claimed,

> the mighty dams which have insulated us against the vagaries of the weather will be empty. The only water that will be available for communities and irrigators next year will be that which flows into the system over next winter and spring. There is ... a clear and present danger that the river will be dry before it finishes its course.

Max Marchetti wonders if his will be the last generation of farmers in this area. He already talks about his farm as a kind of museum:

I couldn't imagine my kids, if farming continues the way it is, becoming farmers. Most of the time, to tell you the truth, I keep the farm going to show them. I really want to show my kids a glimpse of it, and they can take it on or not, but I doubt very much they will.

During lunch in his farmhouse, where the roof has recently fallen in, Marchetti turns on the television and finds a Formula One race: speed, money, sex. In the midst of this desolation, they are like scenes from another planet. "If you can stop a man cutting down a tree," he says, staring at the images of waste on the screen, "why can't you stop this?" Marchetti and his wife have bought SingStar, a karaoke videogame, which they now take wherever they go, to have a sing-along. He's heard of half-a-dozen farmers nearby suiciding in the last six months: "It's sad to think it happens because of the weather."

In a recent editorial in the *Australian*, those "hand-ring[ers]" trying to connect the drought to global warming are ordered to "take a cold shower": "Climate change must certainly be taken seriously but consideration must be based on scientific fact and rational research." For those parties interested, that science and research is here.

On 3 January, the Bureau of Meteorology released its Annual Climate Statement, with data gathered from "a country-wide network of about 100 high-quality, mostly rural observing stations" (it did not include Warracknabeal) and the Volunteer Rainfall Network, a group of more than 5000 Australians who provide the bureau with their rainfall measurements. The bureau announced that "Parts of Southeast Australia experienced their driest year on record, including key catchment areas which feed the Murray and Snowy Rivers, as did parts of the Western Australian coast, including Perth." Temperatures were again nearly half a degree above average, although this was our warmest spring on record, with temperatures 1.42°C above average, and for much of inland NSW it was "as warm or warmer than 2005", our hottest year on record. Paradoxically, in Australia's north-west, the weather was wetter and cooler, with a rain belt stretching from the Pilbara to the Nullarbor. The bureau's senior climatologist, Neil Plummer, says, "Most scientists agree this is part of an enhanced greenhouse effect."

Blair Trewin, from the bureau's National Climate Centre, told me that although an El Niño in the Pacific Ocean had been a dominant cause of the 2006 drought, with some Victorian regions having experienced nearly ten years of "rainfall anomalies", "we are now in unexplored territory." The bureau believes we are seeing the effects of climate change. Dr Trewin says they are less confident talking about other areas of the country, specifically the Murray Darling, in such terms, but that is the conclusion they are leaning towards.

The World Meteorological Organisation announced in December that initial estimates suggest 2006 was the sixth-hottest year since records commenced in 1861. (The ten hottest recorded years worldwide have taken place in the last 12 years.) The WMO's report makes for grim reading: record heatwaves in Australia, Brazil, Europe and the US; prolonged drought in Australia, parts of the Greater Horn of Africa, China, Brazil and the US; severe and historic flooding significantly damaging food stocks, displacing hundreds of thousands of people and leading to landslides; deadly typhoons and cyclones bringing economic losses of US$10 billion to China alone; a 20% depletion of the ozone layer over the Arctic, and the largest ever hole over the Antarctic (29.5 million square kilometres); sea ice declining at the rate of 8.59% per decade or 60,421 square kilometres per year.

Time was, even just a year ago, when sophisticated people, if they noticed the weather at all, thought it much too banal to talk about. But as every day brings news of melting glaciers, shrinking Greenland, coral bleaching, mammoth bushfires, cataclysms or portents of cataclysms, no other subject, including sport, can keep the weather out for long. The effects of global warming are exponential: for a long time, climatic changes seem negligible, then suddenly they appear apocalyptic. Britain's Meteorological Office is already predicting that 2007 will be the hottest year on record.

You would think, with the great song and dance Australians make about the bush, that its survival would be reason alone to make tackling climate change our first priority. Standing in parts of Victoria, the ground now looks blasted, like the site of a battle—which it once was. It was a great battle to clear these lands, one that took heroic labour. The frontier story is a story of surviving drought, and then the rain. The tale is cyclical, elemental. Of course it will rain again. But farmers wonder if it will ever rain again *the way it used to*. They fear the cycle is broken and with it, the story of the Bush. As Max Marchetti says, "The last ten years our rainfall has slowly diminished, but the last five have just been murder, like being shot at. Only nature can win."

Bob Carter

It's good sense to avoid consensus on global warming
The Australian, 10 July 2007

Al Gore's film *An Inconvenient Truth* was launched in May last year. Its message is that global warming is going to roon us all, and the polar bears, too. Initially, the film received eulogistic—and, one might say, generally scientifically ignorant—reviews in substantial newspapers and magazines globally.

As it came to be watched by qualified persons, devastating critiques of the looseness of the film's science began to appear on the internet. More than 20 basic errors, some of them schoolboy howlers, were identified.

From his film, Gore seemed to have lived his life on an imaginary planet where natural change didn't exist, and all change was anyway morally bad. Yet the official science community, represented for example by members of the UN's Intergovernmental Panel on Climate Change, welcomed the film. The public continued to flock to its screening, and platoons of Julie Andrews clones in dirndl skirts danced and sang in the Alpine meadows.

In March, British television's Channel 4 screened another film about climate change that had a different message.

Made by Martin Durkin, and called *The Great Global Warming Swindle*, this documentary explores the science of climate-change alarmism carefully and accurately. The message of *Swindle*, which is to be screened on the ABC this week, is that scientific knowledge does not identify carbon dioxide emissions as an environmental harm, nor does their accrual in the atmosphere cause dangerous warming.

So how is the screening of Durkin's thought-provoking film being received?

Interestingly, in the case of the *Bulletin of the Australian Meteorological and Oceanographic Society*, which published a highly critical film review written by several high-ranking IPCC scientists. As well as six other critical reviews written in response to the British screening of *Swindle*, the BAMOS paper has been widely circulated in influential circles ahead of the Australian screening. For instance, through the deans of science at universities, through the influential lobby organisation the Federation of Australian Scientific and Technological Societies, and through the Australian Marine Sciences Association, among others.

Imagine a well-provendered and equipped military fortress in time of war, for that is what the alarmist, pro-IPCC, climate lobby group represents. Suddenly, loping across the landscape outside the fort, and carrying just a single-shot rifle, appears a lone member of the enemy army.

Does the camp commander respond by sending out a platoon, including a psychologist with a megaphone to check what this naive infantryman is up to? Not on your nelly. Instead, the response is remarkable in its ferocity.

Three panzer divisions come tearing out of the fort—manned, as it happens, by many distinguished scientists who have volunteered for their politically correct duty of suppressing alternative views—blazing away with all they've got. In a trice, the landscape is turned into a moonscape, pockmarked with craters and littered with debris.

Why does this lone gunman represent such a threat to the warmaholic camp? Does it perhaps relate to the fact that on closer inspection several sections of the fortress wall are sagging, undermined by collapse from below and within? How could a lone gunman have effected that? Is it just possible that there are more powerful forces on earth than military and industrial might, or scientific authority? White ants, perhaps; or even scientific logic?

In any event, our lone infantryman is now wandering around, dazed, dirty, half-blinded, and staggering on the rim of a crater; and not a dirndl skirt in sight.

But he's still standing. He miraculously still has four limbs, and what he is saying—that human carbon dioxide emissions are not an environmental hazard—still accords with all the facts and makes complete sense.

For you see, science is not about the triumph of the weight of numbers, nor about consensus, nor about the will of the social majority. An idea such as the greenhouse hypothesis is validated not by shouting but by experimental and observational testing and logical analysis.

And note especially that a hypothesis doesn't care who believes in it, right up to and including environment ministers, heads of state and presidents of distinguished scientific academies. Rather, science requires that to be successful a hypothesis only needs to be clearly stated, understandable, have explanatory power and withstand testing.

It takes one person, not an army, to accomplish that, and the names of those individuals pass down through history: Charles Darwin, Wilhelm Roentgen, Marie Curie, Albert Einstein, Robin Warren and Barry Marshall and their like, mavericks one and all. God bless them.

Despite this reality, every day we find public figures on Australian TV and radio stations muttering about there being "a consensus" on dangerous, human-caused climate change, or that the science of global warming "is settled". Such persons should be referred to the nearest psychologist, and gently dissuaded from inflicting their nonsense—for that is what it is—on the poor public.

Science is never settled, and it is about hypothesis testing against known facts, not arm-waving about imaginary futures that have been created by PlayStation 4 computer buffs. Consensus nonsensus.

Oh, and by the way, it turns out that our infantryman's name wasn't Einstein. It was Durkin. Martin Durkin, and what a service he has rendered.

Clive Hamilton

Who's being swindled here?
New Matilda, 11 July 2007

A few years ago the ABC screened a two-part British documentary about environmentalism entitled *Against Nature*. According to the publicity material, the documentary characterised 'environmentalist ideology as unscientific, irrational and anti-humanist.'

Against Nature created a furore after it was broadcast in Britain, not least for its extraordinary claims that modern environmentalism has its roots in Nazi Germany and that self-interested environmentalists are responsible for enormous suffering in the Third World.

Of course, there is nothing wrong with a documentary that challenges accepted views about the need to protect the environment, including global warming, but *Against Nature* was a series of distortions rather than a sceptical commentary.

Employing a range of editorial devices designed to exclude debate and inflame passions, the program fell well short of accepted journalistic standards. It contrasted images of Third World children dying of horrible illnesses with commentary about how environmentalists oppose dams that would bring clean water and electricity, with the aim of portraying them as callous fanatics.

For example, environmentalists were blamed for preventing construction of the Narmada Dam, although the dam was actually stopped by the Indian Supreme Court after a protest campaign by local residents who would have been displaced by it.

While the affiliations of the environmentalists were shown, the anti-environmentalists were presented as independent experts. One of the most authoritative voices, Fred Singer, was a well-known greenhouse sceptic who today heads an organisation supported by oil companies.

It was as if the ABC were to screen a program reporting on a doctor arguing that smoking does no harm, yet failing to mention that he had been funded by the tobacco industry.

The screening of *Against Nature* here and in the UK was a considerable coup for Right-wing groups that view environmentalism as a threat to capitalism and freedom. But the most remarkable feature of the documentary emerged only after it was shown in Britain. It was revealed that the program makers were linked to an obscure political group named the Revolutionary Communist Party (RCP).

A Trotskyist splinter group, the RCP published a controversialist journal titled *Living Marxism* (later *LM Magazine*), which frequently ran bitter attacks on environmentalism, describing it as a middle-class indulgence or a neo-colonial smoke-screen.

The journal also took contrarian positions on international issues, including opposing sanctions against the apartheid regime in South Africa, support for the Bosnian Serb forces and the Hutu militias and opposition to the ban on land mines.

Several of the people interviewed in *Against Nature* had links to *LM Magazine* and the RCP. The producer and director of the documentary, Martin Durkin, also had close links to the Party.

All of this would be history except for one fact. Martin Durkin is also the writer and director of *The Great Global Warming Swindle*, the documentary that will be screened by the ABC on 12 July.

Durkin has a sorry history. After *Against Nature* was screened in Britain the television regulator pressured Channel 4 into broadcasting an apology because the film distorted or misrepresented the views of environmentalists and scientists who had been persuaded to appear on it.

In another Durkin documentary promoting genetic engineering, two scientists complained that their views had been misrepresented with one saying she felt 'completely betrayed and misled.' A researcher hired to work on a Durkin documentary arguing that breast implants are good for women resigned saying that the program makers had ignored the facts and made misleading claims.

Sure enough, some of those who appeared in *The Great Global Warming Swindle* felt cheated. Professor Carl Wunsch, a leading researcher on ocean circulation and climate, wrote: 'I feel angry because they completely misrepresented me.'

The Times reported that when two eminent scientists collaborating with Durkin on his next film emailed him with concerns about the way the science was presented in *Swindle* they received an expletive-filled tirade. Dr Armand Leroi, from Imperial College London, was called a 'big daft cock' and told to 'go and f*** yourself.'

Durkin has been forced to cut his latest documentary by a third, taking out the more scandalous and indefensible claims.

As for the various 'facts' in *Swindle* put forward to support the thesis that global warming is a giant conspiracy carried out by scientists who want to boost their research funding—every one of those 'facts' has been refuted by eminent scientists. For example:

- the idea that the troposphere has warmed less than the Earth's surface (which would be inconsistent with global warming) emerged in the 1990s but was shown to be based on some incorrect data measurements;
- the claim that volcanic eruptions emit more carbon dioxide than burning fossil fuels is simply untrue; and
- the central contention of the documentary—that the observed warming is due to increased solar activity—has been thoroughly considered and rejected by the consensus process of climate scientists.

The concoction of scientific distortions in *Swindle* led Britain's most prestigious scientific organisation, The Royal Society, to respond publicly by declaring: 'Those who promote fringe scientific views but ignore the weight of evidence are playing a dangerous game.'

Durkin and the other climate denialists hide behind the respectable veil of scientific scepticism. But there is a sharp distinction between healthy scepticism and cynical manipulation of the facts. *Swindle* is not a contribution to scientific debate but dangerous mischief-making in an area where the stakes could not be higher. According to the world's best scientists, if we do nothing millions of people in poor countries will die from crop failures and diseases attributable to human-induced global warming.

Durkin's intervention is not just controversialist; it is political vandalism. The objective is to wreck the fragile progress on climate change with no regard for the suffering it may cause.

In defending his decision to purchase *Swindle*, the ABC's director of television, Kim Dalton, claimed that we should be listening to 'a full range of views.' Does he really believe that? Would the ABC broadcast the lunatic conspiracy theories of American activist Lyndon LaRouche in order to 'hear all voices'? Incidentally, the LaRouche organisation loves *Swindle* and is actively promoting it on university campuses. They understand the ideological purpose of the film, as do the denialists on the ABC Board.

In making judgements about documentary programs shouldn't Dalton require a modicum of credibility and adherence to minimal journalistic standards, as well as looking for good entertainment? If a director is known to have a history of bitter complaints from people he has interviewed, and been censured by the regulators for dishonest practices, does that not ring an alarm bell in today's ABC?

In truth, the programmers at the ABC have been conned by a very clever propagandist. *Swindle* is not about the science, it is a malevolent ideological intervention. If it were to succeed in its goal it would result in enormous avoidable suffering and those who promote or facilitate the documentary would all share in the culpability.

Richard Flanagan

Out of control: The tragedy of Tasmania's forests
The Monthly, May 2007

This story begins with a Tasmanian man fern (*Dicksonia antarctica*) for sale in a London nursery. Along with the healthy price tag, some £160, is a note: "This tree fern has been salvage harvested in accordance with a management plan approved by the Governments of Tasmania and the Commonwealth of Australia." If you were to believe both governments, that plan ensures that Tasmania has a sustainable logging industry—one which, according to the federal minister responsible for forests, Eric Abetz, is "the best managed in the world".

The truth is otherwise. The man fern—possibly several centuries old—comes from native forests destroyed by a logging industry that was recently found to be illegal by the Federal Court of Australia. It comes either from primeval rainforest that has been evolving for millennia or from wet eucalypt forests, some of which contain the mighty *Eucalyptus regnans*. These aptly named kings of trees are the tallest hardwood trees and flowering plants on Earth; some are more than 20 metres in girth and 90 metres in height. The forests are being destroyed in Tasmania, in spite of widespread community opposition and increasing international concern.

Clearfelling, as the name suggests, first involves the complete felling of a forest by chainsaws and skidders. Then, the whole area is torched, the firing started by helicopters dropping incendiary devices made of jellied petroleum, commonly known as napalm. The resultant fire is of such ferocity it produces mushroom clouds visible from considerable distances. In consequence, every autumn, the island's otherwise most beautiful season, china-blue skies are frequently nicotine-scummed, an inescapable reminder that clearfelling means the total destruction of ancient and unique forests. At its worst, the smoke from these burn-offs has led to the closure of schools, highways and tourist destinations.

In the Styx Valley, in the south-west, the world's last great unprotected stands of old-growth *Eucalyptus regnans* are being reduced to piles of smouldering ash. Over 85% of Tasmania's old-growth *regnans* forests are gone, and it is estimated that fewer than 13,000 hectares of these extraordinary trees remain in their old-growth form. Almost half of them are to be clearfelled. Most will end up as paper in Japan.

In logging coupes around Tasmania, exotic rainforest trees such as myrtle, sassafras, leatherwood and celery-top pine—extraordinary, exquisite trees, many centuries old, some of which are found nowhere else—are often just left on the ground and burnt.

The hellish landscape that results from clearfelling—akin to a Great War battlefield—is generally turned into large monocultural plantations of either radiata pine or *Eucalyptus nitens*, sustained by such a heavy program of fertilisers and pesticides that water sources for some local communities have been contaminated by Atrazine, a controversial herbicide linked with cancer and banned in much of Europe. Blue-dyed carrots soaked in 1080 poison are laid on private plantations to kill native grazing animals that pose a threat to tree seedlings. The slaughter that results sees not only possums, wallabies and kangaroos die slowly, in agony, but other species—including wombats, bettongs and potoroos—killed in large numbers, despite being officially protected species.

In 2003 an ageing forester, Bill Manning, was subpoenaed to testify in front of an Australian Senate committee investigating the Tasmanian forestry industry. He methodically began to unravel a tale of environmental catastrophe, of industry connivance and government complicity. His detailed evidence suggested that the forestry industry was not only systematically destroying unique forests, but poisoning the very fabric of Tasmanian politics and life.

No greenie hardliner, Manning was a man who worked for 30 years in the Tasmanian forests and who believes they ought to be logged, but logged so that they remain for the future. Yet he alleged to the Senate committee that forestry management had been corrupted. At the hearing, he painted a picture of illegal destruction on a scale so vast that it was transforming the landscape of Tasmania. Branding what was happening "an ecological disaster", Manning talked of how an "accelerated and unaccountable logging industry" was destroying wholesale native forests "which are unique in the world for their flora and fauna". "The clearfelling is out of control," he told the senators. "The scale of clearfelling in Tasmania is huge."

A whispering campaign about Bill Manning's state of mind began, and in the four years since he ended a career that he loved, by standing up for what he believed, nothing has changed—except for the worse. Today, Tasmania is the only Australian state that clearfells its rainforests. While the rest of Australia has either ended, or is ending, the logging of old-growth forests, Tasmania is the only state where it is secretly planned to accelerate the destruction of native forests, driven by the greed for profit that can be made from woodchips.

As with any epidemic of madness, there sometimes seems no end to the horror. Among Tasmania's many unique plants and animals is the endangered giant freshwater crayfish, one of the largest invertebrates in the world. Although technically protected, its very future is threatened by the frenzy of logging surrounding the creeks where it lives. When a government-appointed expert panel recommended buffer zones of forest be preserved to protect the crayfish, these zones were reduced to a bare minimum, and the areas continue to be logged. "Clearfelling is going on at an incredible rate in their habitat," the crayfish expert Todd Walsh says. "It's going berserk."

Tasmania is an extraordinary land, one that many hoped might become, in the words of the legendary landscape photographer Olegas Truchanas, "a shining beacon in a dull, uniform and largely artificial world". Its remoteness, its wildness, its unique natural world—all seemed to offer the possibility of a prosperous and good future to a state that had for a century been the poorest in the Australian Commonwealth. Instead, over the past three decades Tasmania has mortgaged its future to the woodchipping industry, which is today dominated by one company: Gunns Ltd. And it is Gunns—not the Tasmanian people—that has been the beneficiary of the destruction of Tasmania's unique forests.

Though Gunns was founded in Tasmania in 1875, it was not until 1989, when it became part of the written history of corruption in Tasmania, that many Australians first came to hear of the company, then still one of several Tasmanian timber firms. In that year the then chairman of Gunns, Eddie Rouse, became concerned that the election of a Labor–Green Tasmanian government with a one-seat majority might affect his logging profits. Rouse attempted to bribe a Labor member, Jim Cox, to cross the floor, thereby bringing down the government and clearing the way for the pro-logging former premier Robin Gray and the Liberal Party to resume power. Cox went to the police and the plot was exposed; a royal commission and Rouse's fall from grace and imprisonment ensued. But Gunns continued. Today it is a corporation worth more than a billion dollars, the largest company in Tasmania, with an effective monopoly of the island's hardwood logging, and a darling of the Australian stock market.

Yet Gunns remains haunted by the Rouse scandal. The company's board continues to have among its directors former associates of the late Eddie Rouse. The 1991 royal commission found that director David McQuestin, whose friendship with Rouse it characterised as "obsequious", was not "unlawfully involved as a principal offender" with the bribery attempt, although his "compliance with Rouse's direction in the matter was 'highly improper'"—a "glaring breach of the requisite standards of commercial morality". Robin Gray is also now a director of Gunns; the royal commission found that he "knew of and was involved with Rouse in Rouse's attempt to bribe Cox", and that while his conduct was not unlawful, it was "improper, and grossly so". John Gay, Gunns' managing director in 1989 and now its managing director and executive chairman, was cleared by the royal commission of any involvement with the bribery attempt.

In a dissembling world ever more given to corporate deference to a green image, the company shows an often-unexpected candour. Gunns makes no secret of its enmity towards conservationists and conservation groups. Gunns plans to destroy more, rather than less, Tasmanian native forest. Gunns makes no apologies for what this means. "How do you feel about protected species dying for your business?" John Gay was once asked on national television. "Well, there's too many of them," he replied, "and we need to keep them at a reasonable level." And while the figures for total woodchip production since 2000 are officially secret—like so much else in Tasmania—Gunns' own evidence in support of the pulp mill it proposes for the north of the state reveals that the company plans to double woodchipping, from its present annual levels of approximately 3.5 million tonnes to 7 million tonnes over the next decade.

To evade the ever-growing public anger, the woodchipping industry has had to exercise an ever-stronger control over Tasmanian life. Both major parties in Tasmania, and much of the state's media, frequently give the appearance of existing only as clients of the woodchippers. The state's interest and that of the woodchipping industry are now so thoroughly identified as one and the same that anyone questioning the industry's actions is attacked by leading government figures as a traitor to Tasmania. And it is not only the forests that have been destroyed by this industry. Its poison has seeped into every aspect of Tasmanian life: jobs are threatened, careers destroyed, people driven to leave. And in recent years, its influence has extended further, so that now its activities are endorsed nationally by both the prime minister, John Howard, and the Opposition leader, Kevin Rudd.

Huge money is being made out of destroying native forests, but to maintain what to many is an obscene practice there has evolved a culture of secrecy, shared interest and intimidation that seems to firmly bind the powerful in Tasmania. When the actress Rebecca Gibney, who moved to Tasmania two years ago to raise her family, said in a television interview that she would leave the state if Gunns' proposed pulp mill was built, the former Liberal Party candidate and bottle-shop owner Sam McQuestin made headlines by publicly attacking her as a "serial complainer" whose family made no contribution to the Tasmanian economy and who had no "right to tell the rest of us how to live our lives". McQuestin's family is well known for its contribution: his father, David, is a Gunns director. The attack on Rebecca Gibney was but a public example of something far more widespread and insidious. I witnessed a senior ALP politician make it clear that yet another Tasmanian was no longer welcome in the clearfelling state when the local corporate-communications consultant Gerard Castles wrote an article in a newspaper questioning the government's policy on old-growth logging. "The fucking little cunt is finished," the politician said in front of me and my 12-year-old daughter. "He will never work here again."

To question, to comment adversely, is to invite the possibility of ostracism and unemployment, and the state is full of those who pay a high price for their opinion on the forests, the blackballed multiplying with the blackened stumps. It is commonplace to meet people who are too frightened to speak publicly of their concerns about forestry practices, because of the adverse consequences they perceive this might have for their careers and businesses. Due to the forest battle, a subtle (and sometimes not-so-subtle) fear has entered Tasmanian public life; it stifles dissent, avoids truth.

And how can it be otherwise? The great majority of Tasmanians appear to be overwhelmingly opposed to old-growth logging, and only by the constant crushing of opposing points of view, and the attempted silencing and smearing of those who put them, can the practice continue. And so, nearly two decades after its then chairman failed in his attempt to corrupt the state parliament, Gunns now seems so powerful that Tasmanians joke that their government is the 'gunnerment', and leading national politicians of all persuasions acknowledge that the real power in Tasmania is not the government but Gunns itself.

This goes further than the sizeable donations Gunns makes to both major parties, both in Tasmania and nationally. It goes beyond Gunns' role in election campaigns, such as the $486,000 spent on aggressive political advertising in the 2004 federal election by the Forest Industries Association of Tasmania (FIAT), of which Gunns is the largest member. "A lot of people are intimidated by the employment side of the [Tasmanian forestry] industry," the prominent Liberal Senator Bill Heffernan, from New South Wales, has said, "including some politicians."

But who can blame even the powerful for being scared? The former Tasmanian Liberal leader Bob Cheek recalls how "the state's misguided forestry policy was ruthlessly policed by Gunns", how fearful the politicians were of the forest lobby and what he describes as their "hitmen". In a cowed society, the Tasmanian government often gives the impression of being little more than a toadying standover man for its corporate godfather, willing to undertake any action, no matter how degrading, to help those with the real power.

When, in 2004, the Wyena farmers Howard and Michelle Carpenter had themselves and their property directly sprayed by a helicopter with Atrazine meant for an adjacent Gunns plantation, poisoning their water supply, Gunns' only response was to send the couple two bottles of spring water. Later, when the story became a public scandal, they provided the Carpenters with a water tank which a few months later they removed, though the Carpenter's water bore remained poisoned. To reassure the public that there was no cause for concern, the then water minister, Steve Kons, fronted a media conference at which he loyally drank a glass of water tainted with Atrazine. Steve Kons is now Tasmania's deputy premier.

According to the former federal Labor leader Mark Latham, "They [Gunns] run the state Labor Government, they run [Labor Premier] Lennon ... and old Lennon there, he wouldn't scratch himself unless the guy who heads up Gunns told him to." Latham would know: after all, his own bid to be prime minister ended when he came up against Gunns in the 2004 election. Latham was no conservationist, but the growing national outcry over Tasmania's forests, driven by a long campaign by conservation groups, led him in the week before the election to propose a bold plan to end the logging of the island's old-growth forests, a plan that included an $800-million compensation package for logging workers. Quite extraordinarily, the package was rejected by Tasmanian Labor.

Two days later, the Liberal prime minister, John Howard, flew into Tasmania to announce the indefinite continuation of old-growth logging, along with more extensive subsidies to the logging industry and, as a sop to the green vote, the protection of some areas of old growth. A few areas were victories. Much was a con: areas that were either already reserved; or, as Terry Edwards of FIAT admitted about the north Styx, very difficult to log; or, as in the Weld or the Florentine, later—in an act of arch cynicism—to be logged anyway.

In the most extraordinary images of that election, Howard was cheered by 2000 logging workers at a rally in Launceston, supported by the powerful Construction, Forest, Mining and Energy Union (CFMEU). Within the week Howard would be returned to government, and within a year some of those same workers would be forced out of the industry by Gunns breaking contracts, and looking for new employment in a workforce ravaged by the toughest anti-union laws in Australia's history—introduced by the man they had cheered on to victory.

"We seem to get on better with the Liberals than we do with Labor at the moment," Tasmania's premier, Paul Lennon, told a journalist a few weeks after federal Labor had suffered one of its worst defeats.

The conservationists had foundered and, with Howard's crushing victory, Gunns now had a federal government that felt electorally rewarded for taking the company's side. Gunns had too a state government so committed to it that seemingly no issue in Tasmania could be decided without first being held up to see whether it was good or bad for the old-growth logging industry. And it left federal Labor so terrified of ever touching the issue again that when Kevin Rudd assumed the leadership of the party in 2006, one of his first actions was to express support for the Tasmanian logging industry. But then, as Mark Latham ruefully admitted, "No policy issue or set of relationships better demonstrates the ethical decline and political corruption of the Australian Labor movement than Tasmanian forestry."

The dogs were off the leash and Gunns was now at its most powerful. Within months it made a move that was widely viewed as an attempt to cripple the conservation movement, the last remaining impediment to its ambitions. On 14 December 2004, Gunns filed a 216-page, $6.3-million claim against a group of conservationists and organisations who became known as the Gunns 20. The writ was an extraordinary document that sought to sue a penniless grandmother who had opposed logging in her district; a national political leader, Senator Bob Brown; a doctor who had raised public-health concerns about woodchip piles; prominent conservationists; Australia's leading wilderness-conservation organisation, the Wilderness Society; a film-maker; and several day protesters.

All were joined in what was alleged to be a conspiracy guilty of the crime of corporate vilification. The writ presented a tale of a group of people together seeking, through a series of actions as diverse as protesters chaining themselves to logging machinery to the lobbying of Japanese paper companies, to destroy Gunns' profits. The perversity of the action was staggering: with the immense fortune it had made out of destroying Tasmania's forests, Gunns had launched an action that would, if success-ful, have redefined the practice of democracy as the crime of conspiracy.

An Australian would not have been able to criticise, question or campaign against a corporation, for risk of being bankrupted in legal proceedings brought against them by the richest and most powerful in their society, claiming damage to their corporate interest. No matter how a corporation made its money, be it from tobacco or asbestos or chemicals, all of its actions would have effectively been removed from the realm of public life. Gunns' action was compared with the legal standover tactics that prevails in such countries as Singapore, where those engaged in political opposition are bankrupted and then jailed through such a process of litigation.

If its legal ramifications were enormous but unrealised, its political impact was immediate. While the writ excited a national outcry, garnering comparisons with the McLibel case, in the short term it only served to further intimidate many in Tasmania, and tied up the leading conservation groups and conservationists in a difficult, expensive and all-consuming court case at a moment when Gunns was planning its most controversial action of all. Two days after it issued the writ, Gunns announced its plans for a gigantic $1.4-billion pulp mill, the biggest infrastructure project in Tasmania's history and one of the biggest pulp mills in the world, to be built 36 kilometres from Launceston.

At first, reassuring commitments were given that Gunns' pulp mill would be environmentally friendly: chlorine-free and primarily using plantation timber. Premier Lennon was adamant that the mill would only go ahead if Gunns could prove to an independent government body, the Resource and Planning Development Commission (RPDC), that their proposal conformed to the world's best environmental standards. The process was to be above politics and the RPDC's decision final. But public concern began to grow when it became clear that Gunns was planning something entirely different to what it had originally announced. Gunns now wanted to build a kraft chlorine-bleaching mill—the type that produce dioxins, some of the most toxic substances known to man—fuelled initially by 80% native-forest woodchips.

Then was revealed the shocking news that to feed the pulp mill's gargantuan appetite, Gunns had negotiated a deal (the exact details of which remain secret) with the then Tasmanian forests minister, Bryan Green, that would double the level of woodchipping and accelerate the ongoing destruction of Tasmania's native forests for the next 20 years. (In October 2006 Bryan Green was charged with conspiracy over another secret deal, this time with a building accreditation company run by ex-Labor ministers. He denies any wrongdoing and the case continues.)

At the same time, Tasmanians discovered that while the mill was being assessed Paul Lennon was using a wholly owned subsidiary of Gunns, the construction company Hinman, Wright & Manser, to renovate his historic home. It was a curious choice of builder. Hinman, Wright & Manser is known to be less than enthusiastic in its support of unionised labour, and to be a keen proponent of the Howard government's new workplace-relations laws, of which Lennon had publicly been a vociferous critic. More remarkably, the Gunns "construction division" as it is termed on Gunns' website, is an industrial- and civil-works company that advertises itself as specialising in "larger construction work" such as mines, warehouses, concrete plants, schools, courts, remand centres, nursing homes, hospitals, reservoirs, substations, wharf berths, road bridges and woodchip mills, but makes no mention of home renovation.

Lennon has never answered questions put at the time about what Hinman, Wright & Manser originally quoted for the job, nor whether there were other quotes. Lennon and Gunns have both subsequently said that Lennon paid for the renovations, though the precise sum has never been revealed. Lennon dismissed any questions on the matter as a painful attack on his family's privacy.

The revelations that have since ensued have not been so easily dismissed. In early January 2007, the head of the RPDC pulp-mill inquiry, Julian Green, and the inquiry's leading scientific advisor and a national pulp-mill expert, Dr Warwick Raverty, both resigned, both citing political interference. It has become public knowledge that the RPDC found Gunns' own evidence to be riddled with inaccuracies and errors; that levels of dioxins in the mill's outflow were initially underestimated by a factor of 45; and that the mill, as well as failing to address the concerns of the Australian Medical Association (AMA) about ultra-fine particle pollution, also significantly failed to meet at least three official air-pollution guidelines. Senior scientists questioned Gunns' claims that the 64,000 tonnes of treated effluent pouring daily from the mill into the ocean would not harm Bass

Strait and its marine life. Gunns' modelling for air pollution in the Tamar Valley was so shoddy that it sometimes fantastically predicted that air pollution would be lower with a pulp mill than without.

Pointing out that "no other pulp mill in the world uses the process Gunns proposes," and that its noxious emissions would pour into a densely populated valley already subject to the worst smog in Tasmania, Raverty has since warned that "the risk of producing unacceptable levels of deadly and persistent chemicals known as organochlorines is too high." Raverty, who works for a subsidiary of the CSIRO and has consistently pointed out that he is speaking in a personal capacity about the mill's pollution risk, has claimed that a Gunns executive rang the CSIRO seeking to pressure the organisation into silencing him. The CSIRO has confirmed that Gunns "expressed concerns". Raverty has since said he would welcome the opportunity to appear before a criminal-justice commission or a royal commission into the process, because there needs to be public scrutiny of the "very unethical activities" of the Tasmanian government.

Though the Tasmanian chapter of the AMA warned Tasmania's political leaders that they would be personally accountable for any health problems resulting from the proposed pulp mill, the leaders were listening not to such dire concerns but rather to the Gunns board, with whom Premier Lennon and his kitchen cabinet met on 25 February. Two days later, Gunns told the Australian Stock Exchange it was "confident the necessary government approvals" for its pulp mill "will be obtained within a timeframe which maintains the commercial value of the project".

That same day, Paul Lennon handed the newly appointed head of the RPDC's pulp-mill assessment panel, the former Supreme Court judge Christopher Wright, a typed timeline laying out his demands. "It was plain as the nose on my face," Wright later said, "that he was trying to please Gunns." Describing it as a "completely inappropriate ... attempt to pressure" him, Wright rejected what he termed an "ultimatum" by Lennon to dump public hearings and wind up the assessment by 31 July or face the RPDC being dumped in favour of legislation fast-tracking the process.

And when a fortnight later Gunns withdrew from the RPDC assessment process, blaming delays which John Gay termed "commercially unacceptable", what was commercially acceptable to Gunns became a political imperative for the Tasmanian government.

That Christopher Wright said most of the delays were Gunns' fault was of no consequence. For in a manner that at least is understandable if onerous to Tasmanians, it is clear that in Tasmania Gunns more or less is the law. The woodchippers and their government cronies constantly use the courts against conservationists, but when the courts are used against them the government's response is admirably straightforward: change the law. They changed the law, for example, when Bob Brown sold almost everything he had and took both the Tasmanian and the federal governments to court to prove that under their own laws the logging industry in Tasmania was illegal, because it threatened the survival of endangered species, including the Tasmanian wedge-tailed eagle and the swift parrot. He won, but the government's response was not to enforce the Tasmanian Regional Forest Agreement to protect those species, but simply to alter it so that logging is once again legal.

Faced with the possibility that the pulp mill might not now meet the RPDC pollution guidelines, Paul Lennon simply rushed an act through parliament to establish an entirely new process that seems certain to ensure the mill will be approved by the end of August this year. Though this contradicted what Lennon had so dogmatically maintained for the previous two years about an impartial process that was above politics, the act (drafted with the input of a Gunns lawyer) tellingly allows for the mill to no longer meet the original pollution guidelines. Public consultation has been dispensed with and, most remarkably—and possibly without precedent in the annals of Westminster legislation—the act explicitly provides that the mill will still go ahead even if it is proven that the consultant assessing the project has been bribed.

It had been uncharacteristic of Lennon to even pretend a process mattered more than an outcome, and it seemed cynicism more of a piece with his predecessor, the late Jim Bacon. A one time Maoist, an upper-middle-class alumni of one of Australia's most exclusive private schools, Melbourne's Scotch College, and later, of one of its most infamous unions, the Victorian Builders' Labourer's Federation (BLF), Bacon was for several years a loyal lieutenant of the BLF's leader, the notorious Norm Gallagher. By the time Gallagher was jailed for taking bribes from developers and his union the subject of a royal commission that led to its deregistration, Bacon was ensconced in Tasmania, where the old BLF tactics of espousing a working-class rhetoric while cosying up to the powerful served him well. In 1997 he became leader of the Tasmanian Labor Party.

The following year Bacon was instrumental in brokering the deal that saw the very electoral basis of the Tasmanian parliament altered. Since the 1970s, when the world's first green party was formed in Tasmania, the Greens had been a powerful political minority in Tasmania, securing up to a seventh of parliamentary seats under the island's unique proportional representation system and with it, on occasion, the balance of power.

The 1998 deal was sold to the public as a common-sense measure to reduce the number of parliamentary members. But it was intensely political in effect, because having fewer parliamentarians meant that a higher quota was required by an individual to be elected, thus making it harder for minority parties to win seats and possibly destroying future Green representation—and with it the only real opposition to the woodchipping industry. The former Liberal leader Bob Cheek recalls how Robin Gray, the state's premier in the '80s and now a member of Gunns' board, lobbied him on the night before the vote on the reform. "We've got to stop the Greens, Bob," Gray told him. And they did.

The subsequent election in August 1998 saw the Greens decimated and Jim Bacon's Labor Party triumphant. The Bacon government quickly established itself as the most pro-big-business government Tasmania had ever had. Favoured companies received extraordinary treatment. The privately owned Federal Hotels group, who run the island's two casinos, was awarded a 15-year gaming monopoly—conservatively estimated by Citigroup to be worth $130 million in licensing revenues—free of charge.

But the greatest winner was Gunns. Its shares were languishing at $1.40 when the Bacon government came to power. The company's subsequent growth was dizzying. Within four years, it had recorded an increase of 199% in profits. With the acquisition of two rival companies, Gunns took control of more than 85% of logging in Tasmania. Five years after Bacon won government Gunns was worth more than $1 billion, with shares trading in excess of $12. It had become both the largest logging company in Australia and the largest hardwood-woodchip exporter in the world, its product flooding in from the state's fallen forests.

The state government, which a century ago paid people to shoot the Tasmanian tiger, now provided every incentive to destroy old-growth forest. One of Bacon's first acts was to make 85,000 hectares of previously "deferred forest" available for logging. Gunns paid only paltry royalties to Forestry Tasmania, the public body charged with getting a commercial return from the crown forests that were the very basis of Gunns' record profits. When in 2003 Gunns posted an after-tax profit of $74 million, Forestry Tasmania made a hardly impressive $20 million. By 2005, when Gunns' after-tax profit had soared to $101.3 million, Forestry Tasmania's profit had slumped to $13.5 million. Its projected profit for 2006–07 is break-even: a return of zero dollars, nothing, to Tasmanian taxpayers on the estimated $700-million value of its publicly owned forest estate.

But it wasn't just that public forestry resources were being systematically handed over to a single company's shareholders; it was that much of Gunns' profits were coming out of taxpayers' pockets. On private land, Gunns made a second profit from the federal tax breaks that made tree plantations—with which clearfelled native forests were replaced—one of corporate Australia's favourite forms of tax minimisation from the late '90s.

On top of all this, Bacon's government accelerated a familiar pattern of ongoing handouts to an industry that constantly shed jobs, devastated the environment and sought to manipulate the political system. Between 1988 and the present, the Tasmanian forest industry has received a staggering total of $780 million in taxpayer handouts, $289 million of it since 2005, much of it being used to facilitate further old-growth logging. If an accounting were possible of the taxpayer-subsidised plantation schemes and added to this sum, the real subsidy paid by the Australian taxpayer to an industry that destroys the nation's heritage would approach a billion dollars.

But then, not the least shocking thing about the destruction of Tasmania's old-growth forests is that the state's logging industry is in the end not a commercially viable industry at all, but a massive parasite on the public purse, an industry as driven by ideological bailouts and hidden subsidies as a Soviet-era pig-iron foundry.

Worse still, at the moment when Tasmania was acquiring a global reputation as an island of exceptional beauty, the forces that would destroy much of the island's unique nature had been unleashed. This sad irony, denied in Tasmania, did not escape the more astute of the world's media:

major features began appearing in the *Observer*, *Le Figaro*, *Süddeutsche Zeitung* and the *New York Times*—mounting evidence that what was happening in Tasmania was more and more recognised as an environmental catastrophe of global significance. What might be read about Tasmania's forests in New York or Paris, though, was not information found easily in Hobart or Launceston. Apart from a few brave journalists, a generally craven Tasmanian media rarely questioned or challenged the woodchipping industry during these years. The *Launceston Examiner* ran a four-page feature on Gunns' pulp-mill proposal directly lifted from Gunns' advertising. Necessary fictions were repeated until they became accepted as truth: that, for example, the industry's main concern is sawlogs, when even Forestry Tasmania had admitted that sawlogs are chipped, and had been since 1972. The government's own reports reveal that approximately 90% of Tasmania's logged native forest is woodchipped.

To this day, the forestry industry and the Tasmanian government withhold key information, fudge definitions of forest types and felling practices, and distort statistics to prevent the truth of old-growth logging becoming publicly known, diverting debate into the dullness of disputed definitions and clashing numbers. It's a familiar tactic of sowing semantic confusion that has worked well for the tobacco and oil industries. Beyond it, forests unique in the world continue to disappear.

Jim Bacon's nickname was 'the Emperor', but the man perceived to be the power behind the throne was his deputy, Paul Lennon. Ill-tempered, badly behaved and brutally effective, his political capacity—like that of so many strong-arm leaders—was too often and too easily dismissed. Lennon made no more apologies for his thuggish behaviour (he once shoved a conservationist up against a wall in the middle of a meeting, an encounter he claims not to remember) than he did his enthusiasm for the old-growth logging industry, or his close friendship with the logging baron John Gay. Anyone taking a first-hand look at Tasmania would, he once said, "see a lot of fucking trees".

When Bacon retired in early 2004 because of terminal cancer, Lennon became premier, and any pretence that Gunns might be reined in within Tasmania came to an end. These days, Gunns is everywhere in Tasmania:

there are Gunns shops, Gunns television advertisements, Gunns-sponsored weather bulletins. If you go to watch an AFL game at Tasmania's premier stadium, York Park, you pass through the main entrance, officially and aptly named the Jim Bacon Gates, built by—who else?—a wholly owned subsidiary of Gunns, and come to the Gunns Stand, the largest and most opulently fitted stand in the stadium, much of it paid for, equally aptly, by the Tasmanian government.

With the river of money that had poured in from Tasmania's destroyed forests, Gunns had diversified into businesses in New Zealand and mainland Australia. It set about becoming the main player in the Tasmanian wine industry, with the company itself the dominant producer. That the woodchippers' wines—Tamar Ridge, Coombend, Devils Corner—were not stocked by some shops, bars and restaurants in Hobart because of consumer antipathy was of no concern, for the venture's financial underpinning was the same as for its forestry plantations: tax-minimisation schemes, in which grape-growing qualified for a 100% tax write-off. Yet again, it was Australian taxes at work for Gunns.

Gunns now made no secret of what the cost would be for those who questioned the sanctity of old-growth logging, no matter who they were. During the 2004 federal election, plantation-softwood processor Auspine—a $200-million forestry company based in South Australia that runs two pine sawmills employing 313 people in the northern Tasmanian town of Scottsdale—incurred John Gay's wrath by having the temerity to put forward a $450-million plan in which old-growth logging would be ended immediately, but Tasmania's forest industry would be expanded by 900 new jobs. Gay made it clear that Auspine had been very foolish, saying, "Their comments have been extremely damaging to themselves and their future in Tasmania." Two months later Gunns' hardware stores stopped stocking Auspine timber.

Auspine's pine comes from land owned by Forestry Tasmania, but in 1999 a half-share in their trees was sold by Jim Bacon to an American global investment firm, GMO, for $40 million. In early 2007 it was announced that Auspine had lost its pine supply in a deal that saw the timber go to a new company, FEA, that doesn't even have a sawmill. In this manner over 300 people are to lose their jobs. Though it is the half-owner of the resource, both the state-owned Forestry Tasmania and the

Tasmanian government refused to intervene in the negotiations to help Auspine or its workers. When Paul Lennon finally went to Scottsdale, four weeks after the initial announcement, sawmill workers turned their backs on the man who had always boasted that he stood for the jobs of forestry-industry workers. Increasingly, it appeared to many Tasmanians that the only jobs Lennon really cared about were his own and those of the Gunns directors.

Perhaps predictably, one of the last defences seized on in this battle by politicians on six-figure salaries is that they stand solidly with the working class. But Lennon's routine claim that 10,000 jobs are at stake if old-growth logging ends is without substance, and avoids the truth: jobs have been disappearing in old-growth logging for many years, not because of conservationists but because of mechanisation and Gunns' ability to transfer its losses onto logging workers. While woodchipping destroyed the older labour-intensive sawmill timber industry, the Hampshire woodchip mill in northern Tasmania, the biggest in the southern hemisphere, employs just 12 people. A report in the *Australian Financial Review* in 2004 revealed that the Tasmanian industry in its entirety had shed more than 1200 jobs since 1997.

Like Lennon's previously expansive claims—that, for example, ending old-growth logging in Western Australia had left more than 4000 people unemployed, something categorically refuted by the Western Australian government—the figure of 10,000 jobs is not supported. It is more than seven times the number given by the forest industry's own report on employment in the old-growth-logging sector, commissioned by the Forest Industries Association of Tasmania and written by pro-logging academics in 2004. Old-growth logging—as distinct from the rest of the (much larger) forestry industry—was estimated by a Timber Workers for Forests report in the same year to employ only 580 people. Both figures were arrived at before Gunns sent many contractors to the wall in 2006. Under Gunns' tendering system, contractors were already squeezed hard, with a large proportion of their income servicing debt on loans for the heavy machinery necessary for their work.

When it slashed logging contracts by up to 40% to offset a decline in woodchip sales, logging workers for the first time publicly expressed their growing bitterness towards Gunns and the hefty profits it made while their livelihoods vanished. In response, Barry Chipman of Timber Communities Australia (TCA) denied there was growing resentment within the industry towards Gunns. Presenting itself as the grassroots organisation of those it terms the "forest folk", the TCA has from its inception in 1987 actually been the vehicle of the National Association of Forest Industries (NAFI), which is financed by the logging industry. The TCA's support for the Tasmanian logging industry was once described by John Gay as an "invaluable alliance". Invaluable though it may be, the logging industry does put a price on it: in 2002–03, $723,154 of the TCA's total revenues of $836,977 came from direct industry contributions. In the same year, Barry Chipman's wages were directly paid by the NAFI.

It was "situations like this" Barry Chipman said of Gunns' slashing of contracts, that sorted out the "good operators" from the bad—further incensing those contractors who, acting on Gunns' promises of more work, had taken out bigger loans to purchase better equipment, and now were unable to meet repayments. "Everyone needs to tighten their belt a little bit," Chipman went on. "Any downturn will also be suffered by the company and its shareholders."

But they didn't seem to be suffering much that year at "Launceston's Lavish Lunch", the annual fundraiser of the Launceston branch of the Australian Cancer Research Foundation, held at one of Tasmania's most celebrated historic homes, Entally House. It seems to have been a splendid day for the island's clearfelling contessas, and the Launceston Cancerians—whose committee includes the wives of both John Gay and David McQuestin—later waxed effusively on their website about the event, extending "A big thanks ... to Mr John Gay for opening his house for the function."

Entally House isn't really John Gay's house, of course, just as crown forest isn't really his land. Like the forest, the historic house belonged to the Tasmanian people, but in 2004 the Tasmanian government terminated the National Trust's lease and gave a 20-year lease to Gunns. Plans by Gunns to plant a ten-hectare vineyard in Entally's historic grounds were immediately announced, John Gay declaring that the company was developing a "detailed marketing strategy" for the property, centring on the marketing of its wines. And in this way a unique piece of Australia's heritage became both John Gay's house and a charming marketing platform for Gunns.

The public can still visit Entally House which, technically speaking, they still own. It only costs $8 per adult.

Meanwhile, log-truck driver Gary Coad, who in 2004 was found guilty of assaulting a conservationist and who cheered John Howard when he announced his ongoing support for old-growth logging, was forced out of the industry he had worked in for 30 years. Now, he told a local newspaper, contractors were at "rock bottom", unable to make ends meet. "The biggest problem in the industry," he said, "is Gunns' virtual monopoly", which meant that any contractors who criticised the company could be squeezed out of the business. "We came up [to the Launceston rally] and fought for John Gay's livelihood," continued Coad. "Well, now its time for him to turn around and do the same for us."

But no one—no Gunns director, no Labor or Liberal politician, no CFMEU representative, no 'forest community' advocates—was going to fight for the forest workers, or speak to their feeling of betrayal. Instead, like Kevin Rudd on his 'listening' tour in December 2006, they said that they supported the existing Tasmanian forestry industry—in order, as Rudd put it, that there be "no overall loss of jobs", ignoring the fact that supporting Gunns was exactly what ensured workers would continue to lose jobs, continue to be exploited under Gunns' pitiless tendering system, and continue to suffer.

There is in all this a constant theme: the Lennon government's and Gunns' real mates are not workers, but millionaires. Behind the smokescreen of statistics, beyond the down-home cant of 'timber folk' peddled by the woodchippers' propagandists, past the endless lies, is a simple, wretched truth: great areas of Australia's remnant wild lands are being reduced to a landscape of battlefields, in order to make a handful of very rich people even richer.

Yet giving away such an extraordinary public resource as Tasmania's forests now threatens the state's broader economic prospects. A growing weight of financial analysis suggests that the economics of plantations (with which native forests are being replaced) are not assured, but rather are a huge gamble for Tasmania. The industry's future prospects depend on global pulp prices rising; the government, as the *Australian Financial Review* put it, has "tied the state's economic future to the success of Gunns and its tree farms".

If the future looks dubious, the present is already a failure. The reality is that logging old-growth forests brings little wealth and few jobs to struggling, impoverished rural communities. While Gunns makes its profits primarily in Tasmania, the great majority of the company's shares are owned by mainland institutions. It has been estimated that less than 15% of Gunns' profits remain on the island, where the largest individual shareholder is John Gay himself.

As a consequence of the forestry debate, Tasmania is an increasingly oppressive place to live. Just six days after conservationists had gone public about arson threats in 2004, the historian Bruce Poulson, a prominent opponent of plans to log the historically significant site of Recherché Bay, had the study behind his Dover house, containing decades of research, burnt down in what police described as a "malicious" attack. Ray and Leanne Green had displayed Wilderness Society posters calling for an end to old growth clearfelling in the Styx Valley in their Something Wild Wildlife Sanctuary, half an hour's drive from the valley. They received numerous informal threats, and then had their business burnt out. Cameraman Brian Dimmick was bashed by a log-truck driver who objected to Dimmick filming his vehicle. So it goes in the clearfell state.

It has never been suggested, nor do I wish to imply, that Gunns is in any way responsible for such acts. But the workings of power are not always reducible to orders or even intentions. When a society becomes entrapped in a growing coarsening of public rhetoric, evil finds succour. When vilification is commonplace, when lies are the currency of the day and followers seek to rise through the vigorous anticipation of leaders' unspoken desires, where all are disenfranchised and the most powerless feel what little security they have will be destroyed by those who merely disagree, acts of dubious morality and even of violent criminality become justifiable and appear honourable.

Despite a few years of economic upturn between 2001 and 2006, Tasmania is once more technically in recession, and it remains the poorest Australian state, with the highest levels of unemployment and around 40% of its population dependent on government welfare. New key industries such as tourism and fine foods and wines trade as much on the island's pristine image as they do on the products they sell. There is growing concern in all these industries—in which job growth is concentrated—at the relentless damage being done to Tasmania's name by images of smouldering forest coupes.

It is little wonder that many Tasmanians now worry that the woodchippers' greed destroys not only their natural heritage, but distorts their parliament, deforms their polity and poisons their society. And perhaps it is for that reason that the battle for forests in Tasmania is as much about free speech and democracy—about a people's right to exercise some control over their destiny, about their desire to have a better, freer society—as it is about wild lands.

Of late, Gunns' fortunes have suffered. Its share price has dropped by over a quarter from its record highs of 2005, a reflection of having lost 20% of its market share to South American plantations. At the same time woodchip prices have dropped and a global woodchip glut beckons, all of which leaves Tasmania even more dependent on uneconomic woodchip production.

A recent rally in support of Gunns' pulp mill attracted just 50 people, including Paul Lennon. Gunns' own research shows only one in four Tasmanians supports the island's biggest company. Meanwhile, its pulp-mill proposal meets with growing fury throughout the state. The once-timorous Tasmanian media has begun showing courage in questioning the company's activities; the Gunns 20 writ has been rejected three times, and Gunns' projected legal costs—including the damages it must now pay—run into millions. On throwing it out a second time, Judge Bongiorno described the lengthy writ as legally "embarrassing". Still, Gunns persists with a fourth suit. The eminent QC Julian Burnside, one of the defence counsels, has said, "It leaves you wondering if the purpose is simply to terrorise."

Yet the hope for many Tasmanians of years past—that one or other of the major parties at a national level would act to end the madness of old-growth logging—vanished with Kevin Rudd's Labor Party green light to Gunns. No one could look to a political system now so hopelessly cowed by and enmeshed with the woodchipping lobby to effect change. After a decade of the most pro-corporation national government Australia has ever had, neither major political party has the courage or integrity to stand up to a rogue corporation.

And it is Gunns' determination to do whatever it must to continue old-growth logging that may just condemn both it and Tasmania to a savage vortex: given the history of dependence on government subsidies and the alacrity with which both major parties grant them, Gunns' ability to always shift losses onto others—the government, its workers—means that the company may well continue to prosper. But the price of maintaining the necessary political support is high and ever higher: it demands an ever more determined manipulation of public opinion, an ever more ruthless treatment of public opposition, and an ever more assiduous duchessing and policing of political parties.

For that reason, more Tasmanians are demanding a royal commission into the old-growth logging industry and its relationship with both major political parties. It may find nothing untoward has taken place. It may even find at heart something far more disturbing: that the boundary between what is illegal and what is unethical has now vanished in Australia, and that the spectre that now haunts the nation is not that of an omnipotent state but of a ruthless corporation, beholden to nothing but its own bottom line, inhibited by nobody, liberated by the failure of contemporary politics.

Nothing less than a major investigation with special powers can now clear away the stench that surrounds this industry and shames Australia. Without such an investigation nothing will change, except for the worse, and the rape of Tasmania will continue until one day, like so much else that was precious, its great forests will belong only to myth. Tasmanians will be condemned to endure the final humiliation: bearing dumb witness to the great lie that delivers wealth to a handful elsewhere, poverty to many of them, and death to their future as the last of these extraordinary places is sacrificed to the woodchippers' greed. Beautiful places, holy places, lost not only to them but to the world, forever.

And in a world where it seems everything can be bought, all that will remain are ghosts briefly mocking memory: a ream of copying paper in a Japanese office and a man fern in an English garden. And then they too will be gone.

All information correct as at April 2007

4
Prosecuting the War on Terror

Leigh Sales

Inside the Hicks deal
The Weekend Australian, 28 April 2007

Detainee 002 blindly stumbled from the belly of the plane into the Cuban sun. Blacked-out goggles covered his eyes to prevent him from harming the two crew-cut marines gripping his 163cm frame. He was a high-risk prisoner, like all the others on this flight. A blue surgical mask covered his mouth, and gloves were taped to his hands. Headphones muffled his hearing. Over an orange jumpsuit, he wore what the prisoners called "a three-piece suit": a metal belt with chains attached to leg-irons and handcuffs. It made Detainee 002 walk awkwardly as the marines led him down the plane's rear hatch. The hold reeked of human urine, excrement and body odour. Shackled to the floor and unable to get to the toilet, some of the other accused terrorists had soiled themselves on the 24-hour flight from Afghanistan.

With his sight blocked and hearing muted, the intense heat gave Detainee 002 his first hint that he was at his destination. The sun rarely allowed the US military base at Guantanamo Bay to cool below 32C, even in winter, and the prisoners roasted inside their jumpsuits and restraints.

Marines in Humvees surrounded the enormous grey plane and its valuable human cargo. Some were armed with rocket-launchers and others with machineguns. One manned a grenade-launcher. Camouflaged snipers blended into the surrounding hills and the dull chop of helicopter blades sliced through the air. A gunner hung from a navy chopper, his sights trained on the prisoners as they shuffled out one by one.

It was January 2002, four months after the September 11 terrorist attacks. The soldiers on guard at Guantanamo Bay airport were on extreme alert. They believed the men filing off the plane were conspirators in September 11. The base hummed with jittery energy.

The soldiers' bosses at the Department of Defense in Washington, DC were depicting the first planes to Guantanamo as the terrorist equivalents of *Con Air*. In the film, a gang of rapists, serial killers and pedophiles burst out of their shackles mid-prison transfer and take over their plane. The Pentagon was not risking that on these flights. Guards on the C-17 Globemaster aircraft outnumbered the prisoners two to one. According to the Bush administration, these were ruthless killers ready to slaughter an American at the first opportunity.

"These are people that would gnaw hydraulic lines in the back of a C-17 to bring it down," chairman of the US Joint Chiefs of Staff, General Richard Myers, informed a Pentagon briefing the day the first plane arrived. "These are very, very dangerous people and that's how they're being treated." A reporter asked for detail on the hydraulic-cable incident. That was hyperbole, the general revised.

Just like the soldiers who eyed their every move, the accused terrorists were nervy and tense. Some believed that transfer to the island prison meant they would never be released. Others had never set foot on a plane before and thought that when the noisy machine landed, they would be executed. Detainee 002 shuffled along the tarmac to a white bus, bound for his new home, Camp X-ray. The bus first drove on to a ferry that crossed Guantanamo Bay and then chugged up a dusty road towards Camp X-ray. It entered the camp through a 3.7m steel fence crowned with barbed wire. Marines armed with M16s and binoculars watched every move from a wooden guard tower with an American flag flapping overhead. The bus finally rattled to a stop near a dozen rows of metal cages. The doors hissed open, and guards led the detainees off one by one, ordering them to kneel on the ground just outside their new cells.

By late 2002, the staff in the Office of Military Commissions could not understand why the legal process surrounding the detainees moved so slowly. The team would be told to pull out all stops because the secretary of defence, Donald Rumsfeld, wanted to start trials as soon as possible. But then, nothing would happen. The prosecutors would ask external departments for access to particular files, and the requests would disappear into a black hole. They would telephone other agencies and the calls would go unreturned.

They would refer information up to the office of Pentagon general counsel William Haynes and get nothing back. Some of them started to suspect that Rumsfeld and his deputy Paul Wolfowitz did not actually want to start trials.

"They would give me something to do at 9pm and say you need to do this urgently, work on this because we are going to charge them tomorrow," says one of the former military commission's officials. "I'd stay there till midnight, get it in and then not hear back on it for three weeks." A former prosecutor found the same thing. "The General Counsel's Office had this appearance of fervour and kinetic activity. They really made us work hard to get things done. Then we'd say 'What happened to it?' There was always some third-party bogeyman that could never be identified, holding it up," he says.

Other departments were also perplexed by the delay, particularly the State Department and the National Security Council. By late 2002, State was fielding constant complaints from allies, including Australia, about the indefinite detentions and the failure to charge anyone. The NSC was alarmed by rumblings about the mistreatment of detainees at Guantanamo.

Officials were disturbed by intelligence from the Criminal Investigative Task Force revealing that many of the detainees were not as dangerous as the Pentagon claimed.

Condoleezza Rice and two senior aides in the NSC, senior adviser Elliot Abrams and the general counsel, John Bellinger, started applying pressure to get some of the detainees repatriated.

The NSC felt that the Pentagon resented the interference and adopted a go-slow response. The NSC officials found it difficult to get any detailed information about exactly who was at Guantanamo and why they were being held. There were also constant promises that military commissions were about to start.

"Each time the issue was discussed at high levels over four or five years, officials in the Justice Department or the Pentagon would say they were just around the corner from getting this started," a Bush administration official says.

In reality, the Pentagon was in no rush to start military commissions. Preserving "flexibility" was the top priority. Once trials started, some of that flexibility would be lost. By the end of 2002, there was also a huge amount of negative press surrounding Guantanamo. Why risk any more by holding hearings? What if the first case was weak or, even worse, an acquittal? "In retrospect, it is clear to me that the main obstacle was the General Counsel's Office," the same former prosecutor says. "I wouldn't say there was a smoking gun or diabolical motive. I think they had a very calculated viewpoint that going forward offered nothing but political risk and delaying or stopping the trials offered the best chance of avoiding media exposure on the topics of interrogation and detainee abuse."

The first chief prosecutor, Colonel William Lietzau, was another who recognised that the Pentagon was in no hurry to start legal proceedings at Guantanamo Bay, but suggests a different reason.

"I believe Rumsfeld's primary interest was fighting the terrorists and securing intelligence that could prevent the next terrorist attack," Lietzau says. "Bringing terrorists to trial would take a back seat."

The Department of Defense is an inefficient bureaucracy at the best of times, and its fundamental inertia also played a role in the delay, particularly as the leadership was preoccupied by the war in Iraq. During the latter part of 2002 and the first half of 2003, as planning and then execution of the war were under way, officials in the Office of Military Commissions found it virtually impossible to get access to Rumsfeld. Wolfowitz was almost as difficult to see, and that was even more problematic because he was the acting appointing authority. According to people who attended meetings with Wolfowitz in mid-2003, he could not conceal his lack of interest in beginning military commissions.

"After my first meeting with Paul Wolfowitz, I came out and I said, 'Is anybody looking for somebody else to handle these responsibilities?'" says one senior military official. "It was obvious to me that Paul Wolfowitz was not enamoured with that job because of all his other responsibilities."

Despite the fact that 18 months had passed since the US first detained Hicks and there seemed to be little progress in his case, the Prime Minister was determined to leave him in US hands. The Attorney-General's Department had advised the Government there was probably nothing with which Hicks could be charged under Australian law if he was returned home. The Department of Public Prosecutions confirmed this view once it had seen the Australian Federal Police brief of evidence against him.

When the DPP looked at the brief on Hicks, it decided there were no grounds to press charges in Australia. There were two problems. Where it appeared that Hicks had possibly broken Australian law (for example, by fighting with Lashkar-e-Toiba in Pakistan), there was not enough admissible evidence to prove it. But where the AFP had evidence (for example, showing that Hicks had attended al-Qa'ida training camps), the conduct was not illegal under Australian law at the time.

Partly in response to the Hicks case, the Government introduced terrorism legislation in 2002 covering international conduct. If Hicks went to Afghanistan today and did the things he did in 2001, he would be breaking Australian law. But the Government was adamant that he could not be tried for past behaviour and ruled out retrospective charges.

The decision to rule out retrospective legislation specifically for Hicks dismayed Australia's ambassador to the US, Michael Thawley. From the beginning, Thawley had doubts about leaving Hicks to a US legal process. He agreed the US military had a right to hold Hicks and he believed in the war on terror. But his experience working in Washington made him suspect it would drag on indefinitely. Even with all the problems associated with retrospective legislation, Thawley felt it was a better option than waiting out a US process. The ambassador discussed retrospective charges with embassy staff and with the Prime Minister's office, but he saw very quickly that the idea was going nowhere and abandoned it.

Despite Thawley's concerns, he ultimately agreed with John Howard that a military commission was the only option for Hicks. The officials in Washington and Canberra were well aware of the flaws in the process. But they planned to convince the Bush administration to introduce some changes. By mid-2003, Thawley told his team that its top priority was getting the Pentagon to begin trials. The Australians were to negotiate with the Bush administration to make the process as fair as they could, but speed was paramount. The Government wanted the Hicks and Mamdouh Habib cases resolved.

Thawley was one of the most successful Australian ambassadors ever posted to Washington. A smooth, polished networker, he is equally at home talking about art and travel as he is conversing about economics and foreign policy. Like all good diplomats, he has a keen political sense. Thawley developed incredible access to top Bush administration officials during his posting from 2000 to 2005.

By the time he left, he was so respected that President George W. Bush held a gathering in the Oval Office for Thawley and his wife, Debbie. It was attended by Rumsfeld, Wolfowitz, Vice-President Dick Cheney, Bush's chief of staff, Andy Card, and other top officials. It was a very rare courtesy in Washington.

The source of Thawley's influence was not just his ability and manner, but also his closeness to the Prime Minister. Before going to Washington, Thawley was Howard's international affairs adviser, and US officials in Washington knew that he spoke with the authority of the Prime Minister. Under Thawley, the Australian embassy in Washington was the perfect storm, according to one former staffer. The top officials all shared a discreet, pragmatic approach that went down well in Washington.

The political branch had responsibility for the day-to-day management of the Hicks case. One of the diplomats there, Patrick Suckling, worked desperately to get the Office of Military Commissions moving. He tried to make the Americans understand that the matter was urgent. "Patrick would be in constantly: 'Can you charge him today?' I'd be like, 'We're moving on it. We'll get you whatever we have,'" says one of the US officials closely involved. The Department of Defense repeatedly assured the Australians that things were about to move forward any day. The guarantees were particularly vigorous whenever a minister or the Prime Minister visited. The officials from Canberra would leave believing the process was on track. Then, nothing would happen.

In frustration, the Australians asked allies in other US departments to press the Pentagon to start trials at Guantanamo. They found sympathetic ears in the State Department, particularly its general counsel, William Taft, and the then deputy secretary, Richard Armitage. Staff at the NSC also tried to help, particularly the general counsel, Bellinger, and the senior director for Asian Affairs, Michael Green.

"The Australians felt let down," says Green, who has now left the White House. "The State Department and the NSC spent a huge amount of effort trying to get the Pentagon off its rear end." The Pentagon kept the NSC and the State Department almost as much in the dark as the Australians, according to Armitage. "They were only slightly more frustrated than secretary [of state Colin] Powell and I," he says. He believes the Pentagon treated Australia poorly during that period. "They are incompetent, and this is Rich Armitage on the record," he says. "They can't explain themselves adequately, and their treatment of our allies in general hasn't exactly been stellar."

Armitage's former chief of staff, Randy Schriver, says the State Department found it impossible to get answers. "When we went to the Pentagon, it was like punching a cloud," he says. "You never felt like you were able to get a definite time line; it was very ambiguous."

The Australians' friends were limited in how hard they could pressure the Pentagon on the Hicks case because of something known as command influence. If a senior official leaned on the Pentagon to press charges against Hicks, then the defence lawyers could later argue that the charges were not laid on their merits but because of political pressure. It meant the case could be thrown out if the judge accepted that the President or somebody representing him influenced the process.

Because of fears about command influence, White House lawyers prohibited Green from speaking to the Pentagon on the subject of Hicks. The State Department operated under similar constraints.

How did the Pentagon get away with brushing aside not just a close ally, Australia, but also the NSC and the State Department? One of the most important reasons was that it had the backing of the Vice-President's office. Cheney was immensely powerful in the administration, and he fully supported and helped direct the Pentagon's approach.

A second reason was that Rumsfeld was virtually untouchable in 2002 and 2003. In the first year after September 11, he was so popular that the press touted him as a rock star. The rapid fall of Baghdad in the opening phase of the war in Iraq made Rumsfeld even more powerful. As Iraq slowly unravelled, Rumsfeld's influence waned, ultimately culminating in his resignation in 2006. But well into 2004, the Pentagon and the Vice-President's office exerted the greatest influence in Washington.

The Australian embassy sent all this advice back to Canberra: the Pentagon's obfuscation, the concerns in other agencies, the lack of transparency, the flaws in the process. But by then the Government was so publicly committed to the military commissions that there was little that could be done other than keep pushing the Pentagon to hurry up.

This edited extract, published in The Australian, *was taken from* Detainee 002: The case of David Hicks.

Robert Richter, QC

A trial that was uncomfortably close to Stalinist theatre

The Age, 1 April 2007

David Hicks is coming home. At what price? Let us take stock. The charade that took place at Guantanamo Bay would have done Stalin's show trials proud. First there was indefinite detention without charge. Then there was the torture, however the Bush lawyers, including his Attorney-General, might choose to describe it. Then there was the extorted confession of guilt.

Whatever Hicks may have done, the theatre of a voluntary plea of guilty when the choice is "rot in hell or say it's true so you can go home" is worthy of The Grand Inquisitor. In Stalin's as well as the German show trials of the 1930s, the essence of the display was the public confession, followed by the sentence. The Iranians and al-Qaeda still practise it, but isn't that why we declared a War on Terror?

Then there was the silence. In the show trials, it was enforced by execution. In this instance it is enforced by threats of further punishment in both the US and Australia. The implications of the gag are staggering when added to the wholesale destruction of the rule of law.

Hundreds of years of what constituted the rule of law have been jettisoned so that Howard, Ruddock and Downer can pretend that Hicks is off their election agenda. Forget habeas corpus. Forget retrospective legislation. Forget coerced evidence and confessions. Forget commissions in which guilt has been predetermined. Forget prosecutors being judges in their own cause.

It's OK as long as those who aided and abetted the destruction of these principles are back in office and remain unaccountable and can perpetuate the lie. If they lose office, the true story will emerge—but may no longer have impact.

The deal was simple: Go home. Shut up. If you dare to say you had no choice but to plead guilty, the US Military Commission will find you guilty of perjury and will call in a full seven-year sentence, over and above the five you've suffered unconvicted and uncharged. That will mean the Australian Attorney-General may not release you on licence for another seven years, or will—with the additional gags of control orders and other available means—make sure you cannot tell anyone what happened.

Apart from the loss of fundamental guarantees of freedom, another freedom—speech—is garrotted.

The best thing one can say about the process is that one day there may be a reckoning for this despicable episode, in which Australian ministers, all the way down from the Prime Minister, have been party to the commission of grave crimes under the Australian Criminal Code 1995, divisions 104 (Harming Australians Overseas) and 268D (denying a fair trial), because they have been criminally complicit under section 11.2.

By the time the US Supreme Court strikes down the whole festering sore in a couple of years—which most constitutional lawyers believe it will—we can only hope there will be another attorney-general in Australia who will have the guts to authorise proceedings against those who "aided, abetted, counselled or procured" the commission of the crimes to which I have referred. Let us not forget the war crimes trials after World War II, in which the German Nazi judges who prostituted their duty in the service of the political ideology that put them there were put on trial for what they did.

It may only be then that the full horror of what we allowed to happen to the rule of law in the name of political expediency will be revealed.

Michael Costello

A case with no winners
The Australian, 30 March 2007

The latest turn in the David Hicks saga—his plea of "guilty"—excites exasperation and anger. Exasperation at those who want to turn Hicks into a naive innocent and something of a hero. But more, much more, anger at the barely concealed relief and gloating of the Howard Government and some of its senior ministers.

First, the exasperation.

Hicks was no innocent. The admissions he has made in letters to his family and elsewhere where there has been no duress show clearly that Hicks was engaged in military training and activities with Islamic fundamentalists and was associated at least at a low level with terrorist groups.

To pretend that he is just some fun-loving kid caught up by accident in events he did not understand is wilful blindness. Those who are concerned at the true abuse of civil liberties involved in the Hicks case only weaken their case by making him out to be an innocent who is pleading guilty only in order to get out of Guantanamo and to make him into some sort of folk-hero deserving of admiration and compassion, because the true issue at stake in the Hicks case is this.

There may be strong evidence to support allegations that a person may have committed violent, ugly acts and, on the face of it, deserves legal punishment. But our most basic liberty is the right of all persons, no matter how serious the allegations and however nasty they may be, not to be arbitrarily detained against their will unless they are charged under law and are given a reasonably speedy and fair trial.

The Howard Government is close to achieving its primary goal, which is a political one. Belatedly, Prime Minister John Howard realised that the Hicks case was a serious threat to his re-election. As is Howard's wont in the period leading up to an election, he decided some months ago that he had to clear the Hicks issue out of the way. It looks as though he has succeeded. Whether or not people feel that Hicks only copped a guilty plea as a way of getting out of Guantanamo, the issue will, over the coming months, fade from its current high media profile. While there will be some residual adverse fallout for Howard, most of the vote-changing sharpness of this issue will have disappeared by the time of the next election.

No doubt Howard will feel happy, pleased that once again he has managed to slide out from under. If political adroitness was the only measure of success, so he should.

Indeed, the issue could start to turn around and bite Labor if it is not careful. Those who are determined to see innocence in Hicks will most likely pressure Kevin Rudd to declare that he will seek to find a way out for Hicks from his Australian imprisonment. Rudd will not credibly be able to give such an undertaking because Australian law and our treaty arrangements with the US will not allow it.

But it is not admiration for political skill to which Howard is entitled. Rather, he should feel the anger of all Australians who value the good standing of this country and, more broadly, the standing of the Western world. For Hicks was the object over many years of a deep injustice; held without charge or trial until the US could cobble together some half-baked judicial process. Howard has given our enemies a credible argument that Hicks' trial was a farce and his guilty plea was not genuine but made under duress. For years, Howard ignored the plight of Hicks who, whatever he was and whether innocent or guilty, is an Australian citizen entitled to the protection of his government. Howard let himself and Australia be portrayed as a poodle of George W. Bush.

But worst of all, by not early on protesting not just Hicks' treatment, but the whole jerry-built, ramshackle, ad hoc treatment of prisoners of Guantanamo, Howard and Bush have helped our enemies and alienated allies and potential friends in the very real war against Islamic extremism. That war is not only about military force. It is even more about the force of ideas and values. And by what happened at Abu Ghraib, by its justification of torture and the use of "extraordinary rendition", by its assertion that Guantanamo was a place where law and liberty did not apply, by its exercise of the use of unilateral and arbitrary executive power, the US has done untold damage to its standing.

Howard, by doing nothing to protest even though he was one of the closest allies of the US in the war against terror, has become a de facto partner in those behaviours.

In particular, by failing to understand or address the issues of basic freedoms in the case of Hicks, he has missed the opportunity to assert that Australia at least values liberty first.

Howard has had a significant political victory this week by pressuring the US to quickly fix the issue. But his government's conduct has made Hicks an undeserving hero to many, and much worse, undermined Australia's position in the global fight for our values.

David Marr

Just an ordinary life
The Sydney Morning Herald, 21 July 2007

Mohamed Haneef was about to board Singapore Airlines flight 246 when two police entered the departure lounge of Brisbane International Airport. "You are under arrest for providing support to a terrorist organisation," said Detective Sergeant Adam Simms. The doctor was interviewed first at the airport and then, after midnight, at the Wharf Street headquarters of the Australian Federal Police.

The long arm of the law had reached Haneef from Glasgow where, 47 hours before, his cousin Kafeel Ahmed had driven a burning Jeep Cherokee packed with petrol and gas canisters into the airport terminal. Earlier, two cars packed with explosives had been found in London. British police had also arrested Kafeel's brother, Sabeel, a doctor at a hospital near Liverpool.

The really sexy detail linking the Brisbane doctor to his cousins' alleged crimes was a mobile phone with a SIM card in his name found—it was said—in the wreckage of the jeep at Glasgow airport. That was until yesterday morning when the ABC's *AM* revealed police actually seized the phone from Sabeel Ahmed hundreds of kilometres and many hours away in a little town outside Liverpool. But that was a glitch for the future.

On that first night in Brisbane, Haneef was not panicking. He insisted he didn't need a lawyer and would stick to that for the next three days, saying he could straighten the matter out. But he was tired. Sometime before Haneef was brought a bed at 3am, he told his interviewers he had been trying to ring British police that afternoon to clear up the matter of the SIM card. His calls weren't returned.

Haneef had slept only a few hours when police woke him. Were this an ordinary criminal matter, he would be charged or released at about this point. But police were using for the first time the nation's new anti-terrorism machinery that would allow the prisoner to be questioned for a total of 24 hours over an indeterminate number of days without charges being laid. At 11am, Simms and federal agent Neil Thompson turned on the tape machines for the long interrogation ahead. By this time police had Haneef's phone and financial records from Australia and Britain. While the prisoner was eating breakfast, police had raided his Southport flat, turning up notebooks and diaries. They had yet to strip down Haneef's computer, but they weren't starting cold. They had evidence of a number of social and financial contacts between the detained man and his accused cousins. Yet by the end of that day, they had not unmasked a terrorist.

Haneef emerged from the questioning a nerdy guy with fractured English who has done little in the past decade but study. And whatever else he may have been doing along the way, he has performed to perfection the classic role of the good Indian son—becoming a doctor, supporting his mother, seeing his sister married and marrying well himself. He told the police: "I am the sole carer for my family."

He was 18 when his father, a teacher, died in 1997. With a little money and a scholarship, the son entered medical school in Bangalore. The family lived in an ugly lower-middle-class Muslim quarter of concrete flats. Old neighbours still speak highly of a wholesome and studious boy. His aim was to become a physician, an ambition that took him to England in March 2004. Money was tight. Police seized from his Southport flat an old diary in which he had meticulously noted the sums he borrowed from Indian doctors to stay afloat in England: £180 here, £200 there.

He lived in a boarding house run by Mufeed, an Indian charity that looks after newly arrived trainee doctors and dentists. Police would later say that Haneef told them his cousins Kafeel and Sabeel also lived with him in these Bentley Road digs. Haneef did not say so.

His second cousins—their father was his mother's uncle—were the only family he had in England. He spent four or five days with Kafeel at Cambridge that first summer.

Something is a bit odd here. Haneef says he was "a bit low", having failed an exam. But the Royal College of Physicians has no record of

Haneef failing one of its exams. Kafeel also lent his cousin money: £300 that he didn't want back. "He said: 'Just give it to any of the poor people in India.'"

Haneef spent his first year in England observing and studying. From July 2004 to April 2005 he did unpaid work as a locum registrar at Halton hospital, just outside Liverpool. In May he passed the first round of his physician's exams. It was a life-changing success. What followed was so Indian.

Haneef returned home to bask in his achievement. Now with the prospects of a good job in Britain, he found a wife. Firtous Arshiya came from a family way up the ladder from Haneef's. They lived in a beautiful house in a beautiful suburb of Bangalore. They were modern Muslims. They read. They travelled. Their engagement was announced in July. Then Haneef returned alone to Britain to begin work at the Royal Liverpool Hospital.

His alliance with this family did not come cheap. From his brother-in-law-to-be he borrowed £3000 for the wedding. Here was a source of rich misunderstanding for police who would later be trawling through Haneef's financial records: his brother-in-law is Dr Siddique Ahmed and his second cousin is Dr Sabeel Ahmed. Both figure in records as "S. Ahmed". It could be so confusing.

The wedding took place in Bangalore in November 2005. Haneef told police this was the last time he met Kafeel. The newlyweds returned to Liverpool and moved into a flat in Pembroke Place near the hospital. Haneef got himself a mobile phone with a one-year plan. By December he was making his first repayment to "S. Ahmed": a heavy £550.

He was also supporting his family—or that is Haneef's explanation for a transaction that makes sense to Indians but puzzled Australian investigators. He paid £960 into Kafeel's English bank account in October 2005 on the understanding that his cousin—who was still out in India—would pay the same sum to Haneef's family. The doctor's explanation to the police reads: "He had made arrangements to pay ... in India to my family."

Meanwhile, Kafeel's brother, Sabeel, had turned up in England. Sabeel had been a year or so behind his cousin at medical college in Bangalore. Now he took a job at Halton and often came up to Liverpool to see Haneef and his wife. "He used to visit us," Haneef told the police, "as a family friend on the weekends."

The following spring, Sabeel drove the hire car that took a family party on a tour of Scotland. The passengers were Haneef and his wife, her parents and her brother. They visited Glasgow, prayed at the mosque, but slept that night in a motorway hotel. Oddly, police didn't ask Haneef if they toured the airport.

With his one-year contract at Liverpool drawing to a close in the summer of 2006, Haneef answered an advertisement in the *British Medical Journal* and was accepted for a post at Southport Hospital on the Queensland Gold Coast. He and his wife prepared for the journey to Australia via Bangalore.

Haneef left all his "excess baggage" with Sabeel. As well as dumping books, an overcoat and a picture he'd been given of Mecca's holy shrines, Haneef gave Sabeel's address to his bank—and gave his cousin an 02 SIM card. "There were some free minutes left on the mobile phone. So he said: 'I would like to use that.'" Haneef understood Sabeel would take over the plan and make the phone his own.

Haneef's first interrogation at Wharf Street went from 11am until about 7.30pm with breaks for meals and prayers. The tone was mostly polite. The prisoner was willing. He refused only to give his views on the situation in Iraq and Afghanistan. "I don't like to comment." The two police officers didn't press the point.

Haneef denied ever touching a rifle, ever having any training in firearms, explosives or logistics, or ever being part of a terrorist organisation. He denied any knowledge of the Glasgow attack and the London car bombs. He denied knowing his cousins' friends or their politics. He denied raising money for political causes and denied taking part in anything that could be considered jihad. "Every drop of blood is human," he said. "And I feel for every human being."

The police probed his religious beliefs. Was he Sunni or Shia? "I'm basically a Muslim, that's all." Had he had formal religious training? "No." Where did he pray? Sometimes in a hospital prayer room. Sometimes at the Liverpool mosque and later at the Gold Coast mosque. "I try to go at least once a day."

Much of the questioning involved the financial transactions that bound this young doctor to his family: repayments of his wedding loan, repayments of a small loan to finance his sister's wedding and monthly payments to his family in Bangalore. In Australia he was sending up to $3000 a month from his $70,000 a year salary back home to his family. At every turn, this is a very Indian story.

Haneef began work at the Gold Coast Hospital last September and lived with his wife in a one-bedroom flat in Pohlman Street, Southport. Firtous became pregnant soon after the move and returned to Bangalore in March. "We didn't have enough support here," said Haneef. "We thought it would be better for her to be there with the parents."

Their daughter, Haniya, was born by emergency caesarean on June 26. That day Sabeel "chatted" with his cousin on Yahoo, offering his congratulations on the birth. That was their last contact. A couple of days later the mother and child were back in hospital. The baby had jaundice. Haneef would later claim he was prevented from flying home at this point because there was no cover for him at the hospital.

Here the story lurches into horror. Late on the afternoon of Friday, June 29, news broke in Australia that a car had been found in London stacked with explosive material. Over the next two days a second car was found in London and then the flaming jeep was driven into the Glasgow airport terminal. By Sunday morning on the Gold Coast, Haneef's two cousins had been arrested: a badly burnt Kafeel in Glasgow, and Sabeel working at his hospital in Halton.

Sabeel's mother rang Haneef from Bangalore that morning. British police had rung her looking for him. She said: "There was something wrong with your mobile phone. Someone was misusing the thing." She gave Haneef the number of Tony Webster, one of the British investigators. He left it for a day before ringing.

That Sunday, Haneef got a week's leave from the hospital and rang his father-in-law in Bangalore asking him to arrange and pay for a ticket home. By this time he knew Sabeel was in custody. He says his father-in-law reassured him: "Come here and we'll have support here for you." Haneef was booked to fly late the following night.

Sometime on the Monday, Haneef left his Honda Jazz, some jewellery and a laptop with Dr Mohammed Asif Ali, a colleague at the hospital. This would lead to Ali being detained and questioned under new counter-terrorism powers, for the federal police suspected Haneef was acting "to conceal evidence". (The innocent bystander was released after 24 hours, having been vilified as an associate of terrorists. Ali faces five years in prison if he reveals what happened to him in custody.)

That same busy Monday afternoon, Haneef tried four times to ring Webster's number. Police knew the precise details: three goes between 3.08 and 3.29pm and another at 4.32pm. Haneef said: "I didn't get any response to that number." No mention of this attempt to co-operate with the British police was made in the dossier that convinced the Minister for Immigration, Kevin Andrews, to cancel Haneef's visa on character grounds.

That night Haneef was arrested waiting for his Singapore flight. Why was he leaving on a one-way ticket, asked police? "I going to get a ticket on my own, with my money when I come back," Haneef replied. The interviewing officer later gave the Brisbane bail court an affidavit that stated Haneef "had no explanation as to why he did not have a return ticket".

Before the tapes were turned off on that long first day's interrogation, Haneef told police:

> I haven't done any of the crimes. Just want to let you know. And I don't want to spoil my name and my profession. That's the main thing. And I've been a professionalist until now and I haven't been involved in any kind of extra activities, what sort of activities which you were discussing earlier. And I just want to live in life as a professionalist in the medical profession. That's what I want.

In the afternoon of Thursday, July 5, a hard-bitten Brisbane criminal lawyer named Peter Russo had a call from the Brisbane Watch House to say there was someone in the cells needing a lawyer. "It's not an unusual request," Russo told the *Herald*. "I've been called to the watch house more times than I care to remember." But this wasn't a drunk or a petty crim needing help. It was the man being billed in the press as the nation's most famous terrorist prisoner.

Haneef had spent the best part of two days and two nights since his interrogation waiting in a double cell with a small five-metre by seven-metre yard attached. He had access to magazines but no daily papers. He had made only one phone call, to the Indian consulate, to send a message to his family he would not be arriving on the flight as expected. He had not been questioned again.

Each time the police returned to the magistrate to ask permission to hold him longer, Haneef was offered the right to be represented by a lawyer. He had kept saying no until the Thursday afternoon. So Russo appeared. They spent less than an hour together. Haneef's instructions were simple: "I want to go home."

The secretive nature of the proceedings was quickly apparent when the hearing began at 7pm. Russo was not allowed to hear the police evidence. The magistrate's decision was made in Russo's absence. All he could do was put on record his client had been co-operating. The magistrate decided the prisoner could be held for another 96 hours. Russo's appearance marked a turning point in the case. That night Haneef briefed him and next day Russo rang round the Brisbane bar and engaged Stephen Keim, SC. Their strategy was to force the Government to provide information to explain why it wished to continue to hold Haneef without charge. Keim told ABC *Lateline*: "I went before the magistrate, they handed up the secret information to the magistrate. I said: 'Hey, that's not natural justice. I've got a right to make submissions, I've got a right to know generally what your case is.'"

Huge police resources were being thrown at the Haneef matter. Police were stripping Haneef's computer. "I am told it is the equivalent of reading 31,000 pages of paper to look at the amount of material that actually has to be analysed that has been retrieved through the exercising of search warrants," said the Attorney-General, Philip Ruddock. And the story was a continuing bushfire in the press with a steady series of leaks suggesting Haneef was a darker figure than the Government could ever reveal.

In the end the police folded. Thirteen pages of material were given to Haneef's lawyers: "Material that two days earlier was so secret and so highly protected, I could not get one letter of it," said Keim. Rather than debate the need to continue holding Haneef, police announced on July 13, they would use the last hours allowed to them to conduct a second full-scale interrogation.

The questioning went over 15 hours. Russo was present. About 7.30 next morning, the police told him they would be charging his client under the Commonwealth Criminal Code with intentionally providing a SIM card "to a terrorist organisation consisting of a group of persons including Sabeel Ahmed and Kafeel Ahmed, being reckless as to whether the organisation was a terrorist organisation".

Being charged returned Haneef to the traditional criminal system. His lawyers immediately applied for bail. The *Herald* understands the magistrate queried the logic of anyone giving a SIM card to terrorists: surely its discovery would immediately implicate them in the crimes? Barristers for the Crown argued the phone was intended to be obliterated in the fire that destroyed the Cherokee Jeep at Glasgow airport.

The magistrate, Jacqui Payne, was not impressed. Having considered her decision over the weekend, she granted Haneef bail last Monday. She noted there was no evidence of a direct link between him and the group blamed for Britain's recent failed terrorist plot, nor evidence that Haneef had intentionally provided his SIM card to a terrorist organisation. She observed Haneef was a doctor with no criminal record and a good employment history. She set bail at $10,000 and under stringent reporting conditions, ordered his release.

But the freedom she granted was immediately taken away by the Minister for Immigration. In a move that set off a depth charge in the legal profession, Andrews cancelled Haneef's work visa on "character" grounds claiming to "reasonably suspect Dr Haneef has had an association with persons involved in criminal conduct, namely terrorism".

That power is designed to detain for deportation convicted non-citizens. It has apparently never been used in the past to detain non-citizens pending court proceedings. The president of Liberty Victoria, Julian Burnside, QC, declared this "a serious misuse of power". The president of the Australian Bar Association, Stephen Estcourt, QC, called Andrews's move "a threat to the rule of law".

In the end, the Bangalore doctor chose to remain in prison in Brisbane rather than be shuttled back and forth to the Villawood immigration system in Sydney. He was driven away to his new home on Wednesday, shoeless and in a prison smock, hunched over on the floor of a paddy wagon.

That same morning, details from the 142-page transcript of Haneef's first interrogation was published in *The Australian*. The Prime Minister and Attorney-General were outraged—but for the first time daylight had flooded in on the case. More light will be thrown when the transcript of the second—far longer—interrogation is released to the press, perhaps as early as this weekend.

With the case against the prisoner already looking thin, news broke yesterday morning that the SIM card—the single vivid detail that had seen Haneef interrogated, charged and stripped of his visa—was not in the burning jeep at Glasgow. It had never made it to the scene of the crime but was still where Haneef had left it down south in the possession of his cousin Sabeel—who has not been charged in Britain as a terrorist.

But the collapse of this crucial evidence is not swaying the government. Police Commissioner Mick Keelty urged lawyers and journalists to stop commenting on the case. Kevin Andrews refused to reconsider the scrapping of Haneef's visa because he claims a secret dossier of evidence against the man. Win or lose, he wants the doctor gone. Challenging that decision in the Federal Court is the next round in this saga. The date set is August 8.

Additional reporting by Connie Levett, Joel Gibson and Amrit Dhillon

Paul Kelly

Crisis of trust

The Weekend Australian, 4 August 2007

The periodic collapse of trust among Australia's pivotal institutions—the executive, parliament, the police, the legal profession and the media—is the real story in the Mohamed Haneef affair. The paradox at the centre of this event is that Haneef should never have been charged by the Director of Public Prosecutions, an ill-judged action partly exposed by the media, yet Immigration Minister Kevin Andrews's decision to cancel Haneef's visa was a valid decision on the advice before him.

The idea that the court case was flawed yet the executive action by Andrews was justified seems an impossible concept for much of the media and the legal profession. It is, however, the irresistible conclusion from the saga, which seems to have a long way to run.

This is, in essence, a battle between institutions. The laws in question are the counter-terrorism laws and the *Migration Act*. These are the laws that have dominated much of the struggle between the executive and parliament on the one hand and the legal profession on the other. Beneath the passions aroused by the Haneef affair is a contest over ideas and power.

The Federal Court judge hearing the appeal against Andrews's decision, Jeffrey Spender, raised immediate doubts about the minister's action, saying to the government counsel: "Unfortunately, I would fail the character test on your statements because I have been associated with persons suspected of criminal conduct."

Such remarks are illustrative of much Federal Court thinking towards the executive over the past decade. The Howard Government will not retreat on the Haneef issue. If necessary, it will go to the High Court.

As this saga unfolds, recall the 2002 warning by John McMillan before his appointment as commonwealth Ombudsman that a significant problem in immigration litigation was "overreaching, overzealous judicial review" and that the obligation on courts was to accept "that the merits of administrative decision-making lie with the executive".

That Haneef's case collapsed in the courts does not gainsay that the Australian Federal Police continues to regard him with significant suspicion as inquiries continue. Asked at the end of the week whether the AFP still felt that Haneef may have had some prior knowledge of the London and Glasgow terrorist plots, AFP Commissioner Mick Keelty said "our doubts remain very deep".

Asked whether he still believed that the reasons Haneef gave for his thwarted initial effort to leave the country were just a pretext, Keelty said: "From day one, we thought the reasons he gave were highly dubious."

And that view hasn't changed. The key to Andrews's decision lies in the *Migration Act* and the obligations imposed on him as Immigration Minister by the national parliament.

That such an unremarkable statement tests the limits of credulity reveals how much the public debate has descended into confusion and irrationality.

The blame for that should be shared all around. There are no heroes in this story.

The collapse of the prosecution case against Haneef was an embarrassment to the commonwealth DPP, the AFP and the Howard Government. There is no substitute for these institutions reviewing and improving their performance in the more challenging climate of counter-terrorism. But beware of the false solution propounded by the lawyer lobby that the answer lies in strengthening judicial review against the executive. That is the great myth of our age.

As for Andrews, his depiction in the media degenerated into farce. Rarely has the gap between the person and the fabrication become so wide. Far from being a cunning manipulator of public opinion playing the race and fear cards, Andrews is a fairly ineffective politician but with more backbone than many realise.

Andrews and the immigration minister before him, Philip Ruddock, have cancelled hundreds of visas annually. The rate for Andrews is about half-a-dozen a week. Such power is exercised under law in the public interest and is reviewable by the courts.

There is no universal human right that entitles a person to an Australian visa or to retain a visa. Hopefully, there never will be. As Andrews says, a visa is a privilege granted by the Australian Government on behalf of the Australian people. It is a fundamental responsibility of the executive.

The test for Andrews's action is twofold: was it legal and was it justified on merit?

The July 31 legal opinion from Solicitor-General David Bennett QC finds without qualification that when Andrews cancelled the visa he relied on material that enabled him to validly make such a decision.

Bennett found that Andrews was fully entitled to make this decision. In addition, Bennett found that if Andrews had acted later (after the prosecution had been withdrawn), then he would still have been entitled to make the same decision.

The second test is whether the cancellation was justified. This is a contested issue. The critics say, variously, that Andrews persecuted an innocent man or that he was playing politics. So, what shaped his decision?

Essentially, there were three factors. First, Andrews had on his desk a protected-information dossier from the AFP that included an internet conversation between Haneef and his brother Shoaib that, at the very least, raised serious suspicions about Haneef. This led the AFP to advise Andrews in the second-last paragraph of the document, as summarised by the Solicitor-General, that it "may be evidence of Haneef's awareness of the conspiracy to plan and prepare the acts of terrorism in London and Glasgow".

Consider this: might a responsible immigration minister give weight to such a possibility as flagged by the AFP?

Second, in the final paragraph of the same document, the AFP made it clear that Haneef's attempted departure from Australia appeared overwhelmingly to be on a false pretext. Providing a false pretext for leaving the country (to see his newborn baby) unsurprisingly raised police suspicions. This ignited AFP concerns that Haneef might have some awareness of the terrorist acts. When Andrews reviewed the circumstances of Haneef's attempted departure, he was convinced they were highly suspicious.

Third, Andrews had to exercise his obligations under the *Migration Act*, one of the most scrutinised laws of the past decade. In addition to Andrews and Ruddock, John Howard was familiar with the visa provisions of the act. That would hardly come as a surprise.

The act requires the minister to cancel a visa if he "reasonably suspects" the individual cannot pass the "character test" and cancellation is in the national interest. The act casts a very wide net in instructing the minister about the character test, such failure arising if the person has a criminal record or an "association" with people the minister suspects have been involved in criminal conduct, or if the person poses a risk under another long list of situations not relevant to this case.

The point, as Bennett emphasised in his legal opinion, is that the minister's discretion is extremely wide. Indeed, it is so wide that a precedent exists in the case of the *minister v Wai Kuen Chan* (2001) that the association did not have to involve a nexus between the visa holder and the criminal conduct: that is, guilt or guilty knowledge was not essential. Bennett endorsed this interpretation, saying "that neither knowledge of the associate's criminality nor guilty participation is necessary for a person to fail paragraph (b) of the character test".

In practical terms, the minister must judge how serious the association is and the degree of criminality of the associate (in this case accused terrorists). The criterion the minister applies is not the "beyond reasonable doubt" of the criminal law but the far broader "reasonable suspicion" that Bennett calls "significantly lower than even the civil standard".

Andrews acted on the law. He acted in recognition of his wide discretion in relation to the situation and the relatively low threshold for the test. He acted on the law of the land. These provisions were passed by the national parliament not in a fit of absence of mind but as a matter of policy to vest such powers in the executive in order to protect the public welfare and the national interest. These provisions are upheld by the Coalition and the ALP. Labor supported Andrews's decision.

Andrews was not required to decide whether Haneef was innocent or guilty of any crime. This was not the test. Ministerial discretion to revoke a visa usually follows the conviction of the individual, but this is not required by the law. Andrews was making a judgment about character, not guilt, because that is what the law asked him to do. While Andrews had the discretion, the issue was canvassed by the national security committee of cabinet, where Keelty provided an outline of inquiries. When the committee meeting concluded, Andrews told Keelty his inclination was to revoke Haneef's visa. Keelty backed the decision without qualification. In every discussion with Andrews since that time, Keelty has supported the visa cancellation.

Andrews also discussed the decision with Howard. In effect, he got the green light. Andrews had not the slightest doubt that Howard backed him, and that judgment has been verified since.

Consider the media debate of the past week: it is that Andrews, having acted on this police advice, the wide ambit of the law and the obligations imposed on him as minister, was merely seeking to arouse xenophobia, run a political scare, and should be forced to resign as minister. If this sounds utter nonsense, that's because it is utter nonsense.

The final point is that Andrews did not launch a hunting expedition for material to use against Haneef. The material came to Andrews via the proper channels in the advisory process.

Andrews's errors of judgment were twofold: his timing and his presentation. From the start, the notion of parallel processes was highly dangerous and confusing. Once the court proceedings collapsed, the inevitable media perception was that Andrews was pursuing an innocent man. This perception became almost impossible to shake. His effort to distinguish the court and executive processes largely fell on deaf ears.

As events unfolded, there was a serious concern on the part of Keelty and within the AFP about the parallel processes. Alarm grew within the Government about the political fallout and the rising sense of public distrust of executive actions.

When the prosecution was first launched, Keelty said it was "at the margin". Andrews was surprised the DPP proceeded to court. Eventually the DPP had to withdraw in the most humiliating circumstances. And the public debate was engulfed in a collapse of institutional trust.

In reality, there were no easy options for Andrews. He had considered an announcement before the magistrate's bail decision but that would have only precipitated the outcry that he was trying to intimidate the magistrate.

Alternatively, if Andrews had waited until after the court proceedings before he cancelled the visa, he would have guaranteed an attack along the lines that such a delay suggested he wasn't really serious.

It is apparent, however, that Andrews mismanaged the politics. Having taken the decision, he had only one option: a full-blooded and hardline, no-risk rhetoric on visa holders. He lacked the stomach for this and when he tried it, his effort was feeble.

By the end of the week the Government had regrouped and Andrews had turned defiant.

"I've never been uncertain about the Prime Minister's support at any stage," he said.

The pivotal point for Andrews was his ability via the Bennett opinion to make public not just the computer chat-room conversations involving Haneef but the formal AFP advice in relation to the visa.

Andrews said he was "more certain than ever" about the validity of his decision, pointing to new material: that Haneef did not apply for leave from the hospital when he arrived on the Monday morning but applied only after taking two calls, one from India, and being told about the SIM card problem. At that point he tried to catch the first available plane.

Does any of this prove that Haneef is guilty? Of course not. Does any of this prove that the AFP suspicions are right? Of course not. Most of the time executive decisions are about fine distinctions, not black-and-white situations.

Much of the public debate this week mirrored a legal and media preference for another law: a law that weakens ministerial power and increases the rights of the visa holder. In a robust contribution, Democrats senator Andrew Bartlett said the lesson was "the extreme character provisions of the *Migration Act* combined with mandatory detention". Not a bad analysis.

Naturally, he wants the law rewritten. And this is where the issue should be resolved: in parliament by democratic resort.

As McMillan said in his former capacity as a professor of administrative law, arguments that judicial activism is a superior instrument are "too easily made and too rarely justified". Yes, the executive is deeply fallible, but claims for the superiority of judicial method are undemonstrated and unpersuasive.

In conclusion, the Haneef affair highlights the charade of the so-called politics of fear. Let's say it: terrorism is a political issue. It deserves to be a political issue and it will stay a political issue.

The line from the civil liberties lobby that the Government seeks political advantage from terrorism has as much value as saying it seeks political advantage from education, health or welfare. Of course it seeks political advantage.

The politics of terrorism is driven by the fact that the threat is real, that governments have a responsibility to protect the public and that they will be held accountable if the threat succeeds. Their bias, therefore, is towards counter-terrorism measures. The lawyers and the media are essential checks in this process. But it is the executive that carries the onus of decision-making.

Lawyers and the media may prefer to give the benefit of the doubt to suspects but the public will be unforgiving of a government that does so. Is this how the Australian people want Howard and Kevin Rudd to operate? The answer is obvious.

This is unquestionably so when the issue concerns a visa where the ministerial decision is not about guilt or innocence but a decision about risk.

This goes to the essence of the Andrews decision. He decided, in effect, that Australia would not take the risk that Haneef represented. The Government's preference is for a no-risk policy. This is how Ruddock operated and it is how Andrews operates.

It is Australia's sovereign right to apply such a policy, just as many other nations apply the same policy. The justification, ultimately, is that such firmness is a necessary condition to maintain public support for Australia's huge and non-discriminatory immigration program that, year after year, contributes to a more diverse nation.

Paul McGeough

Misguided US policy a gift to bin Laden
The Sydney Morning Herald, 19 March 2007

It is more the war of error than a war on terror.

Who, four years ago, would have put money on Washington bungling its invasion of Iraq so badly? What might the odds have been, back then, on the terrorist Osama bin Laden surviving to celebrate his 50th birthday?

It is tempting to dwell on tomorrow's fourth anniversary of the start of the US-led march on Baghdad, its specious genesis and the catalogue of mistakes in its aftermath.

But the milestone that demands attention is last week's cyberspace celebration by jihadists of the bin Laden half-century. What does his survival reveal of real progress in this so-called war on terror?

When the US marines lost bin Laden at Tora Bora in Afghanistan in December 2001, the White House resorted to what American commentators call the "bait-and-switch"—if they couldn't find bin Laden, then they would have to portray Saddam Hussein as the real terrorist threat and go after him.

Back then, the White House wanted us to believe that bin Laden's whereabouts did not matter. And by releasing the "A to Z" claim of total responsibility for the whole al-Qaeda box-and-dice last week by Khalid Sheik Mohammed, who is being held by the US at Guantanamo Bay, the new message seems to be that bin Laden simply doesn't matter any more.

There is a sense of deja vu in all this. Remember all the ignored warnings about al-Qaeda before September 11? When, as the former CIA chief George Tenet later conceded, the system was "blinking red"?

Same-same today—intelligence officials alarmed by a remarkable rejuvenation and expansion of al-Qaeda cannot get traction in Washington, so they are backgrounding reporters instead.

The emerging consensus among analysts is that, despite its losses since September 11, al-Qaeda has regrouped and restructured and has opened new bases in Africa and Europe along with its Iraq campaign.

The Lahore-based analyst Ahmed Rashid adds: "[And at the same time, bin Laden] has revived the Taliban movement in Afghanistan and turned Pakistan into 'Terrorism Central'."

The West Point terrorism analyst Bruce Hoffman challenges George Bush's claim that al-Qaeda is "on the run". "Rather than 'al-Qaeda RIP', we face an al-Qaeda that has risen from the grave," he says.

That lack of traction is caused by vast quantities of oxygen being sucked in by the misguided Iraq war—emotional, military, political and diplomatic. It leaves little for a bigger and more disturbing geopolitical picture that has emerged since 2001.

But join the new dots. See how the American President's decisions after September 11 have created a minefield that now extends from the Mediterranean to Islamabad.

The US and its allies, Australia included, are trapped in two "hot" war zones—Iraq and Afghanistan.

Undermanned and underfunded by careless choice, the US is attempting full-scale war and half-baked nation-building on two wild fronts. But it is surrounded by countries—Iran, Syria, Lebanon, Pakistan—that are havens for its enemies just as they are happily indifferent to or deliberately stoking Washington's fires on their borders.

Yet, as the Americans stomp around the region, loose-lipped and guns blazing, they refuse to bite the bullet on Pakistan, where bin Laden hides. On the other hand, amid a disquieting sense of superpower impotence, the Iraq debacle has the entire Middle East on tenterhooks.

When Israel smashed into Lebanon last year, the US Secretary of State, Condoleezza Rice, stood back, recklessly declaring the failed invasion to be the birth pangs of "a new Middle East". Not quite—more a ham-fisted wrecking of the old that has Washington's autocratic allies in the region quaking and its enemies emboldened.

For all its ugly failings, Saddam Hussein's Iraq was the regional keystone. Shiite Iran was held in check by Sunni neighbours on both sides and long-contained Sunni–Shiite tension and resentment were suppressed.

But the invasion of Iraq has wrecked any restraint as the two houses of Islam take sides. The frightening extremism was revealed last month when al-Qaeda, a sworn Sunni enemy of Washington, urged a US nuclear strike on Shiite Iran, another sworn enemy of the Bush White House.

With a vocal Washington lobby urging US strikes on Tehran, the Brookings Institution's Bruce Riedel warns that the hawks are playing into al-Qaeda's hands: "War between the US and Iran would be a tremendous strategic victory [for al-Qaeda] since two of their most deadly enemies would bleed each other. The Sunni Arab jihadist community would kill two birds with one stone."

Despite the White House spin effort, Iraq never was a front in the "war on terror"—but it is now. Despite cocksure predictions that virtually all US troops would be home by July 2003, their numbers have increased and they are bogged down because, as the leader of al-Qaeda in Iraq, Abu Omar al-Baghdadi, puts it: "In order to kill the beast, we must get it to leave its den ... the idiot Bush sent his army to where we laid ambushes."

Saudi Arabia, Jordan and Egypt are terrified by the Shiite ascendancy in Iraq and Shiite Tehran's muscle-flexing. The Gulf states that might have thrown an economic anchor for the new Afghanistan instead are looking much closer to home.

Their obsession with events in Iraq will only be heightened by think-tank conclusions in the US that Washington needs to treble troop numbers in Iraq to cope with the ferocity of full-blown civil war that will kill hundreds of thousands of civilians and reduce millions more to refugees.

Far from putting a lid on terrorism, as Team Bush claimed it would, the Iraq war has provoked a sevenfold increase in fatal jihadist strikes around the world, as counted by Peter Bergin and Paul Cruickshank of New York University's Center on Law and Security.

Inside the Baghdad bunker, the Pentagon's own specialist advisers monitor the US as much as they do Iraq. And their fear now is a Vietnam-style collapse of political and public will at home and the risk of a humiliating retreat—unless they can turn Iraq around within six months.

The odds are stacked against them in that race against the clock.

Just as in Afghanistan, US troop numbers in Iraq are grossly insufficient; a thinning coalition of the dwindling has overtaken the coalition of the willing; the neighbours don't want to help; allies don't care enough; and the central government is weak and corrupt.

Michael Scheuer, who headed the CIA's now disbanded bin Laden unit, figures that once all the support troops in the 36,000-strong US–NATO deployments in Afghanistan are deducted, the allied fighting force is no greater than the Taliban's. And that, he concludes, "[is] far too few in number ... inferior Afghan insurgents have forced far superior Western military forces onto a path that leads towards evacuation".

The Taliban's singular achievement was to impose law and order in Afghanistan. Washington, London and the rest still can't match that, just as they can't match the Taliban's near-total elimination of the opium crop—when it cynically chose to do so.

Increasingly, just as in Iraq, Afghans see the coalition forces from many nations only as Americans; as occupiers; as culturally insensitive; and as cowards who bomb their enemies from the air, killing too many civilians.

But with all the focus on the Middle East, it is in Pakistan that so many of the post-September 11 threads are rooted.

Islamabad's military writ does not extend to the wild tribal regions on the Afghan border from where bin Laden and his resurgent network operate.

Elements in the US and NATO hierarchy increasingly question President Pervez Musharraf's commitment to the fight against terrorism, and to democracy—remember that supposedly is the cause for which more than 3000 Americans have died and US taxpayers have kissed off hundreds of billions of dollars in Iraq.

But Washington plays into Musharraf's hands, sending conflicting messages.

The Vice-President, Dick Cheney, comes to Islamabad to demand that the Pakistani leader do more, but the White House also heaps praise on the democracy-resistant Pakistani leader, last week Washington tut-tutted about Musharraf's crude sacking of Pakistan's chief justice—but then slipped an aid cheque for $750 million in Musharraf's pocket.

When it comes to manipulating Washington's greatest fears, Musharraf is the expert. What a nightmare it would be, his supporters imply from time to time, if the fundamentalists were to elbow him aside and take control of Islamabad's nuclear arsenal. Some US officials show their frustration with Musharraf. But, to use a Bushism, they end up concluding that he is "with 'em" as much as he is "agin 'em".

Last month, the new Director of National Intelligence, Admiral John McConnell, told the US Senate that any new terrorist attack on the US was "most likely" to come from Pakistan.

He said: "Many of our most important interests intersect in Pakistan, where the Taliban and al-Qaeda maintain critical sanctuaries ... [Pakistan] is our partner in the war on terror and has captured several al-Qaeda leaders. However, it also is a major source of Islamic extremism."

But then came the catch-22:

> We recognise that aggressive military action, however, has been costly for Pakistani security forces and appreciate concerns over the potential for sparking tribal rebellion and a backlash by sympathetic Islamic political parties.
>
> There is widespread opposition among these parties to the US military presence in Afghanistan and Iraq. With elections expected later this year, the situation will become even more challenging—for President Musharraf and for the US.

There are reports of covert CIA teams being despatched to Pakistan to kill or capture bin Laden. But the commentator Rashid's sombre reflection on the terrorism master's birthday bash is this:

> Bin Laden has survived half a century due to the failed policies of the US, which declined to chase him down when it was much easier to do so and instead focused on invading Iraq. If he were to die tomorrow, his message and organisation would remain a major threat to the world.

Chris Masters

Mission drift: A report from Afghanistan
The Monthly, December 2007 – January 2008

To arrive in Oruzgan province is to step into both the future and the past. Through the swirling dust and retreating din of the plane's engines appear soldiers in body armour, looking like Galactic troopers from *Star Wars*. Beyond the patch of green that is the Teri River valley there is only flat desert country and a perimeter of tall, bleak cliffs. Soldiers talk of remote mountain settlements that roads and electricity have never reached, of dusty orchards, hand-drawn wells and locals astride donkeys.

Kamp Holland, the main base for Task Force Oruzgan, adjoins the airstrip. The Dutch are in charge, with as many as a thousand Australians their junior partners; inside can be found British and American soldiers, along with newly trained units of the Afghan National Army. Further behind the serried concrete barriers are compounds of Special Forces soldiers with longer hair, cooler sunglasses and looser, non-regulation clothing: the Jedi Knights.

The quarters are largely prefabricated bomb-proof containers, though the crash of incoming missiles is heard only rarely. There is no sound of carousing coming from the local bar; indeed, there is no local bar. Australia and the Netherlands have decided on an alcohol-free campaign. They go to bed early here, and Oruzgan becomes the world's quietest war zone. The only noise is the occasional crunch of gravel as someone heads to a shower cubicle, seeking relief from the heat. Thin shafts of coloured light from soldiers' torches strike through the blackness like benign tracers.

My visit began in late May 2007. It was not yet summer, but at midnight the airconditioning was still welcome. Over here even the tents are climate-controlled. Sleep does not come in large rations. At 2 am on my first morning we were mustered and stumbled towards a convoy of Bendigo-built Bushmasters. I met my driver, a 19-year-old Queenslander, Trooper Brendan Davis. When later I reached my wife by mobile phone, she told me her hairdresser's friend has a son in Afghanistan named Brendan. They are one and the same. Among all the world's nations, Australia is a small country town.

Brendan likes the Bushmaster. They all do: the Americans and British want them, and the Dutch have already bought them. The thinly armoured Humvees and Land Rovers do not offer as much protection from the Taliban's weapon of choice, the homemade mine (or improvised explosive device, as the military calls them). Later, in October, one of Brendan's colleagues, Trooper David Pearce, was killed by a mine while at the wheel of a Light Armoured Vehicle, becoming the second Australian fatality in Afghanistan.

Our pre-dawn convoy set off at an unpredictable time partly for this reason, avoiding roads where explosives may have been secreted through the night. We struck out across country and, after an hour of steady jolting, slowed and regrouped. Dawn broke on an earlier century. I watched as a nomad steered his flock, weaving between the military vehicles with not a glance at this latest invader. Nearby were low-slung Bedouin-style tents, with fierce hounds tethered beside them.

This has long been territory resistant to internal rule, let alone external conquest. But conquest was never the objective, as the various International Security Assistance Force (ISAF) briefings remind us. First, the mantra goes, provide security; second, help with reconstruction; and third, develop governance to a point where Afghanistan can look after itself. And in the early years great strides were made. Operation Enduring Freedom began less than a month after the attacks on the World Trade Center and the Pentagon. By the end of 2001 the Taliban government, which had provided sanctuary for Al Qaeda, had fallen; in 2002 Hamid Karzai won the Afghan presidency in a democratic election; in the following year NATO assumed command of the international forces of the ISAF.

The swift collapse of the old regime was testament to its weak support. While not as corrupt as their predecessors, the village mullahs had proved at least as cruel and violent, reducing Afghanistan to a medieval state. But six years on, neither the Taliban nor Al Qaeda has been vanquished, and the ISAF talks of a long task ahead. Colonel Hans van Griensven, the Dutch commander of Task Force Oruzgan, estimates it will take at least 20 years. One of the British commanders says it may be 30. Although low in numbers, and by Western standards primitively equipped, the Taliban has managed to force a stalemate with the 100,000-strong partnership of the international forces and the new Afghan army. The Taliban fighters have a saying: the foreigners have watches, but the Taliban has time.

Professor William Maley, of the Australian National University, has counted as many as 70 conditions that must be met for individual nations to leave their compounds. "In a fast-moving war," he says, "ISAF becomes choked by the array of caveats." The rules of engagement are never revealed, but to those who spend time in Afghanistan it becomes obvious which nations work on strictly humanitarian endeavours, which avoid fighting at night and which stay away from the more volatile eastern and southern regions. German commanders based in the more stable north, at Mazar-e Sharif, have expressed embarrassment about their inability to venture south. According to the Lowy Institute's Anthony Bubalo, there is a loss of continuity—and not a little shame—when Afghan units trained by them are sent off to battle while ISAF's most professional soldiers and police officers stay behind. Not that you can ever really hide in Afghanistan: at last count Germany had almost ten times Australia's casualties.

Another divide between the coalition partners is in the emphasis they give (in military speak) to kinetic and nonkinetic activity. For non-kinetic, read hearts and minds; for kinetic, fists and boots. The Australian Reconstruction Task Force travels with a bit of both. On the first morning I ventured with the convoy, a long wait followed the spectacular dawn. We paused before a narrow gully. As there was no way around, it was an ideal location for a Taliban attack. After an hour of close inspection by soldiers with mine-detection equipment and a sniffer dog, Flo Jo, the vehicles were signalled forward. This is a war of inches: the exercise was repeated on our return. The soldiers are not alone in taking risks. One Australian dog, Razz, was killed when detecting a mine, which then exploded. Another, Merlin, was run over by a military vehicle.

All this trouble is for the sake of inspecting a range of construction projects being undertaken by the local Provincial Reconstruction Team (PRT). Throughout Afghanistan there arc 34 of these PRTs, involving many of the participating ISAF nations. As in this case, a small group of engineers travels with a larger group of heavily armed infantry. The idea is to do good work, to improve facilities for the Afghans, rather than shoot up the place.

The ultra-cautious approach of the Australians can frustrate their American comrades. But the Australians make no apologies: they see a clear connection between low casualties and disciplined drills. And besides, what is the point of being blown to bits for lack of a little patience?

As we travelled there was occasional discussion amid the troops, who were on the lookout for potential spotters among the locals. Vehicles are commonly seen shadowing convoys, and mobile-phone traffic indicates that reports on the forces' movements are regularly conveyed to the Taliban. A 23-year-old infantry platoon commander from Perth, Lieutenant Wil Langdon, said he has little doubt some locals seen smiling and waving at the soldiers have taken note of the heavy weapons and chosen to leave their AK-47s in the hut. The lot of the locals in dealing with the Taliban and the foreign troops is like that of the prison informant who juggles the competing demands of fellow inmates and prison guards. In order to get on, they peddle information and switch loyalty, trusting their wits to stay alive.

Afghanistan is a nation of tribes. The Pashtun are a majority 45%, and the south is very much Pashtun country. Within the Pashtun there are further divides, principally between the Ghilzai and Durrani communities. The convoy took the long route to the town of Tarin Kowt, which has a population of around 10,000. If the Taliban has a heartland, it is there. The movement's founder, Mullah Mohammed Omar, a Ghilzai, was born in Oruzgan and, it is said, lived in Tarin Kowt during the Soviet occupation.

The Bushmasters threaded through bazaars and narrow roads, laughing children running alongside. The vehicles took up defensive positions again in the compound of the local governor, where the walls are bullet-scarred from a recent battle. The children caught up and gathered round in the way children do. The soldiers counselled me to be careful about giving out prized pens and paper to all those pleading hands. Better to keep a distance, they said. A fortnight later, on 15 June, a suicide bomber struck a Dutch armoured car travelling along the same street. Five of the local children died in the bombing, along with Timo Smeehuijzen, a 20-year-old soldier.

We left the compound on foot, hurrying through back alleys, following an unpredictable route to the local hospital. On the way, women in full burqas shrunk into doorways; soldiers told me they deploy for months without once speaking to an Afghan woman. At the hospital entrance a burly Australian corporal took charge, organising searches of people entering the grounds. Igor Moravcik, or 'Czech', as he is known, is on his third tour of Afghanistan, the first two having been with the Russian Army. His is an awkward job, for a full-body search is hardly the best way to win the trust of a local.

Over the years I have been in many third-world hospitals and interviewed many harried doctors. I recognised the look on one face: it was the physician's version of the soldier's thousand-yard stare. Dr Ajab Noor told me of his own no-man's land, where he risks censure by his government for treating friends of the Taliban and execution by the Taliban for treating friends of the government. Another member of staff said that a dozen medical workers had been killed there in the past year.

An army truck carrying the engineers' equipment was brought up to the back door. A defensive guard of Australian infantry formed as the plumbers and electricians in uniform went about their business. Someone had scribbled "the tethered goat" on a door: the engineers have to put down weapons to pick up mattocks and hammers, drills and tape measures, and they are easy targets. It is hard not to be impressed by these soldiers. When I asked them why they do it, many spoke of simply wanting to do their duty. It sounded neither cloyingly patriotic nor insincere. Captain Liam Hansen, who grew up on the NSW south coast, put it this way: "Helping people who have nothing is a satisfying and humbling experience."

Captain Hansen and his team oversee a $5-million list of projects. Beyond the new wing and kitchen block for the hospital is an all-weather causeway across the Teri River. In the past, during the snow melt, the river became impassable, depriving those on the north of access to medical facilities. People would die waiting, stranded beyond the rushing water. Hansen was gratified to see locals pitching in when a rising river threatened the work that had already been completed.

In addition, the soldiers are overseeing the construction of a training centre, a clinic and schools. Teachers and other government workers habitually receive 'night letters', Taliban warnings of the dire consequences of co-operating with foreigners. A teacher at the Talani School told me that he does his best to resist such intimidation for the sake of the children. He spoke approvingly of the Australians, explaining that in the past, promises from the Canadians and Americans came to little. The Australians have adopted a rapid reconstruction—or what the troops call a *Backyard Blitz*—approach to these projects, recognising the importance of providing results swiftly.

The United States, by far Afghanistan's largest aid donor, had previously operated in Tarin Kowt. A provincial administration building opened in 2006 began to crumble soon after, so extensive were the defects. The construction, undertaken by local contractors, had been improperly supervised. The Australians have had similar difficulties: inspecting work at the Tarin Kowt hospital, Captain Dan Keep, a project engineer from Orange, did a doubletake when he saw a washbasin placed where a kitchen sink should be. Over time a more pragmatic approach has developed, reconciling the gap between the way the foreigners would do it and the way the locals want it. At Kamp Holland there is a regular *sura*, a meeting between local leaders and Australian and Dutch representatives, who negotiate the list of wants.

The individual reconstruction teams are seen as inkblots, the message soaking across the map, beyond the clinics and schools and into the distant hills. Winning trust also has a military advantage. Intelligence on where bombs are made and planted has been more forthcoming over time. Warrant Officer Tony Quirk, from Brisbane, has been to Afghanistan five times. On the wall of the Explosive Ordinance Disposal workshop is a photograph of a younger Quirk, dressed like a mujaheddin. Fifteen years ago he was part of a UN team teaching Afghans to clear some of the 12 million landmines planted by the Russians, a job still unfinished. Crouched over a collection of the latest homemade variations, Quirk explained that many were found because locals pointed them out to soldiers.

The soldiers' days are long: some 16 hours off base. The heat and the weight of the body armour so exhausted me that at one point I slumped in the shadow of a mud wall. I was soon roused by cold soft drinks summoned from somewhere and barbecued-lamb sandwiches the eager crew called "camel burgers". (With equal grace they dubbed me, with my helmet perpetually askew, "Dad's Army".)

When the Dutch first established a presence at Tarin Kowt, they undertook a "conflict analysis", so as to know their enemy. They found that in many instances, fighting in Afghanistan was inter-tribal: Durrani and Ghilzai Pushtuns have been warring there forever. Australian SAS soldiers on missions probing deeper into the hills have found that Taliban fighters are not the only ones involved in battles. In 2005, *Time* magazine reported on an extensive gunfight involving an SAS patrol in 2002; according to the report, the SAS soldiers had been fighting neither the Taliban nor Al Qaeda, but Balkhel villagers guarding their patch.

Defining the Taliban is not easy. In the past years the military nomenclature has included ACM (Anti-Coalition Militia), OMF (Opposing Militia Forces) and simply 'extremists'. The description that most unnerves is the generic 'insurgent', for those drawn from the seemingly infinite ranks of extreme Islam. Replacements come across the porous border with the west of Pakistan, another Taliban heartland. Although technically foreigners, they are not seen so much as outsiders. Pakistan supported the Taliban in its rise to power and was one of the few countries to recognise it as a legitimate government; in the past years, Pervez Musharraf has not denied that the Taliban is sustained from Pakistan's side of the border.

The ISAF identifies three tiers of Taliban membership. The first are the centrally directed global jihadists. The second are often criminals, allied to the Taliban more opportunistically through tribal rivalry or the need to protect illegal interests. The third are locally recruited part-time mercenaries who operate depending on the amount of coercion exerted and the range of available employment.

The hearts-and-minds mission of the international forces is designed to erect a barrier between the top-tier Taliban and the rest of the Afghan people. Within the Provincial Reconstruction Teams there is competition to see which nation can develop the most effective model to do this. One program that has become something of a showpiece is Australia's Trade Training School, at Kamp Holland. Here Australian engineers teach teenage Afghan males trade skills, such as carpentry and small-engine maintenance. The basic course runs for a few weeks, and participants are paid $3.50 a day (two-thirds of the population live on less than a dollar a day, so the payment is not unattractive). When they graduate, each is given a toolkit. Soon after, Australian soldiers sometimes see the kits on sale at the local bazaars, but they accept that some failure is inevitable. The ones who keep the toolkits and begin their own small businesses are less likely to be embraced by the Taliban. And the skills developed help create a local workforce, which can in turn help with the reconstruction projects.

Meanwhile, the Taliban, in pursuit of foreign exchange, has turned the country into the world's biggest drug supplier. Afghanistan now accounts for 93% of the global heroin supply. The base opium paste comes from vast fields of poppies, mostly in the southern provinces; Oruzgan is the third-largest producer. While there has been success in reducing production in the centre and north, in the troubled south-west the reverse has occurred. There, young men can earn as much as $15 a day working the fields. The criminal networks controlling the trade have forged an alliance with Taliban leaders through a mutual need to keep government at a distance. (Government members, though, are known to have their own links to the trade: in 2005, nine tonnes of opium was uncovered in the office of Helmand provincial governor, Sher Muhammad Akhundzada.)

When South African contractors turn up to bulldoze fields as part of a British-sponsored poppy-eradication program, they are directed away from the protected crops to the ones operated by poorer and less-influential farmers. Destroying the fields without compensating local farmers and providing replacement industry plays into the hands of the enemy. Attempts to get farmers to grow less profitable oranges and potatoes have, unsurprisingly, proved futile.

Australia provides $4.5 million to support counter-narcotic efforts, but under ISAF rules the military can't directly engage in eradication. This is seen as a police task, and so far there are few police on the ground. The heroin trade proceeds under the watch of unmanned Predator aircraft and satellites further above. Images show an increase of 17% in the cultivation of poppies in the past year, with production even stronger, growing by 34%. It is difficult not to regard the expansion of these pink fields, which now cover an area of almost 200,000 hectares across the country, as emblematic of the difficulties faced by the Afghan government and the international forces.

Kandahar is the main allied base in the south. It was also the site of the Taliban's last stand in 2001, and the hangars at the air base are still pockmarked from the battle—which, in a sense, persists at the perimeter. In November 2007, Canadian and Afghan soldiers fought off a concerted attack on its north-western districts. Within the confines of the base, though, there is a disconnection from the troubles outside, and ISAF leaders worry about a fortress mentality. A Tim Horton's outlet provides comfort food to the Canadians, and a baseball pitch draws a small and jovial crowd. Joggers pass wearing camouflaged gym outfits, spoiled somewhat by the luminous vests that have become a safety requirement. Road accidents, training mishaps and even Kovco-like unexplained shootings have contributed to the casualty count.

The Taliban's much-touted spring offensive never transpired. British, Canadian and American soldiers did see intense action, but none of it had a decisive effect on the war. Operations north of Kandahar were thought to be pushing the enemy closer to the Australians in Oruzgan. When the Australian Special Operations Task Group (SOTG) returned there in 2007, there was an expectation that it would be kept busy. The SAS, the sharp end of the SOTG, has been back and forth from Afghanistan since 2002. Some of the fighting involving the Australians has been described as the heaviest since Vietnam. Action can erupt suddenly, with enemy fighters massing in swarms. One unnamed commando sergeant won a Star of Gallantry after enduring constant attack by an estimated 200 Taliban fighters. He attributed his survival—after being rushed by the enemy and ducking rocket-propelled grenades for more than six hours—to "being a better shot".

Much of this fighting occurred in the Chora Valley, 15 kilometres from Kamp Holland. A home to Ghilzai Pushtuns, the valley has long been a refuge for the Taliban, and the Ghilzai have resented the greater support being extended the town-based Durranis. In 2006 some 500 soldiers from six nations spent ten days attempting to clear the area. SAS Sergeant Matthew Locke was another to receive a commendation for his role in the fighting. When Locke became the first Australian killed in armed combat, in late October 2007, it was in the Chora Valley. Clearing out the Taliban was beginning to look like holding the tide.

Fighting has continued sporadically since June 2007, when the biggest mass attack occurred, with hundreds of Taliban fighters swarming police posts. A conventional response to these attacks is to call in air and artillery support. When the F-16s streak in and the 60-tonne Dutch Panzer tank begins hurling artillery rounds some 18 kilometres, precision tends to take a back seat, no matter what the military says about 'smart' weapons. At the time it was estimated that about 60 civilians died, along with 70 suspected Taliban fighters and 16 Afghan police. One local said he was forced to bury 18 members of his family, including women and children. President Karzai protested; later, on America's *60 Minutes* program, he called for the banning of all air strikes. In Afghanistan, as in Iraq, the US is seen to be by far the most trigger-happy of international forces.

When I took this up with the ISAF commander, General Dan McNeill, an American, he told me his forces are far more discriminating in the use of air power than is commonly credited. He cited what he said was one of many examples of avoiding striking a compound, which according to intelligence harboured an insurgent leader, because civilians were about 50 metres away.

Sorting out the blame for casualties is a classic fog-of-war problem. The Afghan defence spokesman, General Zahir Azimi, shares his president's anger but acknowledges that the Taliban sometimes uses civilians as shields. Sometimes civilians die due to unavoidable circumstances, in the way they do in all wars. Sometimes the air strikes are the result of false intelligence provided by the enemy. And reports of civilian deaths, particularly estimates of numbers, can prove to be plain wrong when later investigated—even if to say so seems like heresy to a media conditioned to a cynical view of military briefings. A villager is as capable as a uniformed PR officer of twisting truth.

But nothing more damages the Afghanistan mission than yet another incident of civilian bloodshed. The Australian Defence Force, with its strong volunteer tradition and ethos of citizen soldiery, has not managed to avoid error and condemnation. On 24 July, on one of the patrols through Tarin Kowt, a civilian truck driver was shot dead when he drove too close to the Australians. The Bushmasters display signs warning other vehicles to keep their distance, but problems of literacy, not to mention the fact that the signs can't be understood unless the driver is close to them, limit their effectiveness. They seemed not to work the following day, too. It's believed a patrol returned to Tarin Kowt, using loudspeakers to request that people maintain a safe distance. But again a vehicle moved too close; again graduated warnings were given. This time two young children were wounded; one, a little girl, was believed to have lost a hand.

When I talked to soldiers back at the base about that split-second decision when they need to distinguish between a potential suicide bomber and an ordinary citizen, they spoke respectfully of the need for caution and explained that when they return from patrol they are exhausted as much by the mental concentration—the effort of avoiding violent confrontation—as by the physical demands of their work. On 3 May, at a checkpoint outside Tarin Kowt, one of these soldiers noticed something odd in the approach of a young Afghan male. The Australian moved to train his weapon on the man. The action seemed to trigger a premature explosion, killing the bomber and slightly wounding the soldier. Others who were there recounted how pleased they were that no one panicked, that casualties were minimised.

Across Afghanistan, every day, such instant decisions are required. Yet the Australians are one of the nations criticised least for unnecessary violence: indeed, if there is a criticism of the Dutch and Australian forces in Oruzgan, it is that they go in for too much of the touchy-feely stuff.

The Afghan capital, Kabul, houses the headquarters for the international mission and for its sometimes-awkward partner, the Karzai-led government. The drive from the airport concentrates the mind. We were instructed to stop under no circumstances, and our bullet-proof Land Cruiser, its roof cluttered with counter-measure antennae, bulldozed through the busy streets, glancing off a commuter bus before heading into a chicane that slows entry to the restricted zone. The mood is different there. The Milano Bar and Kabul Club offer alcohol to those who are allowed. (The Australians are not, and don't seem to mind.) In the recent past, Friday nights got a little boisterous, but after a British commander reminded his men that some of their comrades were killed while they partied, the beer ration was reduced and a more temperate mindset adopted.

The Australian ambassador, Brett Hackett, says Kabul is "sprawling, messy, dangerous and exciting", a city home to more than 4 million people with infrastructure for about 400,000. Saad Mohseni is over that excitement. He is a member of an Afghan–Australian family that has, among other things, imported to Kabul a kind of Australian sensibility. Having grown up on Triple M and the *7.30 Report*, and encouraged by the prospect of a new Afghanistan, the Mohsenis started their own media mini-empire. Their radio network does well, playing in the main popular music, and their television station, with its *6.30 Report*, is garnering a following. But when coverage displeases the Karzai government, Tolo TV staff have been detained by the attorney-general's office and intimidated by the intelligence agency. Three years after he set up business, Mohseni is weary of the increasing crime, and of police officers shaking down citizens and those in government lining their pockets. President Karzai has referred to the "esteemed" Mullah Omar, signalling a willingness to embrace the Taliban; the way Mohseni sees it, Karzai is bent on "snatching defeat from the jaws of victory".

In Afghanistan, any measure of progress depends on where you happen to be. Some of the provinces, particularly in the north, see little trouble. Visiting the border city of Herat, the Lowy Institute's Anthony Bubalo was struck by the absence of body armour on the Italian soldiers, and the bustle of commerce. There was hope that the Provincial Reconstruction Teams would extend the mandate of the Karzai government beyond Kabul and into the provinces. According to William Maley, "there is no single PRT experience": "some international operators are enthusiastic and productive, while others can't wait to get out of the place." In the comparatively stable Bamiyan province the New Zealanders make progress, while in Kandahar the Canadians have battled to hold the outer districts of the city.

A former American naval officer, Chris Mason, believes these projects are having no strategic effect on the war: "The bottom line is, the PRTs are window-dressing. There is an average of one PRT in the southern insurgency zone for every 1.2 million Pashtuns." Mason believes they would work better if there were more of them and they operated at a district rather than provincial level. In Kabul, Saad Mohseni sees it much the same way. He wants his government to show sufficient capacity to take over the programs, so that locals can feel they are working for themselves and not for foreigners.

For these foreigners, it is a balancing act. They need simultaneously to be tough and gentle: a well-trained soldier with a rifle conducts the most precise form of warfare; but that, of course, means taking risks—not least because some military figures believe killing ten civilians creates a hundred new Taliban fighters. The United States' exploitation of firepower and its aversion to casualties is often counterproductive. (It must be acknowledged that the US, the biggest contributor to the international coalition, has also sustained the highest casualties.) General McNeill knows that establishing a successful society that is not dependent on foreigners will take years. "After decades of war, Taliban rule and another five years of insurgency," he told me, "you may arguably have missed educating two generations, so it is tough to find people right out of the box who have the right qualifications."

The reason for ISAF to stay on in Afghanistan has not changed since 2001. The NATO countries' rationale for intervention was that if they did not go to Afghanistan, Afghanistan would come to them. Since then, the conflict has dragged on longer than World War II. But while William Maley believes that Iraq has become another Vietnam, he does not think the same judgement applies to Afghanistan.

The country is not just a battleground but a training ground for the new ways in which future wars will be fought. Soldiers have always been trained to kill; what Afghanistan has shown is they also need to be diplomats, sewerage engineers and social workers. And many of the Australian soldiers seem to have a talent for this. When they patrol the ancient corners of Oruzgan and see a farmer clearing an irrigation channel, they have been known to get into the mud and help. The Afghan defence spokesman, General Azimi, believes Australia has the right approach: not only hunting out the Taliban leaders and bomb-makers, but also making them less appealing by providing locals with assistance and work. Through curiosity, sign language and a Pashtun phrasebook, these young soldiers— some of whom have come from farms back home—are taking an interest. Although it is difficult to define, there is something in their manner that may be as important to the success of their mission as any space-age weaponry.

5
Australian Values

Tom Keneally

Flattened by a falafel

The Australian Literary Review, February 2007

Recently SBS screened a documentary that analysed Turkish television as a reflection of the concerns of the Turkish people, caught as they are between the blandishments of the US and the European Union, and less secular Muslim regimes to the east.

Turks like to be seen as living in an advanced state, despite, for example, their Government's persecution of novelist Orhan Pamuk, who won the Nobel Prize in Literature last year.

In any case, the program revealed that the most controversial show on Turkish TV was a contemporary drama about a Greek boy who falls in love with a Turkish girl. Their respective families treat their intention to marry as a calamity perhaps worse than death.

Their reaction, at least on the segments of the show I saw, was comic partly because Turkish dramatic acting is more flamboyantly expressive than the muttering methodism that characterises English-language TV. It was unintendedly funny because the crisis seemed by Australian standards so minor a matter.

All the garment-rendings, faintings and howlings to the skies seem out of kilter with their root cause. Though there is no doubting the antiquity of the hostility between the two racial groups, we are not parties to it, and so what was said, instead of sounding like serious statements of self-definition, came across as hilarious.

Even the solemnity of the urbane Turkish TV producers, who told us such a program would have been impossible even 10 years ago, had a comic streak to it.

The question arose: would our Australian solemnities, the issues of ethnicity that often cause the equivalent of garment-rending, fainting and howling, our dances around irrational taboos, seem just as funny to them?

The truth is that behind the tragedy there's often something side-splitting about other peoples' ethnic hysteria, though never about our own. Race bedevils us all; it is the shell game we never tire of playing. It is little more than 10 years since Pauline Hanson's maiden speech to the federal parliament. It threw Australia into a paroxysm. Now the one-time political phenomenon from Queensland, who says she may contest the next federal election, has a new message but with the same purpose: we have gone too far in accommodating Muslims. Also, "diseased South Africans with AIDS" should not be allowed into the country.

This time Hanson has not received the same level of political oxygen. Even John Howard, as much as he made space for her earlier effusions about Asians, has said she is "out of touch". One thing Hanson has always said that is patently true is that many ordinary Australians agree with her. But perhaps Howard feels she has served her usefulness to his Australia.

What has happened to the threat of Asian "white-anting" that she invoked in that infamous maiden speech? What of the resonant line, "I believe we are in danger of being swamped by Asians ... they have their own culture and religion, form ghettos and do not assimilate"? The threats of "their own culture and religion", their ghettos, did not materialise as she and other commentators visualised. Will she at least pause to consider her hysterias of 1996 before demanding our attention for this new threat?

Before moving on to target Islam, shouldn't she and all those who barracked for her acknowledge that Australia was not destroyed by Asians? And if she was wrong about Asians, on what basis, on what extra evidence, does she show that she's not just as wrong about Muslims and "diseased Africans"?

More important, the same questions might apply to the 1984 warnings of Australia's historian laureate (and he's a damned good one too) Geoffrey Blainey. Blainey is the most personable of human beings, gentle in making his point, generous to enemies. And yet his part in the public discourse of Australia as an avatar of contradiction is undeniable.

In March 1984, in a speech to Warrnambool Rotarians, Blainey noticed that "an increasing proportion of Australians seem to be resentful of the large numbers of Vietnamese and other Southeast Asians who are being brought in".

There was a belief that Asians were "a favoured majority". He perceived in government policy a yielding to the fact that "we will have an Asian majority and that the quicker we move towards it the better", and added: "I do not accept the view widely held in federal cabinet that some kind of slow Asian takeover of Australia is inevitable."

He was worried about the impact of such immigration on employment. To be fair to him, he also said: "The danger to democracy does not necessarily come from the Asian migrants themselves. It comes from the tensions imposed on free institutions if the community becomes too divided over cultural and racial questions."

Yet now, more than 20 years later, one can ask whether our free institutions have been endangered by Asian immigration at all. And if not, what has Blainey to say of that? As a commentator he has proved as wide of the mark as Hanson, though both of them have a passionate constituency; in Blainey's case, often from people who haven't read his elegant work.

Purely in language terms, his social commentary is not as deft as his history. His historical works do not use blunt-force phrases such as "Asian takeover of Australia", a line so broad that it ignores the fact of subtle diversities in all our Asian communities, from Indian to Korean, Japanese to Chinese to Vietnamese.

His commentary is an inexact tool compared with the elegance of his writing in books such as *The Rush That Never Ended: A History of Mining in Australia* (1963), *The Tyranny of Distance* (1966) and his latest engaging and humane social history, which Howard gave as a gift to George W. Bush, *Black Kettle and Full Moon: Daily Life in Vanished Australia*.

Writing in *The Australian* in the aftermath of the December 2005 Cronulla riots, Peter Ryan said that event vindicated Blainey. One might respond: Sorry mate, wrong rioters, a quarter of a century later than predicted.

Certainly it would be crass to take smug satisfaction from what happened at Cronulla. What can be said is that the lamentable day and night of public riot and conflict was ended by the energies of good souls in all sections of the Australian community.

And not even the best efforts of rekindling the pernicious flames, which sections of the media seemed determined to do as the anniversary loomed, could call forth those dangerous passions again. The point is that in 1984 Blainey was talking of imminent perils, not 24 hours of argy-bargy at a Sydney beach, no matter how admittedly deep and unresolved many of the causative feelings are.

In *The Rush That Never Ended*, we encounter obscure men, Cornish miners, for example, who on Sundays preach from wagons to huge congregations all taken by mineral dreams, all full of the enterprise and yearning that characterised the second half of the 19th century and the early part of the 20th, doughty participants in the Australian equation, subtly differentiated in assumptions, beliefs and opinions.

Yet there is no subtlety at all in a phrase such as "Asian takeover of Australia". And there's certainly not the same subtlety in Blainey's *All for Australia*, a book that warned of pavements "spotted with phlegm" and skies "filled with greasy smoke and the smell of goat's meat".

This is not to deny that for older Australians the way their suburbs changed under the pressure of immigration was sometimes disturbing, or that more might have been done to mediate between communities, old and new.

It seems astonishing to me that many obviously gifted people can not imagine the more recent immigrants as they do the 19th-century or even mid-20th-century ones, and can not give any weight to their struggles and the drama of their stories.

For many of us the main aspect of the newcomer story is the supposed threat they present to Australian society as we would like to know and identify it. But more of that in a while.

I've always been fascinated by the way we become what we are, and by the way we decide whether another person belongs in our world or not. My first conscious awareness of race was seeing Aboriginal children walking down River Street in West Kempsey, NSW, to go to town.

These were descendants of the Dangaddi. Although I did not know it, the Dangaddi had been sympathetically depicted as a powerful and handsome group by Clement Hodgkinson, surveyor of the Upper Macleay

River. The Cambridge archaeological expedition of the 1890s also photo-graphed many Dangaddi, and so did a Port Macquarie man, Thomas Dick, in the mid-19th century.

One sees from all these illustrations what a striking people they were. But the children who went past our place in River Street were the racially and physically eroded version. Even by the standards of post-Depression Australia, they seemed scabby, skinny, weepy-eyed. At the time I didn't ask who was to blame for their condition. I remember being more interested in why they had to sit at the front of the cinema.

My other childhood experience of race and tribe was the Catholic–Protestant divide, potent in those days and largely an Anglo-Celtic divide. I was very interested in an inchoate way about why we were suspected and considered second-class citizens. Why were there firms that wouldn't employ us? Why were our fathers and uncles full of stories of the others getting promotions quicker than them?

Even in the trenches of France my uncle had written a letter about how someone had been made sergeant-major, but of course that was to be expected: the Masons, you understand.

While at the time people on both sides believed that divide to be a crucial and disqualifying one, in practice the Australian community was turning us into the one sort of man and woman, with shared enthusiasms, hopes, civic virtues and flaws.

By the late 1940s, we found ourselves combined in mistrust of the Balts, southern Europeans and other "reffos". Despite the admirable Good Neighbour Movement, which welcomed and helped the newcomers, the streets of our suburbs, including mine, Homebush in Sydney's west, were full of men and women who believed the arrivals would never become an effective part of Australian society. Their strangeness disqualified them.

I have lived long enough to hear the rhetoric that was used from 1946 onwards deployed against the Muslim community, which is considered in some quarters to be united, unfragmented, homogeneously unappeasable and homogeneously un or anti-Australian.

There is no doubt that the strangeness of newcomers can be a challenge. At Homebush we were shocked when the Calabrians next door saved their night soil for deployment as manure on their tomatoes. Their tomatoes were rip-snorters, but when the Italian mother offered them over the fence to us—well, my progressive mother had to do the best she could. I'm sure the daughters of that Calabrian couple are now living somewhere in the Australian suburbs in overdisinfected, overfumigated manors.

Racial suspicion is an opportunistic beast, a great ruminant that grazes on one set of newcomers and then on another. And "they" are not individuals with personal and complex histories, they are one and indivisible and all in it together. They live in ghettos, they refuse to learn English, they'll never be true Australians.

And we don't believe this with sad dispassion. We believe it passionately, exhaustingly, in a way that raises our blood pressure and blows our karma. And after a lifetime as an Australian I have come to wonder if it is all worthwhile. And I wonder, too, if it is good for democracy, which is always invoked somewhere, to suspect and dislike and exclude. For that sort of undifferentiated frenzy is a gift to demagogues. And that's why I'm rendered uneasy by Hanson and even by Blainey.

That they are entitled to freedom of speech is obvious. But freedom of speech isn't the issue. The issue is whether the sweeping statement, likely to generate disadvantage for a section of the Australian community, and likely in the uncritical to generate hate and vilification, is ever well placed in public discussion of race.

The fostering of an idea of a "they" in the minds of the majority is something we seem to welcome and suck on, a negative version of Henry Parkes's "crimson thread of kinship", which unites our community in a dance of antipathy.

When I was writing *The Great Shame*, I became aware that the first act of terrorism on Australian soil was an attack on the duke of Clarence, youngest son of Queen Victoria, at a picnic held in his honour at the Sydney suburb of Clontarf on March 12, 1868. As the prince passed the enthusiastic crowd, Henry O'Farrell, a self-proclaimed Fenian, drew two pistols and shot him in the back. "I'm a Fenian, God save Ireland!" yelled O'Farrell, who had earlier been treated for mental instability and was not a member of the Fenian movement, the Irish Republican Brotherhood. The prince survived; O'Farrell was hanged at Darlinghurst jail.

The governor of NSW, Lord Belmore, an Ulster landowner, was near the prince and saw the shooting. The state government, which included Parkes, yielded to the temptations of demagoguery and stirred up in the community the belief that all Irish were involved in a plot of deepest Papist dye, to shed the blood of the royal family.

A *Tampa*-level hysteria was let loose. A ridiculous *Treason-Felony Act* was passed, which made the public utterance of republican sentiment punishable by up to 20 years in jail. The Irish, and even some evangelicals who thought the prince had been punished by God for his hedonism, were tailed, questioned, detained, sacked from their jobs. In a riot in Melbourne, an Irishman was killed.

The frantic suspicion deliberately generated would prevail for the better part of a century. Belmore, an enlightened man driven to take colonial jobs to pay off the inherited debt on the Palladian castle in Fermanagh, warned Parkes, the orchestrator of the hysteria, that once the dogs of hate were let slip, they would not easily be kennelled again.

But the political temptation to evoke a useful paroxysm of suspicion was too great. Parkes was quite willing to release O'Farrell's former cellmate from prison and send him around the country to investigate Fenian cells in the bush. In, for example, the fettling gangs of the Great Western Railway and the places where the Irish could always be found: pubs. To the released criminal it was great fun. "Not sufficient funds for Bathurst, send more money," he telegraphed Parkes, who did so.

There are no neat parallels between the past and present, although I think similarities adequately exist here to permit us a wry smile. Most of us can find similar prefigurements of the present; another for me is the report of the Queensland Alien Immigration Commission, set up in the 1920s to inquire into immigrants in north Queensland.

In 1925, commissioner Thomas Arthur Ferry wrote:

The Greek residents of Queensland are generally of an undesirable type and do not make good citizens. They live in the towns and carry on business in cafes, fish shops, boarding houses ... and other less reputable ways.

They are not agriculturalists and add nothing to the wealth and security of the country. They engage in no useful work that could not be better performed without them.

Ferry concluded: "Socially and economically, this type of immigrant is a menace to the community in which he settles, and it would be for the benefit of the state if his entrance were altogether prohibited."

On two successive weeks in 1942, the most dangerous year in this country's history, Norman Lindsay produced brilliant cartoon covers for *The Bulletin*. One depicted Australia as a well-fed, beautiful but vulnerable maiden, sheathed in a long gown, defiant but fraught, likely to be violated in coming days by the Japanese army. The next was of a Digger with his .303 rifle, indomitably facing the same lowering north as his sister.

I confess that I have mentioned these quite magnificent images before, in a speech opening part of the Welcome Wall at Sydney's Maritime Museum. I suggested we had never made up our minds which one of these two was us, the violable maiden or the rock-jawed Digger.

When we triumph, especially in sport, our leaders depict us as the Digger. But in the face of the smell of goat meat in the suburbs, it's the maiden. That's what, without prejudice, I do not understand about Blainey's position. He is undeniably a great singer of the Australian experience. He sings a robust song of robust—not easily beaten—folk. Does he believe that the values generated by these people, the progressive institutions laid down, the vigorous and free discourse, will all be swept away by a little strangeness in a minority?

And how can he doubt, being such a singer of our values, that if the children of a minority are given our freedoms, including equality of education, that its members, too, will become as enamoured as us of life on this continent?

And all the stuff about ghettoes! In the '50s people were frantic about Leichhardt in Sydney's inner west going Italian. In the '70s it was about Cabramatta going Vietnamese. At what stage does a suburb go from being a ghetto to a tourist attraction? Leichhardt's there and Cabramatta's on the way. Yet how much useless hysteria has been spent just on these two?

So can the rock-jawed Digger be knocked out by a falafel? I do not believe so. But why do so many honest people—and in particular those who see themselves as standing up for our history—doubt the capacity of our past to influence the future, and consider that the future is so tenuous it must be hedged by citizenship tests?

Why so little faith in the breadth of what Australia is, in its capacity to go on? Why so little composure about survival? And why so little analysis of the fact that the Ferrys of our history have always been wrong?

And why don't the more popular commentators on ethnic affairs occasionally ask themselves this: Could we be provoking unnecessary fear, unnecessary hostility? In depicting a monolithic "they", do we make it easier or harder for the living, breathing "them" to become the brothers and sisters in the commonwealth we want them to be? Could we be wrong, as our parents and grandparents were often wrong?

And, again, if our economy is so wonderful, wouldn't the children of immigrants want to be participants in it? If we believe in our values, wouldn't the children of immigrants embrace them? They always have.

At the beginning of 2007, I drink to the value of a temperate attitude, of tranquillity rather than unnecessary racial fever. There is a wealth of other stuff, from sovereign corporatism to Iraq to our water crisis to nuclear waste storage, to keep us adequately anxious.

May I paraphrase the wisdom of famous political prisoner and convict John Mitchel, born the son of a Unitarian Presbyterian minister on the Ulster border, transported to Tasmania, escaped to the US. Australia has two kinds of people (so would go the modern version of his adage), and they are not Christian and Muslim. They are those who profit by Australia's divisions and those who suffer for them.

Randa Abdel-Fattah

Veils and Vegemite

The Sydney Morning Herald, Good Weekend Magazine,
17 February 2007

"Do you ever wish you were fully Aussie?"

This question was posed to me by a teenage girl in a Sydney school last year.

"What do you mean by fully Aussie?" I asked.

"Um ... like Anglo, you know?" There was no malice or sarcasm intended. The girl was sincere, and simply curious as to whether I yearned to be liberated from what she saw as the shackles of my hyphenated identity as an Australian-born Muslim of Palestinian and Egyptian heritage, to take refuge in the more convenient and legitimate hyphenated identity of Anglo-Aussie.

My first reaction was to laugh. Unfortunately, her sentiment could not be attributed to a naive, schoolgirl view of Australian identity and citizenship. It was the kind of construction of Australian identity I have been hearing for some time now—from politicians, journalists, radio hosts, public figures, none of whom can hide behind the excuse of puberty or inexperience in life.

When the political rhetoric is spun, demands are made for citizenship tests, Australian values are invoked to justify an "us and them" mentality, some migrants are deemed less Australian for their inability to speak English, a ban on the hijab is called for in secular schools and the deportation of an Australian citizen of Egyptian background is demanded because of outrageous comments he has made, it becomes blatantly obvious who our government and spin doctors have identified as the so-called ideological threat to Australian values.

"Muslim" and "Australian" are widely perceived as being mutually exclusive, as polar opposites. One does not need to adopt a victim complex to arrive at this rather obvious conclusion. Muslims—whether Australian-born, migrants or converts of convict ancestry—are the new Public Enemy No 1. Such an enemy has been constructed because, like it or not, Australians have been undertaking a rather urgent and almost parasitical soul-searching exercise since September 11, 2001. Our status as Australians feeds off the un-Australian status of others. We can only feel truly Australian by measuring ourselves against those we deem to be truly not.

As somebody who falls readily into the category of "other", I am curious as to why Muslims—and indeed people who qualify for the crude misnomer "of Middle Eastern appearance"—are on this side of the deep and bitter chasm that has been created in Australia. There is a fracture in our society and, rather than feel optimistic about it healing, I feel increasingly apprehensive about it becoming worse.

Is it because the criminals who attacked America on September 11, 2001 professed to be Muslim (although their actions clearly abrogated any such claim)? The language of the "coalition of the willing" has only ever been coloured with statements about the "terrorists attacking our way of life" and "our values". By the crude logic of shock jocks and politicians anxious for votes, the purported alliance of the terrorists with Islam renders Australian Muslims and Australians of Arabic background (because the misconception is that every Arab is a Muslim) equally suspect of being antagonistic to "Australian values".

There have been various attempts to define Australian values: a fair go, egalitarianism, gender equality—all values that critics have pointed out are universal human values, certainly not values over which Australia can claim intellectual property rights.

However, the way in which the debate plays out demonstrates that it is not a general values debate. How Muslims view labour laws, free trade, the environment or capitalism has never been at the heart of the issue. The values debate has primarily focused on women's dress and attitudes to certain social norms (such as alcohol, a day at the beach or sexuality). Integration, fitting in, assimilation: it doesn't matter whether you belong to a union or recycle your plastic, it's whether you wear a bikini to the beach, date, or can join in a jovial who-got-more-pissed-on-the-weekend Monday morning water cooler conversation that are the pivotal points that rate you on the 1–10 scale of What Makes You Aussie.

That is why that young schoolgirl asked me whether I ever wished I was fully Aussie. I'd just explained that observant Muslims don't drink alcohol or take drugs, don't have boyfriend/girlfriend relationships and don't wear bikinis or swimsuits to the beach or pools. There were a lot of don'ts in my talk and the girl, rather than seeing these as a matter of personal choice, took pity on me. But her assessment of me as different and weird accurately reflects a widespread wariness among the general population about overt religion.

It is the place of observant Muslims in a secular society that conjures up this irrational fear and the perception that Muslims represent an ideological affront to a secular lifestyle. It is not a Muslim's spiritual beliefs in heaven and hell, the big bang, creationism or Darwinism. It is the hijab, the beard, the call to prayer, the fasting during work hours, the praying during lunch breaks, the self-discipline against indulging (even in moderation, even in tiny doses) in the things our society promotes as normal and acceptable (having a drink, relationships outside of marriage, trying a joint) that seem to me to be the point of divide. For Muslims, such things remain taboo. We are considered outsiders because some of our social norms and moral codes are undeniably different. One could say we are old-fashioned, but we are proudly so.

I don't think the divide that has made Muslims feel like "the other" is based on race, colour or culture. It is a divide based on religious observance. Italians and Greeks may go to church on Sunday or wear a cross around their necks, but most date, enjoy a drink and have the appearance of religious anonymity. The religious observance is not explicit, and that is why their "integration" is perceived as a success of multiculturalism, whereas the Australian-ness of a non-drinking Muslim bloke who steps out of work to go pray at lunchtime, or a woman at the bus stop with a suit and hijab on, is suspect.

Well, what about Orthodox Jewish women, I hear you protest. As a symbol of modesty, they cover their hair with a wig and expose their real hair only to their husbands. And what about nuns who also wear a veil? And Mormons, who have strict dress codes and also do not drink?

So many similarities between Islam and other faiths and yet for every five or more documentaries a week about Muslims, Muslim women or the veil, there are virtually none about the almost identical principles of modesty found in Judaism, or Paul's admonition to women in Corinthians that their hair should be cut off if it is not covered.

It is Islam that has the public fascinated and on edge. Perhaps it is because of the increasing size of the Australian Muslim population. Do we accept people as Australians as long as we can manage the size of their minority status? The less noticeable they are, the more acceptable they become? Time and time again, the values debate has centred on the role of women in Islam (perceived as oppressed) and the role of women in the West (championed as liberated). In the recent past, Prime Minister John Howard has called for "some Muslim migrants to learn English and treat women better in order to fit in with Australian values". He later defended himself, saying he was referring to a small section of the Muslim population.

The qualification was laughable. If the Prime Minister was so genuinely concerned about women's rights in religion, he should not have stopped at Muslims. What of Orthodox Jewish men who each day say, "Blessed art thou, O Lord our God, King of the Universe, who hast not made me a woman"? No headlines about that. And is Christianity so innocent? According to Ecclesiastes 25:19, 24: "No wickedness comes anywhere near the wickedness of a woman ... Sin began with a woman and thanks to her we all must die." Anglican women are still struggling to be ordained in Australia's supposed utopia of female liberation. Our society is notably silent when other religions deny women their rights. And yet, when a Muslim displays a patriarchal, misogynist attitude, the public and our politicians are outraged, as though—God forbid—there are no sexist, chauvinistic non-Muslim men.

That our sports heroes have been embroiled in shocking scandals involving the degradation (and alleged rape and sexual assault) of women is forgotten. That there have been gang rapes perpetrated by Anglo-Australians (whose ethnic identity is never revealed) is ignored. That there have been reports of date-rape drugs being administered on cruise ships is met with silence.

The hypocritical way in which the Sheikh Taj el-Din al Hilaly affair unfolded is a case in point, for while the Sheikh's comments were undoubtedly appalling, the reaction of the Prime Minister, politicians and the media exposed a superiority complex on the part of those who raise Western standards of masculinity as the yardstick. The "us and them" card was whipped out. We respect women. We believe in equality. We stand for liberation. They believe differently. Was the ferocity of public indignation elicited by the words in the sermon, or by the fact that the person giving the sermon was Muslim? After all, comments that imply women invite rape by the way they dress have been made by members of the judiciary. Barristers routinely seek to tender evidence as to the way a rape victim was dressed in order to impugn her credibility. No public or political frenzy there.

The effect of this marginalisation on Australian Muslims frightens me. It is simply naive to think that the political discourse and Aussie! Aussie! Aussie! Oi! Oi! Oi! rhetoric is aimed at empowering Muslims—migrants and the Australian-born—or inspiring a sense of citizenship in them. It is no stretch of my cynicism to see the rhetoric and puffed-up chests of "our values or go home" as an appalling vote-grabbing exercise. Stir up the politics of resentment under the pretence of a celebration of Aussie pride. The result is alienation, defensiveness and, among young Australian Muslims, confusion about one's identity and place in the only country one knows as home.

I know of such confusion because I have felt it many times. The kind of identity politics that has been thrown up by the pressure to define Australian values and identity hit me straight in the eye on a trip I took to Sweden last year. I was invited to speak at the Gothenburg Book Festival in September 2006, and it was there that I befriended a Swedish journalist and rap artist, Nabila, who was raised in Sweden but born in Lebanon to a Kurdish mother and Lebanese father.

As we mingled with other international guests, one person asked Nabila: "Do you feel Swedish?"

"Yes," she replied. "Until you asked me."

When we reflected on her response later that day, I asked her: "What about your Kurdish and Lebanese background? How does it impact on your identity?" She gave me a nonchalant smile and then shrugged. "To be honest, I'm tired of defining myself. Am I Swedish? Am I Kurdish? Am I Lebanese? I'm all of these things, and none. Sometimes I'm more Swedish than Kurdish, sometimes I'm more Lebanese than Swedish. In the end, I'm just me."

Her answer resonated with me. It so perfectly encapsulated an ideal space within which to position one's sense of self. As idealistic and naive as her expression of self-definition was, I longed for the freedom to detach myself from hyphens and labels and the need to prove loyalty to one part of my identity at the expense of the other—something that seemed to underpin the values debate back home. At times I felt intensely Australian; my chest swelled with pride at the sound of an Australian accent in the streets of Gothenburg. Listening to Palestinian writer Suad Amiry talk about her marvellous book, *Sharon and My Mother-in-Law*, I felt intensely Palestinian and craved to walk the streets of Jerusalem again. Eating at an Egyptian restaurant in Stockholm, I instantly connected with the owner and reminisced with him about the chaos and magic of Cairo.

The inconsistency in my emotions and devotions used to faze me. It used to arouse in me a sense of disloyalty and insincerity. But Nabila showed me that there is no weakness in loving many things with equal strength. I returned to Australia conscious, for the first time, of the utter fluidity of my identity. I don't need to feel "fully Aussie". Not because I am not of Anglo background (I don't believe Anglo equals Australian), but because it is an impossible demand of a country founded on immigration to expect a pure demarcation between citizenship and heritage. One's past, whether ancestral or as a migrant, necessarily shapes one's present. The issue is the place of this construction of self in Australia's future.

David Burchell

Trying to find the sunny side of life
Griffith Review 15: Divided Nation

When the historical datelines are being drawn up, the year 2005 may be marked down as the Indian summer of Australia's decade-long economic boom. Truly it seemed as if the sun might never set. Household disposable incomes, measured in dollars, were half as high again as they had been a decade earlier—a deluge of personal wealth we'd not seen since the halcyon postwar years. The dollar values of Australians' homes had more than doubled, while the interest rates they were paying on their mortgages were almost a third lower. Unemployment had fallen from almost 9 per cent in 1995 to little more than 5 per cent in 2005, and the average duration of that enforced leisure had roughly halved (from about six months to three). Housing extensions and renovations were making millionaires of builders across the major cities, while big-screen televisions and "home cinema" equipment were walking off the display floors faster than they could be ordered. "The economy"—that menacing couplet which had quickened the heartbeat of thousands of newspaper readers for decades—seemed to have become what the Romans would have called a *cornucopia*: a horn of plenty.

And yet the monsoon clouds were already gathering on the horizon. In Sydney—an increasingly fractious town wracked by drought, heatwaves and traffic snarls—the apparently weightless property market had begun to reacquaint itself with the force of gravity, and people were watching their real estate magic puddings unaccountably beginning to shrink. Housing affordability had already a hit a historic low, while over the decade from 1995 housing debt rose from about 40 per cent to about 70 per cent of households' disposable incomes. Almost two-thirds of private renters had fallen into a state the statisticians define as "housing stress". As if affected by the endless dry heat, a tone of rancour had crept over the city's baking streets. "Symbolic analysts" and "knowledge workers", those grand but dissatisfied beneficiaries of the boom, argued vociferously over their dinner tables about the nation's moral failings and our shrunken hearts. In the newspapers, there was increasing disputation about the city's status as the main repository for the nation's refugee and family reunion immigration programs. "Ethnic tension", that rough beast we'd associated with South Central Los Angeles or the tenements of Western Europe, seemed to be stirring. The airwaves hissed with anxieties around "home-grown" terror and Islamic extremism, while the dress habits of Arab-Australian women became matters of public notice. And, three times within the space of a year or so, young men—men with different causes, and from different backgrounds, it's true—took to the streets to throw things and words about, attack property and police alike, and generally raise the social temperature. For the first time since the days of the Rum Corps, Sydney had become a riotous place to live.

Late one Friday night, in the dying days of the long hot summer, three young men from one of the most stressed neighbourhoods of that stressed city acquired a late-model white Holden Commodore with a view to taking a joyride. Some minutes later, with an unmarked police car in hot pursuit, the car lost traction at a gentle bend on Eucalyptus Drive, Macquarie Fields, rolled several times and ploughed into a gum tree. Both passengers in the car, Matt Robertson and Dylan Raywood, died instantly. Robertson had been in jail so often his friends couldn't remember his age, but in two weeks he was due to start his first legitimate job, stall-holding at the Royal Easter Show. A year before, Raywood had been selected in the under-seventeen development squad for the Wests Tigers Rugby League Club, part of a program designed specifically to get troubled young players back on track. (The club's football manager admitted: "To be truthful, Dylan wouldn't have made the squad if it was chosen on merit. But the whole purpose of it is to keep kids off the street.") The driver, Jesse Kelly—himself a troubled young man with a precocious criminal record—survived, but he disappeared into the night. His aunt, Deborah Kelly, a formidable woman with a criminal record of her own, took charge of the situation.

According to a later police statement opposing her bail application, Deborah circulated a rival version of events according to which the police had rammed the car into the tree on purpose and then fled the scene. The Glenquarie Estate, a Housing Commission enterprise from the 1970s to accommodate troubled families and their children, is one of the toughest, most crime-wracked localities in Sydney, and relations with the police are generally fraught. Deborah Kelly's account of events sped up and down the laneways of the neighbourhood, and by the Sunday night hundreds of young people had gathered on the street, where they began launching missiles, fireworks and Molotov cocktails at police. The police responded with baton charges. For the next three nights, there were pitched battles along the broad bitumen curves of Eucalyptus Drive. The police donned helmets and shields, and deployed in lines reminiscent of the tactical doctrines of the Duke of Wellington. The local boys fought, posed for the cameras and took souvenirs of the battle. The television film-crews dodged and weaved as they strove to catch the best shots. Outsiders brought in deckchairs to watch the show. And the airwaves of Sydney radio ran fever-hot.

The so-called "law and order debate" nowadays has such a familiar, choreographed quality that it resembles those Balinese shadow-plays which are appreciated in stoic silence by Australian holiday-makers. In the aftermath of the Macquarie Fields riots, the little stick-figures had a busy time of it. The state opposition and the most popular radio personalities united in questioning how the police had allowed the riots to develop in the first place, and in calling for that hardiest of law and order slogans, "zero tolerance". (Exactly how zero tolerance was to be practised on a neighbourhood in which almost everybody seems to fall foul of the law before they reach majority was not explained.) The city's conservative-leaning tabloid, the *Daily Telegraph*, declared "Enough is enough". In sharp contrast, the city's liberal-minded broadsheet, the *Sydney Morning Herald*, offered the familiar "cry of pain" diagnosis: there were "deeper", "underlying reasons" for the riots than mere lawlessness; socio-economic disadvantage was the key.

Yet none of these responses ever seemed really to cut to the heart of the matter. Since, on the one hand, communities whose members routinely plunder and deface public property are rarely healthy places in which to grow up, the first set of responses (zero tolerance, tough love, where are the parents?) always seems inadequate and even perverse. Yet the reflexive incantation of the theme of socio-economic disadvantage—like some journalistic equivalent of a lecture out of Sociology 101—often seems hardly more helpful. Solve disadvantage and you'll solve lawlessness and dysfunction, the slogan seems to say. And then—the tabloid-reading critic might well respond—why not go on to create world peace?

The events in Macquarie Fields, like those in Redfern before and Cronulla after, aroused such controversy in large part because rioting in suburbia seemed—at least prior to the overheated social temperature in Sydney of the last few years—to be strangely out of kilter with Australian mores. In Western Europe, public housing is almost synonymous with public disturbance. The classic tower blocks of inner south and east London, or on the outskirts of Paris—originally built as part of hopeful campaigns of slum-clearance—have defied attempts to foster civic pride. Instead, they have often become graffiti-encrusted, vandalised wind-tunnels, and have provided the cannon-fodder for tribes of neo-Nazi bovver-boys and jihadi-wannabees. In Australia, by contrast, the ambitions of postwar planners turned instead towards fostering private home ownership across the vast green-brown suburban expanses, and (despite the grand dreams of social radicals) inner-city public housing was aimed chiefly at the very poor and the elderly—who generally appreciated what was seen to be their privilege. For every wind-tunnel, there are probably two or three gatherings of neat inner-city window-boxes.

Yet, seen from the historian's point of view, the story of Macquarie Fields has the kind of irresistible logic to it which is often attributed to ancient Greek tragedies. It begins with the changing public housing philosophies of the 1960s and 1970s. As the waiting lists for inner-city public residences grew (and their tenants grew older), planners sketched out miniature suburbs of public housing across the outskirts of all the major cities. Often these neighbourhoods were given pastoral-sounding names like Green Valley or Ambarvale, and it was imagined that they could be designed and laid out like little country villages. At the same time, priority was increasingly directed to providing housing for those defined by new measures of disadvantage as being in crisis—meaning, in many cases, women with kids fleeing violent partners, parents with drug and alcohol problems, or those receiving counselling for behavioural problems—or all of the above. And so, without any explicit policy directive connecting these two movements, the new semi-rural estates became the chief repositories for families in crisis. In the early 1980s, my wife (who was then working in a women's refuge) dropped off an Aboriginal woman and her kids fleeing domestic violence to the then-new Glenquarie Estate, at a house which she recalls only as seeming to be in the middle of nowhere. It felt like dropping a pebble into the ocean.

Up until the mid-1970s, Macquarie Fields was little more than a collection of hamlets loosely following the curve of the Georges River, a half dozen or so kilometres south of Liverpool on the city's south-western verge. If you strayed more than three or four blocks east of Glenfield railway station (as a friend who grew up there recalls it), you'd find yourself wandering through the virgin scrub. Out of this frontier wilderness, the Department of Housing planners carved neat rows of brick-veneer bungalows and angular semi-detached "villas" for a brand-new suburb. But Macquarie Fields was to be more than an ordinary township. It was to be a public housing estate within a suburb: a little island of social experiment locked within the grand suburban sea. And when they came to draft the public housing estate on the suburb's eastern fringe, the planners called upon the ghost of William Morris. Rather than have the kids play on the streets, the architects shaped arcing drives with pastoral names like Eucalyptus, Rosewood and Cottonwood, and sculpted gum-strewn parks with wandering tracks and laneways, like the country lanes of an imagined bygone era. They called it the Glenquarie Estate.

In large measure, the experiment was still-born. Parents in crisis not infrequently reared children in crisis, and some of the children are now, a generation on, becoming crisis-ridden parents themselves. The jobless rate in the suburb is about twice the national average: on the estate it's higher again. Single-parent families are in the majority. Habits of domestic violence and substance abuse are commonly transmitted inter-generationally. It is possible to grow up on the estate nowadays and not know a single adult male who's unquestionably on the straight and narrow. For many, being burgled is a routine occurrence. In the 2564 postcode area in 2005, 114 cars were reported stolen, there were 227 reported burglaries, 457 cases of property damage, and 279 assaults. Given the prevailing relationship with police in the area, the reported figures are probably extremely conservative. Within a couple of decades of the first concrete-pours, the quaint laneways have become unsafe to walk at night, the paired semi-circular drives have turned neatly into amateur racing-tracks, and the paths through the parks make handy escape routes from the police. The neighbourhood has become a kind of monument to good planning intentions gone wrong. Building Jerusalem can hardly have begun more brightly, nor ended with so faint a whimper.

Like a number of my colleagues, I started receiving phones calls from journalists the morning after the first night of riots. My slim claim to expertise rested upon a small book on Western Sydney I'd written a couple of years before. I was inclined to be circumspect. Reporters from the *Sydney Morning Herald* and the ABC dutifully recorded my unremarkable views on the relations between youth, welfare dependency, dangerous driving and property theft. At the end of a *Herald* interview, I happened to mention that south-west Sydney was the national capital of the illicit car-rebirthing industry. Later that day it emerged that the fugitive driver on Eucalyptus Drive was believed to have taken up a career in the car-rebirthing trade. The next day I received a phone call from a television producer on *60 Minutes*, who seemed convinced—on this finest thread of evidence—that I must have the last word to say on the matter.

An appearance on *60 Minutes* is not something to be entertained lightly. The program distils all liberal academia's familiar loathings— low-brow entertainment masquerading as journalism, a knee-jerk conservative social agenda, and for many high-minded critics it provides an unwanted window into the regrettable cultural preferences of the working classes. Partly out of this anxiety, and partly because of a persistent sense that I was "not the right person", I proposed a series of other names, without evident effect. Eventually, with a sense of dread, I agreed to meet the crew early the following week at a house they'd decided—with true *60 Minutes* chutzpah—to rent a few hundred metres from the centre of the troubles.

And so my early morning rural ride down to Macquarie Fields was an unquiet journey. I wanted to believe I'd agreed out of a desire to speak my academic mind to a wider audience—to be the "public intellectual". Yet I struggled with the niggling fear that I was simply along for the ride. My restless mind cycled through the ways in which studious responses might be wrought by the alchemy of TV editing into inflammatory tirades, or absurd overstatements. I meditated upon the hapless Paxton brothers— two teenage boys who, some years before, had ignited an unedifying public debate on dole-bludging when they were filmed by its sister program, *A Current Affair*, refusing to cut their hair for a prospective employer. And, rather like the drowning man, I recalled in fast-forward every impulsive error I'd made since about the age of eight.

The unfurnished house rented by *60 Minutes*, 16 Cottonwood Drive, sits around the corner from Eucalyptus Drive. Except for the uncanny sense that everyone in the neighbourhood had their eyes fastened on a gap in the front curtains, it looked like a quiet backstreet. Outside Number 16, the show's star and presenter, Mike Munro, inimitably dressed in a button-down Ralph Lauren shirt, tight-legged jeans and shiny cowboy boots, was urgently pacing up and down with his mobile phone pressed to his ear. Inside, with the curtains almost drawn, the film crew sat on upturned cartons, tending to their equipment. After Munro read out his improvised questions (some rough outline of which I could see scribbled on an A4 writing-pad) I was shepherded into a Bundy-and-Coke doused Ford Falcon for the short drive around the block to the location. I felt a little like a suspect being led away by the police.

It's the stock in trade of *60 Minutes* to go straight to the emotional heart of things. As with Greek stagecraft and soap opera, the goal is to evoke catharsis in the speediest and most direct manner. They are not unaware of the risks inherent in such an approach—the common criticism that you simply heighten the preconceptions of your viewers, rather than adding to their knowledge. But they see this as simply one more hazard in a risky, no-time-to-stop-and-think kind of business. From *60 Minutes'* point of view, there are two worlds: the world of the participant-actor, and the world of the observer-commentator. They fell into the first category; I was there because I fell into the second. My job was to have scruples (or, if you prefer, to prevaricate); theirs was to act on raw televisual instinct.

And so, of course, they conducted their interviews on Eucalyptus Drive, the interviewee posed in front of a notorious piece of graffiti that proclaimed, a tad vaingloriously, "Cops Kill Kids. We Will Kill You Cops".

The appearance of the *60 Minutes* star and his attendants in any small, tight-knit neighbourhood is inevitably a matter of great moment, and so our staggering progress was interrupted every two or three minutes by the blaring horn of a passing car, or the studiously inconspicuous hum of an unmarked police vehicle. Bus and truck drivers slowed and waved like old friends. Local mums watched from the front fence. ("It's not often we get stars here," said one, appreciatively. "Oh, surely I'm not a star yet," Munro replied, with a winning show of modesty.) The presenter's stage presence was impressive. One young mum with a stroller paused to watch the show from the street corner. When she'd had enough, she told Munro that she hoped they'd get the kids to stop the fighting, as it'd be nice to have a night's sleep for a change. He gave her a serious, knitted-brow look that seemed to suggest that this, like just about anything else, was possible.

As we were winding up the interview, a familiar-looking pair of boys ambled up the street towards us, flashing gap-toothed smiles. Munro waved a greeting and called out brightly: "We've just been interviewing the professor here." One of the boys was Aaron Robertson, Matt's brother, the other was Matt's best mate. Each had been starring on the evening TV news. (Indeed, Aaron succeeded in getting himself arrested three nights running.) Both were about my height and build—which is to say skinny and shorter than average, as so many would-be street heroes are. Each was wearing the hip-hop uniform of baseball cap, baggy polyester tracksuit pants and runners, and an embossed polyester shirt—in the manner of an oversized ice-hockey jersey—with a different slogan. Aaron's best mate was particularly proud of his. Featuring a silver-embossed Uzi sub-machine gun in profile, it had the words "Class War" emblazoned in Gothic script at the top, and had a stirring slogan about resisting the state lettered across the bottom. "I'm against authority," he explained, rather grandly. As he told it, this was the uniform of the new neighbourhood gang, and wearing it was like an initiation rite. He was vague about the shirt's origins: I fancy some anarchist grouplet from the inner-city must have left its calling-card.

The boys seemed cheery enough and entirely at ease. They moved their shoulders jauntily back and forth and bounced up and down on their heels. As Aaron's mate put it, this was pretty much like being a Hollywood film star. They chatted about the events of the last few days, and about the details of Matt's funeral the next day. With a play of secrecy, one of them showed us some improvised firework-weapons—alarming the *60 Minutes* producer, who mistook one of them for a gun. It emerged that *60 Minutes*— which likes to spread money around among potential interviewees—was helping with the funeral costs. Munro asked several times who he should make the cheque payable to. Eventually Aaron angled his head and insisted the money must go directly to his mother. If it went through other family members, he hinted—with a slight movement of the eyebrow—it would probably disappear.

As the camera crew set up, so that Mike and I could be filmed casually strolling up the street, the boys intimated that they had some new business ventures on the go. Right now they had a brand-new stock of razor-scooters going for a song. "Thanks, but I don't have use for a scooter," said Munro, with a polite but firm wave of the arm. The rest of us demurred in turn. The boys smiled, waved and headed back on their way, hands in pockets, deep in conversation. It occurred to me that there was a curious synergy between the flying-by-the-seat-of-one's-pants lives of these boys and the equally improvised modus operandi of the *60 Minutes* crew. Each lived for the moment; each chose their moments of opportunity on pure gut instinct; each had to keep moving lest their past catch them up. It might even be that this was one element in the *60 Minutes* formula for success: the show's stories of the badlands commanded conviction not because of any in-depth research or commitment to veracity, but because (unlike the ironic varsity voices of the ABC) they exude authentic street-smart themselves. "Ah, they're not bad kids," offered Mike as we watched the boys disappear up the road. "That's the worst of it." Then he reminisced, a little wistfully, upon his own youthful adventures in the suburban jungle. Accustomed by now to his talent for personal theatre, I took this meditation rather lightly. As it turned out later, however, this much at least of Mike's patter was the plain, unadorned truth.

After we'd wound up, the *60 Minutes* crew politely offered to drive me back around the corner. It was a five-minute stroll, but when I said I'd walk they looked alarmed. On the way back I passed Caley Park through which the mum with the pram had wheeled off homewards. You could still see the original town planners' bright intentions in the curve of the concrete track that wound through it. The sun was shining brightly through the leaves, there was a light breeze, and some birds in the boughs of the eucalypts were chirping. It was a beautiful autumn day, and strangely I found an old show tune was playing itself inside my head.

> Look for the silver lining
>
> When e'er a cloud appears in the blue.
>
> Remember somewhere, the sun is shining.
>
> And so the right thing to do is make it shine for you.

And then I was crossed by a sudden thought, like a flash of sunlight through the trees. It occurred to me that Matt's mates, far from being proper objects of solicitation and sympathy, actually must feel they had life sussed. They made fast money and paid no tax; they didn't have to queue at Centrelink, or fill out endless job interview forms; they were keeping out of their mum's hair (or maybe escaping her problems); they were high on adrenaline as much as dope or alcohol. So far from resembling welfare "dependants", the mournful passive beneficiaries of academic lore, their demeanour spoke of the adaptive small businessman, the eBay Powerseller, the itinerant entrepreneur. It was tough luck that a brother and a mate were gone forever. But then life here was a dangerous business: better to live it to the hilt than be cowed by it. In a decade or so, each one of them—like their fugitive friend Jesse Kelly—might well be doing some time in jail. But on Eucalyptus Drive you live for the moment, and a decade seems like an awfully long time.

> A heart, full of joy and gladness
>
> Will always banish sadness and strife.
>
> So always look for the silver lining
>
> And try to find the sunny side of life.

"It seems history is to blame," the Englishman Haines blandly observes of Ireland's "Troubles" in James Joyce's novel *Ulysses*. One way or another, it usually is. At the 2005 New South Wales Parliamentary Inquiry into the riots, the Liberal backbencher Charlie Lynn seized upon the testimony of senior staff from the NSW Department of Housing to blame a more recent historical culprit for the Glenquarie Estate's failings—the various "failed attempts at social engineering" which he associated with the social idealism of the '60s and '70s.

The NSW Parliament's Standing Committee on Social Issues is a gathering of larger-than-life individuals, and the inquiry's transcripts are a faithful enough representation of this. There was speechifying aplenty, so much so that expert witnesses sometimes struggled to get a word in. Among the committee's members is the inimitable Charlie Lynn, a former army officer, Kokoda Track tour organiser and Christian youth group activist—a man who takes it upon himself to be the spokesman for the "silent majority" of concerned citizens, alarmed at the dangers lurking on neighbourhood streets. As of November 2006, Lynn had delivered twenty speeches over his ten-year parliamentary career—each devoted to an aspect of the "law and order debate". In 2003 he accused a state government minister of taking sexual advantage of an under-age boy—accusations he subsequently had to withdraw. The chair, Labor Upper House member Jan Burnswoods—a veteran Labor branch and community activist with a fondness for flowers—seems to see her mission as being to demonstrate that Lynn is a fraudulent fool. Treatment which provides Lynn with ample opportunity to present himself as the hapless Mr Smith come to conniving, politically correct Macquarie Street. Chief among the other members is the euphonically named Democrat Dr Arthur Chesterfield-Evans, a former surgeon and anti-smoking activist who interrupted the evidence at various points to quiz witnesses upon the finer points of social policy theory.

In the course of its proceedings, the inquiry interviewed two senior administrators from the Department of Housing, Michael Allen and Clifford Haynes, about the history of the estate. The two men attempted to tell the committee—with all the heroic reserves of patience that only a career in public administration can provide—the tangled story of the estate's genesis in the 1970s and the various attempts to remedy its deficiencies through improvements to the physical environment in the decades since.

Kitchens and laundries had been renovated; houses had been reoriented to face the street; funds had been provided to help around a third of the residents purchase their homes. The longer objective, they explained, was to create greater diversity of tenure and circumstance within the estate, to create a "more balanced community" with people from a wider range of social backgrounds and more diverse sources of income. But this meant overcoming the legacy of large, relatively homogenous housing estates that had been entrenched in the planning of the New South Wales Housing Commission from the 1950s through to the 1970s. More specifically, it meant redrawing the estate to remove the numerous "access ways and cul de sacs" required by the "Radburn model" of estate in favour at the time.

At this point, the indefatigable, history-minded Charlie Lynn leapt up to attract an unsympathetic chair's attention. "I refer to the original Radburn model. When was it introduced? ... Who was the Rhodes Scholar who introduced it? ... Do you see it as a failed attempt at social engineering in the 1970s?" he asked, staccato-style, in a state of genuine agitation. And a jousting match followed between Lynn and Burnswoods as to which party had been in power when "Radburn's" experiment ("Radburn is not a person, it is a town in New Jersey," Allen patiently explained) began.

Lynn's instincts were not altogether misplaced. There is more to the history of the Glenquarie Estate than can be gleaned from government reports alone. But he was surely a little unkind to lay responsibility for the estate's troubles on the now-bowed shoulders of the "flower children". Indeed, if you really want to nab "history" for the troubles of the present, you need to travel a good deal further back than Lynn's historical vision allows. In fact, you'd need to travel back to the late nineteenth century, to the era of the classic social investigators, to the first dreams of slum-clearance and new working-class neighbourhoods studded with oak trees and festooned with flowers. You'd need to begin with a novel like *Looking Backward*, the 1888 time-travelling utopia of American Victorian social visionary Edward Bellamy—the book that pioneered the belief that the psychic wounds of modern industrial society could be healed by a new kind of built community, a city in which work and leisure, culture and industry, and even town and country could be seamlessly harmonised, supposedly combining the best of each with (in the best utopian tradition) the disadvantages of neither.

Bellamy's narrator awakes one morning to find himself in a recreated Boston of the year 2000, a city in which public and private goods intermingle. Want has been abolished, incomes have been equalised, and the mundane traffic in goods has been replaced by universal stores in which the best of everything is available at cost price. It is an image which fairly shimmers even today.

> Miles of broad streets, shaded by trees and lined with fine buildings,
> for the most part not in continuous blocks but set in larger or smaller
> enclosures, stretched in every direction. Every quarter contained large
> open squares filled with trees, among which statues glistened and
> fountains flashed in the late afternoon sun.

Across the Atlantic, one of Bellamy's grandest enthusiasts was a sometime parliamentary reporter, Ebenezer Howard. Drawing upon Bellamy's bright vision, the enlightened factory-town experiments of Christian industrialists such as W.H. Lever and George Cadbury, and the aesthetic principles of the "arts and crafts movement", Howard gathered a movement of professionals and philanthropists to purchase land for the Garden Cities of Letchworth and Welwyn in Hertfordshire. Letchworth was a kind of commune (part Renaissance Florence, part Nimbin): all its citizens owned shares in the civic association, which leased the town's land back to them individually. (It's worth noting that Howard lived in Letchworth from 1905 to 1921, until Welwyn was built, whereupon he moved—and later died—there.)

While the actual Garden Cities varied markedly in pattern according to location (and readiness of funds, which were sometimes tight), Howard seems to have viewed them all as epiphenomena of a Platonic ideal he'd outlined in his 1904 book *Garden Cities of Tomorrow*. And indeed the diagrams there are organised on Hellenic geometrical principles, as a series of concentric circles. There is a central park (derived from F.L. Omsted's massive original in Manhattan) with grand boulevards leading outwards to the city's rim, criss-crossed with concentric-circular avenues of varying designs and functions. The private dwellings are to be "excellently built" in varying individual styles, but with common gardens and "cooperative kitchens". And the churches are "of such denominations as the religious beliefs of the people may determine, to be erected and maintained out of the funds of the worshippers and their friends". The industrial districts occupy the outer rim, where they intersect with the railway lines on which the city's products are conveyed to the wider world. And outside this grand circular gemstone lays a patchwork of private allotments, dairy farms and forests, fulfilling Howard's vision of uniting city and country into a single vision (albeit that, while the city is severely geometrical, the countryside remains illimitable).

Howard's notion was that cities of this kind could be assembled as a network of free-standing social islands, each sufficient to itself for basic needs, but engaged in commerce with others for the exchange of their industrial goods. When one garden city outstripped its bounds, Howard explained, the surplus population would skip over the surrounding countryside to form a new one some miles distant—much, he believed, as Adelaide had at once retained its urban parks, and established its new development in North Adelaide. The sea-lanes connecting this glittering archipelago of progress were the same railway tracks that already carried so many of the nineteenth century's other social hopes. The cities themselves, though, were without mechanical transport: citizens could walk to the central park, or the town halls, concert halls, libraries and museums that surrounded it, or to their workplaces on the periphery as if strolling through pastureland.

Howard's egalitarian democracy, like that of so many of his colleagues and acquaintances, was that of the religiously non-conformist, public-spirited urban professional—the doctrine of the spiritually, intellectually and economically independent. A little like the middle-class Bolsheviks a generation or two later, he envisioned a workers' paradise where the soul was nourished by cheap classical concerts and shapely yet severely functional domestic furniture, where conspicuous poverty and "shoddy" were the twin scourges of humanity.

For this ideal to flourish across the Atlantic—where visions, after all, had more room to flourish, and urban allotments were easier to obtain—it had to be enlarged to cater for less high-minded products of industrialism such as the private motor-car. And so, when a group of similarly minded professionals founded the Regional Planning Association of America in the 1920s, they both drew on the Letchworth model, and reimagined its basic geometry. Clarence Stein's 1929 Radburn Estate in New Jersey, the first Garden City in the United States, resembled a complicated root-system: motorways spawned side-roads, each of which branched off in multiple rootlings towards the rear-facing garages of private villas, which looked outwards towards an encircling tree-lined footway. The car had been accommodated—as, in the new demotic era of motor-transport, it had to be—but only, as it were, through the back door. This pragmatic modification of the Garden City geometry—the harmony of the spheres reduced to a kind of inelegant maze—became the basis for some of the grandest and most fateful experiments in (private and) public housing after World War II.

Australian planners and visionaries had been abreast of the Garden City movement from its early stages. In the interwar years, a prototype public housing Garden City was built on reclaimed land near Port Melbourne, though it failed to bear fruit. At the end of World War II, in the more propitious heyday of nation-building, Walter Bunning was assigned the task of creating a new munitions complex at St Marys, on Sydney's western fringes. Bunning—the main author of the Commonwealth Housing Commission's 1944 report into the country's impending postwar housing needs—was a modernist architect and Garden City enthusiast. Most of the munitions site's workers commuted to the factories by train, but Bunning also constructed some temporary housing across the tracks. And then—as if by way of a casual afterthought—he added a small experimental village, rigorously drawn up on the Radburn model, on the site's eastern fringe. The St Marys Permanent Cottage Area—now heritage-protected for all its few meagre blocks—still stands today, a few kilometres away from the campus on which I work. Within its slender geometric curves lies the strange seed that, thirty years later, blossomed in Macquarie Fields.

Some years earlier, a new private housing development was pegged out in a semi-rural outer western glen by a canny North Shore building firm with the then-chic name Homes De Luxe. It was called Green Valley. The site was later bought by the New South Wales Housing Commission in the wake of nation-building pride, and developed in the 1960s to become the largest public housing estate in the Sydney basin, designed especially for the poorest and most welfare-dependent families. (The Housing Commission commemorated the occasion with a promotional booklet hopefully titled

"Estate of Tomorrow".) Public planners and bureaucrats ("never complain, never explain") leave few records of their governing philosophies, and so we're forced to guess at the process whereby the tidy-town blueprints of Letchworth and Radburn—carefully designed to be self-contained urban entities, each with local factories and processing works—were transmuted into Australia's grandest laboratory experiment in all-commuting-public-rental-accommodation, with no nearby employment, limited public transport and few amenities. According to 1960s researchers at Sydney University, two in five of the original settlers there had no car, while only one in ten could afford a telephone. Once you'd moved there, you were—quite literally—on your own.

Over the course of the 1960s, the phrase "Green Valley" entered Sydney's comic lexicon. The joke lay in pretending that this was indeed a pastoral paradise, as its name seemed to suggest. And, like all the geographical put-downs that litter the folklore of the most unforgiving of Australian cities, this was thought to be irresistibly funny. (In the same idiom—though less maliciously—it's become popular in recent years for Sydneysiders to wear t-shirts claiming "I climbed Mt Druitt"—another of Sydney's "struggle-towns".) By the end of the decade, the estate had already become famous enough to draw sustained comment from the otherwise slightly parochial Adelaide academic Hugh Stretton in his classic *Ideas for Australian Cities* (Georgian House, 1970). Contrasting the still-pristine Green Valley with the unfashionable but striving blue-collar dormitory town of Elizabeth on the northern fringes of his home city, Stretton acknowledged that, of the two: "Green Valley looks better. Its land undulates pleasantly under some mature native trees. Its street planning is more imaginative ... its school buildings are better, it has some attractive pedestrian ways and better and safer pedestrian planning ... and you can't tell its owned from its rented houses."

Here, though, Green Valley's advantages ended. A journey to the beach was a day trip, and most of the residents didn't have cars. There were few jobs in evidence, and poor access to health care. The shopping centre closed early, and the local pub was inhospitable. Unlike Howard's Letchworth, neither doctors nor politicians chose to live there, and the few stories of personal success were "not enough to shake the steady, intelligent desire of three-quarters of its residents to get out of the place". In short, the problem wasn't poor planning, still less a shortage of services (which would "wilt there, for want of paying custom"). Rather, Stretton observed:

> All Green Valley's poverties spring from the poverty of its people, hand picked ... for their comparative incapacity to get on, or get tough, or get well, or get rich, or get things moving; then dumped outside the city walls all together and all alone without work, allies, entrepreneurs, exemplars or defenders.

Substitute the words "Macquarie Fields" for Green Valley in Stretton's choleric judgement, and you may find that you don't need to change a single word. There are still quiet, orderly families on the estate, people who've nurtured their gardens with care, and who still cleave to the bricks and fences bequeathed by the citizenry all those years ago. Jenny Pel, who has lived on the estate since 1977, told *The Age* she was sick of the rioters' endless excuses for bad behaviour. "I love my street. But I'm scared they're going to bulldoze our houses now." But they are outnumbered by those whose "steady, intelligent desire" is to get out of the place. The poor transport, the social and geographic isolation, the resident-body made homogenous in their incapacities by the zany logic of humanely intended social policy—it's all there, with the single signal difference that while Green Valley was meant, in the planners' minds' eye, to be a stepping-stone to a happier and more prosperous future, the Glenquarie Estate seems to have been conceived with no coherent image of the future whatever.

It's a curious fact that, of all the antipodean imitators of the Radburn model, it's the Glenquarie Estate—the last built—which most faithfully adheres to the contours of the original. You can superimpose a projection of Radburn from the 1920s onto the central hub of the Glenquarie Estate—the hub bounded by the now-famous Eucalyptus Drive—without too much violence. The curves and the cul-de-sacs have stayed the same; only their purposes seem insensibly to have changed along the way, a little like the shrunken wings of a flightless bird. The encircling pathways which at Radburn were supposed to mark out each of the neighbourhoods as distinct, and save them from the impending tyranny of motor-transport, have on the Glenquarie Estate mutated into the encircling bitumen curve of Eucalyptus Drive—arguably the city's busiest street-racing circuit. The central "motorway" of the Radburn model, which in the original was meant to serve as an artery to the neighbourhood houses, has been stripped of its pulmonary function, and serves chiefly as a short-cut from one side of the racing-circuit to the other. And the stumpy bucolic "places", meant to provide rear exit-ways from cottages to the street, turned in Glenquarie into back-alleys, quick exit-routes for the apprentices of the neighbourhood academies of property-theft.

Brenton Banfield, the former Mayor of Campbelltown City, grew up on the Glenquarie Estate, and he can still recall the optimism with which the earliest residents greeted their spick-and-span new homes: "Back then it was a place of hope and opportunity. People were living in affordable accommodation. They could save up for a deposit and move out." Over time, those who were well-resourced enough or severely disciplined enough in their family budgeting did indeed move out, creating a perverse process of unnatural selection of those who stayed behind. They were the ones without the capacity to move on, and they felt trapped. In the meantime, the priorities of public housing shifted further, so that few if any of the later arrivals had a realistic hope of escape. As the department's Michael Allen explained to the parliamentarians, when the first concrete was poured at Macquarie Fields, about one in two of the state's public tenants received rental assistance; today, the proportion is close to nine in ten. Back then, seven in every ten public renters were couples with dependent children; today only one in ten is a couple with children—most of the rest are single-parent homes, and more than half subsist on pensions of one kind or another. If you conducted this kind of experiment with laboratory rats, there would be animal activists on hand to demonstrate.

At the same time, the mere existence of 1970s-style public housing estates does not necessarily denote social disaffection. Another witness at the Parliamentary Inquiry was Gary Moore, Director of the NSW Council of Social Service (and alumnus of the tough mid-western Sydney suburb of Lakemba). Asked where he thought Macquarie Fields stood in an imaginary league-table of public housing stress, he surprised many of the committee members by rating it fairly low. After all, there are free-standing estates in parts of Sydney's outer-south west—such as at Minto, a few kilometres further south—with concentrations of public renters as high as nine in ten.

Compared with those, the travails of Macquarie Fields (where almost six in ten residents of the wider suburb are home-owners) may seem relatively small. Yet there are no signs of rioting, or even of widespread lawlessness, there.

Doubtless there is no single explanation for this seeming paradox. Yet it is worth observing that, while Minto is an island of public housing, sufficient unto itself, Glenquarie Estate is effectively a public housing colony within a larger suburb. And in that wider suburb, it sometimes seems, all the good citizens take care of their front lawns, and dearly wish that the troublemakers would simply go away. On some accounts, the hardest aspect of growing up in Green Valley in the 1960s and 1970s wasn't the personal problems of the local community. Rather, it was the opprobrium you carried when you went in search of a job. To be a poor colony of a republic of growing affluence may in its own way be the cruellest fate of all.

The redoubtable Charlie Lynn is himself a social idealist of sorts. He works with Father Chris Riley's "Youth Off the Streets" program—the same program which plans to build a new youth centre on the Glenquarie Estate—and in the parliamentary recesses he leads groups of "troubled kids" up the Kokoda Track, in search of those equally intangible entities, self-discovery and national spirit. Like Mike Munro, perhaps, he seems to view this kind of activity as a street-smart, pragmatic alternative to the unworldly social visions of the welfare-sector left, which must appear to his agitated eye to be inscribed into the concrete of Glenquarie's meandering lanes. In this his instinct may not be entirely misguided. After all, while grand welfare strategies wax and wane, the humbler rituals of self-help and community food-baskets seem to go on forever. Over the march of a century, the maxims of Samuel Smiles seem to have mutated insensibly into those of Oprah Winfrey. But, when all's said and done, Lynn's combat against the mythic Mr Radburn is really a sparring match of idealists, rather than the rhetorically satisfying collision of dream and reality.

In any case, in the end the Garden City model was less unworldly than its historical legacy may suggest. Cadbury, Lever and the rest—like the pragmatic, unromantic founders of Stretton's Elizabeth—had been solid, worldly men, men who just happened, by virtue of their various minority faiths, to be gnawed at by a particular species of Christian conscience.

They built their experimental estates around their own factories, and they possessed the power to provide health and retirement entitlements of a level and kind of their own choosing. (This was, after all, the golden age of the benign planner.) Howard, being a man of more modest means, had not been blessed with all these powers of beneficence, but he was still always canny enough to ensure that his new garden cities possessed an adequate complement of well-paid factory jobs, and that they were gifted with fast and effective transportation links with nearby commercial centres. Likewise, Radburn was built in a long-standing industrial area, with a solid mix of employment types, and a strong leavening of office workers with bank accounts. In this sense, the spiritual descendants of Welwyn and Radburn aren't the denizens of Green Valley or Macquarie Fields, but rather the tidy-town citizens of Glenmore and Harrington Parks in Sydney's outer west—and of all the other so-called "gated communities" that are springing up in the more upwardly mobile reaches of our outer cities. Except that nowadays the tastes of our cultural arbiters have tacked one hundred and eighty degrees, and what would once have been celebrated verdant little private utopias are now decried in the big-city broadsheets as havens of "white flight".

In this respect, the problem wasn't the "Radburn model" as such, but rather the application of a model, founded in the controlled-experiment utopianism of another era, to the circumstances of an entirely different mix of human subjects—not orderly factory workers and their families, but a new class of welfare beneficiaries created out of a new and different world of family chaos, social dislocation and greatly increased substance-dependency. The factory workers of the late nineteenth and early twentieth centuries were a constituency in the process of acquiring serious political and industrial clout, and they had to be reckoned with (by state and employer alike) as potentially dangerous social actors in a new demotic social order. In our era, on the other hand, we've managed to fill our little would-be utopias with a new class of public beneficiaries distinguished by their almost complete dearth of political, financial and televisual leverage of any kind. Howard delighted to reside in Letchworth and Welwyn, the creations of his own mind's eye. And, as Stretton noted, sports stars and other notables were lured by various pecuniary incentives to live in Adelaide's Elizabeth. But no serving politician or planner, then or now, ever went to live in Green

Valley or Macquarie Fields. The locals there can't strike or stop work, or lobby local dignitaries. Forming precinct committees would impress no one. Instead, like the urban "mob" of pre-franchise English cities, they have to throw bricks and break things to make themselves heard.

It's worth noting that, even today, Letchworth Garden City is a busy going concern, choc a bloc with earnest-minded public sector employees, organic food stores and sensible, low-fuel-consumption cars. (Heeding the siren-call of "globalisation", the local factories have mostly moved on, but the equally international tourist industry has obligingly taken their place.) And, even today, the tidy-town residents of Radburn take a proper civic pride in the history of their peculiar burg, where the autumn leaves fall on curving walkways and arrow-straight "motorways" alike. These are towns through whose veins flow money and hope, and whose hearts still tick with that instinct for "community activism" so often found in communities which are thriving, and so rarely in those which logic (and the dreams of radical historians) might suggest should need it more. If things went badly in Radburn or Letchford, you can be sure there'd be tertiary-educated folks hammering down the door of local mayors and government ministers. Neither is ever likely to need the missionary-style community activism of Father Chris Riley or the Salvation Army's food parcels. There may be a sense in which "history" is indeed to blame for failed experiments like Green Valley and Macquarie Fields. But if so, it may be less a matter of commission than omission, less a story of grand folly than of the casually lazy betrayal of good intentions, less the execution of an inexorable vision than of innumerable small-scale instances of amnesia and neglect—all because the people to whom the administrators were ministering were effectively of no political account.

Of all the grand moral disputes of the times, of all the awesome gulfs within our political imagination, that over crime and criminality is perhaps the most primal and profound. It raises, after all, the elemental questions of justice, order, personal accountability and responsibility—the moral touchstones of personal competence and public order beloved by ordinary striving Australians. And it invokes the moral weight and grandeur of our primal human impulses towards caring and interpersonal sympathy—

those ramparts of the liberal moral imagination, and the religiously and professionally driven individuals who form its garrison. Among a generation of citizens for whom the Bible is little more than a childhood echo, it pits the Old Testament against the New, Jehovah against Jesus. Should I love my neighbour as myself? Am I my brother's keeper?

And so, in the days and weeks after the riots, the Glenquarie Estate achieved a strange kind of mythic glamour. According to your allegiance, this little republic of misery became either a vessel for the discharge of elemental human sympathy or a repository for good-citizenly revulsion. Academic social scientists and earnest broadsheet journalists alike shook their heads sadly and asked how it was that boys could be reduced to such a state, and how the acute problems of the area could have been neglected by governments for so long. As it happens, they haven't. As one government minister angrily pointed out, at least forty-five million dollars has been spent on public infrastructure for an estate of four and a half thousand souls in recent years, including a technology centre and a swimming pool, while policing the neighbourhood requires the organisation of a minor military campaign. Since the riots, further public money has been committed to the area, and church groups have plans for a new three million dollar youth centre. At the same time, Sydney's inimitable high-octane radio commentators asked what kind of parenting these kids could have received for them to have gone so bad so early. Where parental discipline had failed, they concluded, youngsters like Jesse Kelly would have to learn the lessons of personal discipline the hard way—through the court system.

Jesse Kelly's biography reads a little like the life-story of the estate. According to newspaper reports, Jesse's birth father disappeared early, his mother found herself incapable of caring for him, and his step-father refused to acknowledge him as a son. When he turned twelve, Jesse's grandparents took him in to their house in Macquarie Fields, but by this stage he was simply too hard to control and they were forced to send him to a special school. (They have nevertheless kept in touch with him throughout his travails.) Like many kids in the area, it's been suggested, Jesse started stealing cars as a form of borrowing; pretty soon he may have moved on to disguising and selling them. As he graduated, he offered a role-model to other young boys in the area for the imagined glamour of the outlaw existence. During the fortnight he remained on the lam after the fatal car-crash, Jesse Kelly's surname was routinely invoked in echo of the much more famous outlaw Kelly—who had of course also hailed from a semi-rural "glen". No doubt this appealed to him. Through friends, he explained cockily to journalists that he was on the run because the police, if they caught him, would show him no mercy. A few days after the fatal crash, a neighbour rather incautiously suggested to the TV news that Jesse should turn himself in. According to the police, Kelly and a group of his friends appeared at the neighbour's house after dark, took apart the man's face with a broken bottle in front of his children, and disappeared back into the night. Yet Jesse's outlaw spirit has the brittle toughness of the lifelong gang member. When, a fortnight after the car chase, he appeared in court charged with two counts of manslaughter, his shoulders dropped and he wept like a lost child.

Thus told, Jesse Kelly's life—like that of so many other boys in the area—is little more than a vessel for the discharge of human sympathy, or else a repository for revulsion. For commentators of all persuasions, he serves—like the monster of the youthful Mary Shelley's imagining—as an exemplary figure. Against his measure, we can find society's claims to inclusion wanting, or lament the waste of a precious life—or else we can use his example as a glass through which to apprehend a decline in societal and personal responsibility, self-discipline and values in parenting. Like refugees from distant lands or the victims of distant wars, his example serves either to rouse our sense of personal conscience, or else to stir our sense of indignity, either to soften our heart or cause us to close it. Such is the power of the personal case, the face with a name to it. Mary Shelley's monster passed solitary hours in the company of Goethe's Romantic tales and pondered his existential plight. It would no doubt make for excellent journalism could Jesse Kelly be persuaded to do the same.

When we debate the fates of communities in crisis, these familiar and even ritualised responses seem to have led us into a series of policy cul-de-sacs. On the one hand, the case for a "zero-tolerance" solution can probably be summarily dismissed. Nothing less than the wholesale evacuation of the estate would be required to bring a "law and order" solution here. That may indeed be a solution—there is an argument that the remaining welfare enclaves like the Glenquarie Estate ought to have been broken up and dispersed years ago. But if it is, it will be one born of the Departments of Housing and Community Services, not the New South Wales Police Service.

On the other hand, liberal-minded sympathy often serves to provide an equally stylised range of responses. Too frequently, there seems to be an almost unbridgeable gulf between the moral imagination of sympathetic journalists and commentators and the actual life situations of those with whom they sympathise—those ingenious, inventive, sometimes malevolent, sometimes fellow-spirited young men of the back streets who make their living as best they may, given where their lives seem to have taken them. Young men who have been selling hot electronics equipment on the streets since early adolescence are soberly advised to take up a trade. Boys who have been disrupting classes for as long as their teachers can recall are earnestly enjoined to stay on longer in school. Kids for whom violence is the indispensable glue of their self-image are guided painstakingly through anger-management counselling.

Military historians have pointed out that, in many cultures, if you want to have a satisfactory battle it's necessary for both sides to agree tacitly on where and how to hold it. Likewise, many of our most bitter political controversies involve a strange kind of conceptual complicity among the warring parties. Defences and critiques of economic deregulation in the 1980s, for instance, alike turned on the assumption that a modern economy could be deregulated, and that the resultant entity would bear a resemblance to the "free market" universe imagined by nineteenth century industrialists. Supporters and opponents of the War on Terror insist upon treating it as a rerun of the Cold War, a kind of ghostly Brezhnevian Groundhog Day. Members of the so-called "welfare lobby" and their opponents too often seem determined to moralise the treatment of poor and dysfunctional communities, so that those who live within them are almost necessarily viewed (according to your preference) as helpless, demoralised and irresponsible, or simply out of control. Jesse Kelly can be enlisted with equal vigour to support any of these interpretations.

No one should under-estimate the corrosive effect on the human spirit of a cocktail of the "stress factors" identified by diligent social investigators such as Tony Vinson. All too often, to be born into an area with (in

Vinson's words) "high rates of low birth-rate babies, high levels of sickness and disabilities, shorter life expectancy, lower school retention rates, low incomes"—all the usual suspects, in other words—is a debilitating experience, draining the self-confidence of those who already lack it, and undermining the life skills of those with a fragile grasp on them.

Commonly, though, people do emerge out of these circumstances with their confidence intact or even lifted by the survival instinct, and their life skills hardened into a kind of granite through long usage. Nor should we trivialise the impact of these success stories. The current Mayor of Campbelltown—which administers the Glenquarie Estate—grew up there, while Labor's "lost leader", Mark Latham, defied at least one of Hugh Stretton's predictions by emerging—with the aid of his local community—as a single "exemplar" from the unforgiving streets of Green Valley.

Sometimes the fact of these success stories is tossed back at the much more numerous non-successes as a mark of reproach: if they could get out of there, why didn't you? (The New South Wales Premier and Police Commissioner both made liberal reference to their own humble upbringings when criticising the Glenquarie rioters.) Yet the harshness of this response simply serves to mask a wider point. On the whole—contrary to some versions of pop psychology which have entrenched themselves as a kind of scientific orthodoxy in liberal opinion in recent years—humans are resilient, resourceful, adaptive, ingenious creatures. Given a chance—all else being well—they'll strive to rebuild their lives after even the most trying experiences. Nor do you have to have your life in perfect order in order to escape cycles of "welfare dependency" or personal dysfunction. Depending on how you measure these factors, tens or maybe even hundreds of thousands of Australians have alcohol and drug dependency problems or mental health issues, but mostly they still strive to raise families responsibly and hold down paying jobs. Given half a chance, they commonly succeed.

In the 1990s, American sociologists—attempting to cut through the familiar moralising debates on welfare "dependency"—strove to measure empirically the responses of welfare recipients to varying policy signals. The results were complex, but their general direction seemed clear. Given a choice, even the poorest and most troubled welfare recipients generally choose to escape their lot by the most reasonable path open to them. Provide single parents with a viable path back into the workforce and they'll take it. Remove "welfare trap" obstacles to accepting unskilled but paying jobs and most people will take those jobs instead. For all but a bohemian few, welfare isn't so much a "way of life" as a pause in life's struggles. Recently, the Australian Housing and Urban Research Institute adopted a similar approach in investigating the relationship between the receipt of housing assistance—which nine in ten public tenants now get—and workforce participation. They found that those receiving rent assistance were significantly less likely to be in paid employment—mostly because it would not make sense for them to take the work. Probing further, they asked unemployed renters how much extra it would cost them to sustain a return to work once their lost entitlements were factored in. The answer was an average of $188. It turned out that the average additional income those renters would have received from taking a paid job was $189 a week. Had they taken those jobs—from their view at least, if not that of taxpayers generally—they would effectively have been donating their labour.

In short, public renters in places like the Glenquarie Estate, like welfare beneficiaries more generally, may be as able as anyone else to do the sums when it comes to making life choices. Turning to petty crime in Macquarie Fields probably makes more sense as a life decision (at least in the short term) than taking a low-paid legitimate job. Only idealists and forward-thinkers would see things differently—and they tend to be in short supply in struggle-towns. Indeed, welfare recipients arguably are more able than most people to make such short-term decisions accurately, since for them the margin between success and failure is narrower, the financial calculation is immediate, predictable and small-scale—unlike the speculative projections of soon-to-be-retired Baby Boomers or mum-and-dad Telstra investors. As in the days of the Victorian social investigators, it seems very likely that "financial improvidence" is a lesser obstacle to poor people's self-advancement than the simple lack of a capital base. (This may well be why Green Valley's most famous son, in his time as opposition leader, chose to champion "micro-finance" schemes for poor families.)

It's tempting to see contemporary Sydney—like the country more widely—as an ocean of affluence studded with small islands of "disadvantage", such as Macquarie Fields, Claymore or Minto. The problem then becomes one of attending to these poor castaways, stranded in would-be garden suburbs, remote communities or regional cul de sacs. And yet, while emotionally gratifying (it appeals, after all, to that old instinct of noblesse oblige which still suffuses the outlook of the concerned professional classes), this is a deceptive vantage-point. To borrow from the terminology of medicine, "treating" disadvantage is rarely a matter of applying a cure—far more often it's the application of a therapy, the aim of which is to soothe the symptoms rather than preventing them. It's not simply that, in our rush to achieve, we've left the poor strugglers behind. The problem is more fundamental than that.

The decisions that created the welfare suburbs which stud our major cities were specific acts of policy, and many of those policies have long since been abandoned. Yet our welfare islands owe their continued existence not to those original decisions alone, but to an entire architecture of policy misdecision which continues to this day. Indeed, you could argue that, rather than having learned from the past, over the decade of our long boom we've simply been reproducing old policy errors on a much larger scale. An historically unprecedented number of those on our welfare rolls today are there not because they are incapable of working or unwilling to work, but because of a series of obstacles placed in their path—often by the same governments which claim to be trying to help them. Employers today demand of those applying for jobs of even limited skills "pieces of paper"—often of decidedly limited practical value—which too many individuals are incapable of acquiring because they fail to complete school. Young men leaving education today without some form of qualification will be condemned to a kind of workforce twilight zone for much of their adult lives. At the same time, benefits and rent assistance are still too often calibrated to taper off as people—often trying to escape from them—start to do better for themselves, so that those who fall out of the mainstream find it hard to drag themselves back in.

Sole-parent benefits and child-care costs sometimes still seem purpose-designed to discourage tens of thousands of mothers from returning to work, and have made unwilling "welfare mums" of thousands of independent-minded divorcees. Economist Bob Gregory has pointed out that female single parents—whose most common life goals are to find new jobs and new partners—don't seem able to find either nowadays, while among married women rates of full-time employment have actually been growing. Meanwhile, as Gregory has observed elsewhere, sanctioned changes to employer behaviour, labour relations and unemployment benefit provisions in recent decades have forced tens (or maybe hundreds) of thousands of older but able-bodied men to recreate themselves as perpetual state dependants and invalids. Indeed, these trends have actually worsened over the course of the ten-year boom. In 1995 the combined total of those on the sole-parent pension and the disability pension was roughly equal to the number of people on unemployment benefits. By 2005, however, the two groups out-numbered those on unemployment benefits by a factor of five to two. And while unemployment rolls have shrunk at an impressive rate (by about twenty-two thousand a year between 1995 and 2005), the sickness benefit roll has grown faster (at twenty-five thousand a year). It's possible that a majority of all those who dropped off our unemployment rolls haven't become employed, but rather have become (at least officially) sick. These are not small, isolated, pitiable fragments of the community. Put together, they add up to an absolute majority of all those on our welfare rolls, and a very considerable proportion of the entire citizen body.

Our contemporary schooling debacle accentuates these difficulties. Until relatively recently, graduates of solid local state comprehensives had a respectable chance of doing better in life than their parents. Increasingly, as ambitious and better-resourced parents defect to other parts of the system, this opportunity seems to be melting away, and with it much of a proud national tradition of self-betterment. In 2002, the Vinson Report into New South Wales state schooling quizzed principals from "low socio-economic status" areas like Macquarie Fields. One principal in outer western Sydney reported that, over the previous two years, no fewer than four-fifths of their existing teaching staff had successfully sought placements elsewhere. Out of the senior staff, the only survivor was the principal himself. Of the current staff, forty-two of the forty-six were in their first teaching appointment. In its final report to the state government, shortly after the Glenquarie riots, the New South Wales Public Education Council examined the placement of beginning teachers in schools across the state. The report noted that one-third of the new teachers who found first jobs in state schools in New South Wales in 2004 were drafted into just 3 per cent of the state's schools—each of which, on average, will have been required to digest at least seven first-time teachers each year. If these schools were the same size as that unnamed western Sydney school documented in the Vinson Report, each one of them would turn over its entire staff every six years or so. As educationist Richard Teese has observed, this is a veritable production line of social incapacity.

Too much of the debate over Australia's new "age of affluence" has been moralised unhelpfully—or, perhaps more precisely, it has been moralised in the wrong way. Our key problems aren't the supposed "time-poverty" of busy knowledge-workers (in any case, as researchers at the University of New South Wales recently pointed out, the most "time-poor" are actually single parents on the workforce's fringes), or supposed enslavement to poor tastes in housing design or "conspicuous consumption" (that old reliable stand-by of disgruntled aesthetes). Those who've achieved high levels of personal and financial independence may mostly be left safely enough to exercise that independence as they see fit. (And if the exercise of that independence causes them psychic trauma, they have an historically unprecedented variety of therapies and spiritualisms of which to assuage it.)

The greater problem is that the new tide of affluence doesn't seem to have brought with it a comparable widening of this experience of personal independence. Australians have always hankered to be able to fend for themselves, but too many are still condemned to hankering. Our incomes may have doubled since the 1970s, but the numbers of those stuck on welfare has stubbornly refused to fall. Unemployment—at least as officially recorded—has halved over that time, yet the numbers of people excluded from the workforce have arguably risen, as the labour market for the unskilled has dwindled. Self-employed tradespeople and contractors nowadays may seem to live in a land of milk and honey, but too many waged employees endure fearful working existences. If we're dissatisfied with our national achievement, this may not be on account of some kind of intangible ennui. Rather, there's a promise there that lies unfulfilled, and the riots in our struggle-towns may only be the most violent indications of it.

Still our debates over work, incomes, tax and welfare continue to roll along the same well-signalled rail lines laid down for our ideological traffic thirty, forty or even fifty years ago. On the left, the size of our welfare outlays, or of our public housing stock, is still too often treated as if it were a marker of our degree of civilisation—as if tending to incapacity were an act of humanitarianism. Clearly, welfare recipients should have the right to a dignified standard of life. And in a society where most citizens aspire to own their own house in their own name, there is no particular electoral incentive for government to care too tenderly for those who cannot, unless others call them to account. Yet it's worth remembering that the advocate's outlook is a partial view. The measure of a civilised society ought not to be the size of its welfare outlays, or of its public housing sector, but rather the success of individuals and families in achieving some stable lifestyle and accommodation which can give them self-reliance and self-respect. To treat the body of public renters and welfare beneficiaries as foot-soldiers in an imagined global war between market and state provision is unfair to the hopeful, if struggling, households who inhabit that "stock" or collect those funds. They don't want to become trophies of a social vision—mostly, they just want to move on.

By contrast, conservatives have always liked to trumpet their rhetorical and ideological commitment to personal striving and independence. Yet in practice this instinct—which is no doubt sometimes sincerely felt—generally loses out to the right's more visceral revulsion against the power of state agencies, even where they can play an active and constructive role in encouraging personal independence, rather than stifling it. If the current federal government leaves behind it a single significant initiative in social policy, it will be the Job Network. In theory, the Network is supposed to "empower" jobseekers by providing them with a choice of job-search providers, and granting them the status of a customer rather than a supplicant to public bureaucracy. In practice, though, it serves in good measure to create and then entrench different categories of the jobless, divided by how expensive (which is to say how unprofitable) they are to help. And since few self-respecting businesses would get into an industry ordered along these peculiar lines, the experience of job-seeking under the Job Network often seems to involve less a change in customer status than a transfer of dependency, from being the supplicant of a government bureaucracy to being the recipient of Christian charity. This is hardly a monument to personal independence. Rather, it is a memorial to the ideological impasse of our times.

On the right, it's been convenient to measure the economic successes of the last decade by the flood of cash they've brought in their wake. The left—as is far too often its wont—has reacted to these claims in a negative, call-and-response manner, either by decrying Australia's affluence as a triumph of poor taste, or seeing it as a kind of financially induced hardening of the moral arteries of the nation. Yet both of these positions, viewed from the wider historical perspective, look myopic. A century ago, Australia's quest for nationhood was measured by the extent to which the entire nation was integrated into a common public life and culture—a life and culture which had been designed, up until that point, chiefly for the enjoyment and satisfaction of the propertied classes. On this measure, the last decade has been a conspicuous historical failure in our national life— a failure made more egregious by the numerous opportunities the wealth and tranquility of the times have offered us. If full citizenship resides in possessing a secure stake in the nation and its culture, we may well have more non-citizens now than we did half a century ago. And their travails may well continue to haunt our mid-summer nights.

In October 2006, after eighteen months in prison for other offences and a turbulent relationship with his warders, Jesse Kelly pleaded guilty in Sydney's Downing Street District Court to two counts of aggravated dangerous driving causing death. This time the newspaper reports made no mention of any crowd of well-wishers outside the court. In his summing-up, Justice Brian Knox SC observed that Kelly seemed to have viewed his long-running cat-and-mouse relationship with the local police as a kind of game—noting, with true judicial sententiousness, that "if it was a game, it was a particularly deadly one for his two passengers". Kelly was sentenced to a maximum jail term of seven years and nine months, with a minimum sentence of five and a half years. In handing down the sentence, Justice Knox concluded: "I do not find there are strong prospects for rehabilitation." After the verdict, Jesse's loyal grandfather, Peter Parker, spoke to reporters outside the court: "I think Jesse accepts the sentence as it stands. But who knows what lies down the road."

6
The Culture Wars

Tom Switzer

Conservatives are no longer losing the culture wars
Quadrant, October 2007

To be a conservative in the journalism profession is a bit like how US presidential candidate Mitt Romney describes what it's like to be a Republican in the liberal state of Massachusetts: you're a cattle rancher at a vegetarian convention. At least until recent times (say, the last five or so years), you were isolated in the newsroom; you were condemned for not conforming to the smelly orthodoxies of political correctness; and your political insights were treated not as a contentious contribution to the editorial conference, but as a flat earther's fit of extremist nonsense. There wasn't their opinion and your opinion; there was their opinion ... and you're insane!

I'll never forget my first week of work in Australian journalism nearly a decade ago. I started work at the *Australian Financial Review* at the height of the waterfront dispute in March–April 1998. My editor called me into his office on the morning that Chris Corrigan and Patrick Stevedores sacked the Maritime Union workers, and instructed me what our editorial line would be, which was along the following lines: "This is a great day for Australian capitalism; at long last, Australia is reaching a big bang end-game in its decades-long quest to remove the shame on its waterfront."

After writing my first draft of the next day's editorial for the editor, I then walked around the floor to meet my new colleagues. They were clearly concerned about the docks dispute unfolding outside our Darling Park office windows. One disturbed journalist asked me: "Comrade, how do you think we are going in the war out there on the waterfront?"

Now, the "comrade" talk naturally astonished me; I had, after all, just returned from Washington, where I had spent three years working at the American Enterprise Institute, and I could never imagine calling my colleagues John Bolton or Jeane Kirkpatrick "comrade", lest they confuse me with some Sandinista! Leaving that aside, I still assumed that my new work friends meant "we" in the sense that we were on message with the company line. So keen to assimilate into my new workplace, I thus plagiarised the editor's refrain: "This is a great day for Australian capitalism!"

My colleagues were bemused. "What on earth do you mean, comrade?" came the reply.

"You know, isn't it wonderful," I said, "that the government and Patrick are staring down the last gasp of old-style union militancy?"

Imagine my surprise when one senior journalist called me aside and warned me that airing such provocative opinions around the office could amount to a workplace dispute—even though I was merely parroting the paper's editorial line! My colleagues, you see, belonged to the journalists' union and so had pledged solidarity with the battling wharfies. Never mind that these battling wharfies had held the country to ransom for decades. Never mind all the notorious unreliability, high cost and long loading delays on our container wharves that made us an international exporting laughing stock. I stood out like a cattle rancher at a vegetarian convention.

The episode, though, made me think: if the sober and august journalists at the nation's leading financial daily had such views about the modern workplace, I wondered how much more entrenched the same attitudes might be among the journalists at the *Sydney Morning Herald* and the *Age*, as well as at the public broadcaster. Former veteran BBC staffer Robin Aitken once lamented he could not raise a cricket team of conservatives among staff at the British public broadcaster. I sometimes doubt if an indoor cricket team could be raised at the other Aunty as well as at many newspapers in Australia.

But in any event, opinions and the public culture have developed and changed over the years since my first day in Australian journalism.

When William F. Buckley Jr revived American conservatism by founding *National Review* in 1955, he said the magazine's job was to stand "athwart history, yelling stop". At that time, conservatism was regarded in polite society as a mental affliction and history did seem to be moving in the wrong direction if you were a conservative intellectual. Later, during the Reagan era and in the 1990s when Republicans gained control of both houses of Congress, American conservatives enjoyed thinking that history was on their side. As *Time* magazine's Michael Kinsley has recently put it: "They saw themselves as riding it like a Bronco, yelling not stop, but faster! faster!"

National Review's birth coincided with the arrival of an important milestone here in Australia. In a cultural landscape that the twenty-six-year-old Owen Harries thought was as flat and unvaried as the proverbial Australian sheep station, *Quadrant* magazine was created to defend cultural freedom. Fifty years ago it planted its banner at what Lionel Trilling called the bloody crossroads where literature and politics meet, and there it remains. Back in those days, Australia's cultural community was very small and isolated, and there was much less diversity and pluralism than in North America or Western Europe. This was the environment into which *Quadrant* was born.

Its first issue was published as Soviet tanks were crushing the 1956 uprising in Budapest and, during the Cold War, *Quadrant* opposed the perverse but comfortable notion that principled liberalism required an anti-anticommunist posture, one that really amounted to neutrality in the conflict between liberal democracy and totalitarianism. In more recent times, it has fought the good fights in the nation's culture wars, combating the political correctness that has poisoned the intellectual class and, until recent years, the political establishment. Above all else, *Quadrant* has been a rallying point for Australian intellectuals and journalists who rejected the prevailing leftism of the times.

Peter Coleman, Geoffrey Blainey, Keith Windschuttle, Jim McAuley, Peter Ryan, David Armstrong, Gerard Henderson, Paddy McGuinness, Roger Sandall, Owen Harries, Hal Colebatch, Frank Devine, David Flint, Dame Leonie Kramer, John Dyson Heydon, Giles Auty, Les Murray and Robert Manne—you know the names and their articles. *Quadrant* has been on the front lines in the culture wars and a trendsetter in the battle of ideas.

One article stands out. In 1994, at the height of Keatingism and a time of rising doubts about the Liberal Party's future, an Opposition front bencher wrote a prescient piece on the culture wars, calling on the Liberal Party to fight "the battle of history with the Labor Party". The author: one John Winston Howard:

> Much of [Paul Keating's] rhetoric about building a so-called new Australia is built on a denigration of our past and its achievements. We are consistently told that Australia's history is a litany of intolerance, bigotry and narrow-mindedness. There are certainly many blemishes, particularly in the treatment of Aborigines, but as all of us know it is hazardous to apply the standards and attitudes of today to the behaviour of earlier generations.
>
> The truth is that, compared with other nations, Australia's behaviour in the area of human rights, personal freedom and general tolerance has been impressive. This is an Australian achievement stretching back over more than 200 years of which we should be positive and proud rather than negative and ashamed. So much of Paul Keating's attack on the national identity is the rhetoric of apology and shame rather than that of praise and gratitude.
>
> In these circumstances, Liberals should become the party of the Australian achievement. There is latent sentiment in the community that legitimate expressions of pride about the past have been stifled, allegedly to show tolerance towards minorities. That tolerance is essential in a fair society, but it is best expressed through the quality of the contemporary treatment of minorities rather than through zealous repudiation of past traditions and achievements.

Just as Bill Buckley did forty years earlier, John Howard was standing athwart history yelling "Stop!" Thirteen years later, it is hard to deny that Howard, as Prime Minister, has put into practice what he preached in *Quadrant*'s pages. Today, Australians increasingly look on their flag with pride, and growing attendances at Anzac Day ceremonies are among many indications of robust patriotism. No longer are Australians told to be ashamed of their country.

Which brings me to the point: the tide is turning in Australia's culture wars. When you look at the way opinion in this country has surged back and forth over the last decade or so, I would suggest that there has been something of a political and cultural realignment of the nation. It's a point that those on the broad Left are conceding, albeit grudgingly, but it's also a point that too many on the Right have not fully realised. Conservatives may not have won the culture wars, but they are certainly not losing any more.

For decades, media sophisticates were able to control the political debate by all kicking in the same direction, like the Rockettes. In recent years, however, it is increasingly clear that the cultural landscape is no longer as flat and unvaried as that proverbial Australian sheep station. Whereas once conservative ideas were swept aside as being outside the boundaries of serious (and morally respectable) consideration, today they represent the political mainstream.

On the great battlefields of history, economics, education, citizenship, national sovereignty and values generally, conservative ideas and those of classical liberalism increasingly, although not of course completely, prevail. When David Marr of the *Sydney Morning Herald* and Clive Hamilton of the Australia Institute warn that the government, allegedly in cahoots with the Murdoch press, is silencing dissent and corrupting public debate, that's code for saying: "We no longer set the terms of the cultural and political debate in this country."

At first glance, this might sound like an odd argument to make. After all, the Australian Labor Party runs all state and territory governments, and Kevin Rudd and the federal Opposition are leading convincingly in the polls. The Left, moreover, still controls the commanding heights of Australian culture—from the arts and university humanities faculties to the Fairfax press and the public broadcaster.

All true. But if conservatives make a realistic assessment of where they are today they at least have some grounds for optimism. Fixate on the opinion polls and the dismal performances of the state Liberal parties across the nation, fixate on *Late Night Live with Phillip Adams* and all those trendy taxpayer-subsidised writers' festivals, and pessimism makes sense. But stand back and look at the grand sweep of change during the past decade, and some of the darkness should lift.

There are two questions that really matter in assessing the state of the culture wars today: In what direction is Australia moving? And how does today's Australia compare with the Australia of, say, the Keating era? The answers to both questions should encourage conservatives.

Start with the direction Australia is moving in: Everything that should be up—incomes, economic growth, the budget surplus, consumer and business confidence—is up, while everything that should be down—unemployment, inflation, even (historically speaking) interest rates—is down. The Australian economy is now in the sixteenth year of the longest economic expansion perhaps, according to John Howard, "since the gold rushes of the nineteenth century". This, remember, at a time of the Asian financial crisis of 1997–98, the US tech wreck and recession of 2000–01, and Australia's worst drought in a century. Today, Australia ranks fifty-third in terms of world population, but it is the world's thirteenth-largest economy, eighth in the world in income per head, up from eighteenth two decades ago. In 2005, a Crosby–Textor survey found more than eight out of ten Australians associated living here with opportunity, confidence and success. Of course, this does not explain the state of the opinion polls, but the point here is that we live in very prosperous times.

The reason for this prosperity: a smart mix of free-market structural reforms and prudent monetary and fiscal policies during the past two decades. If we had heeded the protectionists and economic interventionists—that is, the very people who today complain that their views are being silenced—Australia would well and truly be a banana republic. From the interventionist mindset that delivered economic turmoil in the 1970s, Australia has moved to an era of sounder policy and more durable prosperity.

True, the Prime Minister will all too often throw tax dollars around to targeted special interests with wild abandon, prompting one commentator to call Howard's Australia the Sweden of the South. And it is true there has been some painful adjustment for some Australians; Pauline Hanson's One Nation movement in the late 1990s was, in many ways, a backlash against globalisation and rapid economic change as well as a reaction to the dislocation and, as Joseph Schumpeter famously put it, creative destruction involved.

Still, Australian society now offers unparallelled opportunities. Far from producing Dickensian sweatshops, as predicted by the unions, the workplace changes have produced steady and low-inflation wage growth. Labour unions, once the bedrock of the nation's workforce, are in serious decline while shareholders, small business owners and individual contractors are on the rise. Indeed, not so long ago, Australia passed the point that was reached in the UK under Margaret Thatcher's government where we now have more shareholders than trade union members. A recent study has shown the rewards of the economic miracle have been evenly spread across poorer, middle and richer suburbs and regions.

Of course, Labor partisans keep promoting the old myth that the outstanding prosperity Australia has experienced in the Howard era is directly due to reforms made by the previous Labor governments. And it is true Bob Hawke and Paul Keating did deregulate the financial markets, cut taxes and lower import protection (with, remember, strong bipartisan support led by John Howard).

But if conservatives want the public to get a more accurate picture of the last decade, they should keep highlighting the other side of the Keating legacy: the "recession we had to have", 12 per cent unemployment, 17 per cent interest rates, record high budget deficits and a $96 billion national debt. And they should keep reminding the public that Labor opposed all the government's economic reforms that have kept the good times rolling—including economically conservative policies that helped turn a whopping fiscal deficit into a huge budget surplus.

Now let's compare Keating's Australia with Howard's Australia. To scan the broadsheet newspapers in the 1990s is to understand how Australia has changed—and mainly for the better. In the library, turning the smudgy pages of ten to fifteen years ago, one reads of another world.

Back then there was almost universal consensus in the media about the virtues of Aboriginal welfarism, apologies, treaties, separatism, a politicians' republic, zealous multiculturalism, activist judges rewriting our constitution, and it appeared that the black-armband view of history was the politically approved order of the day. Today, however, things are very different.

Start with the opinion formers themselves. Dennis Glover, a long-time Labor Party speech writer, laments: "Open a major newspaper on any day of the week and you will find Labor has few friends in the world of print." An overstatement perhaps, but not far from the truth. Think about it. Phillip Adams remembers a time in the 1970s when the Left had almost total control of print opinion. He recalls Graham Perkin, the long-time editor of the *Age*, saying: "We really must get a rightwing columnist." And during the Keating era, only a few well-known conservatives or free-marketeers such as Paddy McGuinness, Frank Devine, Alan Wood and John Stone existed in the national media.

Today, by contrast, the ranks of the Right have swelled to include Andrew Bolt, Piers Akerman, Gerard Henderson, Greg Sheridan, Miranda Devine, Janet Albrechtsen, Imre Salusinszky, Sandra Lee, Michael Baume, Dennis Shanahan, Terry McCrann, Michael Duffy, John Roskam, Tim Blair, Christopher Pearson, Paul Gray, Neil Mitchell and Paul Sheehan, who has also published a swag of best-sellers—from *Among the Barbarians* in 1998 to *The Electronic Whorehouse* in 2003.

Robert Manne argues that Albrechtsen, Bolt and Akerman represent "an interesting new phenomenon". He laments: "Even 20 years ago, Australia did not have journalists like this in the mainstream press." A telling confession. One could be inclined to dismiss one voice on this topic, but Manne is hardly alone in fretting and wailing that the Left's near monopoly over the institutions of opinion and information is crumbling. Listen to the following:

> PHILLIP ADAMS: "Our population in the press is so small as to constitute extinction. We are dead parrots ... giving the illusion of life because we are nailed to our perches."
>
> DON WATSON: "Control of both houses is more than a parliamentary triumph; it is final victory in the culture wars. That's the stunning part, and the worst thing for Labor to swallow: the completeness of the ideological victory."
>
> JULIA GILLARD: "Howard has won his culture war, for now. My argument is that it's time for Australians of all political persuasions who don't like this new political correctness—from green on the Left to the small-l liberal on the Right—to wake up to the fact that they have lost the culture war."

And if that is not enough to convince you that the Left is in retreat, then consider that one of the star attractions at both the Sydney and Melbourne Writers' Festivals this year has been a debate between David Marr and Clive Hamilton. The subject: Hamilton's book *Silencing Dissent: How the Australian Government is Controlling Public Opinion and Stifling Debate*.

Now, having a debate about how debate has been shut down may seem a little odd, especially when you consider the many books peddling a similar theme. From *The War on Democracy: Conservative Opinion in Australia* to *Do Not Disturb: Is the Media Failing Australia?*, the message of these countless books is the same. In the words of Hamilton and Sarah Maddison, the Howard government, in cahoots with a "right-wing syndicate" of media commentators, has "systematically targeted independent, critical and dissenting voices" in order "to ensure that its values are the only values heard in public debate".

All of this brings to mind the famous American leftwing lament at the height of McCarthyism. As Leslie Fiedler, the literary critic and liberal anticommunist, once quipped about his paranoid colleagues in the mid-1950s: "From coast to coast, the cry rang out: we are silenced, we dare not speak out!" In other words, far from being silenced, left-wing voices have simply lost their relevance in a cultural landscape that is looking increasingly conservative.

Take indigenous issues. When John Howard took office in 1996, in the wake of the High Court's Mabo decision and Paul Keating's landmark Redfern speech accepting white responsibility for the plight of Australian Aborigines, the imperative was for symbolism rather than substance. More land rights and campaigns against white racism were seen as the solution to the problems of remote Aboriginal communities.

Today, however, the conventional wisdom is very different. John Howard's language of integration and practical reconciliation prevails. The Noel Pearson who once called the Howard government "racist scum" and said John Howard was "totally useless to the nation" now concedes Howard's points that welfare dependency is a blight on the Aboriginal community; that greater individual responsibility, not Aboriginal victimhood, is the way forward; and that more tax dollars and endless negotiation with dysfunctional communities won't provide a long-term fix to the indigenous situation.

Indeed, the recent declaration of a national emergency in Aboriginal Australia puts an end to Nugget Coombs' decades-long experiment of separatism that glorified indigenous culture but was blinded to the modern-day scourges of welfare dependency, substance abuse and boredom. Although doubts have been understandably raised about the intervention leading to unintended consequences in the remote communities, the plan has been widely supported. That has not stopped some journalists, such as David Marr, from lamenting that the plan is a victory for white hardliners.

A decade ago, Robert Manne had a famous falling out with his colleagues and eventually resigned as editor of *Quadrant*—primarily over Ronald Wilson's *Bringing Them Home* report on the stolen generations. But he has nonetheless conceded that *Quadrant*, under his successor Paddy McGuinness, has "marshalled the troops and galvanised the disparate voices of opposition into what amounted to a serious and effective political campaign" against symbolism, gesture politics, unconditional welfare and the rights agenda. Even the *Sydney Morning Herald*, which has long championed an apology, only recently editorialised against such "glib symbolism", saying it was a "practically useless" gesture that would have "no constructive outcome".

Then there's the policy of multiculturalism, which had allowed immigrants of different cultures to settle without expecting them to integrate into society. That policy has not only been openly questioned, but effectively overturned. Integration is now widely regarded as the key to national social cohesion. A new citizenship test requires knowledge of Australian values and history as well as of English. Now Australian citizens must be encouraged to understand Australia's commitment to democracy, equal rights and the rule of law. The government has swapped multiculturalism for citizenship in the title of the Immigration Department. Meanwhile, the nation remains a tolerant multi-ethnic and multi-racial society, sustained, with strong community support, by a non-discriminatory immigration level that is double the rate of Keating-era levels.

It is not as if Australia is alone in moving in this direction of national social cohesion. Other Western democracies are casting aside the old mantra that it doesn't matter whether citizens have a sense of allegiance to their nation and its institutions. Britain, France, Italy, Spain, Germany and Poland are all making prospective migrants sign an integration contract vowing to respect the values of democracy, free speech and respect for all faiths. Some are going even further. Take the erstwhile permissive Netherlands, which was shocked by a Muslim extremist's 2004 murder of Dutch film-maker Theo Van Gogh for producing a movie about the treatment of women under Islam. Now the Dutch are demanding that potential immigrants watch a video that includes images of men kissing and a topless woman emerging from the surf. That's a far cry from Canberra's more modest proposals. Still, gone are the days of unbridled tolerance for the minority and a loathing for the dominant culture or conventional view.

The debate is also starting to shift on education. Performance pay, merit-based policies, more choice, and vouchers that enable parents to spend their public education dollar at any institution they like, increasingly frame today's conversation. The federal government is now questioning the merits of politically correct school curriculum programs such as critical literacy and outcomes-based education that are aimed at finding hidden racism and sexism in great works of literature. And on the history front, the government is sending a message to state education bureaucrats loud and clear: that Australian history should not be taught simply as a story of victims and oppressors, and should not be about imposing today's values on yesterday's events.

Free markets and fiscal rectitude now occupy the moral and policy high ground in Australia. So much so that even the Labor leader has gone to great lengths to describe himself as an "economic conservative". In one television advertisement, Kevin Rudd boasts: "A number of people have described me as an economic conservative. When it comes to public finance, it's a badge I wear with pride." Now, there are good reasons to doubt Rudd's commitment to economic reform, but it says a lot that a modern-day ALP leader feels the need to describe himself as an economic conservative. Whereas thirty-five years ago a Republican president said "We are all Keynesians", these days it appears we are all "economic conservatives".

Even the judiciary is starting to change. From 1987 to 1995, Australia's highest court was transformed from caretaker to creator of the law. According to judges quoted in US academic Jason Pearce's *Inside the Mason Court Revolution*, Anthony Mason's High Court was "hyperactive", "adventurous", "incomparably activist" and it was "composed of judicial legislators [and] controlled by Jacobins". (One Mason court judge told Pearce that critics of the Mabo decision—which rejected the notion of terra nullius and opened the way for recognition of native title rights for Aboriginal Australians—were vociferous rednecks with no sympathy for liberalism.)

These days, however, the High Court appears to subscribe to the conservative view that laws are best made by those most directly responsible to the people through democratic elections. John Dyson Heydon, delivering a *Quadrant* address on the eve of his appointment to the High Court five years ago, detected the changing mindset. "When judges detect particular community values ... as supporting their reasoning," he said, "they may sometimes become confused between the values which they think the community actually holds and the values which they think the community should hold." Radical legal change, he concluded, "is best effected by professional politicians who have a lifetime's experience of assessing the popular will". Quite different sentiments from those of the Keating–Mason era.

As for the republic, it is now so politically irrelevant that even the Labor leader has ruled out a referendum if he becomes prime minister. As Peter Ryan has argued in *Quadrant*: "Where could all the huff and puff (and money) come from to re-inflate that vast hot-air balloon?"

Look at the internal dynamics of the Liberal Party and you will notice a move towards the right. The high command of the party—Howard, Nick Minchin, Alexander Downer, Tony Abbott, Brian Loughnane—are all from the conservative wing. Even Peter Costello is better described as a mainstream conservative rather than a moderate, as his supporters in the party room and the press argue. Also bear in mind that today's small-l liberals such as Petro Georgiou and Marise Payne are further to the right than yesterday's wets such as Ian Macphee and Peter Baume. Witness their broad support for the economic reform agenda as well as their reluctance to fret and wail that Australia is somehow a new international pariah.

As Phillip Adams has lamented, the drought of wets in John Howard's ranks intensifies and the Dick Hamers, Fred Chaneys, Alan Missens represent another era. As he put it in the *Australian* after the death of Don Chipp last September: "In this new world of Right is might, erstwhile wets such as Philip Ruddock, Richard Alston and Robert Hill had to reinvent themselves as reactionaries to survive." Conservatives now also dominate the New South Wales Young Liberals (which the Left had controlled for more than two decades), the Women's Council, and the state executive. That speaks volumes of the cultural sea change in the Liberal Party.

Conservative and populist talkback radio, moreover, has become more popular in the past decade, presumably because many people got sick and tired of being spoon-fed left-liberal dross by the *Age* and the *Sydney Morning Herald*. However strident and overheated they may have been, broadcasters such as Alan Jones, Neil Mitchell, Ray Hadley, Steve Price, Greg Smith and the late Stan Zemanek have proved that conservative talk radio could be profitable as well as influential, and anti-leftists at last found their attitudes and beliefs given forceful expression through a powerful media outlet.

To be sure, the Left has found something to unify it—hatred of John Howard. Technology has given it the means to organise; what the Right found in talk radio, liberals have found in the internet, from GetUp to *Crikey*. Still, these are early days in the online world, and it is only inevitable that more Tim Blairs, Andrew Bolts and Andrew Nortons will produce good quality weblogs from a conservative perspective.

Even the ABC has shown signs of political diversity in the past decade, though conservatives not surprisingly feel betrayed by Donald McDonald. Of the longtime ABC chairman, one high-profile Liberal said:

> As far as Liberals go, the major cultural war of the last twenty years has been against the Left of the ABC, and John Howard has failed to fight it. Donald McDonald has become our equivalent of John Kerr, and John Howard should have known he'd turn on us.

Still, the tremors caused by the new cultural landscape have been felt in the Ultimo and Southbank studios, especially since Mark Scott became managing director a little more than a year ago. No longer, for instance, is there a staff-elected director position on the Board. John Howard once expressed his desire for a "right-wing Phillip Adams" at the ABC. Well, there is now "a right-wing Phillip Adams" in the name of Michael Duffy, who along with Paul Comrie-Thomson provides a welcome corrective, albeit a small one, to the rest of Aunty every week on Radio National. When the provocative Canadian Mark Steyn visited Australia last August, the

ABC broadcast up to ten programs featuring the right-wing polemicist, and treating him, in the most part, with respect and serious consideration. His discussion with Owen Harries at a Centre for Independent Studies forum was broadcast on Radio National. That would have been inconceivable a decade ago. Just as it would have been inconceivable a decade ago to see the likes of Piers Akerman, Andrew Bolt and Gerard Henderson on ABC television every Sunday morning.

Now, none of this is to deny that a soft-Left groupthink all too often colours the output of the public broadcaster. It's just that, as even a long-time ABC critic such as Henderson has conceded: "The ABC has improved since its controversial coverage of the Gulf War [in 1990–91]. The news and current affairs programs are now better balanced than then."

Perhaps nothing better demonstrates the cultural sea change than the history wars. In recent decades, Australian history had been dominated by a negative view of this country based on allegations that British colonialists committed brutal genocide against the Aboriginal inhabitants. This had affected not only our national image during the Keating era; it also affected government policies, by producing a widespread sense of guilt and shame that led to various forms of compensation to indigenous Australians.

Today, thanks to historians such as Keith Windschuttle and Geoffrey Blainey and columnists such as Henderson and Albrechtsen, this black-armband view of history has been challenged and Australians are now under less pressure to feel shame about their heritage. Of course this is not to deny that Aboriginal people have been treated poorly in the past; it's just that Australia's historical failures should not outweigh its successes such as our role as an experimental pioneer of democracy.

The case of Windschuttle is illustrative of the cultural sea change. Writing in *The Fabrication of Aboriginal History* in 2002 and in articles published in *Quadrant* and the *Australian*'s Opinion Page, Windschuttle proved that some academic historians—most notably Henry Reynolds and Lyndall Ryan—had literally made up "facts" to back their claims of a white colonialist genocidal war of extermination against Tasmania's original inhabitants in the early 1800s.

The response from the intellectual establishment was overwhelmingly hostile and downright irrational. Windschuttle was compared, unforgivably, to the Holocaust denier David Irving. Don Watson, Paul Keating's speechwriter, said "Windschuttle should be put in a bag and thrown in the Murray." Three academics wrote a letter to the *Australian* saying they were "deeply concerned that Keith Windschuttle should be given space to attack the credibility of major Australian historians". A book of essays in refutation of the Windschuttle thesis was edited by Robert Manne and published by Black Inc.

And yet throughout the debate, the academic historians failed to rebut convincingly his facts—or rather the serious factual lapses he located in his opponents' scholarship. True, a few small errors were found in his research, errors which Windschuttle acknowledged, but they were minor compared to the many falsehoods peddled by his antagonists. One of Britain's leading writers, Theodore Dalrymple, summarised the academic response best:

> A large and influential part of the Australian academy and intelligentsia actually wanted there to have been a genocide. They reacted to Windschuttle's book like a child who has had a toy snatched from its hand by its elder sibling. You would have thought that a man who discovered that his country had not been founded, as had previously been thought and taught, on genocide would be treated as a national hero. On the contrary, he was held up to execration.

Windschuttle's role in challenging a discipline that had become cosy and insular is a reminder that conservatives are no longer losing the culture wars. Of course, one should never indulge in hubris and arrogance; after all, the battle of ideas is never-ending. Nor should one be contemptuous of ideological opponents, however tempting that may be. As Owen Harries has argued:

> Always bear in mind John Stuart Mill's observation that he who knows only his own position knows little of that. Take particular care to understand the position of your adversary—and to understand it not in a caricature or superficial form but at its strongest, for until you have rebutted it at its strongest you have not rebutted it at all.

Still, conservatives should take some comfort that the public culture has changed during the past decade—and mainly for the better.

Doubting Thomases will warn that my argument here is naive, short-sighted, and fails to accept that ideological pendulums have a tendency to swing back and forth. When you change a government, the tired refrain goes, you change a country. Perhaps, but it is worth bearing in mind that the alternative prime minister, unlike his predecessors, is moving his party towards this new cultural terrain. So Labor's class envy and opposition to more uranium mines are out, for instance, while national standards and performance pay for teachers are in. As a result, Kevin Rudd hopes to convince so-called Howard Battlers to come home to Labor without being embarrassed to tell their friends they are doing so.

Why is Rudd modelling himself as an echo, not a repudiation, of Howard? Because he presumably recognises that the new cultural landscape has shifted to the right during the past decade. Just as Margaret Thatcher helped create Tony Blair's more centrist Labour Party in Britain and just as Ronald Reagan helped lead the Democrats to the more centrist Bill Clinton in the USA, John Howard has pushed the ALP in a more conservative direction.

Historians and political partisans will quarrel over how much of the credit for this cultural sea change should go to Howard. But it is undeniable that at least some of the credit must go to him because—win or lose this year's federal election, and agree with him or not (and I happen to disagree with him on some issues, such as the Iraq war, which I opposed from the outset along conservative realist grounds)—the point is that he has not been afraid to challenge the old assumptions and provoke people into thinking and then arguing about the new attitudes on so many of those issues mentioned here.

Of course, the Prime Minister has been ably supported in this endeavour by long-time cultural warriors such as Peter Coleman, Paddy McGuinness and Tony Abbott. But there has been no better spokesman for this cause than Howard himself.

As a result, my guess is that a lot of Australians now see themselves not as a guilt-ridden nation ashamed of our past, but as a not too badly governed, reasonably prosperous, moderately secure, not too bitterly divided society, facing all the problems of a dangerous world—but facing them with a degree of confidence unimaginable ten to fifteen years ago. The very fact that at all those literary festivals and humanities faculties all over the nation our intellectual elite are whipping themselves into a lather and raging about how Howard has stifled them and silenced debate and corrupted democracy, tells us that at least he has provoked them into thinking and talking about these cultural issues.

More importantly, perhaps they now feel they do not have everything their own way any more, that their ideas have become shopworn, that different cultural attitudes have taken root, that they now have to defend their positions when for the last fifty years or so they had it all their own way. It's hard to imagine that this new cultural landscape won't result in a broader, richer, deeper national debate—something liberals of a John Stuart Mill stripe should welcome. It's also likely to result in a more conservative Australia.

So perhaps it is not surprising that it was John Howard himself who put it best when he declared last year:

> Australians have made a lot of mistakes, we have treated Aboriginal people very badly, and we have our share of racists and bigots. But a lot of the agenda of the cultural Left in this country is basically that the past has been a disgrace, that we've achieved very little, we've become the most materialistic country in the world and that we're mean-spirited. We're pretty awful people and we should be ashamed of ourselves and start all over again. Well, I don't hold that view, and the overwhelming majority of Australians don't hold that view, and they reject it ... We spent too much time in the first half of the nineties pondering whether we had to become less European so we could become more Asian, whether we had to become less British so we could become more multicultural. We had this perpetual seminar on our national identity, contributed to overwhelmingly by the cultural dietitians. I never thought Australians had any doubt as to what their identity was. And I think we've moved on from all of that.

Richard Krygier, the founding father of *Quadrant* more than fifty years ago, would say amen to that. And so do I.

This is an extended version of an address Tom Switzer delivered to the 54th Quadrant Dinner at The American Club in Sydney on 22 August 2007.

Michael Bachelard

Right-wing warriors who changed the workplace

The Age, 15 December 2007

The H. R. Nicholls Society—it sounds like a fusty old men's club and these days that's just what it is. But this association has been one of the most influential non-government groups in the country in the past 20 years.

The name was dreamed up by Ray Evans—an energetic spear carrier in the culture wars—and it brings with it a big ideological sting. Henry Richard Nicholls was a Tasmanian newspaper editor who took on a giant of the Australian left, Justice Henry Bourne Higgins, in a contempt case in the High Court in 1911 and won. Higgins is reviled by the modern right wing as the judge who set the first Australian minimum wage, sufficient to feed a family, which was one of the seminal moments in the construction of Australia's industrial relations and welfare apparatus.

So in January 1986, when Evans and three like-minded men decided to launch an assault on Higgins' legacy, to bring down the industrial relations system as it was then known, Nicholls' was the name they chose to fight under. In its day, this small group of ideologues formed one of the core elements of a movement known as the New Right. Its ideas have dominated policy thinking in the Liberal Party on industrial relations for two decades, and have wrought substantial changes in Australian society that both the Labor and Liberal parties now accept as normal.

The society still exists with 100 or so paying members. It holds annual conferences, and fulminates regularly in the letters and opinion pages of *The Australian Financial Review*.

But the election of the Rudd Government and the round rejection of WorkChoices by voters mean its ability to drive new policy is now almost certainly dead. However, it could reasonably be argued that the H. R. Nicholls Society is a victim of its own success.

"We held our first meeting at a restaurant called Pasta Galore, which no longer exists," Evans said recently. "It was famous in the annals of the '80s because a lot of plots were hatched there."

Evans was then employed as an executive officer at Western Mining, hired by establishment scion Hugh Morgan to "engage in the culture wars and provide him with feedback". "It was a 20-year seminar," Morgan later said of his time as Evans' boss. Also around the table at Pasta Galore that night were former Treasury secretary John Stone, wool brokers' employers federation head Barry Purvis, and a brash young industrial barrister, Peter Costello.

All four men knew the magnitude of the task before them. They had been spurred into action by a report commissioned by the Hawke government, written by Professor Keith Hancock and released late the previous year, that recommended unions be immune from tort prosecutions.

The recommendation was a defensive ploy to counter the work Costello had done in the Victorian Supreme Court in the Dollar Sweets case. There he had set a dangerous precedent for unions by successfully suing the Confectionery Workers Union for contractual interference, intimidation and other common law offences.

This dispute was one of a number fought by employers during the 1980s as they kicked against the restrictions of centralised wage bargaining, the power of the unions and the compliance of the mainstream employer lobby. At the centre of this entire edifice, which writer Gerard Henderson had labelled the "industrial relations club", sat the Conciliation and Arbitration Commission.

In world terms, the 1980s were heady days for the right: Margaret Thatcher and Ronald Reagan were in power overseas, but, while anything seemed possible in terms of deregulation on the world scene, Australia was still, as H. R. Nicholls types saw it, groaning under the yoke of the old Australian settlement.

While Thatcher was boldly declaring in Britain that society did not exist, Hawke, through his policy of consensus and the Prices and Incomes Accord, was seeking to extend the clubbishness he had known as an industrial negotiator at the commission throughout Australian life.

The H. R. Nicholls Society had a much less cosy Australia in mind: in Evans' words, they wanted nothing less than "freedom in the labour market". Their agenda involved abolishing the commission, the award system, and possibly minimum wages. If there was to be a minimum wage it would be set very, very low. Anything above that would be agreed by bargaining in an environment very unfriendly to unions. Voluntary individual contracts would be encouraged, and would take precedence over collectively negotiated agreements. And workers, to increase their loyalty to a company, would have a large portion, say, 30 per cent, of their pay, tied to the performance of the company. This would reduce the incentive to strike, and eliminate unions from the scene.

The overarching desire was to produce full employment by driving down wages.

To do all this, the federal government would take over all the state industrial relations regimes, and legislate for industrial relations under the corporations power in the constitution.

In late 1986, Costello, who formulated the details of these policies in his barristers' chambers in Melbourne, told *BRW* their method for pushing these ideas.

> Basically, we come up with ideas. The Liberals and others say, "Oh no, this is too radical for us. We have to get re-elected." So we put them out into the public debate, writing articles and so on and the newspapers publish them and gradually people begin to talk about the ideas.
>
> Then the Liberals suddenly say, "This sounds like a good idea. Who can we get to help us on this?" And the natural choice is one of us, because we've already been talking about the same thing.

Then Opposition leader John Howard and his industrial relations minister Neil Brown were the Liberals that Costello was referring to. Howard was in the process of purging the "wets" from the party, and the hardliners were rewriting the party's industrial relations policy. In the context of centralised wage fixing, the H. R. Nicholls Society's ideas were truly radical, and they produced enormous resistance from unions and also many businesses.

But, as the years have passed, many of these ideas have been realised, albeit in watered down form. Enterprise bargaining (introduced under

Paul Keating in 1993) was about negotiation at the workplace, leaving the award system as a safety net; Labor and Liberal both now agree to a single industrial relations system under the corporations power; the Industrial Relations Commission and awards are not abolished, but they are neutered; and the arbitration power, which lay at the core of their power, is effectively gone. Minimum wages, at least under WorkChoices, were on their way down in real terms, and unions faced inordinate obstacles to organising their members.

As for individual contracts, they were one of the most important issues in contention at the last election. Employee share schemes were really the only part of the society's early agenda that never flew.

Evans does not recognise the extent of the society's success. He believed WorkChoices was a "disaster," particularly after the introduction of the "insane" fairness test, which grappled working conditions back to the award system.

(Evans is a tireless and, in John Howard's Australia, a fabulously successful culture warrior. He is also the brains behind the Bennelong Society, set up to take on the "Aboriginal industry", and the Lavoisier Group, which argues "that climate change proposals are based on inexact science and would be too expensive for Australia's industry".)

In 2004, one month after Howard beat Mark Latham and won control of the Senate, 20 members of the H. R. Nicholls Society, including Chris Corrigan, and three of the four founding members, wrote to the prime minister urging him to see the "clear need for reforms that extend beyond" the Coalition's election policy in industrial relations. The way to proceed, they said, was to produce a policy paper and start a "wide-ranging national debate", which would "assist in producing a consensus for reform which, in our opinion, should attract the support of a large majority of the Australian people".

For all its radicalism, the society realised the need to build a democratic constituency for radical change, and also believed, perhaps naively, that if the case was argued properly, it would attract public support.

Howard, however, was done with consultation. He simply commissioned WorkChoices and then rammed it through the parliament he now dominated. The rest is history.

Guy Rundle

Goodbye to all that: The end of Australian left-liberalism and the revival of a radical politics
Arena Magazine, April–May 2007

Maybe it was *Jindabyne* that did it. Ray Lawrence's beautifully shot, stylishly directed film hit London as the opening presentation of the London Australian film festival, a flagship event for the presentation/flogging of Australian culture. Having gained five-star reviews from a selection of Australian critics, it was greeted with great expectations. For most of the audience it did not disappoint. And not for the first time in an Australian cinema, one looked around in disbelief to see if anyone else thought what was on the screen was unutterably bogus.

If *Jindabyne* were simply another movie that had gone wrong some-where, it would be of no import. But it is the very manner of its failure, in contrast to the universal praise it has received, that makes it a symbol of a wrong-turning.

Jindabyne begins with a young Aboriginal woman driving along a country road and being persuaded to pull over by a fairly creepy older man in a truck. Before we can find out what has happened to her, we move to the story of Claire and Stewart, an American woman and an Irish man, and their friends, living in Jindabyne.

When four of the men from Jindabyne, including Stewart, set out on a much-looked-forward-to fishing trip, they stumble across the body of the woman seen in the film's opening—clearly violently murdered. Rather than returning to town to report the finding, the men decide to continue their fishing trip, and secure her body by tying it to a tree. When they do finally make a report, all hell breaks loose both publicly and in their relationships.

Tensions rise between the town's Aboriginal and white communities, but the men are reviled by both whites and blacks.

Claire, disturbed by her husband's choice, and feeling distanced from him, becomes increasingly obsessed with making some sort of connection with the Aboriginal community, and with the dead woman's family. With the network of white friendships frayed and riven by the event, Claire tries to persuade her family and friends to come with her to the traditional funeral smoking ceremony. They refuse, but eventually follow her there, where Stewart goes to the father of the woman and asks for forgiveness. The father pauses a moment, and then strikes him, refusing his apology.

That final moment probably saves *Jindabyne* from full-bore mawkishness—an American version would most likely have ended in a deep hug and swelling music. Leaving aside the relatively high quality of the craft, the film follows the usual groove of fully developing the white characters while leaving the black ones as mere functions of the plot— the dead woman's father, friend, etc.—the white community as riven and complex, the black community as whole and undifferentiated. The result is so inevitable that the cultural studies essays could almost have been written before shooting began. The whites are people of culture, politics and history; the blacks are people of nature, pre-political unity, and timelessness.

Jindabyne is not merely an average attempt at political symbolism, as is revealed by the history of the story it tells. It is an adaptation of Raymond Carver's short story 'So Much Water So Close to Home'. In Carver's story the discovery of the woman's body is told flatly by Claire, in retrospect. Her reflection upon it leads into a longer reflection on life's drift, on how even a murder and a scandal fails to really change anything. The funeral is an unremarkable service in a commercial parlour. A woman there weeps privately. There is no collective moment.

Its enormous power comes from the entwining of such mundanity with the incommunicability of Claire's feelings, the impossibility of a public emotion. *Jindabyne*'s transformation of this eight thousand word short story is thus working against its spirit. The dead woman's Aboriginality has charged the event with a meaning it absolutely did not have. Not only has it switched the core moral dilemma from the universal one of gender (which all societies must deal with) to the specific one of race (which many societies do not have to deal with internally), but it turns the question of what the living owe to the dead into what a specific colonial people owe to the colonised. While Carver's story coruscates with new meanings out of its generality, Jindabyne closes it down, drawing them into current political obsessions.

Carver's story was turned into *Jindabyne* by a process that has become common among Australian artists of a certain type over recent years, one both reflective and constitutive of a wider set of attitudes. Thus in Kate Grenville's *Secret River*, a vastly better work, William Thornhill is nevertheless given a subjectivity whose abstract conception of human rights would be unusual to say the least, in settler farmers of the day; in Hannie Rayson's *Two Brothers*, a realist play is distorted into a melodrama that even a Victorian hoofer would have blushed at, in order to stage a confrontation over the refugee issue.

Such works of fiction are matched by programmatic works that have a similar sort of narrowness that is nevertheless presented as an adventurous iconoclasm. One key recent example was Robyn Davidson's *Quarterly Essay* 'No Fixed Address', an account of nomadism, and a reflection through it on the contemporary world. Davidson, the author of *Tracks*, interweaves a story of travelling for several months with the Rabari, a nomadic people based around Rajasthan and facing increasing encroachment on their traditional movements, with a reflection on growing up as a privileged white in Queensland and a relationship, or lack of one, with the Aborigines and a more general account of the history of agriculture, and the unsustainability of current consumption patterns.

For the most part Davidson's account is a long romantic identification with the Rabari, an attribution to them of a virtue and nobility far beyond the ambivalent nature of mere mortals, especially farmers.

They were such noble people because 'great migrations simply could not be accomplished on a ground of deceit. Their success depended upon formal generosity, tolerance and honesty among migrating individuals, families, dangs [small groups], castes and religions'.

The essay itself is a process of falling into a deep romance with her subjects: 'In the months ahead I never once saw one of them show discourtesy to another human being ... They are cosmopolitan in outlook, because they have to deal with difference, negotiate difference.'

They sound too good to be true, and of course they are. Fairly cursory research shows that the Rabari are as liable as any people to use violence—indeed they had to be persuaded by their supporters from attacking farmers encroaching on their nomadic routes—and the condition of women within the group was poor, with high malnutrition and disease rates (from unequal access to food), much lower literacy rates than men, and a higher unnatural death rate almost certainly due to alcohol-fuelled domestic violence. Furthermore there is considerable intra-community conflict around the issue of education, which some see as vital to their continued existence, and others see as a threat to their elder-dominated council structure.

In other words they are exactly like every other kinship society facing the difficult problem of relating to modernity, and with the same mix of qualities that modern people find both positive and negative. Far from being psychologically fluid and mobile, they live amid the dynamic, yet real structures and limits of hierarchy and relationship that such societies reproduce over generations. Davidson's essay wholly misrepresented their way of life.

What's happened to make works such as this not only productible but popular? They are works that rather than letting the material speak to the world through art, impose a series of authors' moral fantasies upon a world that varies utterly from it.

Such programmatic works began to appear as the Howard era got into swing, and the issue of mandatory detention and native title began to occupy centre stage in Australian politics. They came overwhelmingly from a group who felt that a number of prevailing assumptions they could hold about Australia had been shattered.

From the success of the 1967 referendum onwards, through a period of Labor dominance from 1972 to 1996 (and the Fraser government leaving Labor's essential cultural reforms and initiatives in place) it could be assumed that Australia was moving, together, in a direction of pluralism, tolerance and social liberal-mindedness.

Those Labor victories had been built in part on an alliance between the labour movement and a sub-class of left-liberal cultural professionals. Many of the cultural and political initiatives may have cut against the grain of a working class that was largely socially conservative, but the alternative lifestyles were so marginal as to be effectively invisible.

The gradual legalisation of homosexuality, for example, occurred before the economic and social changes of the 1980s produced a visible and cashed-up sub-class of gay men and lesbians, and in a time when such lifestyles were still safely 'held' in mass-media portrayals of mincing queens. In other words a distinct new moral code—that of a left-liberal intelligentsia—was developing in parallel with a substantially unchanged one of the mainstream, protected from substantial scrutiny or conflict by its small size.

By the 1980s, a generation of expanded higher education, of second generation 'ethnic' Australians entering the professions, and the creation of a new, globally cosmopolitan consumer economy—the yuppies—had shifted the gravity of the manner in which values were formed. It was occurring just as working class life, and the particularly stable form given to it by the Australian arbitration system, was losing its cultural centrality.

It was around 1990 that such value systems began to come into conflict, as a variety of measures driven by left-liberal values—sexual discrimination laws, the rise of the notion of 'reconciliation'—come into place. The first half of the 1990s represented a matched battleground between the continuing left-liberal transformation and a counter-attack under the US-imported heading of 'political correctness'.

Rupert Murdoch's transformation of the old *Sun News Pictorial* into the more aggressively culturally right-wing *Herald Sun* coincided with Paul Keating's determination to bring the issue of the republic and the flag to centre-stage.

Whatever the wellsprings of John Howard's victory in 1996, the second half of the 1990s saw a rupture in that long standing political alliance, and the emergence of a values conflict as a real framework for national self-understanding.

It is striking the degree to which the framework has determined the focus applied to various elements within the conflict. When a young Cambodian staged a fake assassination attempt against Prince Charles in 1994, for example, it was in protest at mandatory detention, in which Cambodians had already been held for 12 months. There was little of the later regime that was not already in place, but it simply did not register as a political cause challenging fundamental values.

The period up to 2001, 9/11, the *Tampa* and the election that followed them was primarily one in which such cultural-political issues tended to be fought out in political terms; thereafter, it became clear that events were not an aberration in the direction Australia was taking, but a substantially new one.

The artistic response started to come after the initial political struggle. There were floods of theatre about mandatory detention, in such profusion that the 'refugee play' became a sub-genre. Authors such as Grenville, Andrew McGahan, Rayson, Andrew Bovell and others who had been substantially known for modern urban works turned to epic stories of rural Australia. The quality varied across the spectrum, but they all tended to be as unsatisfying as the various 9/11 novels—pre-Chekhovian once again, unwilling to learn the lesson that there is nothing more dramatic than a bottle exploding offstage which turns out to be a gunshot.

Nor were they willing to formally experiment—indeed the task of taking on the challenge of great events seemed to offer an absolution in which writers could once again turn to dun realism or worse, to reaching for what the poet Philip Larkin once wearily called the 'myth kitty'—the throw-in pile of stock big images.

Interestingly one can contrast Christos Tsiolkas's *Dead Europe*, which whatever else one can say about it, isn't written from the dead superego, but wades through the id, gumboots on. *Dead Europe* uses the events of the story—the undecidable no-choice between a corrupted Europe and a vapid Australia—to deform the genre itself so that realism mutates into vampire horror, form and content playing off each other.

The left-liberal moral fables that mobilised themselves against the Howard government were not of this calibre—unwilling to challenge their own beliefs, to let the work off the leash. Such works started off looking like critique, but their main role was to create a fantasy that could be presented back as a moral fable.

The fantasy was that Australia wasn't really 'like that', that its artists were speaking on behalf of the left-liberal working-class alliance that had transformed a conservative and monoethnic nation in the 1960s, and was in a type of moral exile. Such a position involved smoothing over the real class differences that had arisen between these two groups over the preceding twenty years and which, more than any government policy or conscious mendacity by elements of the press, had served to reshape the political and cultural terrain.

In particular this meant projecting a series of presuppositions specific to a certain class onto the public stage as unquestioned virtues. Yet beneath this process, real relations had changed to such a degree that such projection amounted to a misrepresentation. Chief amongst these was the notion of reconciliation.

No doubt someone somewhere is doing a thesis on the genealogies of 'reconciliation', this concept that seemed to come from nowhere and become an all-embracing term for a certain way of conceiving of race relations politics. Presumably it came via the US civil rights, which in turn had taken it from the driving Christian force within that movement.

Yet the word was always mysterious to many people because of a disjuncture between its religious-political meanings and its everyday one. In its religious-political use the reconciliation ceremony was that of one party asking for confessed sins to be forgiven, and thus being reconciled (to God, to a former victim, etc). In other words, it's the asymmetrical act of one party receiving forgiveness from another.

Yet in the secular sense—usually of personal relationships—reconciliation is a mutual confession of wrongs on both sides, a process which hardly applies in Australian race-relations. One suspects this disjuncture has sat at the heart of the concept of reconciliation for much of the last fifteen years.

At the time of the 1992 Mabo decision it was grounded in a material reality or the possibility of one—a real transfer of land. As that process became bogged down in the late 1990s, and entangled in new judgements, the sense of reconciliation as a distinct act became lost. It was a cloudy concept, wandering far from the brief attention that large numbers of people had given it at one point.

By the first part of the Howard government, when a comprehensive revision of the notion of individual and collective responsibility was being developed—one with a great deal of support—a sense of both angry frustration and of disconnection had taken over. That this was only partly due to the Howard government can be seen by the fact that much of what was pushing Aboriginal issues to one side was the move of multicultural Australia into a firmer position at the cultural centre. Italian–, Greek–,

Vietnamese–Australians and their children could justly say that their relations had been too busy dodging Stukas and napalm to oppress blacks, and there wasn't a whole lot to reconcile about, whatever expressions of fraternity might be made.

One episode of the bizarre SBS series *Pizza* summed that up very well, when one of the characters—a Sydney western suburbs, Lebanese–Australian, would-be gangsta rapper—went down to the 'Old Sydney Town' colonial theme park and performed a one-man re-enactment of the landing of the First Fleet, a sort of Dada restaging of national origins, which indicated the degree to which received history was a weird and distanced event for a clear section of the population. Reconciliation between whom and over what?

By the third Howard term, the notion of reconciliation, if it had occupied any substantial space in the public imagination, was largely gone. The government used 'practical reconciliation' as a figleaf term for a process of official neglect and the beginnings of a policy of population transfer from remote areas, and then pretty much dropped it altogether.

What had taken over on the national scale was what was occurring on the global scale, which was a gradual separation of communities and individuals in a globalised media hyperspace. The notion of a shared destiny between black and white that had developed strongly from the late 1960s was being lost as a sense of shared space was lost. *Pizza*, one of the best things Australia has produced, was so effective because it captured this sense of separate worlds and lives being narrated in a mega-urban no-space, as opposed to those texts which tried to re-synthesise a focus and a unity that was barely there.

The difficult state of rural and remote Aboriginal Australia also served to mark off the community in a different way than the various discussions of partnership, connection, 'one Australia' that had obtained in the Hawke–Keating years.

In a more atomised world accustomed to talking in therapeutic terms, the troubled Aboriginal community could be marked off as 'dysfunctional' and any notion of reciprocity went by the board. They then became the responsibility of the state and an attitude of indifference could be turned towards them.

Much of the rhetoric of such artworks—the overwhelming use of allegory, for example, a town standing for the country, a farm as our history, etc.—was making a bid for telling the big story. These were not specific tales of some people somewhere, which may or may not have wider repercussions, but attempts to put it all down. They were artworks trying to constitute a people they represented, despite the fact that such a body of people had disappeared from behind them.

Reflecting back the world as their creators want it to be, such works can be profoundly embarrassing, impossible to defend, even when one shares even in a most basic way, some of the hopes around which they are formed. They are untough, uncritical, unmaterial works with no real sinew or engagement. Ultimately there is a degree of narcissism involved in them, the 'is' of Australian society disappearing behind the 'ought' reflected back at the writers, for whom the revival of a national progressive project would also form a route back to greater influence in national debates.

A feeling of not really being represented by such works is, in other words, the mark of a profound division within the forces that found themselves yoked together by a common need to oppose the policies of the Howard government.

The formation I've described as the liberal-left is the one that effectively stands for the left in much of the mainstream media—the absolute outer limits of where editors and others will take debate. Many of their political interventions are of a piece with the limits and delusions of the art that represents them.

At times some of it is impossible to defend, and embarrassing, as the self-regarding nature of it leads people into absurdities. David Marr's forensic skills as a journalist deserted him when he argued that to be critical, all journalists had to come from a 'soft leftie' viewpoint. But nor was it much in evidence when he ridiculed any suggestion that the torture at Abu Ghraib could have been shaped by the sadistic violence of recent Tarantino-style movies. Why did Marr reject them? Because it would have suggested a relation between screen violence and behaviour, an absolute left-liberal no-no.

In similar fashion Eva Cox's seeming absolute refusal to acknowledge any evidential foundation to the widespread disquiet around large-scale childcare amounted to a desperate rearguard action against a very deep-seated reaction to a process that had sprung without full reflection upon its consequences.

Others such as Pamela Bone, Julie Szego and Nick Cohen went further, following a wilfully naive military humanitarianism all the way across to an increasingly chauvinistic western suprematism. Few went as far as this, but the left-liberal attitude to the Iraq invasion was always tempted towards a pro-intervention position. Perhaps the epitome of this was playwright Joanna Murray-Smith, who opposed the war prior to the invasion, and then recanted in the first few weeks after the actual nation vs nation conflict had finished and before the insurgency began. Her subsequent views are not recorded.

These, and a range of other moral and political dilemmas were ones in which a simple position could not be successfully 'read off' the left-liberal position, and to try and do so was to simply retreat into nostalgia for a time when political struggles were simpler and more defined. An uncensored media and violence, professionalised and commodified childcare ... these were things that had been fought for in an earlier context, and to not realise that there was now a deep disquiet about the direction of social life, and the way in which a hypermodern society was unfolding was to mark oneself off as irrelevant.

Thus it was too in matters of reconciliation, since it was clear that Aboriginal politics was going in a direction in which there was not only less for white people to do, there was a positive need for disengagement of a sort, so that black people could begin to assert a full autonomy—or reassert it, after it had briefly appeared in the 1970s, and before Aboriginal politics became entangled with a series of government institutions.

For the moment the most visible assertion of Aboriginal autonomy was that of Noel Pearson, who actively pursued a strategy of insulting left-liberals in the hope that they would simply go away. Whether that was strategically smart remains to be seen—the big political partnership that Pearson hoped to renegotiate with sections of the right hasn't really eventuated and Pearson has since had to 'redenounce' the basic racism of the right and the inherited Australian state. More recently he has virtually twinned attempts to get remote Aboriginal societies moving forward, with the US occupation of Iraq, a rather strange benchmarking. The process has left him looking like, well, a bit of a mug.

But the crucial thing was that such a strategy left no place for left-liberalism to put its emotional politics. Why was this? Simply because the liberal-left could see nothing more to be done in their own social realm. Whatever alliance between left-liberals and socialists there had been in the 1970s, the latter movement had long since become either a matter of technocratic social democracy, or an embarrassing source of nostalgia. The identity politics of the 1980s had wiped questions of the economy and class out of public politics to an extraordinary degree (before the late 1990s antiglobalisation moved it back to centre stage), and so a crucial process of critical class reflection by left-liberals was lost.

Within a framework oriented by socialism the class privilege of left-liberal cultural producers was more visible (even, to a degree, masochistically focussed upon)—without it, and with a reorientation to the politics of media and representation, it not only became invisible, but reversed. In an Australia in which, well, almost everyone else had abandoned the liberal progressive idea of what Australia was, left-liberal groupings became, per Brecht's remarks about East Germany, the party who had been failed by its people, and was required to constitute another.

When you are left alone with a media-dominated society in which film festivals, novels, cutting edge design and bars take the place of a grander historical project, you have to pretty quickly start hunting around, consciously or otherwise, for other wellsprings of meaning, and it was only a matter of time before people whose society had pre-modern aspects— whether it was Aborigines or Third World nomads—became a key resource whose lives could be mined for meaning.

Since kinship societies have rich frameworks of correspondence and obligation in which meaning and identity is held in place by its relative invariance over time, they become the perfect other to media professionals whose life practice involves a world in which everything can be re-arranged and connected to everything else, creating a process of diminishing returns. The result is an encroaching nihilistic boredom, held at bay only by a truly monstrous overproduction of culture, and a necessary commitment to transgressive edginess. What would one do, how would one anchor oneself in this flux without Aborigines, who can be reduced to solemn voiceless mourners at traditional funerals, the conflicts and contradictions of their society left unexplored?

With luck, the Howard era is coming to an end this year—although that has been said before. With its passing there will also be the opportunity for a political realignment of sorts. Indeed there will be a whole series of new political questions. Whatever basically humane moves a Rudd government can undertake we presume (we can, can't we?)—the abolition of the 'Pacific solution', the winding down of mandatory detention to a bare minimum of people for a bare minimum of time, withdrawal from Iraq—and whatever hopes we have of a more comprehensive commitment to social investment and social welfare, it is most likely that large parts of the Rudd programme will be modelled on the particular style of the Blair government, and the mix of surveillance and micromanagement that it has deployed in the absence of a comprehensive economic and social reconstruction.

The British 'New Labour' style has been to explicitly encourage the expansion and unleashing of market forces—'we are completely relaxed about people getting filthy rich' as Blair aide Peter Mandelson once remarked—to skimp on the reinvestment desperately needed to refloat areas laid waste by two decades of Thatcherism, and then to manage the lives of people trapped in this entrenched inequality.

Overwhelmingly this has involved handing over a section of the education system to the private sector via 'city academies'—in which private sector consortia and individuals pay to build or establish the school in exchange for being allowed to run it. Effectively this has handed over control to a variety of fundamentalist Christian consortia, and more than a few distinctly odd individuals desperate to use the techniques that made them what they are—neurolinguistic programming and other such—with children as guinea-pigs.

Somewhat contradictorily with this, there has been an emphasis on transforming primary education into a period in which testing, streaming and early intervention have become a fetish, the improvements debatable and the only certain result being a generation of miserable and stressed children. Added to this—largely tokenistic but indicative of a political culture nonetheless—has been the wildly expanded notion of the supervision and suspicion of youth, manifested not only by the notorious ASBO or Anti-Social Behaviour Order (now become, according to a recent report, something that off-message youth compete amongst themselves to get) but also by the idea of intense intervention in allegedly dysfunctional families—the apogee of this being the so-called 'foetal ASBO' in which as yet unborn youth are identified.

At the same time it has introduced programs of fairly creepy socio-emotional engineering, with proposed 'happiness centres', and the offering to violent inner-city youth of massage and aromatherapy programs to help them. All of this has occurred at a time when the government is embarking on a programme of licensing super casinos as a way of regenerating inner cities.

The Blair Government is in other words a morally bankrupt government, which has substituted a form of therapeutic coercion for genuine social reconstruction. Should this sort of process become a central feature of the Rudd era, it will expose a deeper division between those who want to counterpose a more radical vision of social change in the contemporary era. Though left-liberalism has a lot to say about traditional areas of civil liberties, it has no framework to address these more complex issues of social control.

Yet it will most likely make its accommodations with such a government, especially if it re-establishes a favourable attitude to the subsidisation of Australian culture. As Geoff Sharp noted in the previous issue, it is quite possible that a Rudd government will see its role as the extension of a series of hi-tech initiatives, as part of the technophilia which Barry Jones and others have made a central feature of Labor. A whole series of reactionary political challenges posed by the Howard era will have disappeared, and the need to hold a line will not only no longer be there, but the situation will be substantially reversed.

For some time many of us have judged it politically necessary to refrain from criticism of works such as *Jindabyne* and 'No Fixed Address'. But now it's become simply embarrassing, and politically regressive, to not say something more forthright about such works. In some ways, overwhelmingly as far as environmental matters are concerned, the times are moving far more radically than conventional political movements can allow for. There is no excuse to not be as unsparing in criticism of a dead and self-indulgent tradition that happens to hail from the Left, as of the reactionary and corrupted Right that has dominated political life in the country for the past decade.

This is an edited extract of an article that was originally published in Arena's April–May 2007 *edition.*

Mark McKenna

The Anzac myth

The Australian Literary Review, June 2007

On Australia Day last year, I saw English violinist Nigel Kennedy perform at the Sydney Opera House. Kennedy, who cultivates the appearance of a slightly punkish busker-fiddler and is always keen to please his audience, came out on stage and immediately proceeded to play *Advance Australia Fair*.

As he began, everyone rose to their feet and sang the national anthem. This could not have happened 10 years ago. Then, the traditional understated Australian patriotism would have held sway. The audience would have sung along, almost half-heartedly, but now they stood in unison and sang with gusto. What had changed?

One of the defining features of John Howard's decade in power has been his ability to encourage a greater feeling of national pride in the Australian community. During the past 10 years, a new form of Australian nationalism has emerged: unreflective, earnest and often sentimental. Patriotic display has become a civic virtue. Journalists and academics have commented on the new national mood—the flaunting of the flag, the commercialisation of feel-good patriotism—most dating its emergence from the mid-1990s, about the same time that Anzac Day began its resurgence.

Increasingly, Australian society is characterised by the culture of public display: of patriotism and allegiance, of faith and of wealth. The art of modern political leadership is to cast the nation's image, past and present, in that of the leader's political philosophy, to make party-political language and the vernacular of national imagining blend so seamlessly that the only alternative is re-election. Howard has largely succeeded in defining the nation in the image of Australian liberalism: individual freedom, never-ending prosperity and uncritical nationalism. Pride and achievement are his watchwords. As *The Australian*'s Paul Kelly has noted, Howard has made Australian governance "more nationalistic, more different from (and not more similar to) overseas models".

Addressing a citizenship ceremony in Canberra on January 26 this year, Howard told about 100 new citizens that most Australians had a "fundamental pride" in what Australia had achieved. "I welcome all of you to the great Australian family," he said. "It's a wonderful nation. It's the greatest on earth. We think we're pretty good and we are." It would be hard to find a better (or more disturbing) example of the new national pride espoused under Howard.

At the forefront of the new nationalism is Anzac Day. This April 25 witnessed now familiar scenes: footage of the pilgrims at the dawn service at Anzac Cove, still larger crowds at Anzac Day services in the capital cities and the usual rush of political speeches eulogising the sacrifice of the Diggers.

Instead of being the one day of the year that reminds us of the horror of war, Anzac Day has become a day for celebrating national values forged in the crucible of battle, a day that obscures the politics of war and discourages political dissent. Although these changes have occurred on Howard's watch, both the Coalition and the Labor Party have become fond of wrapping themselves in the flag, particularly on April 25.

One of the untold stories surrounding Anzac Day is the manner in which it has served to silence dissent over the Iraq war. As anthropologist Bruce Kapferer remarked last year, Anzac Day is now entrenched as a "symbolic extension of state authority".

Regardless of which political party is in power, the issues involved raise important questions regarding the politics of Australia's military engagements, the use and abuse of military history and the future of our national identity.

In February 2004, Australian Federal Police came to Reconciliation Place on the shores of Canberra's Lake Burley Griffin to confiscate a work by Melbourne-based sculptor Greg Taylor. Taylor's bronze sculpture depicted the Queen and Prince Philip sitting naked on a park bench. The mere thought of royal nudity proved too much for one monarchist who drove from Victoria to the national capital (sledgehammer in boot) and proceeded to decapitate Liz and Phil.

Taylor's next uninvited installation in Canberra—*If the Boots Don't Fit*—aroused similar controversy. On this occasion, he chose as his subject the monarchist PM. Taylor portrayed Howard standing to attention, rifle at his side, in full Anzac regalia—the Digger's uniform, the slouch hat and the old kit bag—all of it about 10 sizes too big for the little Digger. Howard appeared to be swimming in khaki, his chin pointing defiantly upwards, his facial expression reflecting a state of innocent patriotic bliss. Before federal police could confiscate the sculpture, television cameras and press photographers ensured Taylor's work national exposure. The first monument to Howard had captured an essential truth about his politics: his clever exploitation of the Anzac legend.

So far, Howard's use of that legend has been pointed to rather than understood. La Trobe University professor of politics Judith Brett has noted that "Howard is fascinated by the lessons of war, both for individuals and for nations". More recently, Brett's La Trobe colleague Robert Manne has spoken of the "sentimentalised version of the new Australian militarism" that has aided Australia's "faithful service alongside the Americans in the war on terror".

Examples of this new militarism are not hard to find: Howard's leading role in the rituals commemorating military anniversaries (particularly Anzac Day) together with his almost presidential presence at military farewells and welcome home parades. Farewelling troops going to Iraq from Darwin in 2005, Howard sounded more like a sovereign than a Prime Minister. "I wish you godspeed and a very safe return home," he told them.

In the nation's education system, military narratives serve as instructive parables of national virtue for Australian children. In primary schools, children raise the flag each morning, while posters funded by the Howard Government list Australian values against a silhouette of Simpson and his donkey. Brendan Nelson, who was minister for education when the "values in Australian schools" initiative was launched, claimed that if Australia lost sight of what Simpson and his donkey represented, we would "lose the direction of the country".

In public libraries, posters funded by the Department of Veterans' Affairs spell out, against a flag backdrop, patriotic messages such as "We salute their service". Inspired (perhaps by this example?), *The Australian* decided in January this year to award its Australian of the Year award to every serving Australian Digger.

A few days before Anzac Day this year, the postman delivered the latest intelligence from my federal MP, the Liberal member for Eden-Monaro, Gary Nairn. Nairn had been kind enough to send me a fold-out brochure detailing the bravery of the Anzacs. It included a photograph of one Digger at Gallipoli carrying a wounded comrade over his back on their way to the hospital on the beach below. The caption read: "Notwithstanding this unhappy situation, they joked as they made their way down." The inert figure slumped over the Digger's shoulders (behind to camera) hardly looked in the mood for cracking jokes.

Cashing in on the Anzac spirit, the brochure also included a tear-off postcard in case I wished to send a message of support to our troops in Iraq and Afghanistan. Finally, for Anzac Day activities in the kitchen, Nairn remembered to include a recipe for baking Anzac biscuits. Too much Anzac is never enough, especially at a time of increased military expenditure.

In August last year, federal cabinet announced a $10 billion defence boost. During the next five years, there will be a 20 per cent increase in the size of the armed forces. Recruitment numbers are down, so much so that Howard has even singled out school cadets as "one possible source of future recruits", while a new recruitment drive will emphasise "traditional military values", presumably drawing heavily on the Anzac legend.

Nelson, now Defence Minister, confirmed that the army's doors would be open to "tattooed or overweight aspirants". On national radio, one army recruitment officer went so far as to suggest the army would consider taking in people who had smoked marijuana "now and then". To kick off the Government's spending spree, Nelson proudly announced the purchase of new Abrams tanks. Photographed standing underneath their gleaming gun barrels, the beaming minister claimed the tanks would help to protect Australian values.

It seems impossible to deny the broader militarisation of our history and culture: the surfeit of jingoistic military histories, the increasing tendency for military displays before football grand finals, the extension of the term Anzac to encompass firefighters and sporting champions, the professionally stage-managed event of the dawn service at Anzac Cove, the burgeoning popularity of battlefield tourism (particularly Gallipoli and the Kokoda Track), the ubiquitous newspaper supplements extolling the virtues of soldiers past and present, and the tendency of the media and both main political parties to view the death of the last World War I veterans as significant national moments.

Since the early '90s, Australians appear to have lost the ability (or inclination) to debate Anzac Day. It has become an article of national faith and communion, a sacred parable we dare not question, yet another indication of the narrowing of political debate in Australia.

We seem to have lost our critical faculties, politicians tripping over one another to praise the fallen heroes, media outlets whipping up patriotic fervour; the day has become holier than December 25. The history of Australia's invasion of Turkey in 1915 as part of the British Empire (remember the empire?) has been airbrushed from public memory. Anzac Day has been emptied of its historical context and is conveniently remembered as a story of Aussies coming valiantly of age (yet again!).

As one pilgrim told an ABC journalist at the Gallipoli dawn service last year: "It's not about the empire, it's about us."

At times, the rush to embrace the Anzac legend borders on farce.

On the way to the Ashes tour in 2001, Australian cricket captain Steve Waugh led the First XI into the trenches at Gallipoli. There they stood, exactly where Australian soldiers had died in 1915, dutifully wearing their slouch hats in what was little more than a gauche media stunt. Later, Waugh explained to the media that the great lesson of the Anzacs for the present generation was exemplary teamwork.

Australians are encouraged to see the most powerful expression of their identity and values in the field of military endeavour, whether through the memory of the Anzacs or the deeds of our soldiers abroad.

This phenomenon is not necessarily unique to Australia. Deakin University's Joan Beaumont, for example, sees the resurgence of Anzac Day as part of a global trend. Since the end of World War II and the Holocaust, many nations have invested heavily in the public commemoration of past military conflicts. There is probably no better example than Turkey, where more than 2.5 million Turkish visitors are expected at the Gallipoli battlefields this year. Ankara's Islamic Government has recently been keen to play down the role of secular heroes such as Kemal Ataturk, recasting Gallipoli as the successful defence of Islam.

There is a wonderful irony at work here. While the Australian Government is eager to employ the Anzac spirit to galvanise forces in the war against Islamic terror, Ankara is busy reshaping the history of the Turkish victory at Gallipoli to assert Islam in modern Turkey. In both countries, the public memory of the battle for Gallipoli is a plaything of politics.

What is different about Australia, however, is Howard's ability to give a particular inflection to the new militarism, one that increasingly pushes Australia back towards more male-centred and traditional Anglo allegiances that revolve not around the empire but old and trusted friends: Britain and the US.

This idea was powerfully expressed on Australia Day this year when Howard (explaining the Government's position on Iraq) told the National Press Club: "You either stay or you go ... you either rat on the ally or you don't."

Howard sees in Anzac the Australian values to which he believes new citizens should swear their allegiance and that are at stake in the war on terror. As he told the congregation at Gallipoli veteran Alec Campbell's state funeral in May 2002: "We are fighting now for the same values the Anzacs fought for in 1915: courage, valour, mateship, decency [and] a willingness as a nation to do the right thing, whatever the cost."

The right thing, however, in particular a declaration of war, is not a choice between value systems. Nor is it self-evident. It is a matter of political and strategic judgment.

Howard's focus on traditional narratives of nationhood has also narrowed our national mythology, numbing its earlier sensitivity to differences of sex and culture.

As Howard put it on Anzac Day 2003: "On this day, we enrich ourselves ... a nation reveals itself not only by the men it produces but by the men it honours, the men it remembers." And, presumably, by the man who reminds us.

Few other modern liberal democracies define themselves so exclusively through stories of one military engagement as Australia does. The interesting question is why?

The explanation lies in a complex mix of government initiatives and a deep community need for ritual and national communion in an increasingly non-religious age.

In his Anzac Day address in 2001 Howard described the way in which Australians come together on April 25: "All over Australia, all over the world today," he said, "our countrymen and women are gathering, drawn together almost by instinct, by a great silent summons to repay a debt to the past."

Howard's words suggest that Australians follow the sound of the bugle at dawn like sleepwalkers, drawn by a mystical force, a longing for communion they do not fully understand. Like all politicians, Howard would have us believe he is merely reflecting the public will, that the resurgence of Anzac Day is due to a silent organic revolution from below.

Yet only one month before his Anzac Day address in 2001, his Government funded a report, conducted by the RSL, aimed specifically at finding ways to involve younger Australians in the rituals and commemorations of Anzac Day. Through the Department of Veterans' Affairs, the Government has also funded the expansion of Anzac Day initiatives in schools, awarding cash prizes for Anzac-related activities in all primary and secondary schools.

The department's website instructs students to "observe tradition and include veterans in their activities". It also sets out the appropriate order of service for Anzac Day including hymns, prayers, poems, flag-raising protocol and the singing of the national anthem. In case teachers are in any doubt concerning the meaning of tradition, the department obliges by providing a definition: "the continuing, from generation to generation, of beliefs, legends, customs, practices and symbols".

While schoolchildren compete for cash prizes, they are also likelier to encounter television footage of an increasingly militarised Anzac Day commemorative service at the Australian War Memorial in Canberra. The war memorial service has changed more in the past decade than at any other time in its history. Howard, who is often present, parades as a kind of civilian commander-in-chief while military parades and fly-pasts have become the order of the day. In recent years, military swagger has replaced the traditional quietness of Anzac Day.

Since coming to power in 1996, the Howard Government has also invested heavily in the industry of commemoration and encouraged the embrace of the Anzac legend at every opportunity.

Funding of the AWM has been increased significantly, with a rush of new monuments departing from Charles Bean's understated vision for the memorial.

In 2005, Howard nominated Anzac Cove to head a new National Heritage list.

"The land was part of Turkey," he conceded, "but you feel as an Australian it's as much a part of Australia as the land on which your home is built." Australia thus became the first nation to attempt to list the territory of another country as part of its national heritage.

Howard's deep affection for Anzac had led him to ignore the obvious: the Turkish Government would hardly allow part of its sovereign territory to be claimed by another country. At the same time, he seemed to long to possess soil soaked in Australian blood.

The resurgence of Anzac Day is no silent revolution. To think of it as freely constituted is to accept the myth that the Government is simply reacting to community trends. The truth is that the resurgence of Anzac Day has been driven from above and from below.

Praising Anzac Day and "being there" at Anzac Cove on April 25 have become among the primary means of displaying patriotism and loyalty in Australia. Perhaps this is why we find a lack of critical discussion concerning Anzac Day today. Precisely because the Anzac myth has expanded to the point where it has become one of the most important binding agents of our community, many people feel that to criticise Anzac is to criticise Australia.

But we should not make the mistake of placing responsibility for these developments on one political party alone. In 2002, Labor leader Kim Beazley told parliament that Anzac was the "core element of our national psychology". Two years later, the Labor Government in Western Australia enshrined the commemoration of Anzac Day in legislation. More recently, last year Steve Bracks's Labor Government in Victoria supported the recommendations of a parliamentary committee to "enhance commemoration of Anzac Day" and "provide greater support" for activities and projects related to the day.

Under Kevin Rudd's leadership, the federal Labor Party seems intent on outdoing the Howard Government's military nationalism. Labor's present proposal is to commemorate the "successful defence of the Australian homeland" in 1942 by declaring September 6 "Battle for Australia Day". Labor's policy, first announced in 2004, echoes the views of a private lobby group, the Battle for Australia Council.

Speaking last year, Peter Stanley, then a senior historian with the AWM, feared a more insular and nationalised version of Australian history was on the march:

> The Battle for Australia Council's view of 1942 connects several episodes into a single narrative. It presents the defence of Singapore, the conquest of the Netherlands Indies, the battles of the Coral Sea and Midway, the Papuan and Solomons campaigns, and the campaigns that secured Allied victory into a single epic story ... This new emphasis stresses not [World War II] as a whole, not Australia's contribution to Allied victory against Nazism and fascism in the Mediterranean and Europe, but only Australia's defence of itself ... This is an example of historical nationalism ... the product of the emergence of a school of history—and especially military history—that justifies the name nationalist ... It has become the new orthodoxy in Australian military history.

Howard's response has been to support the commemoration of Battle for Australia Day but not at the expense of Anzac Day and Remembrance Day.

At every level of government and across the party spectrum, the respectful commemoration and public observance of the rituals associated with Australia's "civil religion" (as historian Ken Inglis once called it) have become important ingredients of successful politics. Supporting, funding and leading Anzac Day rituals and commemorative military ceremonies have become among the necessary arts of political leadership. That both main parties line up to declare their love of Anzac—politically, neither can afford to be critical of the day—certainly makes it harder to question the celebratory nature that has crept in during recent years.

Nonetheless, important differences remain between the two parties.

While it was a Labor prime minister, Paul Keating, who kissed the ground at Kokoda and gave the memorable Unknown Soldier speech in Canberra, no Labor prime minister (with the possible exception of Billy Hughes) has projected military history to the position of prominence accorded under Howard. Consider the language Howard has used during the past five years to describe the Anzac spirit: "a *creed* to which we can all aspire"; "a great tradition which has shaped the character and the destiny of this country *more* than any other tradition or influence"; one that occupies "the eternal place in the Australian soul" (my italics).

The language pines for tradition, yearns for the mystical, searches for the transcendent moment. Anzac is a myth that is so deep, so sacred, that the powers of human expression will always struggle to give it shape and form, always stumble before its mystery and emotional force.

One of the most fascinating aspects of Howard's lyrical language is his description of the stories of bravery and sacrifice at Anzac Cove as "a wonderful Australian saga". The use of the word saga is revealing. These stories of courage from Anzac Cove, Changi and Kokoda—the stories of men as heroic victims and resisters but never as killers or invaders—have become Australia's national lore, the Australian sagas.

And with each new military engagement, our leaders mine the Anzac sagas to cloak their political decisions in the rhetoric of values, courage, mateship and sacrifice. Since the invasion of Iraq in March 2003, the Anzac legend has been exploited to make the continuation of the campaign appear as a patriotic duty. If you think this is hyperbole, consider these examples.

Peter Cosgrove, then chief of the defence force, on Australian troops in Iraq in 2003:

> Once the ghosts of Anzac past start to talk to our people, they will find that under that hi-tech veneer they are all exactly the same, they will have something to tell their grandchildren: that they were there when Iraq was liberated and a threat of terrible weapons removed from the world.

Treasurer Peter Costello, interviewed by Neil Mitchell in 2003:

There are problems in the world today, just as there were in 1915. You can't turn your back on them ... and young Australians, even today, are serving in the Middle East because they want to make a difference, they want to address some of these problems. And you think back how their grandfathers and great-grandfathers would have felt the same in 1915.

Foreign Minister Alexander Downer, giving the Anzac Lecture, May 5, 2005:

The fundamental values and interests that spurred these young Australians to do what they did on the other side of the world 90 years ago remain the values and interests that animate our societies today and are at the core of the contemporary Australia–US alliance.

And finally, the master mythologiser himself, Howard, who coincidentally chose Anzac Day in 2004 to visit Australian troops for the first time in Iraq, the same year that US President George W. Bush visited American troops on Thanksgiving Day. Anzac Day, Howard said, was simply the "natural time to go". At the dawn service at Baghdad airport, he addressed the Australian troops:

You are seeking to bring to the people of Iraq, who have suffered so much for so long, the hope of liberty and the hope of freedom, and your example, your behaviour, your values, belong to that great and long tradition that was forged on the beaches of Gallipoli in 1915.

Here, fighting for king and country in 1915 provides the rationale for fighting for the US alliance in 2003.

On many occasions, Howard has spoken of the "Australian military tradition", a tradition he believes, remarkably, is not a warlike tradition. As he explains it: "Australians are not by nature a warlike people. We have no tradition of conquest or imperial ambition."

No tradition of conquest? What, then, was the invasion of Iraq in February 2003? Every Anzac Day since the war began in 2003, Howard has attempted to wrap the Iraq campaign in the memory of Anzac. Australia's invasion of Iraq can thus be presented as a just cause, closer to a benevolent exercise in the delivery of democratic aid than the botched and ill-conceived military conquest it has always been. Far from teaching us to cast a questioning eye over authority, Anzac exalts the silent and dutiful soldier over the vocal dissenter.

The more respect and esteem today's military accrue through connection with Anzac, and the more public that connection is made by those in power, the harder it becomes to express disagreement about military conflict without being seen as unpatriotic.

Since 2001, the symbolic repertoire of our politics has diminished. We are witnessing the narrowing of our national mythology to one key legend that encapsulates our values, defines the moment of our nation's birth and gives rise to a military tradition within which those values and ideals are given their most profound expression. When I listen closely to the speeches and vox pops on Anzac Day, I sense a nation in search of a history of melancholy and loss. We have imagined that loss at Gallipoli to be far greater than it was—the British, the French, the Turks, lost many thousands more—and we have removed the site of our history of loss and sacrifice to a foreign shore, creating a myth of nationhood in permanent exile from the land in which we live. If you walk today around Botany Bay or Sydney Cove, you will see remarkably few memorials to the encounters surrounding British settlement. Walk in Canberra and many large Australian towns and you might be forgiven for thinking that the Australian soldiers who climbed the hills of Anzac Cove in 1915 were fighting for Australia's independence. If public memorials are any guide, Australia's national memory has been colonised by stories of war.

Whether it is the Coalition or the Labor Party in power in Canberra, the uncritical embrace of the Anzac legend is likely to continue, a scenario that suggests some disturbing consequences for Australia's future. The more all-consuming the Anzac myth becomes, the less public space exists for understanding the non-military aspects of Australia's history, be it our democratic history, our indigenous history or our intellectual and cultural history. The new love of Anzac is not about Australians paying more attention to their history, as is often claimed; rather, it is about the making of historical myth as a source of national pride and independence, the foundation stone of a new sentimental nationalism.

This is not what the Anzacs fought for. It is what an increasing number of Australians would like to think they had fought for. The Anzacs were not like us. So many aspects of the world in which they lived are fundamentally foreign to our world today.

Late in 2006, I attended a conference on Anzac Day, held at Deakin University in Geelong. There, Andrew Hamilton, who teaches at the United Faculty of Theology in Melbourne, gave one of the most penetrating critiques of Anzac Day I have encountered:

> When we say that people sacrificed their lives for an abstract cause like victory or nationhood, we easily imply that their lives and deaths are given value only by the cause they serve. We lose sight of the preciousness of each human life and equate human value with usefulness. Rhetoric about war is particularly vulnerable to this instrumentalising of human beings because its core business implies that human lives are expendable ... I find more ambiguous the recent nationalist emphases in the celebration of Anzac Day: the proliferation of flags, the singing of national anthems and the desire to make Anzac Day emblematic of Australian values. These things diminish the real humanity of those who have died in order to allow another generation to inflate its image of itself.

The Anzacs did not sacrifice their lives for the Australian nation. The nation has created their deaths as sacrifice to serve its own ends.

On May 18, 1915, less than four weeks after the first landing at Anzac Cove, the NSW Department of Education released a pamphlet for distribution in the state's schools. Its title, Australians in Action: The Story of Gallipoli, revealed the desperate need for deaths on the battlefield upon which the new nation could at last stand proud. This ideal of blood sacrifice was precisely the sense of nationalism that existed at the time.

But after the horrors of the 20th century, should it be ours today? Do we still need to prove ourselves in this way, to continue to accept the myth that our nation was only truly born on the beaches of Anzac Cove, not when the colonies became self-governing, not at Federation? Are our national values defined only when we have to fight for them? When we have an enemy? By sacralising the blood of the Anzacs, do we not forget the blood of Aborigines and settlers spilled in the frontier wars? Do we still prefer our history to be made elsewhere?

The religious symbolism involved in the commemoration of war, from the dawn service on Anzac Day through to the thousands of epitaphs on battlefield gravestones and war memorials across the nation, carries the comforting thought that war is beyond human control, that it is the will of God, the course of history, our cruel and bitter fate.

The rhetoric of our political leaders soars over the top of this religiosity, serving in turn to help us forget the true causes of war. Every war is a result of human and government decisions and it cannot be prosecuted unless we, the people, accept the belief that human life is expendable in the pursuit of military and political objectives.

The only way to do justice to the Australian soldiers who lost their lives—at Anzac Cove, on the Western Front, at Kokoda, in Korea and Vietnam, and in Iraq—is to ensure that their deaths are not exploited. To remember the political, strategic and diplomatic blunders that led to their lives being lost. Not to elevate performance on the battlefield to the pinnacle of our national inheritance but to remember the history of war in all its diversity and changing contexts over time, to remember the pacifists, the deserters, the conscientious objectors as well as those who fought. This is the least we can do.

On February 3 this year, a Saturday, *The Sydney Morning Herald* carried a report from Baghdad of another suicide bomb attack in Iraq. It was a story like many others since the war began, detailing carnage and death on a scale unimaginable for most Australians, the kind of story we cannot bring ourselves to contemplate for too long without giving in to feelings of frustration, anger and helplessness. But this report caused me to stop.

The scene was a crowded market street in the southern city of Hillah. Families walked among the stalls finishing their daily shopping. Mohammed Raad, a 19-year-old high school student, described what happened next. The first explosion ripped through the market, "overturning carts and blowing out shop windows". People ran screaming. In the chaos, a second suicide bomber opened his jacket to reveal a belt of explosives. Seeing him, an Iraqi police officer ran towards him shouting: "Suicide bomber!" In one final act of desperation, he threw his arms around the bomber, shielding others with his own body from the force of the blast. In the words of Raad, he "hugged him and the explosives tore apart both bodies".

For a long time afterwards this image haunted me. I saw the police officer with his arms outstretched, embracing the bomber like a long-lost friend. I saw the flesh of their bodies torn apart and become one in death. I do not know the police officer's name or age. I have no idea if he had a wife, partner or children. I know nothing of his life. But I have read of no greater act of courage in this war. And I am certain there are many more.

If there is such a thing as the Anzac spirit it is epitomised, for me, in the last actions of the Iraqi policeman from Hillah. The Anzac spirit is not uniquely Australian. It is universal. At its best, it is not a national but a human quality. It is found in Palestine and Iraq, in Darfur and East Timor, in Afghanistan and Zimbabwe. If it lives, it lives far from the flag-waving and breast-beating nationalism of recent times, far from the celebration of our national values and the birth of the Australian nation.

7
Howard's Fall

Paul Kelly

The defeat
The Weekend Australian, 15 December 2007

On the morning of Tuesday, September 4, at Phillip Street in Sydney, John Howard began to brief Alexander Downer on the terms necessary for him to quit the prime ministership in a few days.

Howard called Downer to his office from the Quay Grand hotel where Downer was based for the decisive week of Asia-Pacific Economic Co-operation forum meetings. Amid the week's high diplomacy, Howard and Downer had separate meetings on the Tuesday, Wednesday and Thursday to canvass who would lead the Coalition to the 2007 election.

The nuances shifted daily, yet these were frank talks between Howard and his closest cabinet confidant. Their mutual trust sustained tensions arising from their different positions as Howard offered the cabinet the chance to obtain his resignation.

Howard's position was that he preferred to stay and fight the election but he would offer the cabinet an alternative. He was prepared to resign the next week with no partyroom ballot and no political bloodletting subject to conditions. Howard's terms were authentic but daunting. Ultimately they proved too difficult for the Liberal Party in the most intense leadership crisis of Howard's 11 years of power.

"My best judgment is that we will lose the election and I'll lose my seat of Bennelong as well," Howard told Downer. It was a stunning, fateful and, as it proved, accurate judgment. "Bennelong has been a marginal seat for some time," he said. Howard had not forsaken all hope but, as a realist, he was deeply pessimistic.

Downer had been Howard's champion for the entire period. Just 15 months earlier in July 2006, when the mid-term showdown came between Howard and Peter Costello, with Costello asking Howard to quit, the cabinet had rallied to Howard. Downer, Malcolm Turnbull, Brendan Nelson, Tony Abbott and Mal Brough, among others, had insisted that Howard stay. And Howard had stayed.

In his July 31, 2006, letter informing members of his decision, Howard said: "Just as the party now wants me to continue as leader, I accept that it has a perfect right to change its mind if it judges that to be to the party's benefit. If that were to occur I would not be deaf to the party's shift in sentiment."

That shift had come in the first week of September 2007. Downer told Howard: "I don't think we can win. It is probably time to ask ourselves whether we can win with Costello. Probably not, but a change must at least give us a chance. Perhaps we have to give Costello the opportunity." It was a remarkable reversal. Here was Howard's tightest cabinet intimate telling him, perhaps, that his time had come. Downer would maintain this position throughout the crisis week: that the best option was a switch to Costello. Howard sensed the rising unrest. He could absorb such news from Downer without turning against him.

During their talks, Downer saw that Howard was serious about resignation. The confidence that had sustained his four election victories was fractured. Both men were ambivalent. Neither had imagined this situation would arise: serious contemplation of passing the prime ministership to Costello after what they regarded as Costello's incompetence the previous year in trying to force Howard out.

But Howard had come to the precipice and he would make an offer to jump.

His terms were designed to test the mettle of the Liberal Party's senior cabinet ministers and to test their real view of Costello. But there was another more pivotal purpose: to save Howard's face and standing, to uphold his honour. The core condition for Howard's resignation was vesting the political responsibility in the cabinet, not himself. It was one of the most remarkable conclusions about his survival reached by an Australian prime minister. But it was flawed: Howard was saying he would resign, but he wanted the cabinet to carry the responsibility. If it came, it would be a resignation without conviction.

Howard recalled the famous six-man cabinet delegation that visited Bob Hawke on December 12, 1991, to seek his resignation. While Hawke had denied this request in favour of a partyroom contest, Howard was willing to acquiesce.

Howard told Downer:

> If my senior cabinet colleagues publicly own a request for my resignation, then I will resign. In this situation I won't put the party through a leadership ballot. But it needs to be understood that I won't resign in a voluntary decision. I am not prepared to walk away of my own accord. That would be an act of cowardice and it would be seen as an act of cowardice.

Howard believed the time for a voluntary resignation had gone; that was the previous year. He had no regrets about his 2006 decision to stay. He believed it was the right decision at the time. But circumstances, as they do in politics, had changed. Paul Keating had openly predicted that Howard wouldn't quit on election eve because quitting was the coward's option and Keating was right. But Howard had created another option for his cabinet.

He was shaken by that Tuesday's Newspoll showing, in two-party preferred terms, Labor leading 59–41 per cent, akin to a political sledgehammer killing long awaited hopes for a Coalition recovery. The Coalition was facing annihilation.

Howard felt obliged to offer his political head, but his ministers had to become the executioners.

Of course, the optimum time for a transition was long gone. The truth is that Howard still didn't believe in a transition; he didn't think Costello was the party's saviour, but if the cabinet really wanted Costello, then it could have him.

What did Howard think would happen? He later told intimates: "I thought it was unlikely the cabinet would act but I wasn't sure and I thought the question had to be tested." This is probably too much of a subsequent rationalisation. Downer's visceral impression was of Howard's pessimism, yet the situation was complicated because Costello was unpopular and the cabinet was ambivalent about whether a change meant a better election performance. If Costello had been a Hawke the decision would have been easy. Cabinet would have pulled the trigger.

Reviewing the position Downer told Howard: "Costello would be a new face and the age factor wouldn't be there." He felt Costello would be an aggressive leader with the chance to re-brand the government. But the drawbacks were obvious.

"It will look an act of desperation," he said.

Howard suggested that Downer consult cabinet colleagues to see where they stood. It was a sign of Howard's weakness. At this point Downer knew that Howard had opened the door on resignation. While it was not discussed, they both implicitly knew the timetable. With Canadian PM Stephen Harper addressing parliament the next Tuesday, the day for any Howard resignation after a successful APEC meeting would be Wednesday, September 12.

Would this work? As a profound pessimist about the Coalition's electoral fate, Downer thought, yes, it might just fly. At midweek Abbott rang Howard to organise for *The Australian*'s columnist Janet Albrechtsen to see the prime minister. They quickly got on to the leadership and News-poll. Howard told Abbott that he had asked Downer to take soundings on the leadership.

"You should take some soundings yourself," he said to Abbott. There was no doubt in Abbott's mind that Howard was genuine. He suddenly grasped that resignation was a real option. But Howard told Abbott what he told Downer. "I won't just stroll into the partyroom and resign," he said. "The proviso is that this must be the will of the cabinet and party."

For Abbott, it seemed Howard was in "an agony of doubt". They canvassed all options including resignation but settled on none.

Abbott told Howard that, in practice, the two ministers that mattered were Downer and Senate leader Nick Minchin, and he would contact them.

Abbott rang Minchin, whose earlier view on the leadership was known within the inner group. Minchin decided in late 2005 that Howard should resign and felt the 10th anniversary in March 2006 was the best time. But Howard was suspicious of Minchin who, as finance minister, had grown close to Costello. Suspecting that Howard would see him merely as a spear-carrier for Costello, Minchin told colleagues he had asked the two people closest to Howard, Downer and the PM's office chief, Arthur Sinodinos, to make the case, saying: "If you feel it makes sense to mention my name, then do so."

That Minchin, once a Howard loyalist, felt obliged to take such an indirect route testified to the decline of cabinet trust.

Downer did not share Minchin's view but he conveyed it to Howard. When Howard recently checked with Sinodinos, his former aide could not remember any Minchin approach earlier in the term on the leadership.

Minchin now told Abbott: "It would have been best if Howard had gone last year. But it's too late now. The time for change is gone." Minchin even told Abbott he was unsure whether Costello would accept the leadership at such a late stage.

So Abbott rang Costello to make sure. Costello's response was predictable: he complained that he asked Howard to resign the previous year and Howard should have resigned. Yes, he was available if it happened now. When Abbott rang Downer he realised that Downer favoured a change.

Downer was deeply pessimistic about the election. "We're going to lose, but perhaps the loss will be less under Costello," Downer said. "We may even have a chance." Labor's campaign would be disrupted, the Coalition would win new momentum.

Open to the option that Howard might go and struck by the firmness of Downer's position, Abbott left the impression he favoured a change. Perhaps Abbott, the Howard loyalist, was wavering. That was Downer's conclusion; he noted that Abbott wanted a change as well. But Abbott said later there was a difference between being aware that Howard might resign and supporting his resignation, which he did not.

After these talks Abbott took soundings with friends outside politics. One person whose judgment he valued deeply told him: "You people are mad if you panic now and get rid of Howard. That won't save you."

Abbott rang Howard, probably on the night of Wednesday, September 5, to report on the soundings he had taken. He said he believed Howard should remain leader. He reported the views of Minchin and Downer, and Howard seemed unsurprised on either count. It was clear to Abbott that Howard did not believe Downer was working against him. Downer was doing the job Howard requested.

There would be many post-election claims of ministers, apart from Costello, asking Howard to quit. Most are mythical. The truth is that during 2006 most ministers wanted Howard to stay. The reality is that no minister, Costello aside, had been brutal with Howard. In all their talks during the term, Downer had never asked Howard to go.

More recently, not long before the election, Turnbull lamented to Howard that "he should not suffer defeat in Bennelong" and had urged Howard to think about going.

But there had never been any concerted cabinet review or representations.

On Thursday, September 6, after their talks with China's President Hu Jintao, Howard and Downer spoke again about cabinet's views. "I could find out what they think tonight after the APEC business dinner," Downer said. Howard encouraged him. "There's the risk of it leaking," Downer said. But Howard felt it was more pressing to know. "Go ahead," he said. There was an urgency.

Janette Howard was fully aware of her husband's decisions and mood, if not of all his discussions. John spoke to Janette in a seamless dialogue about the leadership. With his survival at stake, Janette was engaged. She would attend the final decisive meeting the next evening.

In his suite at the Quay Grand late on the night of September 6, Downer convened the meeting of cabinet ministers. He noted they ordered a lot of grog and it went on his bill. But Downer felt it was a good meeting, held in good but depressing spirits.

He explained the meeting was at Howard's sanction and request. There were nine ministers—Downer, Philip Ruddock, Nelson, Julie Bishop, Turnbull, Joe Hockey, Ian Macfarlane, Kevin Andrews and Chris Ellison. The ministers unable to attend were Abbott, Minchin, Brough and Helen Coonan.

Downer's opening brief was decisive. It came like a thunderclap. The cabinet was rocked to its foundations and the direction of the meeting was set at the outset. Downer reported that Howard was very pessimistic. He didn't believe he could win the election and didn't believe he could win Bennelong. "That made the decision easy," one cabinet minister said.

The Howard electoral magic within the Liberal Party died that night at 11pm in Downer's suite. "We hadn't given up on the election but now we were being told that Howard felt he was beaten," the same minister says.

Some time later Howard raised with Downer exactly what the foreign minister had said that night, lamenting that Howard's pessimism had been exaggerated in Downer's opening report.

Downer, however, had felt he was true to Howard's mood, stressing that as foreign minister he had much experience in a rapporteur role. He has tried to capture Howard's feelings in his presentation.

One minister made notes of this meeting afterwards and says: "Downer said Howard was prepared to stay and fight, but if the majority of cabinet said he should go, then he would on the basis that the cabinet had taken that position and he had been requested by them." The emphasis Downer gave was heavily on Howard's inclination to leave. But there was a difference in interpretation by ministers present. It is best summarised in these terms: was Howard merely seeking cabinet's green light for his resignation or was he testing whether the cabinet would accept his condition of full public responsibility for his departure? It was a subtle yet lethal difference.

"The impression I had was that Howard was seeking our permission to leave," says one participant pledged to a leadership change. "He wanted to know, if he quit, that cabinet wouldn't be complaining about his walking out on election eve."

Much of the two-hour talk was about how Howard should go and the merit of Costello as successor. There were three noteworthy conclusions. First, only one minister, Ruddock, argued firmly for Howard to stay, saying: "Once the rubber hits the road, people will come back", while another, Ellison, left this impression. So only two of nine ministers wanted Howard, a remarkable sign of lost confidence in the leader.

Second, the clear sentiment of the other seven ministers was that, given the predicament, the best outcome was for Howard to resign of his own volition.

Finally, Howard's proviso was not met; indeed, it was vehemently rejected. Ministers were adamant that Howard must volunteer his resignation, removed from any impression that he had been tapped on the shoulder or was being forced out.

The two ministers most insistent on change were Hockey and Turnbull. Hockey said Bennelong would be a chronic distraction for Howard for the entire campaign. He knew.

He held the adjoining seat of North Sydney and faced a campaign that threatened him. Turnbull was sure the government faced obliteration. Never a Costello fan, he believed Howard's position was utterly lost and a new leader was the only lever left to pull.

Both Hockey and Turnbull said people had stopped listening to Howard; there was no pathway that enabled him to discuss the future. Nearly all ministers felt the people had stopped listening to Howard.

One of the revealing aspects of the debate was the scepticism about Costello. "I was surprised at how many ministers were critical of Costello or had suffered at his hands," Downer reported later to a colleague. Another minister summarised the mood: "Only about 50 per cent of the meeting had any confidence Costello would do better than Howard." Howard was told later that many ministers had their own war stories about dealings with the treasurer.

Yet ministers believed the consequences of having the cabinet depose Howard were lethal. They feared rage and damnation from Howard loyalists and dedicated Liberal voters. Fearful of retaliation from Howard lovers and unsure of Costello's pull, the cabinet refused to take ownership of the decision. "We would have bled to death," one senior minister says.

Ministers settled instead for the view that Howard must summon the courage, do the right thing, hand over to Costello and campaign vigorously for the Coalition's re-election. Aware that Howard's preference had not been met, Downer, before they broke, said: "By the way, Howard wants people to front him directly if they think he should go."

This statement recognised the issue still hung in the balance. So how many ministers subsequently told Howard to leave? Just two: Hockey and Brough.

The bottom line when the meeting broke is best captured in the notes of the diary-keeping minister: "Agree—unless PM says he has decided to go—not on." Decoded, it means the meeting agreed that unless Howard acted voluntarily, then his resignation was not on. This minister told me he left the Quay Grand confident that Howard would not be resigning as PM.

Downer said later that "ministers unanimously felt that demanding Howard's departure would destroy the Coalition in its heartland". Minchin said that Howard's departure could be accepted on only one condition: that it was voluntary and not imposed by cabinet.

"The support of Howard loyalists in the community must be retained," he said.

The next morning Costello rang Downer and the deputy was given a full briefing. Abbott then rang Downer to express "my firm view that we stay with Howard".

At this point Howard and Downer proceeded to meet Russian President Vladimir Putin. On the evening of Friday, September 7, Downer travelled to Kirribilli House to report to Howard. He arrived unsure about the outcome of this meeting. It involved three people: John and Janette Howard and Downer. The atmospherics were important; Downer was on Howard's territory with Howard's wife. This was about politics and family. For the historical record, key aspects of this meeting are contested and, unsurprisingly, the numbers are two to one for one version against the other.

Downer told Howard the cabinet ministers were pessimistic. "They think we are heading for defeat, possibly a bad defeat," he said. Downer said there was a sentiment for change from Howard to Costello. "But there is no way they will own a request," Downer said. "They can't possibly do that." The impact on the Liberal faithful would be too dangerous.

"There were deep reservations expressed about Costello," Downer said. "There is little real confidence that Costello can win. Some ministers think he might do better." Ministers felt the public had stopped listening to Howard and the government.

Downer didn't press Howard to leave but he was struck by the mood change since Tuesday morning. The glint of Howard defiance was back. "You're not a quitter, John," Janette said, reinforcing Howard's instinct.

Howard's belief that he was a superior election leader to Costello was reignited. One version of this meeting has Downer listing the ministers one by one to Howard, leading to the absolutely uncontestable conclusion that the cabinet majority wanted him to retire gracefully at once.

Another version has Downer saying only that "some ministers" favoured the move to Costello. John and Janette Howard have the same recall of this meeting.

There is no dispute, however, on the core point: Downer reported the ministers refused to accept public responsibility for any request for Howard's exit. Howard was meticulous about this. He asked Downer this exact question and he got an unqualified answer.

Howard said that in the situation outlined by Downer he would refuse to walk. His mood was calm, yet there was a visceral touch to his voice. He repeated that he would repudiate the "coward's option". He would never contemplate such retreat, would never voluntarily resign and would never be labelled a coward. He would prefer to face an election defeat.

Downer told Howard he had asked ministers to speak directly to the PM. He depicted a cabinet in consternation. "You should talk to them, you need to talk with them," Downer said. For Howard, it seemed they needed counselling. "Maybe I should leave as well," Downer speculated at one point. Downer felt there was no scope to negotiate; the difference between Howard and his cabinet went to process and honour. Howard's demand mirrored a contradiction: if he resigned, he wanted to save his honour. Yet any such election eve resignation was a situation where honour could not be redeemed.

After an hour Downer left. They had more APEC business in the morning. Both men had the same conclusion: the issue was not quite resolved. Not yet.

For one minister it certainly wasn't resolved. That same day, when Brough heard about the previous night's events, he was incredulous. Brough rang Howard to discover the truth. Howard confirmed his request to Downer to test opinion. For Brough, Howard's admission about Bennelong was a tipping point. If Howard felt he couldn't hold his seat, his position as leader was untenable.

Brough felt Howard must uphold his formula on the leadership, that he would stay only as long as his party wanted him. Obviously, the cabinet no longer wanted him. Brough told Howard he did not think he could win the election and it would be best if he resigned.

While Brough wanted a smooth transition, he was probably the only cabinet minister, even more than Turnbull and Hockey, willing to pursue the issue. Brough told colleagues he wanted the leadership resolved and said, ominously, it must be brought to a head. Brough wanted Downer to convene another cabinet meeting on Sunday or Monday to force Howard out. "In my view this must be finalised by next Wednesday," Brough told colleagues. It was a deadline for action.

Brough accepted Costello would be leader but he would not tolerate Downer as deputy, the option raised at the Thursday night meeting. The partyroom could properly decide this, Brough said.

His alienation from Howard was deepened by Howard's rediscovered assertion. Brough was told that Howard's message would be to say that he was pushed out of the prime ministership by his colleagues, an inflammatory line that Brough saw as designed to pre-empt ministers from moving against him. Brough wanted to rally the cabinet for action.

But Downer would have none of this. He had left Kirribilli on Friday evening aware that he had to make a decision. Should he rally the cabinet against Howard or should he accept Howard's determination to stay, given the cabinet's failure to dictate to him?

For Downer, this was an easy decision. He had high obligations to the Liberal Party that he and his father had served in national governments. Downer would be criticised later for not pulling the plug on Howard. But this begs the real issue and misconceives the situation. Downer was stopped where the cabinet had stopped: lack of sufficient faith in Costello.

This became the unifying narrative that halted action. Howard's ministers would force his departure only if they had confidence in the alternative. The source of their timidity was their uncertainty about Costello.

Downer still favoured a change. He thought, maybe, there was a 5 per cent chance of "a Costello miracle". But these odds weren't good enough to force Howard out.

On Saturday morning Howard put the leadership issue to one side. Again. He and Downer attended the heads of government trilateral security dialogue breakfast at the InterContinental Hotel with US President George W. Bush and Japan's Prime Minister Shinzo Abe. Each leader was in diabolical domestic trouble and Bush resorted to gallows humour, laughing: "Well, here we are, all of us, aren't we trouble, aren't we unpopular."

By the weekend Howard's political calculations had hardened. He examined the consequences of resignation. He calculated that if Costello lost the election there would be two responses: that Howard had abandoned his responsibility to the Liberal Party to stay and fight. He would be attacked for achieving the political liquidation of himself and Costello in one stroke. And, remember, Howard was sure Costello would lose the election.

At the weekend, Downer farewelled the US President, telling him: "When we meet next, I doubt John Howard and I will be holding our current jobs."

On Sunday, September 9, Hockey rang Howard. He said that Downer had asked ministers to speak directly to Howard and that's what he was doing. He felt that Howard should resign, his message wasn't getting through. Howard listened. He was calm and pragmatic, and thanked Hockey for calling.

But Howard was unshakeable; he was shutting down the crisis. He had seen the weakness of the cabinet, he had identified its preference but lack of commitment for Costello. He had regained his confidence.

The family was united. At the weekend he had discussed his future with the family, Janette, Tim, Melanie and her husband. On Saturday he spoke on the phone to Richard, who was overseas. The family did not change Howard's mind, merely confirming his decision.

But Howard's blunder was to reveal publicly that he consulted the family and "they want me to continue". Some ministers were in fuming outrage. "So he rejects the view of his cabinet but listens to the view of his family," one said.

Howard's problem was that the entire process had left him crippled: he asked for an expression of opinion and the cabinet wanted him gone.

Early the following week a frustrated Turnbull had a constant refrain: why had Howard commissioned this process and, when faced with cabinet's answer, refused to leave? Turnbull felt the debate was artificial. Cabinet had given Howard full authority to resign. What else did he want? If Howard was sincere the issue could be negotiated to a resignation solution. Fighting in a marginal seat and close to the environmental issue, Turnbull knew the public was finished with Howard. Turnbull, unlike Minchin, did not feel it was too late. He saw a successful APEC as a platform for Howard's departure with an incoming Costello immediately rebadging the government, starting with Kyoto ratification. But Turnbull, despite his frustration, knew that resort to political pressure was untenable. It had to be Howard's act and this was being withheld.

Howard sought to terminate the crisis at his last APEC press conference on the Sunday, declaring: "Yes, I do intend to contest it (the election) as leader." Costello backers strove to keep the issue alive. Some Costello supporters urged him to confront Howard, but Costello had the sense to stay on ice.

On Tuesday, Minchin and Downer moved to close it down firmly. That day after question time, Downer went to Howard's office and they drew the line. That evening Downer conceded on television there had been a leadership debate the previous week but that it was now behind the party.

There is no gainsaying the final outcome: by September 2007 it was too late for the party to change leaders.

But there is a contested postscript for history. Now retired from politics, Howard has told colleagues that Costello's real chance was in 2006 when Howard and Janette were contemplating their future.

After the 2004 victory the Howards felt their last election was behind them. As 2006 advanced and Howard considered his future he felt it "very probable" that he would retire in the summer of 2006–07. It was a John–Janette position.

There was one event Howard wanted to see. This was the High Court's upholding of the Work Choices law and it happened in late 2006. Downer spoke to Howard periodically in 2006 about the leadership and said late that year he thought it "more likely than not" Howard would have retired during the summer. Yet nobody knows. There is no certainty on this. Post-election claims can be too self-serving. Downer does not know and maybe Howard does not even know. Yet Howard and Downer agree that Costello's pressing of the leadership issue in mid-2006 was a fatal blunder.

This was triggered by News Limited journalist Glenn Milne's revelation of Ian McLachlan's notes of an alleged Howard commitment in December 1994 to hand over the leadership to Costello after two terms. On July 11, 2006, there was a 30-minute face-to-face confrontation between Howard and Costello where Costello sought his resignation and Howard refused.

Such a public clash had three consequences: it hardened Howard against Costello; it turned party sentiment against Costello; and it put Howard under immediate pressure to bring forward his decision and to stay for the 2007 election. Most of the business community wanted Howard to remain, with its doyen, Don Argus, making representations along these lines.

Howard consulted widely and his decision to stay was not just his own. It was the cabinet's and the party's decision. At the time not one cabinet minister proposed to Howard that he should leave.

This reflected the power situation: Costello had neither the numbers to force Howard out nor the ability to persuade him. The Liberal Party's tragic mishandling of the leadership issue over the 2004–06 term is that Howard stayed too long but his deputy never found the mechanism to remove him, by charm or threat.

The reality, however, is that Costello's flaws cannot excuse Howard's misjudgment. His defeat proves Howard should have resigned in 2006 or early 2007. Such a wise decision would have rendered nonexistent the APEC week of remarkable drama.

Paul Keating

Divisive leader who squandered Australia's hopes

The Sydney Morning Herald, 26 November 2007

On Saturday night, when it was clear the Howard Government had been defeated, many Labor supporters around me said: "You must be so happy." But my emotion was not happiness; rather, it was relief.

Relief that the nation had put itself back on course. Relief that the toxicity of the Liberal social agenda—the active disparagement of particular classes and groups, that feeling of alienation in your own country—was over. And over in the only way that could be final: with a resounding electoral instruction of "No more".

In *The Sun-Herald* on November 18, John Howard nominated the putting asunder of political correctness and the celebration of our Anglo-Celtic past as the pinnacle of his social, indeed national, achievement. He was nominating as a virtue political incorrectness of a kind that gave some the right to speak and behave towards others in terms disparaging of their colour, religion, class or social standing. In a country of immigrants, such a view emanating from the Prime Minister is social poison.

Saturday night's victory was not just a victory for the Labor Party; it was also a victory for those Liberals like Malcolm Fraser, Petro Georgiou and Judi Moylan, who stood against the pernicious erosion of decent standards in our public affairs.

The Liberal Party of John Howard, Philip Ruddock, Alexander Downer and Peter Costello is now a party of privilege and punishments. One that lacks that most basic of wellsprings: charity.

The French philosophers had it pretty right with the Enlightenment catchcry of liberty, fraternity and equality. There was not much liberty for the boat people, or fraternity for the Aborigines or the Muslims, or equality for the unionists who believed in nothing more revolutionary than the right to collectively bargain.

Howard says he was the progenitor, the giver, of 11 years of economic growth and, without him or Costello, the growth will evaporate. This result means the public didn't believe him; otherwise they would not have repudiated him. They knew it took more than simply being around and spending up big to create the conditions that have underwritten the longest economic expansion in our history.

Howard's greatest inheritance from the Labor Party was low inflation, the factor that above all others provided the golden thread through those 16 years of growth.

When Howard decided to go after workers with his Work Choices legislation, he did so not out of any economic necessity, as the economic record for wages and inflation attests. He did it simply to break the back of the unions. His motivations were ideological and spiteful, telling us he had learned nothing from the fact that there had been no wages breakout in Australia since the one he detonated 26 years earlier.

Howard proudly mentions his GST as an example of reform, yet its great harvest of money was not spent on education or health or infrastructure. It was largely spent on giveaways, which means it was not necessary in the first place. So cynical was Howard about it he forbade the Treasury from accounting for it in the budget papers, even though it is collected as a federal tax and allocated under Commonwealth policies.

When I turned over the prime ministership to John Howard in 1996 the opportunities presented to him, as the century closed, were unprecedented.

A new-made economy, with open financial, product and labour markets for the first time in our history. Five years' growth already behind us, at an average inflation rate of 2.5 per cent. A universal and compulsory superannuation system, where the previous Labor government had encouraged workers to save 9 per cent of their wages for their retirement. A framework for the movement to an Australian republic with a model designed for acceptance by the Liberal Party.

A set of new international relationships, especially with Indonesia and China, with Australia sitting as the founder of the main piece of political architecture in the Pacific: the APEC leaders' meeting.

As we turned into the new century, what did Howard do with these new opportunities? The short answer is he squandered them.

He took a knife to the new enterprise bargaining wages system the moment he got control of the Senate. He left superannuation jammed at 9 per cent of wages after promising to maintain the commitment I had made to take it to 15 per cent. He connived in the defeat of the republic referendum so that now we are more likely than not to have King Charles and Queen Camilla as our heads of state, as ludicrous as that would be. His triumphalism over East Timor destroyed the relationship Labor had built with Indonesia, which probably can't be rebuilt, or if it can, only after decades. He has attended every APEC leaders' meeting since 1996, but brought not one new idea to it, not even to his own meeting in Sydney this year.

In the end, Howard didn't understand how great his opportunity was and how it could not be advanced by regressive and reactionary policies fuelled by social exclusion and division.

Let us hope the Liberal Party purges itself of its reactionary majority, for Australia cannot afford another prime minister like John Howard.

Geoffrey Blainey

From triumph to a tragic

Herald Sun, 27 November 2007

The defeat of John Howard at the polls will long be remembered. He could not have been defeated without valid fears, widely felt, and silently expressed in the ballot box.

At the same time his reign, second only to that of Sir Robert Menzies in number of years, will eventually be honoured.

While his enemies lick their lips, and while Kevin Rudd deservedly rejoices in his win, John Howard has much to feel proud of.

In more than 11 years in office he never failed to promote the virtues of democracy. Knowing that it takes at least two major parties to run a democracy, he was more willing to give praise to his opponents, at the right time, than were nearly all other major politicians.

Even when he was a very young federal treasurer, serving under Malcolm Fraser, he gave the most generous praise to his Labor predecessor, Frank Crean.

A believer in debate he appeared endlessly on radio, television and wherever there was a listener.

It is slightly ironic that he was defeated by an able and highly articulate candidate who went to some lengths to avoid awkward interviews.

Mr Howard's government had a success in creating jobs, useful jobs, which every prime minister before them would have applauded or envied.

Mr Keating, in his stirring speech on election night of 1993 to his true believers at the Bankstown Sports Club, promised to care especially for the unemployed: we want to get them back to work.

Instead, it was Mr Howard who got them back to work.

While rising inflation and rising interest rates helped to alienate many voters on Saturday, Howard's earlier success in combating inflation, year by year, was impressive.

His predecessors, Bob Hawke and Paul Keating, made several notable economic reforms. But their failure to check inflation, by world standards, was even more notable.

It was the Howard government, which, through Peter Costello as treasurer, implemented in July 2000 the first strong reform of the tax system seen since World War II.

The goods and services tax, understandably, was opposed by the Labor Party and a wide section of the public.

And yet, by a strange turn of the wheel, it was the resultant stream of GST revenue, flowing straight to the states, that enabled Labor governments from the year 2000 to avoid financial crises and so win many elections.

Mr Howard did not sell his economic policies as effectively as in the beginning of his reign. Thus it became the received wisdom that it was China, and its booming economy, that was handing us on a plate our present high level of prosperity.

This is a one-sided myth. China is booming not only because of its own vigour but because Australia had one of the most efficient mining industries in the history of the world, ready to supply China with cheap coal, iron ore and other minerals even before Beijing was wealthy enough to afford them.

The strength of the mineral industry here owed infinitely more to federal and state Liberal ministers, especially to Sir Charles Court in Western Australia, than to Labor governments, some of which obstructed the opening of new mines and ports.

This is one of the reasons why the big swing to Mr Rudd did not eventuate in WA.

It was Mr Howard's triumph at his first election victory in 1996 to sell to these blue-collar and white-collar battlers his economic and cultural message. He knew they were not naturally Liberal voters. This new constituency does not represent a permanent realignment in Australian politics, he wrote in 1996.

And on Saturday they largely deserted him.

His ability to persuade was a secret of his long success. He was one of the outstanding debaters in the nation's history. On any topic, almost without notice, he could speak energetically and persuasively. On the republican issue he was the skilled persuader, after giving the whole nation the chance to make up its mind.

In answering questions he usually was forthright. Not that he was forthright on every occasion.

Who is?

Democratic politics, at times, is the art of camouflage coupled with the art of skywriting.

He was not one of the great formal orators like Menzies or Whitlam, or like Paul Keating when Don Watson wrote speeches for him.

He shunned the set speech handed to him by a writer. But day after day he held his audiences, who listened to every word.

You really have to marvel that John Howard stayed in power for so long.

Except in the two world wars, no other prime minister in our history has had to face such a procession of jolts and setbacks arriving from the outside world.

He faced the dangerous Asian meltdown, which was expected to give our economy a black eye.

He faced the upheavals in Indonesia when President Suharto fell, the chaos in East Timor.

The effects of the terrorist attack on New York in 2001 and the rise of terrorist threats within Australia, the assassinations in Bali, and the crises in Iraq and Afghanistan.

He did not dither.

His government acted.

More and more critics now argue that Australia should not have joined the American alliance in the invasion of Iraq.

But it is too early to judge whether Saddam Hussein should have been allowed to continue to preside, unfettered, over his own torture house.

The American alliance, under Labor and Liberal, has been the backbone of Australia's defences. No previous pair of leaders in Canberra and Washington have enjoyed the kind of personal rapport that united Howard and George W. Bush.

Mr Rudd in his first year in office will probably have a running start, because of that unusual empathy, which Howard established.

Wide criticisms are directed at the Howard government. They extend from its policies on global warming to its policies on Aborigines, both of which are moral mountains on which many of his critics like to stand and do nothing.

Despite the fervent talk, there is no sign that even 5 per cent of Australian voters are seriously prepared to sacrifice part of their standard of living, and even cut down on overseas travel, in order to reduce pollution.

There is now an attempt to dethrone Mr Howard as a major political figure.

Critics say that in losing his own seat of Bennelong, he has suffered a unique humiliation.

Only one other prime minister, Stanley Melbourne Bruce, suffered the same punishment.

That was on the eve of the world depression when, like Mr Howard, he vexed swinging voters by trying to reform the workplace.

Bruce's Liberal seat was Flinders, which in 1929 was a farming as much as a bayside suburban electorate.

What is now forgotten is that Bruce won it back two years later, with ease.

Other political leaders, federal and state, have avoided humiliation by finding a safer seat. Billy Hughes was prime minister in 1917, during World War I, and seemed likely to lose his Sydney seat.

He took the drastic step of moving to the Victorian electorate of Bendigo where he was an easy winner.

In recent years Mr Howard could easily have transferred to a safer Liberal seat in Sydney as the demographics moved against him. Liberal supporters would probably argue it is to his credit that he did not move.

Most likely he concluded it would damage the prospects of his own party if he abandoned his own marginal seat and stood for a safer Sydney seat held by a colleague who had made no mark in Parliament.

The emphatic lesson of Saturday's election is that a successful political regime is bound to be in grave trouble once it approaches its 12th birthday.

Having carried out its main tasks, it loses its sense of purpose and mission.

The crushing defeat of the Hughes and Bruce period of government in 1929, the near-defeat of Menzies in 1961, the resounding end of the Hawke-Keating reign in 1996, and the emphatic defeat of Mr Howard on Saturday are part of the same decisive federal pattern.

In the week after such defeats, the deposed national leader looks for all the world like a headless chook.

But in the end, John Howard will be seen by vast numbers of Australians as one of the great prime ministers.

Paul Sheehan

A contest of ideas, not ideology
The Sydney Morning Herald, 26 November 2007

Ideology is dead in Australia. The electorate made sure of that at the weekend. Australia now has a new leader as conservative as the one the public has just cast aside. The transition was seamless, bloodless and ruthless.

Seamless, because the prime minister-elect has committed himself to policy pragmatism, fiscal conservatism and border security. Kevin Rudd is also the only member of the Labor Party who has regularly attended the federal parliamentary prayer group (dominated by social conservatives like Bronwyn Bishop and Bob Katter).

Bloodless, because the election campaign, at least as contested by the principals, was never grubby or personal but remained a contest of ideas. It was left to a few Liberal hacks to provide the grubby, and a few media commentators to provide the personal, the mean-spirited and the one punch thrown in the campaign.

Ruthless, because the Prime Minister, John Howard, the supposed political master, may have lost his seat in Parliament, while his deputy, the supposed new leader, Peter Costello, self-decapitated as the heir-apparent yesterday, after he had considered the magnitude of the rebuilding that lies ahead.

So the Australian political system, one of the oldest and most stable democracies in the world, has delivered an emphatic change of leadership with a modest change in direction.

The electorate has chosen a Labor leader who locked his party's utopian left wing in a broom closet for the election campaign, and is giving every indication he intends to keep them there. In his final keynote address of the campaign, not once did he mention the words unions, Aborigines, indigenous, apology, refugees or multiculturalism.

It's taken almost 40 years to learn from mistakes and apply the necessary discipline. What rolled over the Howard Government in the past eight months was Labor 3.0, built on the experiences of Labor 1.0 and Labor 2.0.

Labor 1.0 was the Whitlam government. After emerging from 23 years in the wilderness in 1972 many of its members behaved like pigs at a trough and it was rejected overwhelmingly by the public in 1975. Labor 2.0 was the Hawke–Keating government, vastly more sophisticated and accomplished, but eventually undone by arrogance and the culture wars, as Paul Keating, Gareth Evans, Nick Bolkus and Robert Tickner led the charge of "racism" every time anyone dared to question its misguided policies on immigration or Aboriginal affairs. It took 10 years for Labor to recover.

Labor 3.0 is encapsulated by Rudd's refusal to contest the culture wars with Howard. The rhetorical tendencies of firebrands like Julia Gillard, Peter Garrett and the trade union ideologues have been conspicuously tempered or measured, or non-existent, since Rudd took charge. On Saturday night, we had the spectacle of Stephen Smith, a senior member of Rudd's shadow cabinet, complaining about "the worst excesses, the ugly face of unionism, which hasn't helped us at all". He was referring to Labor's relative failure in Western Australia.

The utopian Left inside Labor and the Greens will have to come to terms with the reality that Australia will soon have a Labor prime minister who has a temper, an iron will, a fierce intellect and an enormous mandate, who has given the Australian electorate what it wanted. What it wanted was an end to the excesses and the hollowness of the Howard Government, not a deviation from policy pragmatism.

The conventional wisdom is that Howard was too old, stayed too long, exhibited political hubris; the Work Choices legislation bit too deep and went too far. All true, but the Government's problem went deeper. There was a hollowness to its policies, a formulaic cynicism, as if tax cuts and handouts were enough to buy the electorate's loyalty.

We are better than that. Australians are living at a time of systematic greed in the corporate sector, where record profits are skimmed by huge fees, huge salaries and huge payouts for corporate executives. The privatisation of Telstra did the Howard Government no favours. None of this sits well with an electorate that is expected to absorb longer hours, higher debt, greater job insecurity, spreading road tolls and accelerating change as the burdens of prosperity.

There was also a shocking absence of vision in Howard's last year, personified by his almost wilful blindness on the greatest issue facing this country—climate change and water. Howard's responses were belated, begrudging and piecemeal to the very end. In the keynote address that launched his 2007 election campaign, not once, in 4400 words, did he utter the words "climate change". All he offered was this almost throwaway comment: "We need to have a lower-carbon future but we need to do it in a way that does not destroy jobs, does not weaken the great coal industry ..."

It was conservative pragmatism taken too far. It gave Rudd an effortless space in which to appeal to younger voters as a man whose time had come rather than a man whose time had passed.

In this seamless, bloodless, ruthless transition, two men who deserved to be prime minister will now never get the chance. One is Labor's Kim Beazley, who in 1998 beat John Howard in both the campaign and the popular vote but lost the election. His second chance was destroyed by the events of September 11, 2001, which ruined his campaign. Peter Costello also deserved better. He dominated Federal Parliament for the past decade and led Australia through an era of historic prosperity.

Nine months ago this column implored John Howard to do the moral thing and step aside, and give Costello his chance to shine as prime minister. The party wouldn't allow it to happen. It chose timidity when Labor chose boldness. And so the grim reaper finally caught up with the leader who chose to join the invasion of Iraq and the misbegotten, misnamed and mishandled "war on terror".

Andrew West

More than just a light on the hill
The Sydney Morning Herald, 22 December 2007

Shortly after 9am one Sunday Kevin Rudd slipped quietly, but not unnoticed, into a pew at the back of St John the Baptist Anglican Church in the gentrified Brisbane suburb of Bulimba. The man who had been Prime Minister for just six days was late, but his sons, Marcus and Nicholas, were inside.

The priest had read the Collect for the Day and the congregation had just finished the first hymn. Two bodyguards stood at the doors of the unprepossessing weatherboard church, and outside a television crew waited for Rudd to emerge. He has been a parishioner of St John's for more than a decade, but it was only after he became Labor leader late last year that the media began filming his Sunday devotions.

Rudd, our most publicly Christian prime minister in almost a century—since his Queensland Labor predecessor, Andrew Fisher, who was a stern Presbyterian Sunday school teacher—has an active faith that shapes his world view. "He understands that his faith relates to what he does on a day-to-day basis," says Father John Milburn, the rector of St John's. "And God prepares us all for what we have."

On this particular Sunday the message to Rudd was clear. Isaiah, chapter 11, seemed to speak directly to him: "He shall not judge by what his eyes see, or decide by what his ears hear; but with righteousness he shall judge the poor and decide with equity for the meek of the Earth."

Paul's letter to the Romans, chapter 15, exhorted the faithful to "live in harmony with one another"—a theme Rudd embraced in his conciliatory acceptance speech on election night—while St Matthew's gospel spoke of humility before a Lord who was coming to sort the wheat from the chaff. Milburn's sermon, meanwhile, preached that "if redemption of the world is going to happen, it must come from the top down".

Was it a message to his newly influential parishioner? "No," he insisted later.

> I haven't changed the way I've been preaching at all. It just so happens—and I've been very aware that he's been there—that the readings for the past few weeks have been about serving other people, about God getting really uptight if the Israelites forgot about the weak, the orphans, the dispossessed and the outcast.
>
> Now, Kevin's been sitting there and I've been thinking, "I don't know if this cap fits you or not," because he never discusses this with me, but he listens very carefully. But I don't know that my preaching would affect him more than others because [the sentiment] is already in his heart.

Still, even one of the hymns, "The Servant King", reinforced the theme. "I did smile at that," Milburn confesses.

Rudd was raised a Catholic but told his biographer Robert Macklin that, as a teenager at De La Salle College in Brisbane, "there was no particular sense of personal faith". His Catholicism involved Mass three mornings a week, classroom prayers and memorising the catechism.

But at the age of 17, Macklin told the *Herald*, Rudd "made a deliberate decision that he would be a Christian. He was embarking on a spiritual journey."

This kind of conscious awakening to a faith gives Rudd a profound connection with the growing community of evangelical Christians, who believe that the dramatic, clarifying experience of being "born again" is often necessary to becoming a Christian.

When Rudd went to Canberra to attend the Australian National University, he started attending the Uniting Church—liberal in theology, activist in politics, often informal in worship—but drifted towards Anglicanism after meeting Therese Rein. When they married in 1981, it was in the most establishment of Canberra's churches, St John's, Reid.

He appears to have worshipped as an Anglican ever since, although without ever having been formally received into the church in a ceremony in which the priest blesses the new communicant. (Rudd's office could not answer this question and, for the record, declined two requests for an interview, citing his mammoth workload.)

The Anglican Primate of Australia, Brisbane's archbishop, Philip Aspinall, suggests that Rudd may have found intellectual freedom in Anglicanism, with its three pillars of scripture, reason and tradition, and a history of accommodating Catholic and evangelical styles of worship. It offered, perhaps, some wiggle room.

"Political life is about listening to the different sides and finding a way forward, and I think Anglicanism is a bit like that," Aspinall says.

> We have no one centre of authority. There is no one who can tell you all the answers. We don't have an infallible book, in which you can look up all the answers, or an infallible pope, who can tell you all the answers. It's a matter of drawing on the various sources and coming to conclusions yourself, not in a simplistic or individualistic way but in the company of the church.

Nurtured in the Brisbane diocese, Rudd would have found just enough of the Catholic ritual and social teaching on issues such as the "preferential option for the poor" that have ostensibly influenced his politics. (In the last week of the election campaign, for example, Rudd focused on homelessness.)

"Within Christianity some branches emphasise individual salvation and faith," Aspinall says. "In contrast is the social emphasis, which is about the importance of social justice, relationships and reconciliation. It's a false dichotomy to pit one against the other"—evangelicals have long been committed to justice, going back to the anti-slavery movement—"but, on the spectrum, Catholic Anglicanism emphasises the social aspects a bit more than some other branches of Christianity."

In 2005, speaking to Geraldine Doogue for ABC TV's *Compass*, Rudd aligned himself clearly with the Christian Socialist Movement, using the pronoun "us". He has since insisted he is not a socialist per se, but the antecedents and objectives of the movement commit it to closing the wealth gap within and between nations, and breaking down concentrations of economic power.

In a lecture later that year to the University of NSW's New College, and in a later article for *The Monthly*, Rudd named Dietrich Bonhoeffer, the German theologian and martyr to the anti-Nazi cause, as his hero. Bonhoeffer believed it was the duty of the Christians to not only identify with the "marginalised, vulnerable and oppressed" but also to "jam the spoke in the wheel" of state power when it oppressed its citizenry. If Rudd is true to the calling of his heroes, he could find himself challenging the abuse of power, in all its manifestations.

Aspinall believes it is a responsibility of Christians in leadership. "Leaders have to stand up for truth and what's right, and that sometimes involves rough and tumble with vested interests who stand to lose something," he says. "That comes out of the prophetic tradition. Part of the wealth that's generated through corporate and business activity has to be directed to caring for the most vulnerable and the weakest, and ensuring everyone gets a share of that prosperity."

There are two ways to read Rudd's blending of faith and politics.

The first—and, in fairness, the way most people who know him read it—is that Rudd's values really are driven by the Old Testament prophets crying out for justice, and the example of the radical Christ, who consorted with the despised of his day—tax collectors, prostitutes, criminals and lepers—and who overturned the tables of the money lenders in the temple.

The second, less charitable, view is that after the 2004 election Rudd saw the strategically important, if not particularly large, evangelical vote and decided he wanted a slice of it for Labor. Rudd talked to this author in 2005 about the Faith, Politics and Values working group he had established within the Labor caucus. To supporters of the Christian-inspired Family First party, which had sent preferences to the Coalition in several decisive seats, he asked: "What do you get from the Liberals that you don't get elsewhere?"

His political motive was blatant. "The challenge was made sharply manifest by Family First having adopted a 2004 election political posture that was no different from being a wholly owned subsidiary of the Liberal Party," Rudd said.

Bruce Baird, the leading Liberal moderate who retired at last month's election, befriended Rudd as a fellow member of the Parliamentary Christian Fellowship. "I think Kevin's faith is genuine and not for synthetic or political reasons," Baird says.

"On the issue of RU486 [the so-called abortion pill], he did discuss it seriously with people on the Christian scene in Canberra."

Baird and Rudd voted for a bill that denied the then health minister, Tony Abbott, the right to determine if RU486 was made available to women.

For Baird, one of the most telling signs of Rudd's faith and his willingness to let it shape his politics is his involvement with the fellowship. While up to 50 MPs might attend the parliamentary prayer breakfast to hear guest speakers such as Sydney's Catholic archbishop, Cardinal George Pell, or the World Vision chief, Tim Costello, it is a committed core who gather for bible study every Monday night when Parliament is sitting.

"They're not confessional, as such," Baird says,

> but they are quite personal encounters that go to the implication of what it means to be a Christian with a heavy public burden. We talked a lot about how to respond to Christ's call for humility and servanthood and the conflict with our role as politicians and having to push yourself forward.

Baird was impressed with Rudd's deep biblical knowledge—one of the Prime Minister's staff, who asked to remain anonymous, says Rudd, like Kim Beazley, carries a small Bible on his travels, and he studies the writings of Paul.

Dr Mark Harding, dean of the Australian College of Theology and a Princeton-educated expert on Paul's scriptures, says Rudd's affinity with Paul suggests an inclusive approach to governing.

> It is in Paul's writings that we find the famous injunction that there is neither Jew nor Greek nor slave nor free, male nor female, but all are one under Christ Jesus. That was a very powerful statement in a world divided then, and still today in many ways, by gender, ethnicity, race and social class.

If theologians and church leaders set a high bar for Rudd, others say there is a way to navigate the difficult shoals of politics and faith. Brian Howe, a Uniting Church minister, served as deputy prime minister to Bob Hawke and Paul Keating. Raised with the Methodist passion for social justice, he took comfort in the writings not only of Bonhoeffer but his contemporary, Reinhold Niebuhr, a Lutheran cleric and author of *Moral Man and Immoral Society*. Niebuhr developed the theory of Christian Realism.

"He recognised power and saw how it related to hubris, and the way people in politics were driven by primal forces that sometimes they could not control," Howe says.

As an idealist struggling to build, as Blake wrote, the new Jerusalem, Howe was often frustrated by the compromises of realpolitik. "I always concluded that it was better to live to fight another day and that, by compromising in the short term, you protected those causes that really mattered to you."

If Rudd, who is, by all accounts, possessed of much self-respect, is tempted by the hubris of which Howe warns, he need only to return to St John the Baptist in Bulimba. "For Kevin," Father Milburn says,

we hope this will be a place to come home to. While the office of prime minister is absolutely respected in the parish, Kevin's always been a member of the congregation. We know him, so becoming prime minister is very much as though he, like others in the parish, has just switched jobs.

Pamela Williams

A right royal mess: How Howard led Libs into chaos

The Australian Financial Review, 11 December 2007

From the prime ministerial suite in the white-angled splendour of Parliament House, and from the gabled elegance of Kirribilli House in Sydney, John Howard ran both the country and the Liberal Party.

It was an unrivalled grip on power. By the time of the 2007 election campaign, Howard, his wife Janette and a tiny coterie of close family and friends were nicknamed the "Royal Family" by some Liberal insiders due to their influence over the party and over campaign matters both large and small.

Now, as the family leaves behind the prestige of Kirribilli and Howard's shattered aura of invincible power, his role in sidelining the Liberal organisation is also coming under the spotlight.

Like a house of cards, everything has collapsed, leaving the party structurally and financially vulnerable.

The Liberals' fortunes are teetering, caught between massive campaign spending costs and seriously reduced fund-raising.

The situation is so fraught that one insider told *The Australian Financial Review* the party was "unviable".

So much had been spent on the campaign that staff at the federal directorate faced a slash and burn, he said, before adding a devastating assessment of the organisation John Howard professed to love: "The party's broke. They're smashed up. And it's mayhem."

Another insider was less emotional as he too conceded a need for belt-tightening at the federal office. But he insisted the campaign had been fully funded. He said the problem the party faced now was in long-term fund-raising.

The Liberals' federal treasurer, Mark Bethwaite, has been the butt of some criticism for his fund-raising efforts, especially given his well-known commitment to sailing. His time on the water was judged—perhaps cruelly—to have taken time away from his fund-raising efforts.

As the party's finances veered south over the past year, Bethwaite's predecessor as treasurer, businessman John Calvert-Jones, put his shoulder to the wheel, together with former federal president Shane Stone. These two got on the phone and tramped boardrooms with their odd mix of connections, Melbourne old-school charm and Top-End chutzpah.

One important Liberal symbol remains safe. In Canberra, the party's headquarters, R. G. Menzies House, has no mortgage, courtesy of the tight management of another former federal treasurer, Ron Walker, who changed the rules to make it difficult to borrow against the property. Unlike Liberal state branches around the country that sold off property when the going got tough, Walker put a fence around the Canberra headquarters by vesting it in a structure requiring a special party meeting and a 96 per cent vote in favour before a mortgage could be raised. To secure the party finances and keep the National Australia Bank's beady eyes off the property, Walker personally guaranteed the party's million-dollar debts.

While Walker ran the money side of things, former federal presidents Tony Staley and later Shane Stone steered the organisation with a strong hand. Staley was a former Liberal minister, who, together with Walker and former party director Andrew Robb (and later Lynton Crosby), were the backbone that steered Howard to power. Staley also was a ruthless operator who knifed two floundering Liberal leaders, John Hewson and Alexander Downer, in the early 1990s.

That was a time when the party organisation had clout and power. It was an era that worked to the massive benefit of Howard in his bid for the leadership and ultimately the prime ministership. But things changed.

Those who give can take away. Howard, faced with the high profile of the key organisational figures, and their well-known role in his elevation, steadily dismantled the struts. During his reign he placed, or supported, the appointment of people who would not rock the boat—in the administrative level, the cabinet, the ministerial level, the party organisation and the federal executive. Gradually he pulled the net tight.

Over the years as Howard became the party's supreme commander, many of the old practices broke down. The federal executive, once playing a commanding role itself, was sidelined and largely ignored by Howard. The federal election campaign, with Howard controlling the strategy, was a revelation of the steady deterioration of the party organisation over a long period of time. One insider said yesterday there had been at best only one federal executive meeting in the past year.

"Increasingly this all became a Howard operation, with his small coterie," said a party-machine man yesterday. "As a consequence, the organisation was marginalised and the competitive tension between the organisation and the parliamentary party was lost. There was no counterbalance."

Today the position of Liberal federal president is held by Chris McDiven, a strong Howard loyalist, elected with his support in 2005 and generally regarded as someone who would never rock Howard's boat. Her predecessor, Stone, was known as a hard-head who exercised power in a two-step relationship with federal director Lynton Crosby, the successor to Robb.

Stone had authority. But McDiven was mainly known for being the first female president of the party—with little or no authority. By contrast, Stone played a role inside the campaign headquarters in the recent election campaign, as well as his external role with Calvert-Jones to shore up the party fund-raising.

McDiven's most critical act as Liberal president came during the Asia-Pacific Economic Co-operation forum in September when Howard's own cabinet tapped him on the shoulder. The prime minister was regarded as the biggest impediment to re-election and his cabinet colleagues believed that he should stand down for the good of the party. Howard called their bluff, warning that if they wanted him out they would have to tear him down in public.

McDiven addressed the issue in a formal way by staring down those in the party's upper echelons who wanted the federal executive to get involved or even to hold a meeting on the issue. This was not the role of the executive, she made clear to those who pressed. When it was most needed, she would not exercise her authority to bring the weight of the organisation in behind the cabinet. In the past, the organisation was not afraid to push back. But increasingly, the Royal Family ran the operation.

Now McDiven is in the spotlight herself as aggressive warriors from the parliamentary party seek revenge against the party executive. McDiven's failure to act during APEC certainly helped Howard to outfox his colleagues and cling to power—if only briefly. But in the end, McDiven was not responsible. She believed in doing nothing. Some say she was there for that very purpose. Blame should be more fairly split between Howard and his family on the one hand; and, on the other, a cabinet paralysed by his glare and a backbench in thrall to his coddling.

McDiven has told party colleagues she understands the need for change and will not recontest the president's position at the next federal council meeting in the middle of next year.

But McDiven is now caught up in the game-plans of others. She has been targeted by the NSW Liberals' hard-line Right—oddly, she is a moderate as well as a Howard supporter. The NSW faction has been working actively for the party's national right wing to push McDiven out in the federal executive meeting tomorrow.

This is a strategy with more than a few clever wrinkles. The former foreign minister, former leader and now vocal backbencher Alexander Downer wants the job—although he nonchalantly plays down his interest. Under the Liberal rules a casual vacancy could be filled by a simple vote of the executive. If McDiven steps aside tomorrow, Downer could be in on a show of hands.

But if McDiven sticks to her guns, and sees out her term, then the position will not be vacant until next year. Downer would probably face a number of rivals for the job. Thus there is some urgency among Downer's backers to see off McDiven ASAP.

"The bullying pressure on Chris was huge last week," said one annoyed executive member yesterday. "The Right is trying to gather a push to move a motion of no-confidence in her on Wednesday. It will make it very difficult for Brendan Nelson attending a first federal executive as leader with all these deep divisions."

Aside from his support from the Right faction—and his decade-long reputation as Howard's closest confidant in the parliamentary party—Downer's push for the job has run into questions about whether as a sitting member of parliament, he would have a conflict of interest. One interested observer posed this question yesterday regarding Downer's candidacy:

> If a large part of the problem has been caused by the head of the parliamentary party suppressing the organisation, then to give it to a strong member of the parliamentary party—who is close to Howard—is this right? And being who he is, would Downer become an alternative source of power in the party?

Melbourne Liberal powerbroker Michael Kroger has also been touted as a candidate. Supporters say Kroger's deep knowledge of the party's history and dynamics would make him an important candidate, while detractors argue that he can be a divisive figure.

Given the pressures, it seems likely a new process to overhaul the organisation will emerge, postponing the push for a hasty beheading of McDiven. Once such changes are established, McDiven might make way for a successor who is the result of a more reflective process than the current drop-your-gun-and-put-up-your-hands strategy.

One thing is certain: the party needs a president more in the mould of Stone, a forceful personality who did not put his hands over his eyes and hope it would all just go away.

Howard's iron rule in the end became a rod for the party's back. The presidential nature of his era affected even the most obscure corners of both the party organisation and the campaign strategy.

At the high end of the election campaign planning, Howard's personal dominance meant that the party was unable to grapple with the major campaign issue of climate change—for fear of embarrassing their leader. Kyoto was the symbol of all that was wrong on the Liberal side. To ratify the protocol might have been merely symbolic, but it was the symbol the government needed—of youthful vision and a strong, committed gaze into the future.

Former environment minister Malcolm Turnbull talked to his colleagues all year about ratifying Kyoto. Listening carefully to voters in his marginal seat, Turnbull knew what Kyoto represented.

But Howard was a non-believer and the government was seen through that prism. Ratifying Kyoto seemed like a political stunt to Howard, although some who had his ear on the subject insist he gave it considerable thought.

But the problem was Howard's own history. The question of ratifying the Kyoto Protocol first went to cabinet in early 2002. Howard was immediately opposed to ratification. When Turnbull became environment minister, he too, like several of his predecessors, wanted to ratify Kyoto. He raised the subject privately with Howard's ally, Alexander Downer, who took the view that for political purposes it might have been the right thing to ratify Kyoto way back in 2002, but not now.

Downer told Turnbull that to ratify Kyoto three months before an election—after five years spent arguing that it was weak and hollow and bad policy—would have made Howard a laughing stock. Howard was not going to do a backflip. When Turnbull raised the matter three months ago at the end of a cabinet meeting, it was dismissed. Some took the view that the protocol should not be ratified, full stop. Others thought it was a good idea, but too late. Yet others thought it would look like weakness for Howard. For Howard, not ratifying Kyoto would ultimately become as much of a symbol as ratifying it became for Kevin Rudd.

For Rudd, this was a stroke of seriously good luck. It might be just slogans to the Liberals, but for Labor, Kyoto was part of a mix of imagery conjuring up youth, energy and a way forward. It was the gleam in Rudd's eye.

On the Liberal side, developing anything approaching a future strategy was an uphill battle. Howard was opposed to the whole theory of special forward plans. It went against the grain. And he did not like being tied down by someone else's ideas.

"There was no plan, nothing to sell, no future agenda," said one campaign worker this week. "And even if there were, Howard had told voters he was not going to stick around to see it through. Howard seemed to believe that people would vote for him simply on his record. He believed they would come to their senses."

Howard complained to those around him that Rudd's campaign was just a string of slogans. They meant nothing, he said. There was no detail. "Howard simply didn't get it," said the campaign worker. "For Rudd, the slogans made up a picture of the future. It might not have had much more detail than 'broadband' and 'computers in schools', but it all actually stood for something."

Federal director Brian Loughnane was always trying to produce a seven-point plan or a nine-point plan for the future. But Howard did not believe in the snappy slogans and he didn't want any fancy plans. Two and a half weeks was expended trying to get Howard to agree to a plan. There were hundreds of policies to choose from, but the strategists were unable to get Howard to commit to a clear vision to espouse.

Loughnane persevered and finally a nine-point plan was mailed to voters. But then in the last week of the campaign, Howard produced a five-point plan during a speech in Sydney. What happened to the missing four points (from the earlier nine-point plan) was anyone's guess. And as one irate insider remarked, the new five-point plan included "reconciliation", which had not even been in the original nine-point plan. "It was a nightmare," said the campaign worker.

By the end of the campaign, insiders say Loughnane was tearing his hair out, trying to keep Howard on message, trying to keep some semblance of the campaign strategy on track. Perhaps his mistake was in not standing up to either John or Janette Howard earlier. Loughnane took the path of least resistance, but in this he was not Robinson Crusoe.

And the nation, as soon became clear, had stopped listening to Howard. The government had been almost 12 years in office, with an ageing and immovable 68-year-old leader. Howard was no longer even a credible salesman for a future plan—not least because he was retiring. Howard himself was tired too. Outwardly he put on a show of strength with the awkward ritual of his morning walk. But inside the campaign, there were claims that he had fallen asleep during more than one campaign briefing.

Howard's wife and closest confidant, Janette, had become so entrenched in the campaign structure that few dared to challenge her opinions. Her views were imposed in even minor matters such as lighting and the colours in advertising brochures. One bitter campaign worker said last week: "While the ALP was running a professional campaign, the Liberals were doing Homebake."

In the end, Howard's old modus operandi ran out of steam too. Spending his way back to power had been the hallmark of every election for this veteran politician. But suddenly, spending was out of fashion. Former treasurer and longtime leadership aspirant Peter Costello had tried his best to tie up the money with a massive tax cut strategy, working on the basic assumption that if you cut tax, you can't spend it.

But Howard then wanted a massive health policy on top of the tax cuts. He planned to spend billions of dollars taking over district hospitals across the country.

Costello fought and fought. Finally, with the coup of Rudd's tactical announcement that big spending was out, and health minister Tony Abbott's personal campaign implosion, Costello won.

He pared back Howard's plans for even more generous child-care rebates. It was a constant war between the treasurer and the big spenders led by Howard, the prime minister who believed that ultimately only he could draw the ace. But in the end, Howard's strength was proved ephemeral. The man who misplayed the electorate so badly did not even have the membership ticket to vote for a new party leader. The man who believed he could hold the vote around the whole country could not even hold his own seat. And when he fell, he took the party with him.

Contributors

Randa Abdel-Fattah is a 28-year-old Australian-born Muslim of Palestinian and Egyptian origin. She is an award-winning author who also works as a lawyer and human rights activist. Her next novel, set in Palestine, will be released in October 2008. Randa lives in Sydney with her husband and their two-year-old daughter.

Phillip Adams is a columnist, broadcaster and filmmaker. Adams has been contributing to Australian and international media for more than fifty years. He has presented ABC Radio National's *Late Night Live* for eighteen years and currently contributes two weekly columns to *The Australian*.

Michael Bachelard is a reporter in the Investigative Unit of *The Age*. He covered federal politics for *The Canberra Times* in 1996, and has written about industrial relations on and off since 2000 for both *The Australian* and *The Age*.

Geoffrey Blainey is Australia's pre-eminent historian and has served on federal government committees since 1967, when Harold Holt was prime minister. He has published more than thirty books, including the highly acclaimed *A Short History of the World*.

Judith Brett is Professor of Politics at La Trobe University. She has written extensively on the history of the Liberal Party, including the multiple award–winning *Robert Menzies' Forgotten People, Australian Liberals and the Moral Middle Class: From Alfred Deakin to John Howard*, and most recently 'Exit Right: The unravelling of John Howard', *Quarterly Essay 28*, December 2007.

David Burchell teaches in humanities at the University of Western Sydney. He is author of *Western Horizon: Sydney's heartland and the future of Australian politics*, editor of books on politics, ethics and rhetoric, and author of articles on a range of historical and political themes. He also writes regularly for *The Australian*.

Bob Carter is a marine geologist and environmental scientist with forty years' professional experience. He has held academic positions at Otago University and the University of Adelaide, is an Honorary Fellow of the Royal Society of New Zealand

and is currently a Research Professor at James Cook University in Queensland. He has published more than 100 papers in international science journals, is a newspaper columnist and has made regular appearances on radio and television.

Michael Costello is Managing Director of ACTEW Corporation and Chairman of Ecowise Environmental Pty Ltd. He was previously deputy managing director of the Australian Stock Exchange, and has held a number of diplomatic posts including ambassador to the United Nations. He was chief of staff to Kim Beazley MP and Bill Hayden MP and was Secretary of the Department of Foreign Affairs and Trade and the Department of Industrial Relations. Michael is also a weekly columnist for *The Australian.*

Pat Dodson is an Aboriginal leader and activist and was chairman of the Council for Aboriginal Reconciliation from its inception in 1991 until 1997. He is a former royal commissioner into Aboriginal Deaths in Custody and is currently the Founding Chairman for Lingiari Foundation, a leading research and development organisation that seeks the advancement of Indigenous affairs.

Richard Flanagan's bestselling and multi–award winning novels are published in twenty countries. They include *Death of a River Guide*, *Gould's Book of Fish* and *The Unknown Terrorist.* Flanagan also directed a feature film based on his novel *The Sound of One Hand Clapping,* and recently collaborated with Baz Lurhmann on the screenplay of his new epic, *Australia.* In 2004, Tasmanian Premier Paul Lennon declared that 'Richard Flanagan and his fictions are not welcome in the new Tasmania'. He lives in Hobart.

Michelle Grattan is currently Political Editor of *The Age.* She has covered federal politics since the 1970s. She edited *Australian Prime Ministers* and wrote *Back on the Wool Track.*

Clive Hamilton is the author of several books including *Scorcher: The dirty politics of climate change.* Until recently he was the executive director of the Australia Institute.

Chloe Hooper's first novel, *A Child's Book of True Crime*, was a New York Times Notable Book. She has won a Walkley Award for her writing on the 2004 Palm Island death in custody, and her book *The Tall Man: Death and life on Palm Island* will be published in June 2008.

Paul Keating was prime minister of Australia from 1991 to 1996 and treasurer from 1983 to 1991. Mr Keating's social and economic reforms include compulsory superannuation, financial sector deregulation, floating the Australian dollar, engaging with Asia, establishing the APEC leaders' meeting, and reforms in education, training, the labour market and the arts. He worked towards an inclusive social policy and argued the case for Australia to become a republic.

Paul Kelly is Editor-at-Large of *The Australian* and was previously editor-in-chief. Paul has covered governments from Gough Whitlam to John Howard and comments on ABC Television for *The Insiders* program. He is the author of six books including

The Hawke Ascendancy, The End of Certainty and *November 1975* and the co-editor of *Hard Heads, Soft Hearts*. He is a former Graham Perkin Australian Journalist of the Year, holds a Doctor of Letters from the University of Melbourne and has been a Kennedy School Fellow at Harvard University.

Tom Keneally is one of Australia's most successful writers. He is the author of more than thirty works of non-fiction and fiction, including *Schindler's Ark*, for which he won the Booker Prize and which was later made into the Academy Award–winning film *Schindler's List*. He is the recipient of two Miles Franklin awards.

Tony Koch is Chief Reporter with *The Australian* newspaper in Queensland. He has been writing about Indigenous issues for twenty-five years, and has won four Walkley awards. In 2006, he received the Graham Perkin Award for Australian Journalist of the Year.

Marcia Langton is Professor of Australian Indigenous Studies in the School of Population Health at the University of Melbourne. She is co-editor of two published collections on agreements with Indigenous people: *Honour Among Nations* and *Settling with Indigenous People*. Her doctorate is a study of the Aboriginal land tenure system of eastern Cape York Peninsula.

Hugh Mackay is a psychologist, social researcher and writer. He is the author of eleven books, and has been awarded honorary doctorates by Charles Sturt, Macquarie and New South Wales universities. He is a fellow of the Australian Psychological Society and received the University of Sydney's 2004 Alumni Award for community service. He is a newspaper columnist and a frequent broadcaster on ABC Radio. His latest book is *Advance Australia...Where?*.

Simon Mann is a staff writer for *The Age*, and a former deputy editor of the newspaper. From 1999 to 2002 he was Europe correspondent for *The Age* and *The Sydney Morning Herald*, during which time he was awarded a Walkley Award for his coverage of the conflict in Kosovo.

Robert Manne is Professor of Politics at La Trobe University and Chair of the Editorial Board of *The Monthly*. He is the author of *The Petrov Affair, In Denial: The stolen generations and the Right* and *Left, Right, Left*. Most recently, he is the editor of *Dear Mr Rudd: Ideas for a better Australia*.

David Marr writes for *The Sydney Morning Herald* and *The Age*. Over a long career he has written biographies on Patrick White and Sir Garfield Barwick, reported for ABC Television's *Four Corners* and presented *Media Watch*. With Marian Wilkinson he wrote *Dark Victory*, an account of the Tampa elections of 2001. His *Quarterly Essay* 'His Masters Voice: The corruption of public debate under Howard' was published in 2007.

Chris Masters is ABC's *Four Corners*' longest serving reporter. Chris has won four Walkley awards, including the prestigious Gold Walkley for a report on the sinking of *The Rainbow Warrior*. He is the author of *Inside Story, Not for Publication* and *Jonestown*, which was named Biography of the Year by the Australian Book Industry Association in 2007. In 2004 he was appointed Adjunct Professor at RMIT University and in 2006 was awarded an honorary doctorate in communication.

Paul McGeough is *The Sydney Morning Herald*'s chief correspondent, and has been reporting on international crisis and conflict since the 9/11 attacks on the US. A former editor of *The Herald*, he is currently writing a book on Hamas. He has twice been named Graham Perkin Australian Journalist of the Year and has won numerous Walkley awards.

Mark McKenna is a Senior Research Fellow in History at Sydney University. His *Looking for Blackfellas' Point: An Australian history of place* won the Douglas Stewart Prize for Non-Fiction and the Book of the Year in the New South Wales Premier's Literary Awards in 2003. He is currently writing a biography of Manning Clark which will be published by Melbourne University Publishing in 2009.

George Megalogenis is a senior writer with *The Australian* newspaper based in Melbourne. He spent eleven years in the Canberra press gallery between 1988 and 1999, is the author of *Faultlines* and *The Longest Decade* and a regular panellist on the ABC's *The Insiders* program.

Glenn Milne is the Political Editor for News Limited's Sunday publications. He has been a chief political correspondent for the Seven Network and in 1997 he won a Walkley Award for his coverage of the Thredbo landslide disaster. Milne serves as a Vice President and Director of the National Press Club and is a regular panellist on *The Insiders* and *Meet the Press*.

Louis Nowra is a playwright, novelist and screenwriter. His new novel *Ice* will be published in late 2008.

Noel Pearson has been strongly involved in campaigning for the rights of Cape York Aboriginal people and played a pivotal role in the establishment of the Cape York Land Council in 1990. He was a member of the Indigenous Negotiating Team during the drafting of the *Native Title Act* in 1993 and was chairman of the Cape York Land Council between 1996 and 1997. Today, he works as a Team Leader with Cape York Partnerships. In 2004 he became the Director of the Cape York Institute.

Matt Price was a political commentator and sketch writer with *The Australian* who also wrote regularly about his beloved Fremantle Dockers. A former Western Australian editor of *The Australian*, he was also a frequent blogger, regular guest on the ABC program *The Insiders* and author of the 2003 book *Way to Go*. Price passed away in November 2007.

Robert Richter, QC, is a Melbourne barrister specialising in criminal law and associated fields. He was appointed Queen's Council in 1985 and was chairman of the Criminal Bar Association of Victoria between 1986 and 1989. He was president of the Victorian Council for Civil Liberties between 1994 and 1996.

Guy Rundle is currently the US Correspondent for *Crikey* online daily. He was co-editor of *Arena Magazine* between 1992 and 2006, is a frequent contributor to a wide range of Australian publications, and the writer of a number of hit stage shows with the satirist Max Gillies.

Leigh Sales is the ABC's National Security Correspondent and anchors the prestigious *Lateline* program in the absence of Tony Jones. She won a Walkley Award in 2005 for her coverage of Guantanamo Bay and her first book, *Detainee 002: The case of David Hicks*, won the George Munster Award for Independent Journalism.

Paul Sheehan is a columnist and senior writer for *The Sydney Morning Herald*, where he has been day editor, chief of staff and Washington correspondent. His work has appeared in *The New York Times*, *The New Yorker*, *The Atlantic Monthly*, *Foreign Policy*, *The Best American Essays 1997* and *The Best Australian Essays 2000* and *2002*. His two previous books are *Among the Barbarians* and *The Electronic Whorehouse*.

Russell Skelton is a senior correspondent for *The Age* based in Sydney. A former deputy editor (business) and Japan correspondent for the paper, he has been regularly reporting on Indigenous issues since 2005. He received a Quill Award for investigative journalism and a United Nations association peace award in 2007 for a series on town camp violence in Alice Springs.

Tom Switzer is the Senior Policy Advisor to the Leader of the Opposition, Dr Brendan Nelson, and the former opinion page editor of *The Australian*. He is a former editorial writer at *The Australian Financial Review* and assistant editor at the American Enterprise Institute in Washington. He is also a regular contributor to *The Wall Street Journal* and *Quadrant* magazine.

Andrew West, a journalist at *The Sydney Morning Herald* and columnist for *New Matilda*, is the author of *Bob Carr: A self-made man* and *Inside the Lifestyles of the Rich and Tasteful*, a study of social class in contemporary Australia. He is a graduate of the University of Sydney and Columbia University in New York City.

Marian Wilkinson is Environment Editor for *The Sydney Morning Herald*. She has reported on national and international affairs for *The Herald*, *The Age*, *The Australian* and the ABC's *Four Corners*, and has received numerous awards for journalism including a Walkley and a Logie. She is the author of several books, including *The Fixer: The unauthorized biography of Graham Richardson* and *Dark Victory* with David Marr.

Pamela Williams is the National Correspondent and Associate Editor of *The Australian Financial Review*. She is a former news editor of the paper and a former executive producer on the ABC's *7.30 Report*. Williams has won Walkley awards for investigative journalism, business journalism, and the coveted Gold Walkley. She has also won the Graham Perkin Australian Journalist of the Year Award and is the author of *The Victory*.